The Gnostic and Esoteric Mysteries of Freemasonry, Lucifer, and the Great Work

+

Los Misterios Gnósticos y Esotéricos de la Masonería, Lucifer y la Grand Obra

Éliphas Lévi
Samael Aun Weor
Arnoldo Krumm-Heller

EDITOR'S NOTE:

The capitalization and punctuation have been duplicated (as much as possible) from the originals in order to preserve the Authors' styles. All pictures, footnotes, the items in [brackets] and the "quotes" which appear at the beginning and end of the book have been added by the present Editor in order to help clarify and provide insight into this text's subject matter.

This text contains a collection of materials from different sources which are given together in order to provide access to information that may not have been seen before as well as to see how this enriches one's understanding of these subjects.

The Masonic Legend of Hiram Abiff which we have included here is from the first book of Éliphas Lévi's *Le Grand Arcane ou Occultisme Dévoilé* *["The Great Arcanum or Occultism Unveiled"]* that consisted of three books. Levi finished writing it in 1868, but it was not published until after his death in 1898. The first book from *Le Grand Arcane* has been previously published on its own as *Livre Des Splendeurs* *["Book Of Splendours"]* and was described by Levi as "Le mystère hiératique ou les documents traditionnels de la haute initiation" ["The hieratic mysteries or the traditional documents of high initiation"].

Some of the materials from Samael Aun Weor are transcriptions of recorded lectures (from *El Quinto Evangelio* ["*The Fifth Gospel*"]), published in 2000, as well as from his books.

The materials from Arnoldo Krumm-Heller are from his *Revista Rosacruz* ["*Rose-Cross Magazine*"], which was published between 1927 - 1936.

The Gnostic and Esoteric Mysteries of Freemasonry, Lucifer, and the Great Work = Los Misterios Gnósticos y Esotéricos de la Masonería, Lucifer y la Grand Obra

© 2015 by Daath Gnosis Publishing (A.S.P.M.)
ISBN 978-1-105-19656-0
All Rights Reserved. Printed in the United States of America.

Based on the books, articles and lectures of Eliphas Levi, Samael Aun Weor, and Arnoldo Krumm-Heller.

First Edition December 2011 (Private printing)
Second Edition October 2012
Third Edition April 2013
Fourth Edition July 2013
Fifth Edition December 2014
Sixth Edition July 2015

Table of Contents

1) Introduction to the Symbolism of Esoteric Masonry............... 1

2) The Magical Origins of Freemasonry..... 5

3) The Legend of the Three Traitors of Hiram Abiff................ 11

4) Esoteric Explanation of the Symbolism in the Masonic Legend............. 39

5) Gnostic Explanation of the Symbolism in the Masonic Legend............. 49

6) The Rose-Cross Secrets of Occult Masonry................ 65

7) Esoteric Explanation of Baphomet, the Devil, Masonry and Religion.............. 95

8) The Synthesis of All Religions............ 111

9) The Shadow of God........................ 135

10) Esoteric Explanation of the Symbolism of Satan, the Devil, Lucifer, the Serpent and the Astral Light............... 157

11) Lucifer and the Arcanum A.Z.F.......... 177

12) The Gnostic Mystery of Lucifer.......... 191

13) The Luciferic Roots of the Great Work 237

Editor's Appendix............................ 267
- The Book of James
- The Three Traitors and the Three Gunas
- Love, Death and Resurrection
- Gnostic Secrets of Esoteric and Occult Masonry
- Speculation of the Editors regarding some Masonic Signs
- Some Names of God in Masonry
- Some Masonic Words of Interest
- Some Masonic Plates, Codes and Alphabets

Contenido

1) Introducción a al Simbolismo de Masonería Esotérica................ 1

2) Origen Mágico de la Francmasonería...... 5

3) La Leyenda del los Tres Traidores de Hiram Abiff................ 11

4) Explicación Esoterico del Simbolismo en la Leyenda Masónica............... 39

5) Explicación Gnóstico del Simbolismo en la Leyenda Masónica............... 49

6) Los Secretos Rosa-Cruz de la Masonería Oculta................ 65

7) Explicación Esoterico del Baphomet, el Diablo, la Masonería y la Religión............ 95

8) La Síntesis de Todas las Religiones...... 111

9) La Sombra de Dios........................ 135

10) Explicación Esoterico del Simbolismo de Satán, el Diablo, Lucifer, el Serpiente y la Luz Astral................ 157

11) Lucifer y el Arcano A.Z.F................. 177

12) El Misterio Gnóstico de Lucifer.......... 191

13) Raíces Luciféricas de la Gran Obra..... 237

Apéndice del Editor........................ 267
- El Libro de Santiago
- Los Tres Traidores y las Tres Gunas
- El Amor, la Muerte y la Resurrección
- Secretos Gnósticos de la Masonería Esoterica y Oculta
- Especulación de los Editores sobre algunos Signos Masónica
- Algunos Nombres de Dios en la Masonría
- Algunas Palabras Masónicas de Interés
- Algunas Laminas, Código, y Alfabetos Masónicos

"There are two types of Kabalists, intellectual Kabalists and intuitive Kabalists."

-from the Author's Preface from *Esoteric Course of Kabalah* by Samael Aun Weor

"The Intuitive [one] knows how to read what the Master does not write and [knows how] to hear [what] the Master does not say."

-from Ch. 62 of *Tarot & Kabalah* by Samael Aun Weor

"Hay dos clases de Kabalistas: Kabalistas intelectuales y Kabalistas intuitivos."

-del Prefacio del Autor del *Curso Esotérico de Kábala* por Samael Aun Weor

"El Intuitivo sabe leer donde el Maestro no escribe y escuchar donde el Maestro no habla."

-del Cap. 62 de *Tarot y Kabalah* por Samael Aun Weor

"...It is unfortunate, then, that the brother Masons know nothing. Until the "G" is put there by Gnosis. In the triangle there is the "G" of Gnosis, [the "G"] signifies Gnosis, but they do not know it. [Masonic] Initiation is magnificent. The Initiation for the degree of Master [is] tremendous: They put you inside [a] symbolic coffin, meaning that in order to be [a] Master one must die in oneself. There you have it from a wooden coffin, the whole Lodge dressed in black and the whole thing, and then they take [you] out from there and [to] the ceremony... but it turns out [to be] very good, symbolically, [it] says it all!"

-from 'ETHICAL AND ESOTERIC RECOMMENDATIONS' (Lecture #258, page 2651) in *The Fifth Gospel* by Samael Aun Weor

"...Es lamentable, pues, que los hermanos masones ya nada sepan. Hasta la "G" está puesta ahí de la Gnosis. En el triángulo ahí está la "G" de la Gnosis, significa Gnosis; pero no saben. La Iniciación es magnífica. La Iniciación del grado de Maestro formidable: Lo meten a uno entre el ataúd simbólico, significando que para llegar a ser Maestro tiene que morir en sí mismo. Ahí lo tienen entre un ataúd de madera, toda la Logia vestida de negro y toda la cosa, y luego lo sacan de ahí y la ceremonia... pero resulta que, ¡muy bueno, simbólico, dice todo!"

-del 'RECOMENDACIONES ÉTICAS Y ESOTÉRICAS' (Conferencia #258, página 2651) en *El Quinto Evangelio* por Samael Aun Weor

"The BRAHMINS are not TWICE BORN, but symbolically they are. Nor is the MASTER MASON truly a Master, but symbolically he is. The interesting thing is to reach the SECOND BIRTH and the problem is one hundred percent sexual."

-from 'SCORPIO' in *Esoteric Treatise of Hermetic Astrology* by Samael Aun Weor

"Los BRAHMANES no son DOS VECES NACIDOS, pero simbólicamente sí lo son. El MAESTRO MASÓN tampoco es MAESTRO de VERDAD, pero simbólicamente sí lo es. Lo interesante es llegar al NACIMIENTO SEGUNDO y el problema es sexual en un ciento por ciento."

-del 'ESCORPIO' en *Tratado Esotérico de Astrología Hermética* por Samael Aun Weor

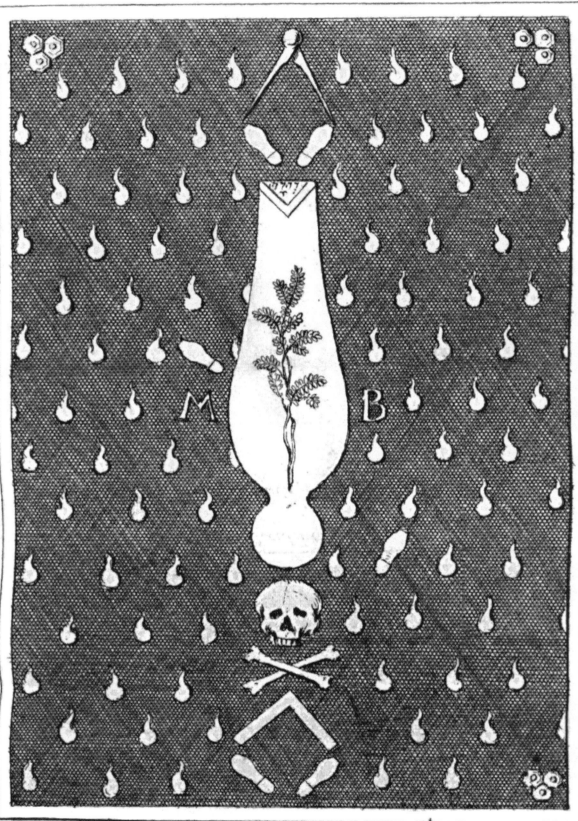

Plan de la Loge du Maître.

*Introduction
to the Symbolism of
Esoteric Masonry*

*Introducción
a al Simbolismo de
Masonería Esotérica*

| Introduction to the Symbolism of Esoteric Masonry | Introducción a al Simbolismo de Masonería Esotérica |

Extracts from the INTRODUCTION of HISTORY OF MAGIC[1]
by Eliphas Levi

…The kingdom of God is not an arbitrary[2] empire, neither in respect to man nor for God himself.

> "A thing is not just because it is willed by God," said St. Thomas, "but God wills it because it is just."

The divine balance rules and necessitates eternal mathematics.

> "God has made all things with number, weight and measure."[3]

Here is the Bible speaking.

Measure a corner of creation, and make a proportionally progressive multiplication, and all [of] infinity will multiply its circles filled by universes which will pass in proportional segments between the ideal branches and crosses of your compass; and now suppose that from whatever point of the infinite above you, a hand holds another compass or square, the lines of the celestial triangle will necessarily meet those of the compass of science in order to form the mysterious star of Solomon.

---

[1] The present English extracts of the Eliphas Levi's "HISTOIRE DE LA MAGIE" have been translated directly from the original French language and so the English footnotes refer to their corresponding French text (which is not in this Text) and therefore may not correspond to the Spanish.
[2] Literally 'arbitraire' means "arbitrary, unreasonable, uncontrolled"
[3] This is from a book of the Old Testament called *Wisdom*, which is not in most modern English translations, but is in the Latin Vulgate, Wycliffe, Geneva, and Douay-Rheims Bibles: "Yea, and without these, they might have been slain with one blast, persecuted by their own deeds, and scattered by the breath of thy power: but thou hast ordered all things in measure, and number, and weight." - Wisdom 11:21

Extractos de la INTRODUCCIÓN del HISTORIA DE LA MAGIA
por Eliphas Levi

…El reino de los Cielos no es un imperio caprichoso respecto del hombre ni respecto de Dios.

> "Una cosa no es justa porque Dios la quiera", dijo Santo Tomás, "sino que Dios la quiere porque es justa".

La balanza divina rige y exige, una matemática eterna.

> "Dios creó todas las cosas con número, peso y medida."

Aquí está hablando la Biblia.

Mídase un ángulo de la creación, efectúese una multiplicación proporcionalmente progresiva, y toda la infinitud multiplicará sus círculos, poblada por universos, pasando en segmentos proporcionales entre los simbólicos brazos extendidos del compás. Supóngase ahora que, desde un punto cualquiera del infinito que está encima de nosotros, una mano empuña otro compás o escuadra; entonces las líneas del triángulo celestial se encontrarán necesariamente con las del compás de la ciencia y formarán allí la misteriosa estrella de Salomón.

"You will be measured," says the Gospel, "with the measure that you yourselves have used [to measure]."[4]

God does not enter into battle with man in order to crush him with his grandeur, and he never places unequal weights in his balance…

"Con la vara que midiéreis, seréis medidos", dice el Evangelio.

Dios no pugna con el hombre para aplastarlo con Su grandiosidad; jamás pone pesos desiguales en Su balanza...

---

[4] See Matt 7:2 and Mark 4:24

*The Magical Origins
of Freemasonry*

*Origen Mágico
de la Francmasonería*

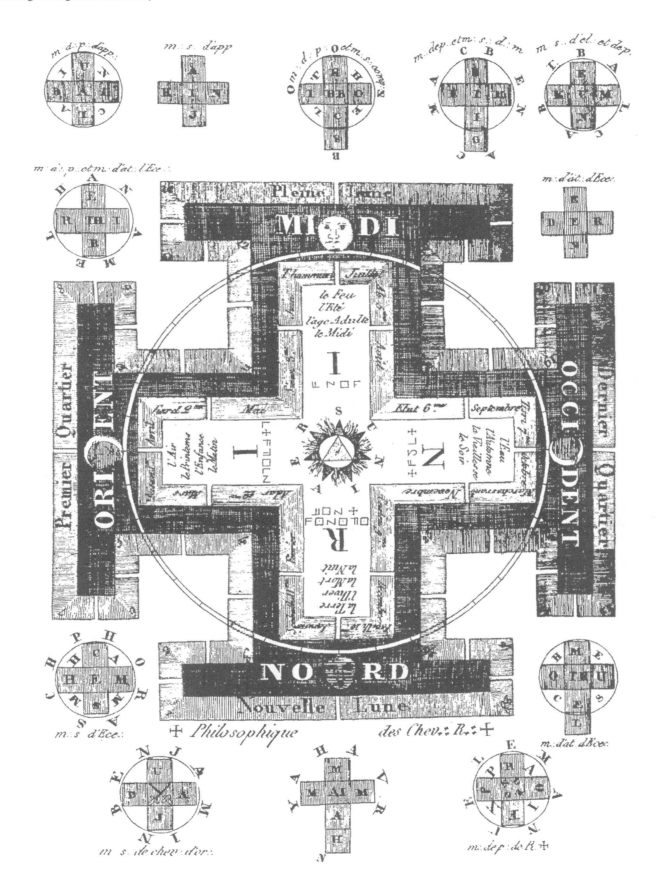

| The Magical Origins of Freemasonry | Origen Mágico de la Francmasonería |

| Extracted from Ch.7 of Book Five of
HISTORY OF MAGIC[1]
by Eliphas Levi, entitled:
"MAGICAL ORIGINS
OF FREEMASONRY" | Extracto del Cap.7 del Libro Cinco de
HISTORIA DE LA MAGIA
por Eliphas Levi, titulado:
"ORIGEN MÁGICO
DE LA FRANCMASONERÍA" |

That great kabalistic association, known in Europe under the name of *masonry*, appeared in the world all of a sudden at the moment when protests[2] against the Church had just succeeded in dismembering christian unity.

The historians of this order do not know how to explain [its] origin: some give its mother [as] a certain association of masons who were formed for the construction of the cathedral of Strasburg; others give its foundation [to] Cromwell[3], without asking themselves if the rites of english masonry from the times of Cromwell were not [more likely] organized against this leader of puritanical anarchy; [and] there are enough ignorant [persons] in order to attribute [the origins of masonry] to the jesuits, [and] if not the foundation [then] at least the continuation and direction of this long secret and always mysterious society.

La gran sociedad cabalistica conocida en Europa bajo el nombre de Masonería apareció repentinamente en el mundo cuando la rebelión contra la Iglesia logró desmembrar la unidad cristiana.

Los historiadores de la Orden se hallan en dificultades cuando buscan explicar su origen. Según algunos, provino de una cofradía de masones que se unieron para construir la catedral de Estrasburgo. Otros atribuyen su fundación a Cromwell, sin detenerse a considerar si los Ritos de la masonería inglesa en la época del Protector no se desarrollaron más probablemente como un contragolpe hacia este jefe de la anarquía puritana. En fin, algunos son tan ignorantes que atribuyen a los jesuítas el mantenimiento y dirección, si no la invención, de una sociedad conservada largo tiempo en secreto y envuelta siempre en el misterio.

---

[1] The present English extracts of the Eliphas Levi's "HISTOIRE DE LA MAGIE" have been translated directly from the original French language and so the English footnotes refer to their corresponding French text (which is not in this Text) and therefore may not correspond to the Spanish.
[2] Literally 'protestation' means "protest, protestation, outcry; remonstrance; furor"
[3] Oliver Cromwell (1599 - 1658) was an English military and political leader who overthrew the English monarchy and temporarily turned England into a republican Commonwealth, and served as Lord Protector of England, Scotland, and Ireland.

| The Magical Origins of Freemasonry | Origen Mágico de la Francmasonería |

Setting aside this last view (which refutes itself) we can reconcile the others by admitting that the Masonic Brethren borrowed their name and some emblems of their art from the builders of [the] Strasburg cathedral, and that they first publicly organized themselves in England, thanks to radical institutions and in spite of Cromwell's despotism[4].

It may be added that they took the templars[5] as [their] models, the rose-cross[6] as [their] immediate fathers and the johannites[7] as [their] ancestors.

Their doctrine is that of Zoroaster[8] and of Hermes[9], their rule is progressive initiation, their principle is equality regulated by the universal hierarchy and fraternity; they are successors of the school of Alexandria[10], heir of all the ancient[11] initiations; they are the trustees of the secrets of revelations and the zohar; the object of their worship is truth represented by the light; they tolerate all beliefs and only profess a single philosophy; they only seek truth, [they] only teach reality and want to progressively bring all intelligences [or intelligent understandings back] to reason.

Dejando a un lado esta última opinión, que se refuta por sí misma, podemos conciliar las otras, admitiendo que los Hermanos Masones tomaron su nombre y algunos emblemas de su arte de constructores de la catedral de Estrasburgo, y que su primera manifestación pública tuvo lugar en Inglaterra, debido a las instituciones radicales y a pesar del despotismo de Cromwell.

Puede añadirse que los templarios fueron sus modelos, los rosacruces sus progenitores inmediatos, y los sectarios juanistas sus antepasados más remotos.

Su doctrina es la de Zoroastro y Hermes, su ley es la iniciación progresiva, su principio es la igualdad, regimentada por la jerarquía y la fraternidad universal. Son sucesores de la escuela de Alejandría, y de todas las iniciaciones antiguas, custodios del Apocalipsis y del Zohar. La verdad es el objeto de su culto, y representan a la verdad como la luz; toleran todas las formas de credo, profesan una sola filosofía, buscan únicamente la verdad, enseñan la realidad, y su plan consiste en dirigir toda la inteligencia humana, mediante pasos graduales, dentro del dominio de la razón.

---

[4] Literally 'despotisme' means "despotism, tyranny, absolute power and control; dictatorship"

[5] The Knights Templar (or the Order of the Temple) were among the most famous of the Western Christian military orders.

[6] The Rosicrucians (also called the Rose-Cross Fraternity) are largely associated with Esoteric Christianity and the legendary Christian Rosenkreuz.

[7] The Johannites were a sect of Gnostic Christians who emphasised John the Baptist's writings and teachings.

[8] Zoroaster was an ancient Iranian prophet and the founder of Zoroastrianism.

[9] Hermes Trismegistus is the Greek name for the Egyptian god Thoth, often called the scribe of the gods. Thoth was called the heart (which the ancient Egyptians considered as the seat of intelligence and the mind) and the tongue of the sun god Ra, as well as the means by which Ra's will was translated into speech.

[10] The Catechetical School of Alexandria (founded in 190) was and is a place for the training of Christian theologians and priests in Alexandria.

[11] Literally 'antique' means "antique, ancient, age-old; vintage"

| The Magical Origins of Freemasonry | Origen Mágico de la Francmasonería |

The allegoric goal of freemasonry is the reconstruction of the temple of Solomon; the real goal is the reconstruction of social unity through the alliance of reason and faith, and the reestablishment of the [universal] hierarchy, according to science and virtue, with initiation and ordeals[12] for degrees.

Nothing is more beautiful, [as] can be seen, nothing is greater than its ideas and its tendencies, [but] unfortunately the doctrines of unity and of submission to hierarchy are not preserved in universal masonry; there was soon a dissenting[13] masonry[14] (opposed to orthodox masonry) and the greatest calamities of the french revolution were the result of this separation[15].

The free-masons have their sacred legend, it is that of Hiram, completed by that of Cyrus[16] and Zerubbabel[17].

El fin alegórico de la Francmasonería es la reconstrucción del Templo de Salomón; el fin real es la restauración de la unidad social mediante una alianza entre la razón y la fe, y la vuelta al principio de la jerarquía, basada en la ciencia y en la virtud, el sendero de la iniciación y sus pruebas que sirven como escalones de ascenso.

Se apreciará que nada es más bello, nada más grande que tales ideas y consagraciones; desgraciadamente, las doctrinas de unidad y sumisión a la jerarquía no fueron mantenidas en la masonería universal. Además de la ortodoxa, surgió la masonería disidente, y las peores calamidades de la revolución francesa fueron resultado de este cisma.

Ahora bien, los francmasones tienen su leyenda sagrada, que es la de Hiram, completada por otra relativa a Ciro y Zerubabel.

---

[12] Literally 'épreuves' means "test, trial, examination; proof, print; pull, crucible"
[13] Literally 'dissident' means "dissident, rebel, nonconformist"
[14] Editor's note: Levi may be referring to the Grand Orient de France (GODF) which is the largest of several Masonic organizations in France and the oldest in Continental Europe, founded in 1733. The GODF practices Continental style Freemasonry (also called "Liberal Masonry"), which does not require a belief in Diety for its members. This is in antithesis to the English or "Anglo" tradition of Freemasonry, which requires their members to profess a belief in deity. The Anglo-Masonic Jurisdictions withdrew recognition of the Grand Orient over this issue, and they now deem the GODF "irregular".
[15] Literally 'scission' means "scission, division, split; separation; fission"
[16] This could be Cyrus II of Persia (600 BC - 530 BC), commonly known as Cyrus the Great, also known as Cyrus the Elder, who was the founder of the Achaemenid Empire.
[17] Zerubbabel was a governor of the Persian Province of Judah (Haggai 1:1) and the grandson of Jehoiachin, penultimate king of Judah. Zerubbabel led the first group of Jews (numbering 42,360) who returned from Babylonian Captivity in the first year of Cyrus, King of Persia. Zerubbabel also laid the foundation of the Second Temple in Jerusalem soon after.

*The Legend of
the Three Traitors
of Hiram Abiff*

*La Leyenda del
los Tres Traidores
de Hiram Abiff*

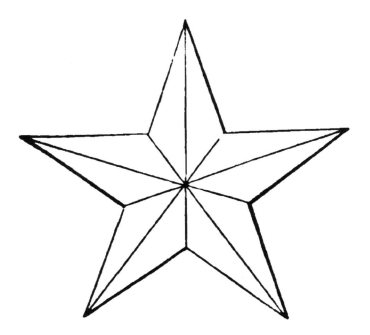

Extracts from Part Three of
THE BOOK OF SPLENDOURS[1]
by Eliphas Levi, entitled:
"THE FLAMING STAR"

Masonic Legends

Extracts from a Ritual
Manuscript of the Eighth Century

FIRST LEGEND

Solomon, the wisest of all the kings of his time, wanting to build a temple to the Eternal, assembled together in Jerusalem all suitable workers for the construction of this edifice.

He had an edict published throughout his kingdom which spread itself over the entire land: that whosoever wished to come to Jerusalem to work on the construction of the temple would be [well] received and well rewarded[2], on condition that he be virtuous, full of zeal and courage and not subject to any vice.

Soon Jerusalem was found [to be] filled with a multitude of men who knew the noble virtues of Solomon and who asked to be registered for the work of the temple.

Extractos de la Parte Tres del
LIBRO DE LOS ESPLENDORES
por Eliphas Levi, titulado:
"LA ESTRELLA FLAMÍGERA"

Leyendas Masónicas

Extractadas de un Ritual
Manuscrito del Siglo VIII

LEYENDA PRIMERA

Salomón, el más sabio entre los reyes de su tiempo, queriendo erigir un templo al Eterno, hizo reunir en Jerusalén a todos los obreros necesarios para construirlo.

Mandó publicar un edicto en su reino, que se esparció por toda la tierra: que quien quisiera ir a Jerusalén para trabajar en la construcción del templo sería bien recibido y recompensado, con la condición de que fuera virtuoso, henchido de celo y de valor y no sujeto a ningún vicio.

Pronto Jerusalén se encontró lleno de una multitud de hombres conocedores de las altas virtudes de Salomón que solicitaban hacerse inscribir para los trabajos del templo.

---

[1] The present English extracts of the Eliphas Levi's "LIVRE DES SPLENDEURS" have been translated directly from the original French language and so the English footnotes refer to their corresponding French text (which is not here) and therefore may not correspond to the Spanish.
[2] Literally 'récompensé' means "recompense, reward, award; payoff, reimbursement, repayment; retribution; return"

Solomon, being assured of a large number of workmen, made treaties with all the neighboring kings, in particular with the king of Tyre, to the effect that he might select from Mount Lebanon all the cedars and other woods which were suitable to him, as well as other materials.

The work[3] was already begun when Solomon remembered a man named Hiram, the most knowledgeable man of his time in architecture, [who was] wise and virtuous, [and] whom the king of Tyre liked[4] a lot for his great qualities.

He perceived also that so great a number of workers could not conduct [their work] without a lot of difficulty and confusion; also the work was beginning to be greatly hampered by the discussions which prevailed among them; [so] Solomon resolved, then, to give them a worthy[5] chief [capable] of maintaining good order, and made the choice of this [to be] Hiram, an Ethirian by nationality; he sent deputies loaded with gifts to the king of Tyre, in order to implore[6] him to send the famous architect named Hiram.

The king of Tyre, charmed by the high notion that Solomon showed him, accorded him, sending him Hiram and his deputies filled with riches and amity for Solomon, and to tell him that, despite the treaty that they had made together, he accorded Solomon an alliance forever, placing at his disposition all that could prove useful to him in his kingdom.

Salomón, contando con un gran número de obreros, hizo tratados con todos los reyes vecinos, en particular con el rey Tiro, para que pudiera escoger del monte Líbano los cedros y las maderas que le convinieran, así como otros materiales.

Habían ya empezado las obras, cuando Salomón se acordó de uno llamado Hiram: el hombre más experto de su tiempo en arquitectura, sabio virtuoso, por quien el rey de Tiro conservaba singular estima debido a sus grandes cualidades.

Se apercibió también de que tan gran número de obreros no podía dirigirse sin grave dificultad y confusión; además las obras comenzaban a resentirse por las continuas discusiones que reinaba entre ellos. Salomón resolvió darles un jefe digno para mantenerlos en buen orden, y con tal efecto eligió a Hiram, tirio de nacimiento. Envió expresamente diputados cargados de presentes al rey de Tiro, para rogarle que le enviara aquel famoso arquitecto llamado Hiram.

El rey de Tiro, encantado del elevado concepto que Salomón tenía de él, se lo concedió, y le envió a Hiram y a sus diputados a los que colmó de riquezas, expresándoles su sincera amistad por Salomón, añadiendo que, además del tratado que ambos habían concertado, le concedía una alianza ilimitada y que podía disponer de cuánto le fuera útil de su reino.

---

[3] Literally 'ouvrages' means "work, sewing, handiwork"
[4] Literally 'aimait' means "like; love; fancy, cherish, engage; care"
[5] Literally 'digne' means "dignified, worthy; proper, staid"
[6] Literally 'prier' means "pray; plead, implore; entreat, request"

The Legend of the Three Traitors of Hiram Abiff	La Leyenda del los Tres Traidores de Hiram Abiff
The deputies arrived in Jerusalem, accompanied by Hiram, on July 15… a beautiful summer day.	Los diputados llegaron a Jerusalén, acompañados de Hiram, el 15 de julio…, uno de los hermosos días de verano.
They entered into Solomon's palace.	Entraron en el palacio de Salomón.
Hiram was received with all the pomp and magnificence due his great qualities.	Hiram fue recibido con toda la pompa y la magnificencia debidas a sus elevadas cualidades.
The same day Solomon gave a festival for all the workers in honor of his arrival.	El propio Salomón dio una fiesta a los obreros para conmemorar su llegada.
The next day, Solomon assembled the council chamber to settle matters of importance; Hiram was among them and [was] received with favor; Solomon said to him before all in attendance:	Al día siguiente, Salomón reunió la cámara del consejo para arreglar los asuntos de importancia; Hiram fue admitido en ella recibiendo los plácemes de todos los concurrentes.
	Salomón le dijo, en presencia de todos:
"Hiram, I chose you as chief and great architect of the temple, as well as for the workers.	"Hiram, yo os escojo por el jefe y arquitecto mayor del Templo, así como de los obreros.
I give you full power over them without them needing another opinion [other] than yours; thus I regard you as my friend to whom I would confide the greatest of my secrets."	Os trasmito mi potestad sobre ellos, sin que haya necesidad de otra opinión que la vuestra; así que os miro como a un amigo a quien confiaré el mayor de mis secretos".
Next they left the council chamber and went to work, among all the workers, where Solomon himself said in a loud and intelligible voice, [while] showing Hiram to them:	En seguida salieron de la cámara del consejo y fueron a los trabajos, donde el mismo Salomón, dijo ante todos los obreros en voz alta e inteligible, mostrando a Hiram:
"Here is the man I have chosen as your chief and to guide you; you will obey him as you would me, I give him all power over you and over the work, those who will become rebellious to my orders and to his, will [fall] under penalty [and will] be punished in whatever manner he judges appropriate."	"He aquí el que he escogido, por vuestro jefe para guiarnos; le obedeceréis como a mí mismo. Le concedo amplio poder sobre vosotros y sobre las obras. Bajo pena, a aquellos que no obedezcan mis órdenes y las suyas, de ser castigados de la manera que él crea conveniente".
Then they made a tour of the jobsite; [and] everything was put into Hiram's hands, who promised Solomon to put everything in to good [working] order.	En seguida inspeccionaron los trabajos; todo se puso bajo las órdenes de Hiram, quien prometió a Salomón llevarlos con el mejor orden.

The following day, Hiram assembled all the workers and said to them:

"My friends, the King, our master, has charged me with the custody of maintaining [order among] you and of regulating all [the] work of the temple.

I have no doubt that all of you are filled with zeal to execute his orders and mine.

There are those among you who merit distinguished salaries; each one of you may attain this through evidence, which will show[7] the future of one's work.

It is for your own rest and to distinguish your zeal that I am going to form three classes out of all of you who are workers: the first will be composed of apprentices, the second of those of companions[8], and the third of those of masters.

The first will be paid accordingly, and will receive their salary at the door of the temple, at column J.

The second, also at the door of the temple, at column B.

And the third in the sanctuary of the temple."

Al día siguiente, Hiram reunió a todos los obreros y les dijo:

"Amigos míos: el Rey, nuestro señor, me ha confiado el cuidado de dirigiros y regular los trabajos del Templo.

No dudo que a ninguno de vosotros os falte el celo para ejecutar sus órdenes y las mías.

Entre vosotros hay algunos que merecen salarios más elevados; cada uno podrá alcanzarlo mediante las pruebas sucesivas de su trabajo.

Para tranquilidad y premio a vuestro celo, voy a formar tres clases de obreros: la primera estará compuesta por aprendices, la segunda de oficiales y la tercera de maestros".

"La primera será pagada como tal, y recibirá su salario a la puerta del Templo, en la columna J".

"La segunda, también a la puerta del Templo, pero en la columna B".

"Y la tercera, en el santuario del Templo".

---

[7] Literally 'donnera' means "give, hand; give out, deal; tender, pitch, donate; bestow, present; play, render, contribute, furnish, impart, mete, yield"
[8] Literally 'compagnons' means "companion, company, fellow, escort, helpmate, journeyman"

Payment was found to be greater according to rank, [and] each of them was found to be happy to be under the authority of such a worthy chief.

Peace, friendship and harmony[9] reigned among them; the respectable Hiram, wanting for all things to exist in good order, and not wishing for any confusion among the workers, applied to each rank signs, words and grips[10] by which its members could recognize each other, with prohibition to all from confiding these to any others without the express permission of the king or of their chief; thus they received their salary only upon giving their sign, and in such a way so that the masters were paid as masters, the companions as companions, and the apprentices as apprentices.

In accordance with such a perfect rule, each [class of workers] were[11] in peace, and the work continued as Solomon desired it should.

But could so fine an order remain for long without upset[12] and without revolution?

No. In fact, three companions, pushed by greed and envy to receive the pay of masters, resolved to know the word [of the master]; and as they could only obtain it from the respectable master Hiram, they formed[13] the design to get it from him [either] in good will or by force.

Se aumentaron los salarios según los grados, y cada cual se consideraba dichoso de hallarse bajo el mando de tan digno jefe.

La paz, la amistad y la concordia reinaban entre ellos. El respetable Hiram, queriendo que todo marchase en buen orden y para evitar confusiones entre los obreros, aplicó cada uno de los grados, signos, palabras y toques para reconocerse. Con la prohibición de comunicarlo sin permiso expreso del rey Salomón y de su jefe. De modo que cada uno recibiría su salario de acuerdo con su signo, de suerte que los maestros serían pagados como maestros, así como los oficiales y los aprendices.

Ajustándose a una regla, tan perfecta, todo desarrollaba en paz y las obras continuaban según los deseos de Salomón.

¿Pero, podía persistir tan hermoso orden?.

No, en efecto, tres oficiales, impulsados por la avaricia y el deseo de percibir la paga de los maestros, resolvieron conocer la palabra, y como ésta no la podían obtener más que del respetable maestro Hiram, concibieron el propósito de arrancársela, de grado o por la fuerza.

---

[9] Literally 'concorde' means "concord, harmony, amity"
[10] Literally 'attouchement' means "touch, contact"
[11] Literally 'régnait' means "prevail, predominant, reign"
[12] Literally 'trouble' means "trouble, turmoil; disorder, confusion; disquietude, disturbance; perturbation, agitating, disquiet; upset, commotion"
[13] Literally 'formèrent' means "shape, form; train, discipline, fix; groom, develop; mold, make"

| The Legend of the Three Traitors of Hiram Abiff | La Leyenda del los Tres Traidores de Hiram Abiff |

Since the respectable Hiram went everyday into the sanctuary of the temple, in order to make his prayers to the Eternal, around five o'clock in the evening, they agreed together to wait for him to exit, [and then] to demand of him the word of the masters; and there being three doors to the temple, one to the east, one to the west and the other to the south, they divided themselves between these three doors, one armed with a ruler, one with a lever[14] and the other with a mallet; [and] so they waited for him.

Hiram, having finished his praying, wanted to exit through the door of the south, where he encountered one of the traitors, armed with a ruler, who stopped him and demanded the word of the master.

Hiram, astonished, explained[15] to him that it was not in this way that he might obtain it and that he would rather die than give it to him.

The traitor, enraged[16] by his refusal, struck him with his ruler.

Hiram felt he had been struck [and], stunned from the blow, withdrew and tried to exit through the door of the west, where he encountered the second traitor who demanded the same as the first.

Como el respetable Hiram iba diariamente al santuario del Templo para dedicar una plegaria al Eterno, hacia las cinco de la tarde, convinieron en esperarle a la salida, para preguntarle la palabra de los maestros. Y como el Templo contaba con tres puertas, una a oriente, otra a occidente y la tercera al mediodía, esperaron uno con una regla, otro con una palanca y tercero con un mazo.

Terminada su oración, Hiram intentó salir por la primera puerta, en la que encontró a uno de los traidores armados de la regla, que le detuvo, preguntándole la palabra de maestro.

Asombrado Hiram, le manifestó que no era de aquella suerte como lo conseguiría y que moriría antes de decírselo.

El traidor, furioso por la negativa, le asestó un golpe con su regla.

Hiram, aturdido por el golpe, se retiró dirigiéndose a la puerta, en la que encontró al segundo traidor que le hizo la misma pregunta que el primero.

---

[14] Literally 'levier' means "prise, lever", like a crowbar, that is: 'A solid body, moveable around a fixed point (point of support), allowing a force applied to a resistance to be multiplied.'
[15] Literally 'représenta' means "depict, portray, represent; describe, explain, picture; perform, play, act out; relieve, stand for, account for"
[16] Literally 'outré' is defined in french as 'poussé au-delà de la mesure' meaning "pushed further than measure" or "pushed beyond measure", note that the ruler is a measuring device.

Hiram still refused [to give] him [the word], which [also] enraged this traitor who struck him a blow with the lever, that made Hiram stumble [back inside], [and] withdraw towards the door of the east; but the third traitor, who was waiting for him there, stopped him and demanded of him the same as the preceding ones.

Hiram told him that he preferred death rather than to declare to him a secret he did not yet merit.

This traitor, offended[17] by his refusal, gave him so great a blow with his mallet that he killed him.

As it was still day, the traitors took the body of Hiram and hid it in a pile of waste north of the temple, waiting for night in order to transport it further away.

In fact, as soon as it was night, they transported it out of the city, to a high mountain, where they buried it, and since they had decided that they would take it even further away [at another time], they planted on the grave an acacia branch so as to be able to recognize the place, and then all three of them returned to Jerusalem.

The respectable Hiram was in the habit of going daily, first thing in the morning, to Solomon, to give him an account of the work, and to receive his orders.

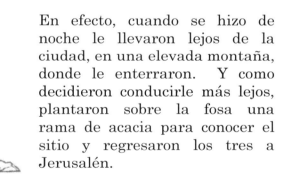

Hiram la rehusó igualmente, lo que también enfadó al traidor, que le golpeó con la palanca. Tambaleándose, Hiram intentó retirarse por la puerta de oriente por la que creía seguro poder salir. Pero el tercer traidor que le esperaba allí le dirigió la misma pregunta que los anteriores.

Hiram le contestó que antes prefería morir que declararle un secreto que aún no merecía.

Indignado por su negativa el traidor le dio tan terrible golpe con el mallete que lo dejó muerto.

Como aún había luz, los traidores cogieron el cuerpo de Hiram y le ocultaron en un montón de escombros al norte del Templo, esperando la noche para transpórtale más lejos.

En efecto, cuando se hizo de noche le llevaron lejos de la ciudad, en una elevada montaña, donde le enterraron. Y como decidieron conducirle más lejos, plantaron sobre la fosa una rama de acacia para conocer el sitio y regresaron los tres a Jerusalén.

El respetable Hiram iba todos los días, al levantarse Salomón, a darle cuenta de las obras y recibir sus órdenes.

---

[17] Literally 'indigné' means "indignant, deem unworthy, take offense"

| The Legend of the Three Traitors of Hiram Abiff | La Leyenda del los Tres Traidores de Hiram Abiff |

Solomon, not seeing Hiram on the following day, sent one of his officers to fetch him, but the man returned saying he had searched everywhere and that no one had been able to find him.

This answer saddened Solomon, who went himself to look for him in the temple and had a thorough search made of the whole city.

The third day, Solomon, having gone to pray in the temple's sanctuary, came out by the eastern door.

There he was surprised to see a few traces of blood; he followed them to the pile of waste in the north; he had it searched and nothing else was found, except that it had been recently disturbed.

He trembled with horror, and took it as a sign that Hiram had been murdered.

He went back into the temple to weep at the loss of such a great man; then he went into the court of the temple, where he called together all the masters and said to them:

"My brothers, the loss of your chief is certain."

At these words, each of them fell into a deep sadness, which brought about a long period of silence[18], interrupted at last by Solomon, saying that nine from among them must resolve to leave to search for the body of Hiram, and bring it back into the temple.

Este, no viendo a Hiram al día siguiente, le mandó llamar con uno de sus oficiales, que le dio cuenta de que se le había buscado por todas partes y que nadie había podido encontrarle.

Tal respuesta afligió a Salomón que quiso buscarle por sí mismo en el Templo, y mandó practicar indagaciones precisas en toda la ciudad.

Al tercer día, al salir Salomón de elevar sus plegarias en el santuario, lo hizo por la puerta oriente.

Sorprendiéndole ver huellas de sangre; Las siguió hasta el montón de escombros del norte, mandó cavar y allí no halló otra cosa sino que había sido recientemente removido.

Se estremeció de horror y aseguró que Hiram había sido asesinado.

Volvió a penetrar en el santuario del Templo para llorar en él la pérdida de tan grande hombre; en seguida volvió al atrio del Templo, donde mandó reunir a todos los maestros y les dijo:

"Hermanos míos; la pérdida de vuestro jefe es cierta".

Ante estas palabras cada uno se unió en un profundo dolor, lo que produjo un silencio bastante prolongado, que Salomón interrumpió diciendo que era preciso que nueve de ellos se resolvieran a partir para buscar el cuerpo de Hiram y conducirle al Templo.

---

[18] Literally 'calm' means "quiet, calm, peaceful, still; cool, restful, unmoved, leisurely, steady; composed, dispassionate; sedate, uneventful"

Solomon had scarcely finished speaking when all the masters wanted to go, even the oldest, without regard for the difficulty of the trail[19].

Solomon, seeing their zeal, told them that only nine of them would leave, [and that] they would be chosen by the voice of the ballot.

Those whom chance selected for the search were so transported by joy that they undid their sandals so as to be more agile, and set out on foot[20].

Three took the road to the south, three [took] that of the west, and three [took] that of the east, promising to one another to meet in the north on the ninth day of their walk.

Eventually one of them sat down to rest, and finding himself quite tired and wishing to stretch out on the ground, took hold of an acacia branch for support; but the freshly planted branch, remained in his hand, [and] this, of course, surprised him, and it was then that he saw a rather large space of newly turned earth and took this as an sign that Hiram was buried in this place.

His strength was renewed; [and] animated by courage, he went to rejoin the other masters who were meeting back up as the nine had promised each other.

He took them to the place that he came from, and said what he knew, and they put themselves to excavate that earth, [being] all animated with the same zeal.

In fact, the body of the respectable Hiram was buried there, and when they discovered it, they were seized with horror, recoiling back and trembling.

---

[19] Literally 'chemin' means "path, way, road; course, line; trail, walk"
[20] Literally 'en marche' means "moving; walking; up, operational, up and running"

Salomón apenas terminó de hablar, cuando todos los maestros quisieron partir, hasta los más viejos, sin pensar en la dificultad de los caminos.

Viendo si celo, Salomón les dijo que no partirían más que nueve que serían elegidos por escrutinio.

Los agraciados dieron muestras de alegría, se despojaron del calzado para estar más ágiles, tres emprendieron la ruta del mediodía. Tres la de occidente y tres la de oriente, prometiendo reunirse al noveno día de su partida.

Uno de ellos, hallándose extenuado de fatiga, quiso descansar y al querer sentarse se agarró a una rama de acacia que encontró cerca para ayudarse; pero aquella rama, colocada allí ex profeso, se le quedó en la mano, lo cual le sorprendió. Y viendo entonces un gran espacio de tierra recién removida, presumió que Hiram pudiera hallarse en aquel sitio.

Recuperó nuevas fuerzas; animado de valor fue en busca de los otros maestros reuniéndose los nueve conforme habían convenido.

Les condujo al sitio de donde venía, les refirió lo que sabía, y animados todos del mismo celo, se pusieron a remover aquella tierra.

En efecto, allí estaba enterrado el cuerpo del respetable Hiram, y cuando le descubrieron se horrorizaron, retrocediendo y estremeciéndose.

Then sorrow took hold[21] of their hearts and they wept a long time; but at last they found again their courage; one of them went into the grave and took hold of Hiram by the index [finger] of the right hand, wanting to raise him.

But Hiram's flesh was already decomposing and smelled foul, which made him fall back, saying:

'Iclingue[22]', which means 'he stinks'.

Another took hold of him by the finger next to the index: but the same thing happened to him as had happened to the first, and he withdrew, saying *'Jakin[23]'.* (The response is: *'Boaz[24]'.)*

The masters consulted each other.

Since they did not ignore that in dying Hiram had preserved the secret [word] of the masters, they resolved to change it, and [decided] that the first word uttered when the body was raised from the grave would serve as the new word.

---

[21] Literally 'empara' means "appropriate, take without permission"
[22] If this is the correct word it could be spelled: יכלנגו or יכלינגו, but this could also be a typo for "Isch'ngi" ישעי *Salus mea.* [meaning 'my Salvation'].
[23] "Jakin (Jachin), name of one of the columns of the temple of Solomon… Heb. יכין *firmus, stabilis, rectus, preparatio.* [meaning solid, steadfast, right, preparation] ([From the] root כון *Coun*)… Although one should write Jachin, and pronounce the *ch* like *k*, the spelling Jakin prevailed, no doubt, to avoid ambiguity in the pronunciation." from *Manuel Maçonnique ou Tuileur [Masonic Manual or Tyler]* (1820) by André Claude Vuillaume
[24] "Booz, is the name of one of the columns of the temple of Solomon… Heb. בעז Bogaz (*in fortitudine*) formed from עז chald. (*fortis*) and the preposition ב (*in*)… The English pronounce it Boaz, and they are right, but the pronounciation Booz, conforming to the latin tradition, has prevailed in France. Some write Bohaz ou Bohoz, which is a mistake, the ע can not be pronouced with an 'h'…This word is interpreted as: the strength is in God." from *Masonic Manual or Tyler* (1820) by André Claude Vuillaume

---

El dolor embargó sus corazones y permanecieron largo tiempo en éxtasis; pero recuperando el valor, uno de ello penetró en la fosa tomó a Hiram por el índice de la mano derecha, queriéndole levantarle.

Hiram cuya carne ya corrompida se disgregaba, olía mal, lo que le hizo retroceder diciendo:

Iclingue, que significa "huele mal".

Otro le cogió por el dedo que sigue al índice y le sucedió lo mismo que al primero, y se retiró diciendo: *Jakin* (se responde *Boaz*).

Los maestros se consultaron.

Como ignoraban que al morir, Hiram, había conservado el secreto de los maestros, resolvieron cambiarlo, y que la primera palabra que profirieran al retirar el cuerpo de la fosa, fuera la usual en lo sucesivo.

The Legend of the Three Traitors of Hiram Abiff	La Leyenda del los Tres Traidores de Hiram Abiff
Then, the oldest one of them entered the grave and gripped the good Hiram just above the wrist of the right hand, pressing his chest against the cadaver's, his knee and his right foot pressed together, the left hand behind the cadaver's back and against its right shoulder, and in this way he lifted Hiram from the grave.

His body made a muffled[25] sound which frightened them, but the master, still full of courage, cried out:

'Mac-Benack[26]', which means, 'the flesh comes away from the bones'.

Then they repeated the word one to another while embracing each other, [and] took up the body of the respectable Hiram and carried it to Jerusalem.

They arrived in the middle of the night, but the moon was exceedingly bright, [and] they entered into the temple where they put down the body of Hiram.

Solomon, informed of their arrival, came to the temple accompanied by all the masters, [who were] all attired in white gloves and an apron, where they gave the last honors to the respectable Hiram; Solomon had him buried in the sanctuary and had a gold plate placed on his tomb, [which was] triangular in shape, whereon was engraved in hebrew the name of the Eternal; then he rewarded the masters with compasses of gold which they attached to their garments by means of a blue ribbon; and they exchanged the new words, signs and grips. | En seguida el más viejo de ellos entró en la fosa, cogió al respetable Hiram y le sacó agarrándole de la muñeca derecha, apoyando el pecho contra el suyo, así como la rodilla y el pie del mismo lado y con la mano izquierda sujetándole por los hombros, levantando así a Hiram de la fosa.

Su cuerpo produjo un ruido sordo que los asustó, pero el maestro, siempre sereno, exclamó:

Mac Benak[27], que quiere decir "la carne abandona los huesos".

En seguida se repitieron el nombre los unos a los otros y cogiéndole del brazo tomaron el cuerpo del respetable Hiram y le llevaron a Jerusalén.

Llegaron de noche, con luna llena y entraron en el Templo, donde depositaron el cuerpo de Hiram.

Informado Salomón de su llegada, acudió al Templo, acompañado de todos los maestros, de guante blanco y delantal, rindieron al respetable Hiram los postreros honores. Salomón le mandó inhumar en el santuario e hizo colocar sobre su tumba una placa de oro, de forma triangular, en la que estaba grabado, en hebreo, el nombre del Eterno. Después, recompensó a los maestros con un compás de oro, que llevaron en el ojal de sus trajes, pendientes de una cinta azul, y se comunicaron las nueve palabras, signos y toques... |

---

[25] Literally 'sourd' means "deaf, surd, voiceless;"
[26] "מק-בנה, *mak-b'nah* (and not *mac-benac*, as it is [sometimes] taught), which signifies *oedificantis putrido, filius putrificationis*, [from the] root, מק and בן… Mak-Benah (and not *Mac-Benac*) which is interpreted as : *The flesh leaves the bones*" from *Masonic Manual or Tyler* (1820) by André Claude Vuillaume

[27] La palabra Hebrea es actualmente "*mak-b'nah*", מק-בנה, *oedificantis putrido, filius putrificationis*, que se interpreta como: "*la carne deja los huesos*".

These same ceremonies are done when pulling the candidate from a coffin, at his reception.

The password is *Gibline*[28], the name of the small village nearest to where Hiram's body was buried.

Se hacen las mismas ceremonias al retirar al candidato de su ataúd, durante la recepción.

La palabra convenida es *Gibline*, el nombre del lugar en cuya cercanía estaba encerrado el cuerpo de Hiram.

---

[28] "This word *Giblim* serves as the password for the *Master* [Degree] of the French Rite. It is written in Hebrew Ghebolim גבלים, which means *Termini* [end]. By the adoption of this word, what is meant to be expressed is that the *Master* is the *Terme*, the *End* of true Masonry. Some authors want to write Ghiblim גבלים (the Giblians), because this [group of] people were employed by Solomon for the construction of the Temple; from which comes the name *stone Cutters* ארג-בלים, but we prefer the first interpretation." from p.122 of *Thulier des Trente Trois Degrés [Tyler of the Thirty Three Degrees]* (1813) by François-Henri-Stanislas of the Aulnaye

"Ghiblim... From the hebrew גבלים [meaning] *termini* [end]. The ghiblians, which this name designates, were tasked by Solomon to cut stones for the construction of the temple. There are rituals where it is written *giblim*, not paying attention that the *ghimel* (ג) is always a hard g pronunciation." from *Masonic Manual or Tyler* (1820) by André Claude Vuillaume

[Extracts from Part Three of
THE BOOK OF SPLENDOURS
by Eliphas Levi, entitled:
"THE FLAMING STAR"

Masonic Legends

Extracts from a Ritual
Manuscript of the Eighth Century]

SECOND LEGEND

[Extractos de la Parte Tres del
LIBRO DE LOS ESPLENDORES
por Eliphas Levi, titulado:
"LA ESTRELLA FLAMÍGERA"

Leyendas Masónicas

Extractadas de un Ritual
Manuscrito del Siglo VIII]

LEYENDA SEGUNDA

Having buried the body of Hiram in the sanctuary with all the pomp and magnificence due to so great a man, Solomon assembled all the masters together and said to them:

"My brothers, the traitors who committed this murder must not go unpunished, we can discover them, this is why I command you to carry out a search with all the ardor[29] and circumscription[30] possible; and when they are discovered, that no harm at all should befall them; they should be brought to me alive, so that I may reserve the custody[31] of vengeance for myself.

Habiéndolo mandado Salomón inhumar el cuerpo de Hiram en el santuario del Templo, con la pompa y magnificencia debidas a su rango, congregó a todos los maestros y les dijo:

"Hermanos míos; los traidores que han cometido este asesinato no pueden quedar impunes. Se les debe descubrir, para lo cual os declaro que las investigaciones deben llevarse a cabo con todo el ardor y la circunspección possible. Y en caso de que sean descubiertos, que no se les haga daño alguno, trayéndolos vivos, para reservarme la satisfacción de la venganza.

---

[29] Literally 'ardeur' means "ardor, eagerness; heat, flame; keenness, mettle, vehemence; vim"
[30] Literally 'circonspection' means "circumscription, prudence, wariness"
[31] Literally 'soin' means "care, carefulness, custody, concern, heed"

To this effect, I command twenty-seven among you to carry out this search, taking care to execute my orders."	A este efecto, ordeno que veintisiete de vosotros partan para llevar a cabo esta investigación, poniendo especial cuidado en ejecutar mis órdenes".

Each of them wished to leave in order to avenge the death of their respectable master; but Solomon, always just in his desires, repeated that only twenty-seven were needed, and that nine would take the eastern road, nine the southern road, and the others the western road, and that they would all be armed with clubs against whatever dangers they might encounter.

As soon as he had them named by the voice of the ballot, those who were chosen left with the promise to carry out the orders of Solomon point by point.

The three traitors, Hiram's murderers, who had resumed work on the temple after having committed their crime, were seized by fear, seeing that Hiram's body had been discovered, [and] they imagined that very soon thereafter Solomon would have some research done to know those who had murdered him; which were in effect the wishes of Solomon, [this] they learned from other companions, who were to do the research.

They left Jerusalem at nightfall, dividing themselves into three parties, so that since they would not be together, they would be less suspicious and discoverable.

Each took flight, going far from Jerusalem, to hide themselves in foreign lands.

The fourth day of walking was scarcely over when nine of the masters found themselves, utterly fatigued, [and] surrounded by the rocks of a valley at the foot of the Lebanon mountains.

Todos querían partir, para vengar la muerte, de su respetable maestro, pero Salomón siempre respetando sus acuerdos, les repitió que era preciso fueran veintisiete, tomando nueve la ruta de oriente, nueve la del mediodía y nueve la de occidente, y que irían armados de mazas, para defenderse de los peligros que pudieran ocurrirles.

En seguida los designó por escrutinio verbal, y los elegidos partieron con la promesa de seguir punto por punto las órdenes de Salomón.

Los tres traidores, asesinos de Hiram, que habían vuelto a los trabajos del Templo, después de su crimen, viendo que se había encontrado el cuerpo de Hiram, se imaginaron que al punto ordenaría Salomón practicar investigaciones para saber quiénes le habían asesinado.

Como en efecto, conocieran por otros oficiales las órdenes de Salomón, que eran de practicar investigaciones, salieron de Jerusalén, al anochecer, y se separaron, a fin de que, no yendo juntos, fueran menos sospechosos.

Cada cual emprendió la huida, alejándose de Jerusalén, para ir a ocultarse en tierras extrañas.

Apenas expiraba el cuarto día de marcha cuando nueve de los maestros se encontraron extenuados de fatiga, en medio de las rocas, en un valle, al pie de las montañas del Líbano.

The Legend of the Three Traitors of Hiram Abiff | La Leyenda del los Tres Traidores de Hiram Abiff

They rested there, and as it was becoming[32] night, one of them stood guard ahead [of the others], and [kept] watch, so as to not be taken by surprise.

His affection [for the job of watchman] caused him to walk some distance away from his companions, so much so that he perceived a tiny light through the crack of a large rock; he was surprised and he trembled, but at last took courage and ran to the spot, resolved to find out what it was.

As soon as he drew near, a cold sweat broke out all over his body in seeing the entrance of a cave from where the light was shining.

Courage soon seized him and he resolved to enter.

The entry was very narrow and very low, so that he entered [with] the body curved[33], the right hand in front of the forehead[34] to avoid the pointy rocks, the feet one in front of the other, making as little noise as possible[35]; he finally succeeded in this way [in arriving] at the end of the cave, where he saw a man lying down, asleep on his hands.

Descansaron allí, y como comenzaba a anochecer, uno de ellos quedó vigilando, a fin de no ser sorprendidos.

Su misión le obligó a alejarse un poco de sus compañeros, divisando a lo lejos una lucecita a través de la hendidura de una roca. Se estremeció, sorprendido, pero ya más tranquilo, corrió a aquel sitio resuelto a conocer lo que era.

Apenas se hubo acercado, un sudor frío invadió todo su cuerpo, viendo la entrada de una caverna, de la que salía aquella luz.

Recuperado nuevo ánimo, resolvió penetrar.

La entrada era estrecha y muy baja, de modo que penetró con el cuerpo encorvado y la mano derecha en la frente para evitar los salientes de la roca; avanzando los pies, uno tras otro, y produciendo el menos ruido possible. Llegando, al fin al fondo de la caverna donde vio a un hombre acostado y dormido sobre sus manos.

---

[32] Literally 'entrée' means "entering"
[33] Literally 'courbé' means "awry, crooked, curved, stooping, bent"
[34] Literally 'front' means "forehead, brow; face, front;"
[35] Literally this would read "making the least noise that he could"

He soon recognized him as one of the workers at the temple of Jerusalem, one of the class of companions, and did not doubt that he had come upon one of the murderers, [but] his wish to avenge the death of Hiram made him forget Solomon's orders, and he armed himself with a dagger which he found at the feet of the traitor, he plunged it through his body, then cut off the head.

This act finished, he felt himself especially[36] thirsty, when he perceived a spring that flowed at the traitor's feet, he quenched his thirst, and exited the cave, the dagger in one hand, the head of the traitor [in the other], which he held by the hair; in this way he returned to find his comrades, who shuddered with horror as soon as they perceived him.

He told [them] what had occurred in the cave and how he had found the traitor who had sought refuge [there].

But his comrades told him that his great zeal had caused him to disobey the orders of Solomon[37].

Recognizing his mistake, he remained mute[38], but his comrades, who [put] great hope [in] the kindness of the king, promised to obtain from him his grace.

They immediately took the path to Jerusalem, accompanied by he who still held the traitor's head in one hand and the dagger in the other, they arrived [in Jerusalem on] the ninth day after they had [originally] left.

Al punto le reconoció como uno de los obreros del Templo de Jerusalén de la clase de oficiales y, no dudando que se trataba de uno de los asesinos, el deseo de vengar la muerte de Hiram le hizo olvidar las órdenes de Salomón, y armándose de un puñal que encontró a los pies del traidor, se lo clavó varias veces en el cuerpo y acto seguido le cortó la cabeza.

Terminada esta acción se sintió atacado de una sed devoradora cuando apareció a los pies del traidor un arroyo, en cuyas aguas aplacó su sed, saliendo de la caverna con un puñal en una mano y en la otra la cabeza del traidor, que llevaba por los cabellos. De este modo fue a buscar a sus camaradas, quienes al verlo se estremecieron de horror.

Les contó lo sucedido en la caverna, y de que modo había encontrado al traidor que se había refugiado en ella.

Pero sus camaradas le dijeron que su celo exagerado los colocaba en el trance de faltar las órdenes de Salomón.

Reconociendo su falta, permaneció cohibido, pero sus camaradas, que todo lo esperaban de la bondad del rey, le prometieron obtener gracia.

En seguida reanudaron el camino de Jerusalén, acompañados del que aún continuaba con la cabeza del traidor en una mano y el puñal en la otra, llegando al noveno día de haber partido.

---

[36] Literally 'pressé' means "hurried, rushed; pressing, pressed; eager"
[37] Literally this would read "that the grand zeal had placed him in the circumstance of failing the orders of Solomon."
[38] Literally 'interdit' means "forbidden, prohibitive, unallowable"

They arrived at the moment in which Solomon was closed up within the sanctuary of the temple with the masters, since they had the custom of doing [this] every day at the end of their work, to repent [the loss of] their worthy[39] and respectable master Hiram.

They entered, then, all nine of them, that is to say, eight together, and the ninth still holding the head in one hand and the dagger in the other; and shortly after he cried three times: '*mecum*[40]', which signifies *vengeance* [or "With me comes vengeance!"], and each time he make a genu-flexion[41].

But Solomon trembling [at the sight] of this spectacle said to him:

> "Wretch! What have you done?
>
> Did I not tell you that I reserved the custody of vengeance for myself?"

Immediately all the masters placed one knee on the ground and cried: 'Be merciful to him!' saying that it was his too-great zeal alone which had caused him to forget his orders.

Entraron en el momento en que Salomón estaba encerrado en el santuario del templo con los maestros, como acostumbraba a hacerlo todos los días a la terminación de los trabajos, para recordar con dolor a su digno y respetable arquitecto Hiram.

Penetraron los nueve, es decir, ocho reunidos, y el noveno llevando siempre el puñal en una mano y la cabeza en la otra, gritando por tres veces: *mecum*[42], que significa *venganza* ["¡Conmigo viene la venganza!"], y cada vez hacían una genuflexión.

Pero Salomón, estremeciéndose ante aquel espectáculo, le dijo:

"¡Desgraciado!. ¿Qué has hecho?.

¿No te había dicho que me reservaras el cuidado de la venganza?".

Entonces, todos los maestros, rodilla en tierra, gritaron: "¡Gracia para él!", afirmando que su excesivo celo le había hecho olvidar sus órdenes.

---

[39] Literally 'digne' means "dignified, worthy; proper, staid"
[40] The Hebrew word is actually "necum" or "nekum". נקם (Strong's H5358) 'nâqam' or 'naw-kam'. A primitive root; to grudge, that is, avenge or punish: - avenge (-r, self), punish, revenge (self), X surely, take vengeance. "Nekam! (heb. נקם *ultio*, vengeance! And not *necum* or *nekum*, as seen in some books or regulators.)" from *Masonic Manual or Tyler* (1820) by André Claude Vuillaume
[41] Literally 'génuflexion' means "genuflection, bowing, kneeling"

[42] La palabra Hebrea es actualmente "necum" o "nekum". נקם (Strong's, H5358) 'nâqam' o 'naw-kam'. Una raíz primitiva; de rencor, es decir, vengar o castigar: - vengar (mi), castigar, venganza (mi), X seguramente, tomar venganza.

Solomon, full of kindness, pardoned him, and ordered that the traitor's head be exposed on the end of an pole covered[43] with iron at one of the doors of the temple, in sight of all the workers, which was immediately executed, while awaiting the discovery of the two other traitors.

Salomón lleno de bondad, le perdonó, ordenando que la cabeza del traidor fuera expuesta en el extremo de una pértiga guarnecida de hierro, en una de las puertas del templo, a la vista de todos los obreros, lo que al punto fue ejecutado, esperando descubrir a los otros dos traidores.

---

[43] Literally 'garnie' means "fill, cover; garnish, dress, decorate"

[Extracts from Part Three of THE BOOK OF SPLENDOURS by Eliphas Levi, entitled: "THE FLAMING STAR" Masonic Legends Extracts from a Ritual Manuscript of the Eighth Century]	[Extractos de la Parte Tres del LIBRO DE LOS ESPLENDORES por Eliphas Levi, titulado: "LA ESTRELLA FLAMÍGERA" Leyendas Masónicas Extractadas de un Ritual Manuscrito del Siglo VIII]

THIRD LEGEND / LEYENDA TERCERA

Solomon, seeing that the traitors had divided themselves, believed it would be difficult to discover the two others; consequently he had an edict published throughout his kingdom in which it was prohibited for anyone to take into their homes whomever it [may] be, unless they already knew them or they had a passport, and promised large rewards to those who might bring the traitors to Jerusalem or give knowledge [of their location].

An unknown [man], who worked in the quarries of Tyre was well acquainted with a foreign man who had taken refuge in a cave near the quarries, [and] who had confided in him his secret, making the worker promise to rather have his tongue pulled out than to reveal it.

Since this man came daily to the neighboring village in order to find supplies for the traitor who was in the cave, he found himself precisely in the village at the moment when king Solomon's edict was published, [and] seriously reflected upon the reward that it promised to those who discovered the murderers of Hiram.

Viendo Salomón que los traidores se habían dividido, creyó que sería difícil descubrir a los otros dos, y, en consecuencia, mandó publicar un edicto en todo su reino, por el que prohibía dar hospitalidad a ningún desconocido que no fuera provisto de pasaporte; prometiendo grandes recompensas a los que pudieran traerle los traidores a Jerusalén o darle noticias de ellos.

Un obrero que trabajaba en las carreteras de Tiro, sabía de un hombre extranjero que se había refugiado en una caverna, próxima a la carretera, quien le había confiado su secreto y haciéndole prometer arrancarse la lengua antes que revelarlo.

Como aquel hombre venía todos los días a la ciudad vecina a buscar víveres para el traidor que estaba en la caverna, encontrándose precisamente en la ciudad cuando la publicación del edicto de Salomón, echó cuenta sobre la recompensa prometida a los que descubrieran los asesinos de Hiram.

The Legend of the Three Traitors of Hiram Abiff	La Leyenda del los Tres Traidores de Hiram Abiff
Personal interest overtook[44] his fidelity to the promise he had made.	El interés pudo más que la fidelidad a la promesa que había hecho.
So, he left, taking the path to Jerusalem upon which he encountered the nine masters deputized to search for the guilty ones, [and] whom, perceiving that their presence made him change color, asked him where he came from and where he was going.	Entonces salió y tomó el camino de Jerusalén. En el cual encontró a los nuevos maestros comisionados para buscar los culpables, quienes apercibiéndose de que su presencia le hacía cambiar de color, le preguntaron a dónde iba y de dónde venía.
The unknown [man], made a gesture of tearing out his tongue, placed a knee on the ground, and kissing the right hand of the one who interrogated him, said:	El desconocido, haciendo ademán de arrancarse la lengua, hincó la rodilla en tierra, y besando la mano derecha del que le interrogaba, respondió:
"Since I believe, upon seeing you, that you are the envoys of Solomon searching for the traitors who murdered the architect of the temple, I must tell you that even though I promised [to keep a] secret, I can do nothing else than follow the will of king Solomon, who indicated [this] to us by an edict that he has just published.	"Como me creo que sois los enviados del rey Salomón para buscar a los traidores que han asesinado al arquitecto del Templo. Tengo que deciros que a pesar de haber prometido el secreto. No puedo obrar de otro modo que obedecer las órdenes del rey Salomón que se indican en el edicto que acaba de mandar publicar.
One of the traitors you seek is a day's walk from here, [he has] taken refuge in a cave, among the rocks, around the quarries of Tyre, near a large bush.	Uno de los traidores que buscáis está a un día de camino de aquí, refugiado en una caverna, entre rocas, en las cercanías de la carretera de Tiro, próxima a un gran zarzal.
A dog is always stationed at the entrance of the cave who warns him and informs him as soon as he sees someone approaching."	Un perro está siempre a la puerta de la caverna, que le previene cuando alguien se acerca".
The masters, upon hearing this, told him to follow them and to direct them near to this cave.	Al escuchar este relato, los maestros le dijeron que les siguiera y les condujese hasta las proximidades de aquella caverna.
He obeyed and took the masters to the quarries of Tyre, where he showed them the place where the traitor was.	Este obedeció y condujo a los maestros a la carretera de Tiro, desde donde les mostró el sitio en que estaba el traidor.

---

[44] Literally 'emporta' means "take, take away, carry away, carry off, carry out, sweep, carry"

The Legend of the Three Traitors of Hiram Abiff	La Leyenda del los Tres Traidores de Hiram Abiff
It was the fourteenth day of their walk that they discovered the traitor; as night fell, they perceived the bush, the weather was overcast and a rainbow had formed[45] above, making it seem to burn[46].	Era el decimocuarto día de su marcha cuando le descubrieron. Al anochecer vislumbraron el zarzal; el tiempo estaba borrascoso, y al pronto lució el arco iris.
Having stopped to look at this phenomenon, they discovered the cave.	Habiéndose detenido para presenciar el fenómeno, descubrieron la caverna.
They approached, seeing the dog asleep, [and] took off their shoes to deceive its vigilance.	Acercándose, apercibieron entonces al perro dormido y para burlar su vigilancia se quitaron los zapatos.
A few of them entered into the cave, where they surprised[47] the sleeping traitor.	Una parte penetró en la caverna, donde sorprendió al traidor dormido.
They bound him, choked[48] him, and led him back to Jerusalem with the unknown [man] who had indicated to them [the traitor's hiding place].	Le ataron, le sujetaron y le llevaron a Jerusalén, con el desconocido que se los había indicado.
They arrived on the night of the eighteenth day following their departure, at the moment when the work was ending.	Llegaron el decimoctavo día de su partida, por la tarde, en el momento en que terminaban los trabajos.
Solomon and all the masters were in the sanctuary of the temple, as was their custom, to repent [the loss of] Hiram.	Salomón y todos los maestros, como de costumbre, estaban en el santuario del Templo para recordar con pena a Hiram.
They entered presenting the traitor to Solomon, who interrogated him and made him admit his crime.	Penetraron en él y presentaron el traidor a Salomón, quien le interrogó y le hizo confesar su crimen.
Solomon condemned him to have his body opened, his heart torn out, his head cut off, [and] placed at the end of a pole covered with iron, placed at one of the doors of the temple, same as the first, in sight of all the workers.	Le condenó a que le abrieran el cuerpo, arrancaran el corazón, cortaran la cabeza y la colocaran al extremo de una pértiga de hierro, en una de las puertas del Templo, lo mismo que al primero, a la vista de todos los obreros.

---

[45] Literally 'donnait' means "give, hand; give out, deal; tender, pitch, donate; bestow, present; play, render, contribute, furnish, impart, mete, yield"

[46] Literally this would read "which rendered it ardent". The word 'ardent' in French means "burning, fiery, flaming, ardent; fervent; raging, yearning; fierce; earnest, warm; live, torrid, hot-blooded"

[47] Literally 'surprit' means "surprise, overtake; startle, amaze"

[48] Literally 'garrottèrent' means "garotte, choke to death, strangle"

And his body was thrown on a garbage dump to serve as food for animals.

Solomon then rewarded the unknown [man] and sent him back, satisfied, to his country, awaiting the discovery of the third traitor.

Y su cuerpo fue arrojado al muladar para servir de pasto a los animales.

Salomón recompensó al punto al desconocido y le envió satisfecho a su país, esperando que se descubriera al tercer traidor.

[Extracts from Part Three of **THE BOOK OF SPLENDOURS** by Eliphas Levi, entitled: "THE FLAMING STAR"	[Extractos de la Parte Tres del **LIBRO DE LOS ESPLENDORES** por Eliphas Levi, titulado: "LA ESTRELLA FLAMÍGERA"
Masonic Legends	Leyendas Masónicas
Extracts from a Ritual Manuscript of the Eighth Century]	Extractadas de un Ritual Manuscrito del Siglo VIII]

FOURTH LEGEND / LEYENDA CUARTA

The last nine masters had begun to despair [that they would not] be able to discover[49] the third traitor, when, on the twenty-second day of their walk, they found themselves lost in a forest of Lebanon, and were obliged to cross over multiple perilous places.

They were obliged to spend the night there; as a consequence they chose places convenient to be able to rest safely from the ferocious beasts which inhabited that wilderness.

The next day, as the sun[50] was beginning to appear, one of them went out to discover the place where they were.

From a distance he caught the glimpse of a man with an axe who was resting at the foot of a rock.

Los nueve últimos maestros desesperaban ya de encontrar al tercer traidor, cuando al vigésimo día de su marcha se hallaron perdidos en una selva del Líbano y obligados a franquear varios sitios peligrosos.

Se vieron forzados a pasar allí la noche, eligiendo para ellos sitios cómodos para guarecerse de las bestias feroces que poblaban aquellos desiertos.

Al día siguiente, al amanecer, uno de ellos fue a reconocer el sitio en que se encontraban, advirtiendo a lo lejos a un hombre armado de un hacha, que descansaba al pie de un peñasco.

---

[49] Literally 'rencontrer' means "meet, run into, encounter; face, pass; contest; come across; experience"
[50] Literally 'jour' means "day, daytime"

| The Legend of the Three Traitors of Hiram Abiff | La Leyenda del los Tres Traidores de Hiram Abiff |

It was the traitor they were searching for, who, having learned of the arrest of his accomplices, was fleeing into the wilderness to hide, and seeing that one of the masters was coming towards him, [and] recognizing him from having seen him at the temple of Jerusalem, [so] he got up and went towards him believing he had nothing to fear from a single man; but upon perceiving the eight other masters who were approaching at [a] great pace, he turned and fled with all his strength, which made him recognizable as guilty and showed[51] to the masters that this could be the traitor that they were searching for; which excited the masters to pursue [him] with vigor.

Finally the traitor, fatigued by the pitfalls which he crossed in fleeing, was obliged to wait for them with [a] firm foot, resolving to defend himself and die there rather than to let himself be taken [alive].

As he was armed with an axe, he threatened to not spare any of them.

Paying no attention to his recklessness[52], the masters, armed with their clubs[53], approached him, telling him to give himself up.

But stubborn[54] in his sentiments, he mixed himself up in the midst of them and defended himself with fury[55] for a long time, without being able to wound a single one [of them], the masters only warded off the blows that he delivered, since they did not wish to do any harm to him before bringing him back to Jerusalem and presenting [him] alive to Solomon.

Era el traidor que buscaban, que habiéndose enterado de que sus cómplices estaban detenidos, huía al desierto para ocultarse. Y viendo que uno de los maestros se dirigía hacia él, le reconoció por haberle visto en el Templo de Jerusalén. Entonces se levantó y salió a su encuentro, creyendo que nada debía temer de un hombre solo. Pero observando de lejos a los ocho restantes que se acercaban a grandes pasos, huyó precipitadamente, lo que le descubrió como culpable e hizo sospechar a los maestros que pudiera ser el traidor a quien buscaban, decidiéndoles a perseguirle.

Al fin el traidor, fatigado por los obstáculos que franqueaba para salvarse, se vio obligado a esperarles a pie firme, resuelto a defenderse, prefiriendo morir antes que dejarse coger.

 Como estaba armado de hacha, amenazaba con no respetar a ninguno de ellos.

Despreocupados de su temeridad, los maestros, armados con sus malletes se aproximaron a .él, invitándole a rendirse.

Pero obstinado en defenderse luchó y se defendió con furor largo tiempo, sin poder herir a ninguno. Los maestros se limitaron a parar los golpes que les asestaba, porque no querían hacerle daño antes de conducirle a Jerusalén y presentarle vivo a Salomón.

---

[51] Literally 'dire' means "say, tell; mention, put, state; admit"
[52] Literally 'témérité' means "temerity, adventurousness, recklessness, hazard"
[53] Literally 'massue' means "mace, spiked club used as a weapon; spice ground from the outer shell of the nutmeg"
[54] Literally 'opiniâtre' means "obstinate, stubborn; relentless, pertinacious, obdurate; stiff, wilful"
[55] Literally 'fureur' means "fury, fit of rage; violence"

And to achieve this easier, half of them rested themselves, while the others fought.

Night was beginning to fall when the masters, fearing that the darkness would allow the traitor's escape, attacked him all together, seizing him at the very moment he wished to precipitate himself from the height of a boulder to the bottom.

Then they disarmed him, bound him and directed him back to Jerusalem where they arrived on the twenty-seventh day [after the initial start] of their walk, at the same moment that Solomon and the masters were in the sanctuary, doing their prayers to the Eternal and regretting [the death of] Hiram.

The [returning] masters entered and presented the traitor to Solomon, who interrogated him, and since he was unable to justify himself, he was condemned to have his belly opened, his entrails torn out, his head chopped [off], and the rest of his body thrown into the fire so it could be reduced to ashes and thrown to the four corners of the world.

His head was exposed at the end of a pole covered with iron.

Their names were written and attached to each pole, with similar instruments to those they made use of to assassinate Hiram.

The heads rested for three days in view of all the workers of the temple.

All three had been from the tribe of Judah: the oldest was named Sebal, the second, Oterlut, and the third, Stokin.

Para mejor conseguirlo, la mitad de ellos descansaba, mientras los otros combatían.

Empezaba la noche cuando los maestros, temiendo que las tinieblas facilitaran la fuga del traidor, le atacaron todos unidos y se apoderaron de él en el momento en que intentaba precipitarse desde lo alto de una roca.

Entonces le desarmaron, le ataron y le condujeron a Jerusalén, donde llegaron al vigésimo séptimo día de su partida, al fin de los trabajos cotidianos, en el momento en que Salomón y los maestros estaban en el santuario para elevar su plegaria al Eterno y recordar con pena a Hiram.

Los maestros entraron y presentaron el traidor a Salomón, quien le interrogó; y como no podía justificarse, fue condenado a que le abrieran el vientre y sacaran las entrañas, tras cortarle la cabeza y arrojar el resto del cuerpo al fuego para ser reducido a cenizas, aventando éstas a los cuatro puntos cardinales.

Su cabeza fue expuesta, como la de los otros dos, al extremo de una pértiga con la punta de hierro.

Sus nombres estaban escritos sobre cada pértiga, con útiles parecidos a los que habían usado para su crimen.

Las tres cabezas quedaron durante tres días expuestas a la vista de todos los obreros del Templo.

Los tres eran de la tribu de Judá; el más viejo se llamaba Sebal, el segundo Oterlut, y el tercero Stokin.

The third day, Solomon had a great fire lit in front of the main entrance, and had the three heads, the instruments and the names thrown into it, and had it all burned until it was entirely consumed.

The ashes were scattered to the four corners of the world.

Everything being achieved, Solomon directed the work on the temple with the assistance of all the masters, and all peace was restored.

Al tercer día, Salomón mandó encender una gran hoguera ante la entrada principal y arrojar en ella las tres cabezas, los útiles y los nombres, siendo todo quemado, hasta consumirse por completo.

Las cenizas fueron lanzadas a los cuatro puntos cardinales.

Terminado lo cual, Salomón dirigió los trabajos del Templo con asistencia de los maestros y todo siguió en paz.

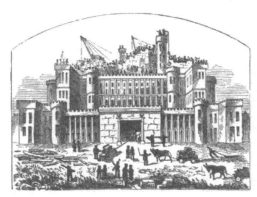

*Esoteric Explanation
of the Symbolism
in the Masonic Legend*

*Explicación Esoterica
del Simbolismo
en la Leyenda Masónica*

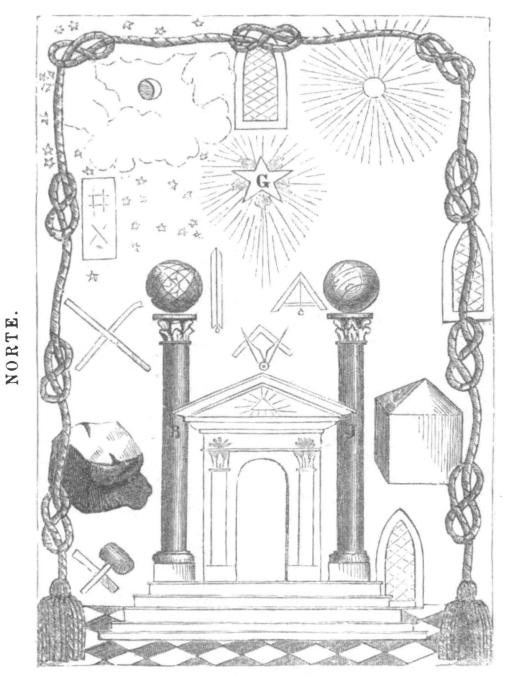

Extracted from Ch.7 of Book Five of HISTORY OF MAGIC[1] by Eliphas Levi, entitled: "MAGICAL ORIGINS OF FREEMASONRY"	Extracto del Cap.7 del Libro Cinco de HISTORIA DE LA MAGIA por Eliphas Levi, titulado: "ORIGEN MÁGICO DE LA FRANCMASONERÍA"

…Solomon is the personification of supreme science and wisdom.

The temple is the realization and the figure of the hierarchical kingdom of truth and of reason upon the earth.

Hiram is the man [who has] reached[2] the empire through science and through wisdom.

He governs through justice and through order, while giving to each according to their works.

Each degree of the order possesses a word which expresses intelligent understanding[3].

For Hiram there is only one word, but this word is pronounced in three different ways.

One manner is for the apprentice, and pronounced by them it signifies nature and is explained by work.

Another manner is for the companions, and for them it signifies thought [and] is explained by study.

[And yet] another manner is for the masters, and in their mouth it signifies truth, [a] word which is explained by wisdom.

…Salomón personifica a la ciencia y la sabiduría supremas.

El Templo es la realización y el emblema del reino jerárquico de la verdad sobre la tierra.

Hiram es el hombre que, mediante la ciencia y la sabiduría, alcanzó el imperio.

Gobierna con justicia y orden, retribuyendo a cada uno según sus obras.

Cada grado guarda correspondencia con una palabra, que expresa su sentido.

Para Hiram la palabra es una sola, pero se expresa de tres maneras.

Una es para los Aprendices y estos pueden expresarla; significa la Naturaleza y es explicada por la Obra.

Otra es para los Compañeros; en su caso significa el pensamiento y es explicada por el Estudio.

La tercera es para los Maestros; en su boca significa la verdad y es explicada por la Sabiduría.

---

[1] The present English extracts of the Eliphas Levi's "HISTOIRE DE LA MAGIE" have been translated directly from the original French language and so the English footnotes refer to their corresponding French text (which is not in this Text) and therefore may not correspond to the Spanish.
[2] Literally 'parvenu' means "reach, attain; get through; upstart, one who has risen suddenly in rank or status"
[3] Literally 'intelligence' means "intelligence, cleverness; wit, brilliance, cunning; understanding"

This word is that which is used to designate God, the real name of which is ineffable and incommunicable.	En cuanto a la palabra en sí, se usa para designar a Dios, cuyo verdadero nombre es impronunciable e incomunicable.
Thus there are three degrees in the hierarchy, like there are three doors to the temple;	Así hay tres grados en la jerarquía y tres entradas en el Templo;
There are three rays in the light;	Hay tres modalidades de luz;
There are three forces in nature;	Y tres fuerzas de la Naturaleza;
These forces are symbolized by the ruler, which unites, the lever which raises[4] and the mallet [or hammer] which affirms.	Estas son simbolizadas por la Regla que mide, la Palanca que eleva y el Mazo que consolida.
The rebellion of brutal instincts, against the aristocratic hierarchy of wisdom, successively[5] arms itself with these three forces with which it diverts[6] harmony.	La rebelión de los instintos brutales contra la aristocracia jerárquica de la sabiduría se arma exitosamente con estas tres fuerzas y las vuelca para sus fines personales.
There are three typical rebels:	Hay tres rebeldes típicos:

The rebel of nature;
The rebel of science;
The rebel of truth.

El rebelde contra la Naturaleza,
El rebelde contra la Ciencia, y
El rebelde contra la Verdad.

They were symbolized in the hell of the ancients by the three heads of Cerberus.

En el Hades clásico fueron representados por las tres cabezas de Cerbero.

They are symbolized in the Bible by Korah, Dathan and Abiram.

En la Biblia, por Koran, Dathan y Abiram.

In the masonic legend, they are designated with names which vary according to the rites.

En la leyenda masónica se distinguen por los nombres que varían en los diferentes Ritos.

The first, who is ordinarily called *Abiram* or [the] murderer of Hiram, hits the great master with the ruler.

El primero, que habitualmente se llama *Abiram*, o asesino de Hiram, es quien golpea al Gran Maestro con la regla.

This is the history of justice put to death, in the name of the law, by human passions.

Esta es la historia del hombre justo inmolado por la pasión humana bajo la pretensión de la ley.

---

[4] Literally 'soulève' means "lift, raise, trigger; rouse, press"
[5] Literally 'successivement' means "successively, one after the other"
[6] Literally 'détourne' means "divert, turn away, hijack, avert, steal away, deter, embezzle, misappropriate, deflect, shunt, siphon, stage"

Esoteric Explanation of the Symbolism in the Masonic Legend	Explicación Esoterica del Simbolismo en la Leyenda Masónica
The second named *Miphiboseth*, from the name of a ridiculous and disabled [person who made] claims [to] the royal [linage] of [King] David, struck Hiram with the lever or with the square[7].	El segundo, denominado *Mephibosheth*, luego ridículo y débil pretendiente del trono de David, ataca a Hiram con la palanca o la escuadra[14].
It is thus that the popular lever or square of an insane[8] equality becomes the instrument of tyranny in the hands of the multitudes and awaits the royalty of wisdom and of virtue, even more sadly than [it does for] order[9].	Así la escuadra o la palanca populares de la igualdad insensata se convierten en instrumento de la tiranía en manos de la multitud, y atacan, con mayor fiereza aún que la regla, la realeza de la sabiduría y la virtud.
The *third* finally defeated[10] Hiram with the mallet. Just as the brutal instincts do, when they want to create order in the name of violence and fear by crushing intelligence.	En fin, el tercero remata a Hiram con un mazo. Así actúan los instintos brutales cuando procuran establecer el orden, en nombre de la violencia y el miedo, aplastando a la inteligencia.
The acacia branch on Hiram's tomb is like the cross on our altars[11].	La rama de acacia sobre la tumba de Hiram semeja la cruz sobre nuestros altares.
It is the sign of the science that outlives[12] science ; it is the green branch which announces another spring.	Es un signo del conocimiento que sobrevive al conocimiento mismo; es la verde ramita que presagia otra primavera.
When man has disturbed the order of nature enough, Providence[13] will intervene in order to reestablish [order], like Solomon [did] to avenge the death of Hiram.	Cuando los hombres han perturbado de esta manera el orden de la Naturaleza, la Providencia interviene para restaurarlo, como Salomón para vengar la muerto del Maestro Constructor.
He who assassinated with the ruler, died by the dagger.	Quien asesinó con la regla, perecerá con el puñal.

---

[7] Editor's note: Levi mentions that the second companion struck Hiram "with a square, others say with a lever."
[8] Literally 'folle' means "mad, crazy, out of one's mind; insane, terrific; daft, demented, maniac"
[9] Literally 'règle' means "ruler, measure; rule, common practice; period (of a cycle)"
[10] Literally 'achève' means "finished, terminated, completed; defeated, destroyed"
[11] Literally 'autels' means "altar, aisle; communion table"
[12] Literally 'survit' means "survive, live on; outlive"
[13] Providence means 'a manifestation of divine care or direction'. It is also considered 'the foreseeing care and guidance of God', especially when conceived as omnisciently directing the universe and the affairs of humankind with wise benevolence.

[14] Nota del editor: Levi menciona que el segundo compañero Hiram golpeó "con una escuadra o, como dicen otros, con una palanca."

He who has struck with the lever or square, will die under the axe of the law.

This is the eternal stop of the regicides[15].

He who triumphed with the mallet, will fall victim to the force which he has abused, and will be strangled[16] by the lion[17] [of the law].

The assassin [who struck] with the ruler, is denounced by the same lamp which illuminates and by the source[18] where he quenches his thirst[19]. That is to say, that we will apply the pain[20] of the [law of the] talion[21] to him.

The assassin [who struck] with the lever will be surprised when his vigilance is at fault[22] like a sleeping dog, and he will be delivered by his accomplices; for anarchy is the mother of treason.

The lion who devours the assassin with the mallet, is one of the forms of the sphinx of Oedipus.

And the one [who] will deserve[23] to succeed Hiram in his dignity [is the one] who will have vanquished the lion.

---

[15] Literally 'régicides' means "regicide, murder of a king"

[16] Literally 'étranglé' means "strangle, choke, throttle; strangulate, suffocate, garotte; overlie"

[17] Editor's note: Levi mentions that "The third assassin was killed by a lion, which he had to vanquish in order to take his cadaver, other version say that he defended himself with axe blows against the masters, who finally achieved his disarming and brought him to Solomon, who made him atone [for] his crime."

[18] Literally 'source' means "spring, source, fountain; well, fountainhead"

[19] Literally 's'abreuve' means "drink, consume liquids;"

[20] Literally 'peine' means "pain, sentence, penalty; grief, sorrow, bitterness; ache, heartache, infirmity, pains"

[21] The 'law of the talion' (Latin: lex talionis, literally "The law of retaliation.") refers to the principle 'an eye for an eye', meaning that a person who has injured another person receives the same injury in compensation.

[22] Literally 'en défaut' means "at fault, find fault"

[23] Literally 'méritera' means "deserve, worth, merit, worth it, claim, earn, rate"

Quien atacó con la palanca o la escuadra, expiará su crimen con el hacha de la ley.

Esta es la sentencia eterna que cae sobre los regicidas.

Quien asesinó con el mazo será víctima del poder que empleó malamente.

Quien mató con la regla es traicionado por la misma lámpara que le alumbra y por el arroyuelo del que bebe. Esta es la ley de represalia.

Quien destruyó con la palanca es sorprendido cuando su vigilia fracasa como un perro dormido, y es entregado por sus propios cómplices, pues la anarquía es madre de la traición.

Quien golpeó con el mazo es devorado por el león, que es una variante de la esfinge de Edipo.[24]

Mientras que quien venza al león merecerá suceder a Hiram.

---

[24] Nota del editor: Levi menciona que "El tercer asesino fue muerto por un león, y hubo que matar a la bestia antes de poder apoderarse del cadáver. Otras versiones dicen que se defendió con un hacha cuando los Maestros cayeron sobre él, pero que lograron desarmarle y conducirle ante Salomón quien le hizo expiar su crimen."

The rotten corpse of Hiram shows that forms change, but that the spirit remains [the same].	El cuerpo corrupto del Constructor indica que las formas pueden cambiar mas el espíritu subsiste.
The source of water flowing near the first murderer, recalls the flood that has punished the crimes against nature.	El manantial en la vecindad del primer asesino recuerda el Diluvio que castigó los crímenes contra la Naturaleza.
The burning bush and rainbow skies which help[25] discover the second assassin, represent the light and life, denouncing the attacks against [upright] thought.	La zarza ardiente y el arco iris que delatan al segundo asesino tipifican la vida y la luz denunciando el pecado de pensamiento.
Finally the vanquished lion represents the triumph of the spirit over matter and the final submission of strength [or force] to understanding.	Finalmente, el león vencido representa el triunfo de la mente sobre la materia y la sujeción absoluta de la fuerza a la inteligencia.
Since the beginning of the work of the spirit to build the temple of unity, Hiram has been killed many times, and he always resurrects[26].	Desde la alborada del trabajo intelectual por el que fue erigido el Templo de la unidad, Hiram fue asesinado a menudo, pero siempre se levantó de entre los muertos.
Adonis is killed by the boar, Osiris is assassinated by Typhon.	Es Adonis destruido por el jabalí, Osiris asesinado por Tifón.
This is Pythagoras outcast[27], it is Orpheus torn [apart] by the Bacchantes, it is Moses abandoned in the caves of Mount Nebo, [and] it is Jesus put to death by Caiaphas, Pilate and Judas.	Pitágoras proscripto, Orfeo despedazado por las Bacantes, Moisés abandonado en las cavernas del Monte Nebo, Jesús crucificado por Judas, Caifás y Pilatos.
The true masons are those who willfully persist in constructing the temple, according to the plan of Hiram.	Ahora bien, son masones de verdad quienes buscan persistentemente reconstruir el Templo de acuerdo con el plan de Hiram.
This is the great and principle legend of freemasonry; the others are no less beautiful nor less deep, but we do not believe we should divulge the mysteries, since we have only received initiation from God and from our work, [therefore] we look at the secret of high freemasonry as our own.	Esa es la leyenda grandiosa y principalmente de la masonería; hay otras no menos bellas y profundas; pero no creemos justificado divulgar sus misterios. Aunque sólo hemos recibido la iniciación de Dios y de nuestras indagaciones, mantendremos los secretos de la francmasonería trascendental tal como lo hacemos con nuestros propios secretos.

---

[25] Literally 'font' means "make, build, draw up; play, take; do, work; cook; prepare, perform; handle, transact"
[26] Literally 'ressuscite' means "come back to life, resurrect, revive"
[27] Literally 'proscrit' means "outcast, homeless, ostracized"

[We have] attained a scientific degree through our efforts which imposes silence [upon] us, [and] we believe [that] we are better suited[28] by our convictions than by an oath.	Habiendo llegado, por nuestro esfuerzo, a un nivel de conocimiento que impone silencio, nos consideramos más comprometidos por nuestras convicciones que por un juramento.
Science is a nobility[29] which obliges[30], and we do not demerit the crown prince of the rose-cross.	La ciencia es nobleza que obliga, y de ningún modo dejaremos de merecer la principesca corona de la Rosa-Cruz.
We also believe in the resurrection of Hiram!	También creemos en la resurrección de Hiram.
The rites of freemasonry are intended to transmit the memory of the legends of initiation, [and] to preserve it among the brethren.	Los Ritos de la masonería tienden a transmitir un recordatorio de las leyendas de la iniciación y a preservarlas entre los Hermanos.
One might ask us how, if freemasonry is so sublime and so holy, could it have been banned[31] and so often condemned by the Church.	Ahora bien, si la masonería es tan santa y sublime, puede preguntársenos cómo es que tan a menudo la Iglesia la proscribió y condenó; pero ya hemos replicado a estas preguntas al mencionar sus divisiones y profanaciones.
We have already answered this question, by talking about the splits and the defilements[32] of freemasonry.	
Freemasonry is gnosis, and the false gnostics have had the real ones condemned. Which has forced them to hide themselves, it's not the fear of the light, the light is what they want, what they seek, [and] what they adore.	La masonería es la Gnosis y los falsos gnósticos provocaron la condenación de lo verdadero. Esta fue ocultada, no por miedo a la luz, sino porque la luz es lo que anhelan, buscan y adoran.
But they fear the profaners[33], that is to say, the false interpreters, the slanderers[34], the skeptics with [their] stupid laugh, and the enemies of every belief and of every morality.	Pero temieron el sacrilegio, o sea, a los falsos intérpretes, a los calumniadores, al ludibrio de los escépticos, a los enemigos de toda creencia y toda moralidad.

---

[28] Literally 'engagé' means "bind, commit, engage; secure, pledge; retain, insert, run"
[29] Literally 'noblesse' means "nobleness, nobility, lordliness; greatness, grandeur"
[30] Literally 'oblige' means "oblige, force; bind, push, constrain; shove, commit"
[31] Literally 'proscrite' means "banish, proscribe, prohibit"
[32] Literally 'profanations' means "profanation, defilement, desecration, pollution"
[33] Literally 'profanateurs' means "profaner, blasphemer"
[34] Literally 'calomniateurs' means "calumniator, slanderer"

Anyway, in our present time [there are] a great number of men who believe themselves to be free-masons, [yet they] ignore the meaning of their rites, and have lost the key of their mysteries.

They do not even comprehend their symbolic pictures[35], and understand next [to] nothing of [their] hieroglyphic signs, which are illustrated[36] on the carpets of their lodges.

These pictures and signs are the pages of a book of the absolute and universal science.

They can be read with the help of the kabalistic keys, and they hide nothing for the initiate who possesses the clavicles of Solomon.

Freemasonry has not merely been profaned, but has even served as [a] veil and pretext for conspiracies of anarchy, through the occult influence of the avengers of Jacques de Molay, and of those who continued the schismatic[37] work of the temple.

In place of avenging the death of Hiram, they have avenged that of his assassins.

Además, en la actualidad, hay muchos que piensan que son masones pero no conocen el significado de sus Ritos, habiendo perdido la Clave de los Misterios.

Interpretan erróneamente hasta sus dibujos simbólicos y los signos jeroglíferos que blasonan las alfombras de sus Logias.

Estos dibujos y signos son las páginas de un libro de la ciencia absoluta y universal.

Pueden leer por medio de las claves cabalísticas sin que quede nada oculto para el iniciado que posee ya las de Salomón.

La masonería no fue meramente profanada sino que sirvió de velo y pretexto de conspiraciones anárquicas que dependían de la influencia secreta de los vengadores de Santiago de Molay y de quienes continuaron la labor cismática del Templo.

En lugar de vengar la muerte de Hiram, vengaron la de sus asesinos.

---

[35] Literally 'tableaux' means "picture, drawing, canvas; board; table, chart". These are often called "tracing boards" in modern freemasonry.
[36] Literally 'historiés' means "storiated, historiated, decorated with animals, flowers, or other designs that have a narrative or symbolic purpose."
[37] Literally 'schismatique' means "schismatic, guilty of attempting to form factions; causing the formation of opposed factions"

The anarchists have taken the ruler, the square and the mallet, and have written upon them the words liberty, equality, fraternity.[38]

That is to say: liberty for desires[39], equality in degeneration[40] and fraternity for destruction.[41]

These are the men whom the Church has justly condemned and will always condemn.

Los anarquistas retomaron la regla, la escuadra y el mazo, escribiendo en ellos las palabras Libertad, Igualdad y Fraternidad[42]:

Libertad, es decir, para toda codicia, Igualdad en la degradación, y Fraternidad en la labor de destrucción.

Esos son los hombres a los que la Iglesia condenó con justicia y condenará eternamente.

---

[38] Editor's note: In Ch. 2 of Book 2 of *The Key to the Great Mysteries*, Levi says "While the world does not comprehend these three words: *truth, reason, justice*, and these: *duty, hierarchy, society*, the revolutionary motto *liberty, equality, fraternity*, will be nothing but a triple lie."

[39] Literally 'convoitises' means "desire, covetousness; greed, cupidity; lust"

[40] Literally 'bassesse' means "baseness, sordidness; servility, vileness, tawdriness, wretchedness"

[41] Editor's note: Levi says in his Preliminary Discourse to his second edition of *Dogma and Ritual of High Magic* that by giving new definitions to terms, concepts and ideas (or misinterpreting them), subversive persons are able to manipulate any organization. "The tactics of the heretics and the materialists have always been to misuse words in order to pervert things; [and] when the authority avenges herself, by condemning the heretics, [and] the truths wrongly interpreted by them and which serve them as teachings, then they accuse the authority of apostasy [a total departure from their principles]. You [who] call liberty the most condemnable license, you [who] call progress a tumultuous and subversive movement; the Church disavows you, and you bitterly accuse her of being the enemy of progress and of liberty!"

[42] Nota del editor: En el Cap. 2 del Libro 2 de *La Clave de los Grandes Misterios*, Levi dice: "Mientras el mundo no comprenda estas tres palabras: *verdad, razón, justicia*, y también aquéllas de: *deber, jerarquía, y sociedad*, la divisa revolucionaria *libertad, igualdad, fraternidad* no será más que una triple mentira."

*Gnostic Explanation
of the Symbolism
in the Masonic Legend*

*Explicación Gnóstica
del Simbolismo
en la Leyenda Masónica*

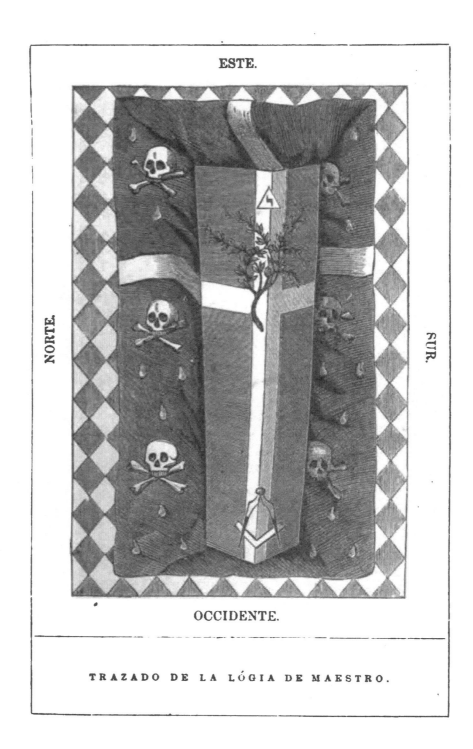

Chapter 4 from
THE MOUNTAIN OF JURATENA
by Samael Aun Weor

"THE THREE TRAITORS OF HIRAM ABIFF"

The three traitors of Hiram Abiff are called Sebal, Ortelut and the third [is] Stokin.

The three traitors should be decapitated.

The heads should be tossed into the fire and the ashes thrust to the four points of the earth, to the four winds.

These three traitors are the Black Dragon with three heads. The three rebels.

The first is the rebel of nature, the second is the rebel of science and the third is the rebel of the Truth.

These Three rebels in the Bible are: Korah, Dathan and Abiram.

The first is the one who struck Hiram with the ruler, so the righteous are killed in the name of Law and Order.

The second one struck Hiram with the lever [or crowbar], this is like the prejudices and beliefs of each epoch leading to the death of the great initiates.

The third finished off Hiram with the hammer, so this is like the violence of any epoch [which] assassinates the righteous and prohibits the diffusion of the Secret Doctrine.

These three traitors control the three bodies called: Astral, Mental and Causal (Willpower).

The great clairvoyants have studied these three vehicles, but disgracefully they have not studied what is within them.

The Astral is controlled by Sebal, the father of desire. The Mental is controlled by Ortelut, the horrible demon of the Mind and the Body of Willpower (Causal [Body]) is controlled by Stokin, the terrible demon of ill-will.

These three traitors constitute that which is called the Prince of the World.

The sacrificed[1] victim is always the internal Christ of all men who come to the world.

Hiram is our Internal Christ.

Hiram is the Sun King.

The King is dead, long live the King!

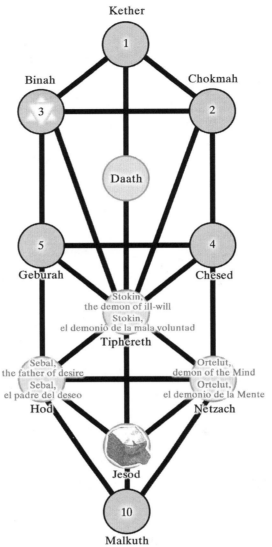

Christ was assassinated by three traitors: Caiaphas, the high priest, Judas Iscariot and Pilate.

It is necessary for us to resurrect[2] the Christ inside ourselves.

This is only possible by decapitating the three traitors.

The twenty-seven Masters who left to search for the first traitor divided themselves into three groups of nine.

---

[1] Literally 'inmolada' means "immolate, sacrifice"
[2] Literally 'resucitar' means "resuscitate, bring back to life, pull back to life, revive;"

Los grandes clarividentes han estudiado estos tres vehículos, pero desgraciadamente no han estudiado lo que hay dentro de ellos.

El Astral está controlado por Sebal, el padre del deseo. El Mental está controlado por Ortelut, el horrible demonio de la Mente y el Cuerpo de la Voluntad (Causal) está controlado por Stokin, .

Estos tres traidores constituyen eso que se llama el Príncipe de este Mundo.

La víctima inmolada es siempre el Cristo interno de todo hombre que viene al mundo.

Hiram es nuestro Cristo Interno.

Hiram es el Rey Sol.

El Rey ha muerto, ¡viva el Rey!

Cristo fue asesinado por tres traidores: Caifás, el sumum sacerdote, Judas Iscariote y Pilatos.

Nosotros necesitamos resucitar al Cristo dentro de nosotros mismos.

Esto solo es posible decapitando a los tres traidores.

Los veintisiete Maestros que salieron a buscar al primer traidor se dividieron en tres grupos de nueve.

Gnostic Explanation of the Symbolism in the Masonic Legend	Explicación Gnóstica del Simbolismo en la Leyenda Masónica
These three groups went[3] to the East, to the South and to the West.	Estos tres grupos practicaron por el Oriente, por el Mediodía y por Occidente.
This reminds us of the three doors of the temple: Man, Woman, Sex.	Esto nos recuerda las tres puertas del templo: Hombre, Mujer, Sexo.
Only by descending into the ninth sphere (sex), can we find the Prince of this World, in order to decapitate him.	Solo bajando a la novena esfera (el sexo), podemos encontrar al Príncipe de este Mundo, para decapitarlo.
The Masters find the first traitor hidden inside the cavern of desire. Then the Master decapitates the first traitor.	Los Maestros encontraron al primer traidor escondido entre la caverna del deseo. Así el Maestro decapita al primer traidor.
So the Master presents him to King Solomon leading in one hand the dagger and in the other [hand] the head of the first traitor.	Así el Maestro se presenta ante el Rey Salomón llevando en una mano el puñal y en la otra la cabeza del primer traidor.
This is how the Master exclaims: "With me comes vengeance[4]!"	Así es como el Maestro exclama: "¡Conmigo viene la venganza[8]!"

M K N

NaKaM

Avenge or punish, revenge, take vengeance

Vengar o castigar, revancha, tomar venganza

The second traitor was found by the second group of nine Masters, [that traitor] got inside the cavern of the mind, at whose door is always the dog of the desire.	El segundo traidor fue hallado por el segundo grupo de nueve Maestros, metido dentro de la caverna de la mente, a cuya puerta está siempre el perro del deseo.
The Masters took the prisoner to Solomon, this happened on the eighteenth day after [their] departure, in the late afternoon[5] and in [the] moments in which the work on the Temple had ended, Solomon had[6] the body opened, his head cut off and the heart pulled out[7].	Los Maestros lo llevaron prisionero a Salomón, esto sucedió a los dieciocho días de la partida, en la tarde y en momentos en que terminaban los trabajos del Templo, Salomón le hizo abrir el cuerpo, le cortaron la cabeza y le arrancaron el corazón.

---

[3] Literally 'practicaron' means "practice, play; carry out, perform"

[4] Editor's suggestion: Kabalistically analyze the three letters of the Hebrew word for 'vengeance', נקם, Nun=14 Kuf=19 Mem=13.

[5] Literally 'tarde' means "afternoon, evening; late, after-hours"

[6] Literally 'hizo' means "do, carry out, execute, make, perform, effect, realize;"

[7] Literally 'arrancaron' means "pull out, break off, pluck, break away, drag up, pluck off, pluck out, pull up, rip away, rip off, rip out, tear away, uproot, wrest;"

---

[8] Sugerencia del editor: Analizar kabalísticamente las tres letras de la palabra Hebrea sentido 'venganza', נקם, Nun=14 Kuf=19 Mem=13.

These eighteen days remind us of arcanum eighteen of the Tarot.		Estos dieciocho días nos recuerdan el arcano dieciocho del Tarot.

These eighteen days remind us of arcanum eighteen of the Tarot.

Really the secret and hidden enemies of the mind watch[9] us to divert us from the path of Initiation.

Only nine Masters found the second traitor.

Only down in the ninth sphere do we get to decapitate the second traitor.

The third group of nine Masters found the third traitor and had to defend themselves with much courage[10], because the third traitor heroically defends himself with the axe of ill will.

The most serious [of all this] is [that] the third traitor attempts to throw himself into the abyss, ill will and disobedience always make us fall into the abyss.

The three heads were placed on three poles garnished with iron at the door of the temple, then they were cast into the fire.

We have to descend into the ninth sphere (sex), to behead the three traitors of Hiram Abiff.

All the great initiates from the past had to descend to the ninth sphere.

The secret key is the Great Arcanum.

This Arcanum is sexual.

There must be the sexual connection.

Estos dieciocho días nos recuerdan el arcano dieciocho del Tarot.

Realmente los enemigos secretos y ocultos de la mente nos acechan para desviarnos de la senda de la Iniciación.

Solo nueve Maestros encontraron al segundo traidor.

Solo bajando a la novena esfera logramos decapitar al segundo traidor.

El tercer grupo de nueve Maestros encontró al tercer traidor y tuvo que defenderse con mucho valor, porque el tercer traidor se defendió heróicamente con el hacha de la mala voluntad.

Lo más grave es que el tercer traidor intentaba lanzarse al abismo, siempre la mala voluntad y la desobediencia nos hace caer al abismo.

Las tres cabezas fueron colocadas sobre tres pértigas guarnecidas de hierro a la puerta del templo, luego fueron echadas al fuego.

Tenemos que bajar a la novena esfera (el sexo), para decapitar a los tres traidores de Hiram Abiff.

Todos los grandes iniciados del pasado tuvieron que bajar a la novena esfera.

La clave secreta es el Gran Arcano.

Este Arcano es sexual.

Debe haber conexión sexual.

---

[9] Literally 'acechan' means "watch, be on the lookout for, lurk, pry, spy on, watch carefully for;"
[10] Literally 'valor' means "courage, manhood, valor, bravery, gallantry, grit, grittiness, pluck, derring-do, stoutheartedness, valour;"

In the union of the phallus and the uterus is the key, the important thing is [for] the couple to withdraw before the termination[11] of the sexual act, before the spasm, before the physiological orgasm, to avoid the ejaculation of the semen, not to spill the semen inside the womb, nor outside of it.

The restrained desire transmutes the seminal liquor into subtle seminal vapors that, in their turn, are converted into solar and lunar energies, positive and negative [energies].

These electro-magnetic energies ascend through two fine ganglionic cords that are coiled in the spinal medulla.

These energies rise up to the chalice, that chalice is the brain.

In this way the brain is semenized.

In this way the semen is cerebrized.

This sexual secret is the Arcanum A.Z.F., the entrance into Eden can be achieved[12] with this Arcanum.

Eden is sex itself.

We went out of Eden through the door of sex, [and] only through that door can we enter Eden.

No one can enter Paradise through false doors, we have to go [in] through where [we] went out. That is the Law.

---

[11] Literally 'terminar' means "finish, be done with, be finished with, conclude, end, terminate, be through with, stop, wind up;"

[12] Literally 'logra' means "achieve, accomplish, get, get in, obtain, succeed in, arrive at, attain, get to, realise, realize, hack out; manage to, be able to, get around to, get to, manage, have just the chance to;"

En la unión del phalo y el útero se halla la clave, lo importante es retirarse la pareja antes de terminar el acto sexual, antes del espasmo, antes del orgasmo fisiológico, para evitar la eyaculación del semen, no hay que derramar el semen ni dentro de la matriz, ni fuera de ella.

El deseo refrenado transmuta el licor seminal en sutilísimos vapores seminales que a su vez, se convierten en energías solares y lunares, positivas y negativas.

Esas energías electro-magnéticas ascienden por dos finos cordones ganglionares que se enroscan en la médula espinal.

Esas energías suben hasta el cáliz, ese cáliz es el cerebro.

Así el cerebro se seminiza.

Así el semen se cerebriza.

Este secreto sexual es el Arcano A.Z.F., con este Arcano se logra la entrada al Edem.

El Edem es el mismo sexo.

Nosotros salimos del Edem por la puerta del sexo, solo por esa puerta podemos entrar al Edem.

Nadie puede entrar al Paraíso por puertas falsas, tenemos que entrar por donde salimos. Esa es la Ley.

When solar and lunar currents of our seminal liquor make contact with the coccyx near the triveni, then the igneous snake of our magical powers awakens.

The ascending flow of the energy of the Third Logos along our spinal column, is the flaming sword with which we decapitate the Prince of this World.

With the Arcanum A.Z.F., every human being can awaken the Kundalini and become a great Master of the White Lodge.

[Also see Chapters 43 - 48 of *Tarot and Kabalah* by Samael Aun Weor for more information on this Topic.]

Cuando las corrientes solares y lunares de nuestro licor seminal hacen contacto con el coxis cerca del tribeni, entonces despierta la culebra ígnea de nuestros mágicos poderes.

El flujo ascendente de la energía del Tercer Logos a lo largo de nuestra médula espinal, es la espada flamígera con la cual decapitamos al Príncipe de este Mundo.

Con el Arcano A.Z.F., todo ser humano puede despertar el Kundalini y convertirse en un gran Maestro de la Logia Blanca.

[También ver Capítulos 43 - 48 del *Tarot y Kabala* por Samael Aun Weor para más información sobre este Tema.]

Extracted from Chapter 29 from THE THREE MOUNTAINS by Samael Aun Weor	Extracto del Capítulo IXXX de LAS TRES MONTAÑAS por Samael Aun Weor

"THE NINE DEGREES OF MASTERY" / "LOS NUEVE GRADOS DE LA MAESTRÍA"

It is urgent, and unpostponable to capture, to apprehend, to grasp[13] in an integral form, the deep significance of the nine Masters that went looking for HIRAM and his murderers.

Capturar, aprehender, captar en forma íntegra, unitotal, la honda significación de los nueve Maestros que se fueron en busca de HIRAM y de sus asesinos, es urgente, inaplazable.

Unquestionably none of the nine Masters went to the regions of the North, but intelligently organized [themselves] into three groups of three [each], they distributed themselves to the East, the South and the West.

Incuestionablemente ninguno de los nueve Maestros se fue por las regiones del Norte, sino que inteligentemente ordenados en tres grupos de a tres, se repartieron respectivamente al Oriente, al Mediodía y al Occidente.

Ostensibly it was this last [group] who achieved [the] discovery [of] the grave[14] and the murderers.

Ostensiblemente fueron estos últimos los que lograron descubrir la tumba y los asesinos.

This symbolic esoteric pilgrimage of the nine Masters refers specifically in consequence, to the individual pilgrimage that every Initiate must undertake in "The Second Mountain", going through nine successive stages or degrees totally enumerated and defined in the nine spheres:

Esta simbólica peregrinación esotérica de los nueve Maestros, se refiere específicamente en consecuencia, al peregrinaje individual que todo Iniciado tiene que efectuar en "La Segunda Montaña", pasando por nueve etapas o grados sucesivos totalmente enumerados y definidos en las nueve esferas:

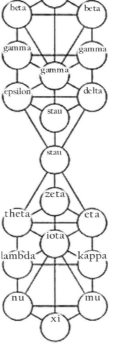

MOON [zeta]
MERCURY [eta]
VENUS [theta]
SUN [iota]
MARS [kappa]
JUPITER [lambda]
SATURN [mu]
URANUS [nu]
NEPTUNE [xi]

LUNA [zeta]
MERCURIO [eta]
VENUS [theta]
SOL [iota]
MARTE [kappa]
JÚPITER [lambda]
SATURNO [mu]
URANO [nu]
NEPTUNO [xi]

---

[13] Literally 'captar' means "perceive, apprehend, capture, grab, grasp; gain; get, detect; understand;"
[14] Literally 'tumba' means "tomb, grave, burial place;"

We can and even must issue[15] the following announcement:

> "Only through these intimate pilgrimages from sphere to sphere are we in a position to enliven and revive inside of ourselves the Secret Master, HIRAM, SHIVA, the Husband of our DIVINE MOTHER KUNDALINI, the ARCH-HIEROPHANT and ARCH-MAGICIAN, the particular, individual, Monad, our Real Being…"

It is one thing to be a Master and another, certainly much different, to achieve perfection in Mastery.

Any Esotericist who makes the "TO SOMA HELIAKON"[16], the "Wedding Garment[17] of the Soul", in the "Forge of the Cyclops" converts themselves, by such a motive, into a Man and thus a Master; however, perfection in Mastery is something very distinct…

---

[15] Literally 'emitir' means "emit, beam, cast, discharge, flash, free, give forth, give off, gush, issue, send out, throw off, flash off, pour forth, release; broadcast;"

[16] Editor's note: Compare Ch. 41 of *Tarot & Kabalah* "This famous clothing is the Egyptian Sahu, or the To Soma Heliakon in latin, that is to say, the Body of Gold of the Solar-Man, the Wedding Garment with which to attend the Banquet of the Easter Lamb. So it is necessary to comprehend that in order to have that body, the Great Alliance is needed, the work in the Ninth Sphere between Man and Woman."

[17] Literally 'Traje' means "suit, clothes, clothing, costume, dress, gown, outfit, attire, get-up, getup, toilet, toilette;"

Extracted from Chapter 27 of
THE THREE MOUNTAINS
by Samael Aun Weor

"THE HOLY SEPULCHER"

...In a distant epoch from my present existence I had not even died in myself, [and] I continued with the Ego very much alive; the sepulcher was then merely symbolic, like the coffin of a Masonic Lodge...

I did understand, though, in an integral manner, the sepulchral symbolism; I knew that I had to die in myself in order to have the right to the resurrection of "HIRAM ABIFF", the Secret Master, inside my heart temple...

Extracto del Capítulo XXVII de
LAS TRES MONTAÑAS
por Samael Aun Weor

"EL SANTO SEPULCRO"

...En aquella lejana época de mi presente existencia, ni siquiera había muerto en mí mismo, continuaba con el Ego bien vivo; el sepulcro era entonces meramente simbólico, como el ataúd de toda Logia Masónica...

Comprendía sí, en forma íntegra, el simbolismo sepulcral; sabía que debía morir en mí mismo para tener derecho a la resurrección de "HIRAM ABIFF" el Maestro Secreto, dentro de mi templo corazón...

Extracted from Chapter 15 of
THE THREE MOUNTAINS
by Samael Aun Weor

"THE THIRD INITIATION OF FIRE"

...Among the Mysteries of the Great cathedrals the Holy Sepulcher is never absent[19] and it is evident that mine could never be missing in the Initiation.

At the instant in which I am writing these lines, [there] comes to my memory the Initiatic moment of Ginés de Lara.

There was, effectively, no maiden of "Great Lineage", daughter of the founder of the Monastery, to accompany him, at that esoteric instant of the notable initiate, nor was there [the] "Good Man" [or] the actual Master Guide[20], who led him to the Sancta Sanctorum or Adytum of that temple, where the neophyte found, in the center of a very rich room of marble, a sumptuous sepulcher hermetically closed, and whose heavy lid Ginés, obeying the Master, easily lifted with his hands, and he saw within[21], to his great surprise, his own physical body.

Different from Ginés de Lara, I saw in the sepulcher my own Astral Body; I then comprehended that I had to go through the esoteric resurrection.

Unquestionably we must resurrect[22] the Great Master Mason HIRAM ABIFF in Ourselves.

"The King is dead". Long live the King!

---

[19] Literally 'falta' means "lack, absence, deficiency, shortage, scarceness, scarcity, shortness;"
[20] Literally 'Guía' means "guide, lead; direct; govern; navigate; steer; train"
[21] Literally this would read "and he saw it the same"
[22] Literally 'resucitar' means "resuscitate, bring back to life, pull back to life, revive;"

Extracto del Capítulo XV de
LAS TRES MONTAÑAS
por Samael Aun Weor

"LA TERCERA INICIACIÓN DEL FUEGO"

...Entre los Misterios de las Grandes catedrales no falta jamás el Santo Sepulcro y es evidente que no podía faltar el mío en la Iniciación.

En instantes en que escribo estas líneas, viene a mi memoria el momento Iniciático de Ginés de Lara.

No había, efectivamente, en aquel instante esotérico del insigne iniciado, doncella alguna del "Gran Linaje", hija del fundador del Monasterio, acompañándole, ni más "Ome Bueno" que el propio Maestro Guía, quien le condujo hasta el Sancta Sanctorum o Adytia de aquel templo, donde el neófito halló, en el centro de una riquísima estancia de mármol, un sepulcro suntuoso, herméticamente cerrado, y cuya pesada tapa levantó fácilmente con sus propias manos Ginés, obedeciendo al Maestro, y vio en el mismo, con gran sorpresa suya, a su propio cuerpo físico.

A diferencia de Ginés de Lara, yo vi en el sepulcro a mi propio Cuerpo Astral; comprendí entonces que debía pasar por la resurrección esotérica.

Incuestionablemente debe resucitar en Nosotros el Gran Maestro Masón HIRAM ABIFF.

"El Rey ha muerto". ¡Viva el Rey!.

A realistic, crude, legitimate, authentic Resurrection is only possible in the Second Mountain.

In these paragraphs we are only emphatically referring to the symbolic Initiatic Resurrection.

I had to stay astrally inside the Holy Sepulcher for a space of three days before the above mentioned Symbolic Resurrection.

The descent to the dark[23] abode[24] of Pluto was indispensable, after all the symbolic processes of resurrection [had taken place].

I had to begin some tenebrous[25] recapitulations within the deepest[26] entrails of the Earth; where the Florentine Dante encountered the city of Dis[27].

The progressive ascension was slowly realized through the diverse strata of the submerged mineral kingdom...

The scenic, vivid, progressive, ascendant recapitulation was indispensable for the total knowledge of Oneself, of the Myself.

To recapitulate ancient abysmal errors tends to be useful when one is trying to dissolve the EGO...

To know our own psychological errors is certainly urgent, [and] imperative...

Resurrección realista, cruda, legítima, auténtica, sólo es posible en la Segunda Montaña.

En estos párrafos sólo nos estamos refiriendo enfáticamente a la simbólica Resurrección Iniciática.

Dentro del Santo Sepulcro hube de permanecer astralmente por espacio de tres días antes de la mencionada Resurrección Simbólica.

El descenso a la oscura morada de Plutón fue indispensable, después de todo el proceso simbólico resurrectivo.

Recapitulaciones tenebrosas hube de iniciar entre las entrañas más profundas de la Tierra; allí donde el Dante Florentino encontrara la ciudad de Dite.

La ascensión progresiva se realizó lentamente, a través de los diversos estratos del reino mineral sumergido...

Recapitulación escénica, vívida, progresiva, ascendente, fue indispensable para el pleno conocimiento del Sí Mismo, del Mí Mismo.

Recapitular antiguos errores abismales, suele ser útil cuando se trata de disolver el EGO...

Conocer nuestros propios errores psicológicos, es ciertamente urgente, inaplazable...

---

[23] Literally 'obscura' means "dark, dim, obscure, darkish, dusky, shadowy, darksome, subfusc;"
[24] Literally 'morada' means "dwelling, abode, home"
[25] Literally 'tenebrosas' means "murky, obscure, dark, gloomy, shadowy, mirky, tenebrous;"
[26] Literally this would read "most profound" or "most deep"
[27] In Dante Alighieri's "The Divine Comedy" and Virgil's "Aeneid", "Dis" is the City of the Dead.

Extracted from pages 2585-2586 of THE FIFTH GOSPEL:

"TRANSCENDENTAL ESOTERIC INITIATIONS[28]"

Master: ..."Each exaltation [is] always preceded [by] a humiliation".

"IF ONE WANTS TO ASCEND, ONE MUST FIRST DESCEND", in order to be able to have the right to ascend.

Disciple: You may want to say, [then that] the womb of Heaven...

M. Is below; the Inferno is the womb of Heaven!...

D. Then, the sepulcher of Hiram Abiff is in the same Ninth Sphere?

M. Well, the SEPULCHER OF HIRAM ABIFF HAS TO [BE] SEARCHED [FOR] IN OUR OWN ANIMAL DEPTHS; the Sepulcher is there...

D. Is [he] our Christ, in truth Master?

M. HIRAM ABIFF IS OUR REAL BEING, he is the Lord, [he] is the Secret Master, [is he] not?

Extracto de páginas 2585-2586 de EL QUINTO EVANGELIO:

"INDICACIONES ESOTÉRICAS TRASCENDENTALES[29]"

Maestro. ..."A cada exaltación le precede siempre una humillación".

"SI UNO QUIERE SUBIR, DEBE PRIMERO BAJAR", para poder tener el derecho a subir.

Discípulo: Quizás quiera decir, la matriz del Cielo...

M. ¡Está abajo; el Infierno es la matriz del Cielo!...

D. Entonces, ¿el sepulcro de Hiram Abiff está en la misma Novena Esfera?

M. Pues, el SEPULCRO DE HIRAM ABIFF HAY QUE BUSCARLO EN NUESTROS PROPIOS FONDOS ANIMALES; allí está el Sepulcro...

D. Es nuestro Cristo, ¿verdad Maestro?

M. HIRAM ABIFF ES NUESTRO REAL SER, él es el Señor, es el Maestro Secreto, ¿no?

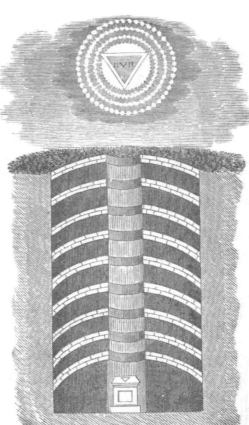

---

[28] This extract is from part of a question and answer session.

[29] Este extracto de parte de a preguntas y respuestas sesiones.

He is in the "sepulcher" and the "sepulcher" is ourselves, [it] is our own Deep Animal Depths; he is very dead and [IT] IS NECESSARY TO RESURRECT[30] HIM...

D. In the texts of Philosophical Masonry, those people still say that they are going to find Hiram Abiff; and we know that Hiram Abiff is [the symbol for] Resurrected Masters.

They say that when [they] find Hiram Abiff, he is going to resurrect Masonry again.

And if he is resurrecting in us, because in Gnosis there are already Masters, and these Resurrected Masters are precisely Hiram Abiff, then they are still waiting for this thing...

M. Well, "The King is dead; [long] live the King". One has to search for him, the King, Hiram Abiff, within ourselves, and one has to resurrect him within ourselves.

In such a way that, while Hiram Abiff is not resurrected, we are dead.

The important thing is to resurrect him.

One has to search for the Golden Fleece which is below, in the World [of the] Infernos.

If we do not look for it below, we are lost...

Él está en el "sepulcro" y el "sepulcro" somos nosotros mismos, son nuestros propios Bajos Fondos Animales; él está bien muerto ahí y HAY QUE RESUCITARLO...

D. En los textos de la Masonería Filosófica, esta gente todavía dicen que van a encontrar a Hiram Abiff; y nosotros sabemos que Hiram Abiff son los Maestros Resurrectos.

Ellos dicen que cuando encuentren a Hiram Abiff, va a resucitar nuevamente la Masonería.

Y si ya está resucitando en nosotros, porque en la Gnosis ya hay Maestros, y estos Maestros Resurrectos son precisamente Hiram Abiff, entonces ellos todavía está esperando esa cosa...

M. Pues, "El Rey ha muerto; viva el Rey!" El Rey, Hiram Abiff, hay que buscarlo dentro nosotros mismos, y hay que resucitarlo dentro de nosotros mismos.

De manera que, mientras no resucite Hiram Abiff, muertos estamos.

Lo importante es resucitarlo.

El Vellocino de Oro hay que buscarlo es abajo, en los Mundos Infiernos.

Si no lo buscamos abajo, estamos perdidos...

---

[30] Literally 'resucitarlo' means "resuscitate him, bring him back to life, pull him back to life, revive him;"

*The Rose-Cross Secrets
of Occult Masonry*

*Los Secretos Rosa-Cruz
de la Masonería Oculta*

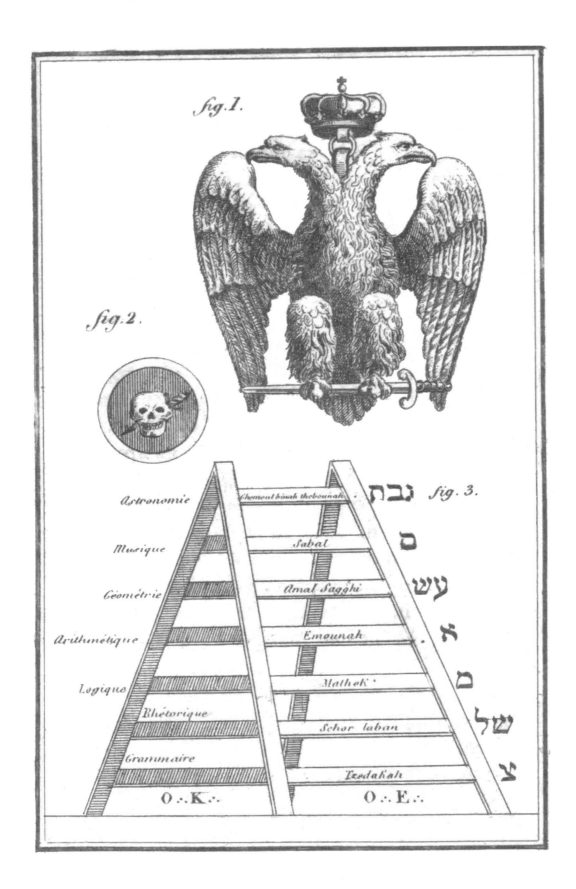

Editor's Note about Arnoldo Krumm-Heller (Huiracocha)

Krumm-Heller was a Mason and member of the Memphis-Mizraim branch of High Grade Masonry. This Rite had 97 degrees and was established in France in 1881 from the combination of two so-called 'Egyptian' Rites: the Rite of Memphis and the Rite of Misraïm. The Rite of Misraïm is said to have been popularized by Cagliostro in the late 1700s and was introduced in France in 1814. The Rite of Memphis was introduced in France in 1839.[1] Eliphas Levi mentions this association in one of his letters to his disciple Baron Spédalieri in 1862, saying:

> "Eckhartshausen[2] belonged to the occult Masonry of the Misraim rite, and he was the grand master therein. This rite was profaned in France by the materialistic disciples of the mysterious Cagliostro. The rite of Misraim was affiliated with the Joannites or Templars of whom the actual Grand Master was the baron of Szapari. Their doctrine materialized itself and was corrupted…"

Krumm-Heller says in his book *Logos, Mantram, Magic* (1930) at the end of the Section entitled 'EVERYTHING RADIATES':

> "I, who have nearly half a century of study in these matters behind me, who possess the highest degrees of masonry 3-33-97 … declare for myself [that] in vocalization, in the use of mantrams and [of] *prayer*, [and] through the awakening of the sexual secretions, exists the only path to arrive at the goal and all else, that is not here, is a miserable waste of time."

---

[1] Editor's note: See *Esoteric Studies in Masonry Vol. 2* for more information about these Rites from J-M. Ragon.
[2] Karl von Eckartshausen (1752-1803) was a German Catholic mystic, author, and philosopher.

Krumm-Heller has a unique perspective on the subject of Masonry which is evident in the following three articles. But there is something that must be remembered: Krumm-Heller speaks with the language and terminology of his time and perspective (the end of the Age of Pisces, prior to beginning of the Age of Aquarius).

Krumm-Heller talks about the same subjects and topics that we discuss in Gnosis, but he just uses different terms to describe them. Do not let this confuse you in your studies. Remember to extract what is useful and discard what is useless, so that you can benefit from anything.

THE SECRETS OF MASONRY 1

Dr. Arnold Krumm Heller

Often it has been requested of me that I write on occult Masonry, but I have always refused because I have thought that I should not have to waste any[4] time [with this].

But, lately, Leadbeater has published[5] a book on Masonry[6], just as Heindel had done before [him], and so I have resolved to exit[7] from silence.

When reading these works, just as the one by Jinaradasa[8], I have said to myself: either these authors do not know anything about occult Masonry or maybe they know and they do not want to speak [about it].

What is more probable is that thousands and thousands of masons are going to the Lodge[9] dedicating themselves to a very beautiful humanitarianism, but in order to [not] over salt them [with] Masonry and [so as to] make more practical work [possible, they are] being enlisted into the salvation army with the degree of lieutenant.

SECRETOS DE LA MASONERÍA I

Dr. Arnold Krumm Heller

Muchas veces se me ha pedido que escriba sobre la Masonería oculta, pero siempre me he negado porque he creído que no debo perder el tiempo.

Pero, últimamente, Leadbeater ha lanzado un libro sobre Masonería[10], lo mismo como lo había hecho antes Heindel, y entonces he resuelto salir del silencio.

Al leer estas obras, lo mismo como la de Jinaradasa[11], me he dicho: o estos autores no saben nada de Masonería oculta o si saben no quieren hablar.

Lo más probable es que sean como miles y miles de masones que acuden a los Talleres dedicándose a un humanitarismo muy hermoso, pero para ejercerlo les sale sobrando la Masonería y harían obras más prácticas enrolándose en el ejército de salvación con el grado de alférez.

---

[4] Literally 'el' means "the; he; it; one"
[5] Literally 'lanzado' means "throw, cast; send; sling; aim; shoot; pitch; release; launch; dart, dash"
[6] This would be either *Glimpses of Masonic History* (1926), later republished as *Freemasonry and its Ancient Mystic Rites*, or *The Hidden Life in Freemasonry* (1926).
[7] Literally 'salir' means "exit, leave, go out; appear, come into view; escape; enter; hatch, emerge from an egg; defray, pay, cover the expenses of; project; quit; lead; win"
[8] Curuppumullage "Carlos" Jinarajadasa (1875-1953) was a freemason, theosophist and president of the Theosophical Society Adyar. Jinarajadasa's interests and writings included religion, philosophy, literature, art, science and occult chemistry.
[9] Literally 'Talleres' means "atelier, artist's studio or workroom, workshop; mill, works; garage; pit"

[10] Esto sería tanto *Historia Secreta De La Masoneria*, o *Los Grandes Secretos de la Masoneria*, ambos publicados en 1926.
[11] Curuppumullage "Carlos" Jinarajadasa (1875-1953) fue un masón, teósofo, y cuarto presidente de la Sociedad Teosófica (ST). Sus intereses y escritos incluyen religión, filosofía, literatura, arte, ciencia y química oculta.

For some years, the theosophists have been installing masonic bodies that they call, I believe, [masonry] of adoption [or adoptive rite masonry][12] and in them they receive women and when practicing their ritual they give some quite accurate symbolic explanations, which always means a step forward, but what they know and [what] they say is nothing compared[13] with the true secrets of the Fraternity.

We must not forget that Masonry, [just] as much as the catholic religion, in its rites and ceremonies, is nothing more than recollections[14] of the Real Art or Magic.

It says [in] one of the first phrases of the ritual of initiation that in order to be [a] mason [one] is required to be free man and of good moral [standing][15].

So it is necessary TO BE [A] MAN and not [a] woman.[16]

When the theosophists put women in our works [they] do not know what they have done.

It is not that I see women as less, no; without her we would be nothing nor [would] we obtain anything and I think that women must participate in all the social affairs just like men, in everything… except in Masonry; where it does not fit.

---

[12] Editor's note: Adoptive Rite Masonry has existed in France since at least the mid-late 1700s, and was not created by the Theosophical Society, but they may have their own flavor.
[13] Literally 'en comparación' means "in comparison"
[14] Literally 'reminiscencias' means "reminiscence, recollection of past events and experiences"
[15] Literally 'buenas costumbres' means "good customs or good habits", but when these two words are used together it means "moral or morality"
[16] Editor's note: Krumm-Heller is entitled to his opinion, but let us remember that the emphasis is on being a "free man". "Free", meaning having a free-will and therefore free from vices and bad habits, or, we could say, those who's soul is free from the dominion of their passions. And "man", meaning a man in the complete sense of the word, a Causal Man, that is: to have the superior existential bodies of the Being. So if we understand the meaning of the term "free man", then we see the true purpose of freemasonry and that a woman can possess these things as well.

Hace algunos años, los teósofos han instalado unos cuerpos masónicos que llaman, creo, de adopción[17] y en ellos reciben a las mujeres y al practicar su ritual dan algunas explicaciones simbólicas bastante atinadas, que siempre significa un paso adelante, pero lo que saben y dicen no es nada en comparación con los verdaderos secretos de la Fraternidad.

No olvidemos que la Masonería, tanto como la religión católica, en sus ritos y ceremonias, no son más que reminiscencias del Arte Real o Magia.

Dice una de las primeras frases del ritual de la iniciación que para ser masón se requiere ser hombre libre y de buenas costumbres.

De manera que es necesario SER HOMBRE y no mujer.

Al meter los teósofos a las mujeres en nuestros trabajos no han sabido lo que han hecho.[18]

No es que yo mire a menos a la mujer, no; sin ella nada seríamos ni nada lograríamos y opino que la mujer debe participar en todas las cuestiones sociales igual que el hombre, en todo… menos en la Masonería; allá no cabe ella.

---

[17] Nota del editor: la Masonería Adoptiva ha existido en Francia al menos desde mediados de los años 1700, y no fue creado por la Sociedad Teosófica, pero que puede tener su propio sabor.
[18] Nota del Editor: Krumm-Heller tiene derecho a su opinión, pero recordemos que el énfasis está en ser un "hombre libre". "Libre", que significa tener una voluntad libre y, por tanto, de vicios y malos hábitos, o, nosotros podríamos decir, aquellos que tiene alma es libre desde el dominio de sus pasiones. Y "hombre", lo que significa un hombre en el sentido completo de la palabra, un Hombre Causal, es decir: que tiene los cuerpos existenciales superiores del Ser. Así que si comprendemos el significado del término "hombre libre", entonces vemos el verdadero propósito de la masonería y una mujer puede poseer estas cosas así.

The woman will never be able to assume the functions of man as creator.

[She] can imitate, [she] can help, but [she] cannot create because [she] needs the creative gland, the prostate[19], having been born without it and the mason must have [the] prostate when he wants to dedicate itself to masonic and experimental magic.

The eminently wise Standemeyer[20] in his work "Magic as Experimental Science", says:

> "We have certain nervous centers that we must excite in the experiments.
>
> With them we can awaken and exteriorize our magical forces."

These centers are in intimate relation with our endocrine glands and they, in their turn, are susceptible to being provoked into functioning in a given sense with the oppression of certain arteries or the suppression of other nervous centers.

The practice of how to do all this is locked up[21] in the giving[22] of the signs, grips[23] and passwords of Masonry.

How insignificant sometimes is the grip that is required!

La mujer nunca podrá asumir las funciones de hombre como creador.

Puede imitar, puede ayudar, pero no puede crear porque le falta la glándula creativa, la próstata[24], por haber nacido sin ella y el masón debe tener próstata cuando quiere dedicarse a la magia masónica y experimental.

El eminente sabio Standemeyer en su obra "La Magia como Ciencia Experimental"[25], dice:

> "Tenemos ciertos centros nerviosos que debemos excitar en las experiencias.
>
> Con ellas podemos despertar y exteriorizar nuestras fuerzas mágicas"

Estos centros están en íntima relación con nuestras glándulas endocrinas y éstas, a su vez, susceptibles a ser provocadas a funcionar en un sentido dado con la opresión de ciertas arterias o la supresión de otros centros nerviosos.

La práctica de cómo hacer todo esto está encerrada en el manejo de los signos, toques y palabras de pase de la Masonería.

¡Cuan insignificante es a veces el toque que se requiere!

---

[19] Editor's note: Of course Krumm-Heller is neglecting that women have a corresponding "gland" and internal organ which also perform a creative function, being the Ovaries and the Uterus.
[20] This appears to be referring to Ludwig Staudenmaier's *Die Magie Als Experimentelle Naturwissenschaft* (1912) which has not been translated into English.
[21] Literally 'encerrada' means "locked-up, shut-in, closeted, constrained, locked, pent-up;"
[22] Literally 'manejo' means "handling; driving, conduction, operation, conduct;"
[23] Literally 'toques' means "touch, feel; knock, beat, tap, brush, light touch, flick;"

[24] Nota del Editor: Por supuesto Krumm-Heller es descuidar que las mujeres tienen una "glándula" correspondiente y el órgano interno que también realizan una función creativa, siendo los Ovarios y el Útero.
[25] Esto parece estar refiriéndose a el libro *Die Magie Als Experimentelle Naturwissenschaft* (1912) por Ludwig Staudenmaier

The Rose-Cross Secrets of Occult Masonry	Los Secretos Rosa-Cruz de la Masonería Oculta
The treatments of Dr. Asuero[26] have proven, who when slightly interrupting[27] the trigeminal nerve, heals diabetics[28] in the act and quadriplegics throw their crutches [away].	Lo prueban las curaciones del Dr. Asuero[32], quién al herir ligeramente el nervio trigémino, logra que los diabéticos sanen en el acto y que los paralíticos tiren sus muletas.
Who among the masons present has ever suspected that such things existed behind our grips?	¿Quién de los masones actuales ha sospechado jamás que tras de nuestros toques existieran tales cosas?
And, nevertheless, in Turkish Masonry and in the Rite of Memphis and Mizraim the key is exhibited[29] with complete clarity.	Y, sin embargo, en la Masonería Turca y en el Rito de Memphis y Mizraim está expuesta con toda claridad la clave.
The ancient rites, and those which are from the ninth century, give the practices mentioned with all the details: the days in which to do the practices, the grips, how [they are done], [and] in the same manner, their association with vocalization.	Los ritos antiguos, y los hay desde el siglo noveno, dan las prácticas mencionadas con todos los pormenores: los días en los que hay que hacer las prácticas, los toques, como, asimismo, su asociación con la vocalización.
All this is indicated in the masonic calendar.	Todo ello es señalado en el calendario masónico.
They give instructions on the awakening of the chakras, that a mason of the middle ages called[30] "flames" and in those times the neophytes had to learn to magically handle the passwords of the first and the second degrees.	Dan instrucciones sobre el despertar de los chakras, que un masón de la edad media denomina "llamitas" y ya en aquellos tiempos los neófitos tenían que aprender a manejar mágicamente las palabras de pase del primer y segundo grado.

In Rosario [Argentina] they have come back to realize this ancient rite, but nowadays [something] curious [happens]; they do not have [anything] more than the [masonic] patent issued in Italy, but they are missing[31] what [is] essential: the KEY, because those degrees precisely lack it.

En Rosario han vuelto a realizar este rito antiguo, pero ahora viene lo curioso; no tiene más que la patente expedida en Italia, pero les falta lo esencial: la CLAVE, pues precisamente esos grados carecen de ella.

---

[26] Dr. Fernando Asuero (also known as Don Fernando) was a well-known Spanish physician (1886-1942), who practiced in San Sebastian and was famous for his ability to cure many "incurable" disease, sometimes simply by touching the patient's trigeminal nerve.
[27] Literally 'herir' means "injure, wound, hurt, pierce"
[28] Literally 'logra que los diabéticos sanen' means "manages to heal the diabetics"
[29] Literally 'expuesta' means "expose, exhibited, on exhibit, on show, on view; expound; set out, explain; display"
[30] Literally 'denomina' means "name, denominate, denote, designate, entitle; call"
[31] Literally 'falta' means "lack, absence, deficiency, shortage, scarceness, scarcity, shortness; need, want;"

---

[32] Dr. Fernando Asuero (también conocido como Don Fernando) fue un célebre médico español (1886-1942), que ejerció en San Sebastián y era famoso por su habilidad para curar muchas enfermedades "incurables", a veces con sólo tocar nervio trigémino del paciente.

They wanted me to give it to them[33], but, despite my [efforts], it was not possible.

When I was giving a conference in the beautiful halls the Union Lodge Number 17[34], a brother who presided [there] launched [himself] into a discourse, from [the] title of my presentation, [which] proved with complete clarity that they don't know [much] beyond what is in Masonry itself and in its relation with the Rose Cross Fraternity, and at that time I said to myself: "here you should not reveal anything, because they are not yet mature for these things".

[They want] the ancient and sacred Rite [of Masonry] to be handled the way the Scots handle it, [but] I am not ready for that, since they have converted [their Masonic system] into a corpse[35].

The masonic brothers can be sure that I, as [a] ROSE CROSS adept, am a mason, not by the diplomas that I own (because sometimes these are not worth [the cost of] the paper that has been spent on them). No, I am [a] mason because I have comprehended the great secrets of the Order.

The vowels I A O, which are locked up in the passwords of the first degrees, must be pronounced in combination with the grips and immediately the sanguineous current of our organism undergoes an instantaneous modification and it puts us into [a] condition for provoking psychic phenomena.

---

[33] Litearlly 'que yo se la diera' means "that I give it to them"
[34] "Logia Unión Nº 17" is in Rosario, Argentina and seems to be a "Free and Accepted" (York Rite) Masonic Lodge. It appears to have opened on October 11th 1860 and was still operating in 2011 according to the *Gran Logia de la Argentina de Libres y Aceptados Masones* website.
[35] Literally 'pues lo han convertido en un cadáver' means "they have converted it into a corpse"

Han querido que yo se la diera, pero, malgrado mío, no fue posible.

Al dar yo una conferencia en los hermosos salones de la Logia Unión Número 17[36], un hermano que presidía, a título de presentación mía, lanzó un discurso en el cual probó con toda claridad que no saben allá lo que es en sí la Masonería y sus relaciones con la Fraternidad Rosa Cruz, y entonces me dije: acá no debes revelar nada, pues aún no están maduros para estas cosas.

Que el Rito antiguo y sagrado se maneje como se maneja el Escocés, para eso no me presto, pues lo han convertido en un cadáver.

Los hermanos masones pueden estar seguros que yo, como adepto ROSA CRUZ, sí soy masón, no por los diplomas que poseo, pues éstos no valen a veces el papel que se ha gastado en ellos. No, yo soy masón porque he comprendido los grandes secretos de la Orden.

Las vocales I A O que están encerradas en las palabras de paso de los primeros grados, deben pronunciarse en combinación con los toques e inmediatamente la corriente sanguínea de nuestro organismo sufre una modificación instantánea y nos pone en condiciones de provocar fenómenos psíquicos.

---

[36] "Logia Unión N ° 17" se encuentra en Rosario, Argentina, y parece ser un "Libre y Aceptado" (Rito de York) Logia Masónica. Parece haber inaugurado el 11 de octubre 1860 y fue todavía en funcionamiento en 2011 de acuerdo con la página web del *Gran Logia de la Argentina Libres y Aceptados Masones*.

A turkish master mason who was[37] with me [for] a time, took a rabbit[38] and he put his fingers upon him in the form that the apprentice mason must make, and immediately the little animal was put into [a] state of catalepsy[39], soon he did the same with a boy of 20 years, whom I believed was dead, but [it] was enough to give him the hand as [the] master [mason does] for [him to], instantaneously, return to himself.

[For] years and years I have experimented in the laboratory with the masonic subjects and every day I have been more [and more] convinced that we are truly possessors of a real, grandiose, [and] superior art with which we can teach official science.

Will I be able to let the brother masons participate in that which I have discovered? The future will say and I [will be] seriously happy to be able to do so.

What I can assure [you of] is that if you have seen me cure [a] paralyzed[40] [person], [or a] blind [person], like [Doctor] Asuero, and many [other so-called] incurable patients, sometimes very instantaneously, I did not learn it in the school of medicine, but [by] meditating on the intimate subjects of Masonry, where I found much more, so much more, than is commonly suspected.

Un maestro masón turco quién actuó un tiempo conmigo, tomaba un conejo y le ponía los dedos en la forma como debe hacerlo el aprendiz masón e inmediatamente el animalito se puso en estado de catalepsia, luego hizo lo mismo con un muchacho de 20 años, quién yo creía muerto, pero bastó darle la mano como maestro para que, instantáneamente, volviera en sí.

Años y años he experimentado yo en el laboratorio con los asuntos masónicos y cada día me he convencido más de que realmente somos poseedores de un arte real, grandioso, superior a lo que nos puede enseñar la ciencia oficial.

¿Podré dejar participar a los hermanos masones de lo que yo he descubierto? El porvenir lo dirá y yo seria feliz en poderlo hacer.

Lo que puedo asegurar es que si me han visto curar paralíticos, ciegos, como Asuero, y muchos enfermos incurables, en algunas ocasiones instantáneamente, no lo aprendí en la escuela de medicina, sino meditando sobre los asuntos íntimos de la Masonería, donde encontré mucho más, muchísimo más, de lo que comúnmente se sospecha.

---

[37] Literally 'actuó' means "act, perform; play; appear; operate; proceed; sit"
[38] Literally 'conejo' means "rabbit, cony, animal with long ears and long hind legs, any of several small species of rodent from the family Leporidae; fur of a rabbit;"
[39] Literally 'catalepsia' means "(Medicine) catalepsy, muscular rigidity and lack of contact with the environment (associated with schizophrenia); trance"
[40] Literally 'paralíticos' means "paralytic, palsied, paralyzed;"

The dualism represented by the two columns of the temple signify the two aspects of the consciousness, that is to say, the conscious Self and the subconscious [Self][41].

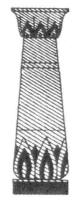
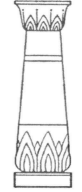

Masonry has always appealed to reason and has applauded France when [it] excluded God glorifying Reason in a woman.[42]

Our Reason certainly is, like the consciousness, the divine voice in us, but we cannot listen to its dictations clearly, since we are put to sleep by our vices and bad habits, our prejudices and preoccupations and it is necessary to liberate [ourselves] from them.

We have been guided by our instincts too much, forgetting that we have intuition as [a] prominent divine factor, which can guide us, but intuition does not work[43] [for us] if we do not do magical exercises, [we should] study [the] movements before [we do the exercises] and this has always been [the] privilege of the initiatic societies.

El dualismo representado por las dos columnas del templo significa los dos aspectos de la conciencia, es decir, el Sí[44] consciente y el subconsciente[45].

La Masonería ha apelado siempre a la razón y ha aplaudido a Francia cuando excluía a Dios glorificando en una mujer a la Razón.[46]

Nuestra Razón seguro que es, como la conciencia, la voz divina en nosotros, pero no podemos escuchar sus dictados claramente, por estar adormecidos por nuestros vicios y malas costumbres, por nuestros prejuicios y preocupaciones y es menester liberarla.

Nos hemos guiado demasiado por nuestro instinto, olvidando que tenemos la intuición como factor divino prominente, que nos puede guiar, pero esa intuición tampoco actúa si no hacemos ejercicios mágicos, movimientos estudiados de antemano y que han sido siempre privilegio de las sociedades iniciáticas.

---

[41] Editor's note: In Gnostic Psychology we could also call these two sides the Light and the Darkness or the Being and the Ego, the Bonded Cathexis and the Loose Cathexis.
[42] Editor's note: It is unclear exactly what Krumm-Heller is referring to, but possibly that the *Grand Orient de France* (GODF) believes in 'freedom of conscience' and this allows them to admit atheists. So he may be referring to the idea that the Absolute is Reason which is a concept that is mentioned in some of the higher degrees.
[43] Literally 'actúa' means "act, do something, take action; perform on; act out; perform, play-act;"

[44] Originalmente "el Ego". Nota del Editor: Huiracocha no se refiere al ego como se utiliza en la Psicología Gnóstica, pero al nosotros total.
[45] Nota del Editor: En la Psicología Gnóstica también podríamos llamar estos dos lados la Luz y la Oscuridad o el Ser y el Ego.
[46] Nota del Editor: No está claro exactamente qué Krumm-Heller se refiere, pero posiblemente que el *Gran Oriente de Francia* (GODF) cree en la "libertad de conciencia" y esto les permite admitir ateos. Así que él puede estar refiriéndose a la idea de que el absoluto es razón que es un concepto que se menciona en algunos de los grados superiores.

| The Rose-Cross Secrets of Occult Masonry | Los Secretos Rosa-Cruz de la Masonería Oculta |

Then, these exercises and everything that we do, like [the] steps and movements, in the different masonic degrees, are not only psychotechnical[47] practices, but they are [also] practices that can take us to a superior state [of consciousness] from the commonly known [state of consciousness]…

The masonic catechism[48] says that a Masonic Lodge represents the Universe and that we admire the Great Architect of the Universe.

It has also been called the Macrocosmic Universe, putting it in front of us (we who are the Microcosm), signifying that we are a synthesis of the great All[49], and since we do not have a way to study the Universe, the Mason must occupy himself with the study of their SELF in order to start [his study of] the secrets of the Universe by analogy.

Our SELF is represented for the Mason by the dualism of their columns, the "J" and the "B" columns.

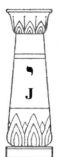

The [letter] "J" should be [the letter] "I", because this vowel has always been the representation of the SELF in the primitive languages, and it has preserved itself in the German in the "Ich", in the English "I", the French "Je", the Italian "Io", and the Spanish "Yo". We could follow with other languages[50].

Pues bien, estos ejercicios y todo lo que hacemos, como marchas y movimientos, en los diferentes grados masónicos, no son solo prácticas psicotécnicas, sino que son prácticas que nos pueden llevar a un estado superior al del comúnmente conocido…

El catecismo masón dice que una Logia Masónica representa el Universo y que se admira al Gran Arquitecto del Universo.

Se ha llamado también al Universo Macrocosmos, poniéndolo frente a nosotros, que somos el Microcosmos, siendo así que significamos una síntesis del gran Todo, y estando por nuestro modo de ser incapacitados para estudiar el Universo, el Masón debe ocuparse del estudio de su SÍ[51] para arrancar los secretos del Universo por analogía.

Nuestro SÍ[52] está representado para el Masón por el dualismo de sus columnas, la columna J y la B.

La Jota debe ser I, pues esta vocal ha sido siempre la representación del SÍ[53] en los lenguajes primitivos, y se ha conservado en el Alemán en el Ich, en el Inglés I, en el Francés Je, en el Italiano Io, y en el Español Yo. Podríamos seguir con otros idiomas.

---

[47] Litearlly 'psicotécnicas' means "psychotechnical, pertaining to the use of psychological knowledge in practical applications"
[48] Literally 'catecismo' means "catechism, an elementary book containing a summary of the principles of the philosophy or religion, especially as maintained by a particular group, in the form of questions and answers."
[49] Literally 'todo' means "all, whole, total; all in all; everything"
[50] Literally 'idiomas' means "languages, tongues, idioms; dialects;"

[51] Originalmente "su YO". Nota del Editor: Huiracoccha no se refiere al yo como se utiliza en la Psicología Gnóstica, pero al nosotros total.
[52] Originalmente "Nuestro YO".
[53] Originalmente "del YO".

But the [letter] "I" not only has symbolic value, but [also has] real [value], through its sound, and the apprentice [Mason] must learn the articulation of the "I" well in order to awaken the inherent force in the sound of this vowel, which is always in intimate relation with the Tattwa, reflected in the Atmosphere and in the magnetic centers of the body.

For these things the dualism must be conscious.

The columns are separated; one represents the subjective SELF and the other the objective [SELF].

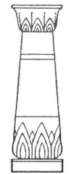

When we say: "I enter through the door", we generally confuse our two Selves, and thus we do not realize the true situation of the Universe.

The apprentice Mason should accustom themselves to the following way of thinking: "I take my body through that door".[54]

Equally when speaking, [one] should think: "I make the "I" sound with my vocal cords."

There is a difference between the internal Self which speaks and the external Self which pronounces.

For the exercise of meditation the Turks advise the apprentice masons to take a grain or a seed and meditate upon it, [on] the potentiality which [is] locked up [inside of it], [and] the faculty to be developed, [which] will come to be [a] flower, plant and tree, thanks to the impulse of the Great Architect of the Universe.[55]

Pero la I no solo tiene valor simbólico, sino real, por su sonido, y el aprendiz debe aprender bien la pronunciación de la I para despertar la fuerza inherente al sonido de esta vocal, que está siempre en íntima relación con el Tatwa, en la Atmósfera refleja y en los centros magnéticos del cuerpo.

Para estas cosas el dualismo debe ser consciente.

Las columnas están separadas; la una representa el SÍ[56] subjetivo y la otra el objetivo.

Cuando decimos: "yo entro por la puerta", confundimos generalmente nuestros dos Sí Mismos[57], y así no nos damos cuenta de la verdadera situación del Universo.

El aprendiz Masón debería acostumbrarse al siguiente modo de pensar: "yo llevo a mi cuerpo por esa puerta".[58]

Igual cuando habla, debería pensar: "yo hago sonar la I por mis cuerdas vocales".

Hay una diferencia entre el Ego interno que habla y el Ego externo que pronuncia.

Para el ejercicio de la meditación aconsejan los turcos a los aprendices masones que tomen un grano o una semilla y mediten sobre ella, la potencialidad que encierra, la facultad de desarrollarse, de llegar a ser flor, planta y árbol, gracias al impulso del Gran Arquitecto del Universo.[59]

---

[54] Editor's note: Compare what Gurdjieff says in Ch.9 of *In Search of the Miraculous* about the Transformation of Impressions, "In an ordinary psychic state we simply look at a street. But if we remember ourselves, then we do not simply look at the street; we feel that we are looking, as though saying to ourselves: 'I am looking'. Instead of one impression of the street there are two impressions, one of the street and another of ourselves looking at it."

[55] Editor's note: Compare the exercise given in Ch. 85 of *Tarot and Kabalah*

[56] Originalmente "el YO".
[57] Originalmente "nuestros dos Egos".
[58] Nota del editor: Compare lo que dice Gurdjieff en Ch.9 de *Fragmentos de una Enseñanza Desconocida* sobre la Transformación de las Impresiones, "En un estado psíquico ordinario, simplemente miro a la calle. Pero si «me recuerdo a mí mismo», no miro simplemente a la calle, yo siento que la miro, como si me dijera a mí mismo: «Yo miro». En vez de una impresión de la calle, tengo dos impresiones: una de la calle y la otra de mí mismo mirando a la calle."

[59] Nota del Editor: Comparar el ejercicio dado en Cap. 85 de *Tarot y Kabalah*

Then they will take an imitation of a grain or seed, as we see [in] the wax or rubber imitation fruit.

[If] that occult power did not reside [in the seed or grain], [then] the Great Architect of the Universe would not act.

That takes care of the real and unreal things, that living or dead aspect of things.

The black and white floor represents the day and the night, in relation to our Self [either we are] in state of vigilance and [or we are] in a sleeping[60] state.

Luego hacen tomar la imitación de un grano o semilla, como vemos las frutas imitadas de goma o de cera.

Es que no reside ese poder oculto donde no actúa el Gran Arquitecto del Universo.

Así se hace cargo de las cosas reales e irreales, de ese aspecto vivo o muerto de las cosas.

El piso blanco y negro representa el día y la noche, en relación con nuestro Ego en estado de vigilia y en estado dormido.

---

[60] Literally 'dormido' means "sleeping, asleep"

Rosicrucian Magazine Year VI
Berlin, May 27, 1932
No. 02

Occult Masonry
By Krumm-Heller

If we study the Ancient Mysteries, of which Masonry is undoubtedly a continuation, we will constantly observe that its symbolism is separate[61] from its legitimately[62] real philosophical value.

If the [purpose of the] Mysteries was to know a supra-physical World, this was because it truly exists and [because this] is where one goes after death, while the ordeals[63] that are still maintained in apparent form, [in the ancient Mysteries, they] were real and highlighted some aspect [of the work that is needed to reach that supra-physical World].

It is not possible that Masonry is divorced from the source from which it sprung, that its symbolism only exists metaphorically[64] and that the "I"[65] [י], for example, one of the columns, [is] only a vowel taken at random when another quite different [letter] could have been taken.

The Aleph [א] of the Hebrews, which represents man between two worlds, would have lent itself beautifully to fulfill[66] this symbolism in a most perfect way.

---

[61] Literally 'apartado' means "separate, divide; alienate; distract; avert, turn away; lure away, allure"

[62] Literally 'verdadero' means "legitimate, legal, lawful; acceptable; correct, sound; incorrupt, perfect"

[63] Literally 'pruebas' means "evidence, proof; test, exam; experiment, trial; audition; demonstration; correction"

[64] Literally 'de modo metafórico' means "in [a] metaphorical way"

[65] Editor's note: This is most likely refering to the Hebrew letter י (Iod/Jod/Yod) corresponding to the letter I, the first letter of the word "Jakin".

[66] Literally 'llenar' means "fill; cover; pack; stuff; crowd; occupy; equate"

Why, let us ask, was the "I" [י] taken for one column and the "B" [ב] for [the] other and why then are [the] words [Jakin and Boaz] which start with those letters [the names of] the columns of the Temple of Solomon?

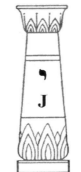

The finishing apprentices could give us a wealth of responses [which] would rectify[68] our ignorance and we would have to hide [because of] embarrassment[69] since we, 33rd degree [members], did not know these things and asked such childish questions.

But... we, ignorant 33rd [degree members] and companions of the other ignorant 33rd [degree members], we know that there is something more and that's what our companions ignore...

The symbols, we [can] say, are worth nothing in themselves if their meaning is not known, but the "I" [י and] the "B" [ב] are realities and there are concrete ways[70] for those who know [how] to read.

We have signs, grips[71] and passwords.

Something that at first seems silly and childish, may have been invented in a more complicated way and, nonetheless, these grips, these signs and the words, have not been respected...

Do you not think that all this could be an expression of something occult?

Such is, indeed, the case.

Por qué, nos preguntamos, fue tomada la I [י] para una columna y la B [ב] para otra y por qué se encuentran luego palabras [Jakin y Boaz] que comienzan por esas letras las columnas del Templo de Salomón?

El último de los aprendices podría darnos un cúmulo de respuestas anulando nuestra ignorancia y tendríamos que escondernos apenados ya que nosotros, grado 33, no supiéramos esas cosas e hiciéramos preguntas tan infantiles.

Pero... nosotros, ignorantes 33 y compañeros de los demás ignorantes 33, sabemos que hay algo más y eso es lo que ignoran nuestros compañeros...

Los símbolos, decimos, no valen nada de por si no es lo que ellos significan, pero la I [י y] la B [ב] son realidades y allí están de modo concreto para quien sabe leer.

Tenemos señas, tocamientos y palabras de paso.

Algo que a simple vista parece necio e infantil, pudiendo haber inventado de una manera más complicada y, sin embargo, no se hizo quedaron respetados esos tocamientos, esas señales y esas palabras...

No se piensa que todo esto pueda ser la expresión de algo oculto?

Así es, en efecto.

---

[68] Literally 'anulando' means "annul, cancel; revoke, rescind; defeat, overcome"
[69] Literally 'apenados' means "ashamed; grieved; pained"
[70] Literally 'modo' means "way, mode; manner; line; wise; digit; mood"
[71] Literally 'tocamientos' means "act of touching"

The signs, are seen.

The grips, are [they] not felt?

The words, are heard...

Then surely you need to See, Feel[72] and Hear something which is ignored and which is, much later, to be perceived in its entirety.[73]

The "I" ['] sees it, but does not feel nor hear it and we must, we absolutely must, feel and hear it.

To do this, the ancient Masons had a section of secret instructions where they taught how to practically Feel an "I" ['], [and] a "B" [ב], that is to say, a Vowel and a Consonant.

Each of these senses, taken separately, are important in order to fulfill that which is desired[74] and this is the reason[75] you need the cooperation of the three [senses].

Now let's take a piece of wood with a very interesting figure [that is] painted[76] bronze and we would not doubt that what we see before our eyes is truly shaped in bronze.

Until we touch it [we do not know its content], and the touch tells us that in reality [either] it is metal, [or] that it has the properties of wood[77].

But one look convinces us that the work is of bronze, dropped to the ground and then the sound is what shows us our mistake.

---

[72] Literally 'Sentir' means "feel, sense; hear; bear; be sorry, regret"
[73] Editor's note: Compare "TO KNOW MEANS TO SEE, HEAR AND TOUCH THE GREAT REALITIES." from Ch. 9 of *Tarot & Kabalah* by Samael Aun Weor
[74] Literally 'desea' means "desire, wish for, want; covet"
[75] Literally 'causa' means "cause, factor, reason; principle, purpose;"
[76] Literally 'pintamos' means "paint; picture; depict, portray; decorate; stain"
[77] Literally 'tal es la propiedad que puede dársele hoy a una pieza de madera' means "that it has the property that can now be given to a piece of wood"

Las señas, se ven.

Los tocamientos, no sienten.

Las palabras, se escuchan...

Luego, se necesita indudablemente Ver, Sentir y Oír algo que se ignora y que hay que percibirlo, más tarde, en toda su extensión.[78]

La I ['] la vemos, pero no la sentimos ni la escuchamos y es preciso, absolutamente preciso, sentirla y oírla.

Para ello, los antiguos Masones, tenían una sección de instrucciones secretas donde enseñaba prácticamente el modo del Sentir una I ['], [y] una B [ב], es decir, una Vocal y una Consonante.

Cada uno de estos sentidos, por separado, es importante para llenar lo que se desea y esta es la causa de que se necesite el concurso de los tres.

Hoy podemos tomar, una pieza de madera con la figura que mas interese, la pintamos de bronce y ante nuestra vista no podemos dudar que aquello que vemos no sea una verdadera talla en bronce.

Hasta la tocamos, y el tacto nos acusa que en realidad allí existe el mental, tal es la propiedad que puede dársele hoy a una pieza de madera.

Pero una vez convencidos de que la obra es de bronce, la tiramos al suelo y entonces el sonido es el que nos demuestra nuestra equivocación.

---

[78] Nota del Editor: Comparar "POR SABER SE ENTIENDE, VER, OÍR Y PALPAR LAS GRANDES REALIDADES." del Cap. 9 de *Tarot y Kábala* por Samael Aun Weor

Behold two senses were powerless to perceive the truth and [we] needed to use a third.

As for the sign of [the] Apprentice. [Masonry] could change and use, for example, the [sign] of the Fascists whose salute is more airy and arrogant, but, nonetheless, the Masons have to use their own [sign], that which is peculiar to them, bringing the right hand up to the throat where the organ of the voice is [and where it] flows[79] with more or less intensity [according to how] this organ is constricted[80] or loosened[81].

This, no doubt, has a significance.

The Sign is combined with the voice, but this is in ourselves and we must observe that we are not alone, our brothers are with us from which our SELF is but an extension and we need the help of others in order to fulfill with them what is wanted: the sign and the word...

But Ah!, then we speak...

Masonry is not useful for anything[82] when [it is taken] alone because we need another, a companion, a brother, who will be Touched by the sign...

And if we did not have anyone for this purpose, where [would one] find him?

Note that there is always Another, another who can not be seen, another who is enclosed within ourselves and it is this other [one] who must recognize [the sign]...

Ved aquí que dos sentidos eran impotentes para percibir la verdad y hubo necesidad de utilizar un tercero.

En cuanto a la señal de Aprendiz. Pudiera cambiarse al uso, por ejemplo, de los Fascistas cuyo saludo es más airoso y arrogante, pero, sin embargo, los Masones han de utilizar el suyo, el que le es peculiar, llevando la mano diestra a la garganta donde radica el órgano de la voz la cual brota con mayor o menor intensidad según se aprieta o se suaviza ese órgano.

Esto tiene un significado indudable.

La Seña se combina con la voz, pero esto es en nosotros mismos y hemos de observar que no estamos solos, está con nosotros nuestros hermanos de entre los cuales nuestro SÍ[83] no es mas que una prolongación y necesitamos el concurso de los demás para llenar con ellos lo que pretende la seña y la palabra...

Pero Ah!, nos decimos entonces...

La Masonería no nos sirve de nada estando solo pues necesitamos otro, un compañero, un hermano, el que habrá de ser Tocado con la seña...

Y si no tuviéramos a nadie para este fin, donde hallarlo?

Tened en cuenta que siempre hay Otro, otro que no vemos, otro que va encerrado en nosotros mismos y es a ese otro al que hay reconocer...

---

[79] Literally 'brota' means "sprout, burst forth; grow quickly; cause to sprout"
[80] Literally 'aprieta' means "tighten; screw; constrict; press; grasp, grip; quicken; snuggle; subtend"
[81] Literally 'suaviza' means "ease up, abate; relax; subdue; soften"
[82] Literally 'no nos sirve de nada' means "does not serve us for anything"

[83] Originalmente "nuestro Yo". Nota del Editor: Casi con toda seguridad Krumm-Heller refiriéndose a nosotros total, y no el "yo" psicológico como se utiliza en la Psicología Gnóstica.

This brother [of] our's who goes with us through life, is our Internal Master[84], to whom the sign, the word and the grip are given, in order to achieve certain hidden effects that will lead to another degree, [in] the other plane: the astral [plane] itself.

Few know of it and it is better that way. We ourselves can not divulge it.

The Key is conquered through internal preparation or is given to the chosen by the Master in [the] Superior Room.

[The] only [reason] we have[85] to write the above, [is in] an effort to arouse the curiosity of those who study and encourage all to meditate.

In Constantinople, I was recognized in Occult Masonry and saw the effects of our signs based on[86] [the teaching of] a Guru (Master) between columns and [who was] giving masonic instructions.

At the conclusion of the session[87], the astral spectrum was dissolved and all the participants[88] took this phenomenon as natural.

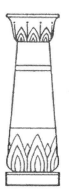

---

[84] Editor's note: Literally 'Altar Ego Astral' means "Astral Alter Ego", but Krumm-Heller seems to be referring to our Inner Being, the Master in us, using a term that was in fashion at the time, but now is easily confused because of the Gnostic understanding of the term 'Ego'. Consider this: "The Intimate [or Inner Being] is the ardent flame of Horeb. According to Moses, he is the Ruach Elohim who was fashioning the waters in the beginning of the world, the Sun King, our Divine Monad, the 'Alter ego' of Cicerone." from Ch. 3 of *The Revolution of Beelzebub* by Samael Aun Weor and "The disciple must learn the masonic salutes from his own Intimus [or Inner Being]: the "Internal Master" must teach them to him." from Ch. 8 of *Zodical Course* by Samael Aun Weor
[85] Literally 'lleva' means "carry, transport; take; convey; wear; win; lead; bear; spend; hunch, hump; heave; carry off; deliver; live through; encroach on"
[86] Literally 'apareciendo' means "appear, come into view; emerge, come out; show up, turn up; loom up; intervene; develop"
[87] Literally 'tenida' means "meeting, session; uniform"
[88] Literally 'asistentes' means "attendant; assistant, auxiliary; participant"

Ese hermano nuestro que va con nosotros por la vida, es nuestro Maestro Interno[89], a quien hay que dar la señal, la palabra y el tocamiento, pues lograr ciertos efectos ocultos que nos lleven al otro grado, el otro plano, al astral mismo.

Pocos saben de ello y es preferible que así sea. Nosotros mismos no lo podemos divulgar.

La Clave se conquista mediante la preparación interna o la da el Maestro den Camara Superior al elegido.

Sólo nos lleva al escribir lo que antecede, un afán de despertar la curiosidad de los que estudian y animan a todos a la meditación.

En Constantinopla fui reconocido en la Masonería Oculta y vi los efectos de nuestras señales apareciendo un Guru (Maestro) entre columnas y dio instrucciones masónicas.

Al concluir la tenida, el espectro astral se disolvió y todos los asistentes tomaron ese fenómeno como natural.

---

[89] Nota del Editor: Originalmente está escrito 'Altar Ego Astral', pero Krumm-Heller parece referirse a nuestro Ser Interior, el Maestro en nosotros, usando un término que estaba de moda en el momento, pero ahora es confuso con el entendimiento gnóstico del término 'Ego'. Considere esto: "El Íntimo es la llama ardiente del Oreb. Aquel Ruach Elohim que según Moisés labraba las aguas en el principio del mundo, el Rey Sol, nuestra Mónada Divina, el 'Alter ego' de Cicerón." del Cap. 3 de *Revolución de Bel* par Samael Aun Weor y "El discípulo debe aprender los saludos masones, de su propio Intimo: el "Maestro Interno" deberá enseñárselos." del Cap. 8 de *Curso Zodical* par Samael Aun Weor

In any [Masonic] Lodge in Spain or America [this] would have scared some, others would have ignored the spiritualist centers and few, very few, would have tried to repeat it, but we in our Rose Cross Lodges will do so.	En cualquier Logia en España o América unos se habrían asustado, otros habrían ignorado a los centros espiritistas y pocos muy pocos habrían tratado de repetirlo pero nosotros en nuestras Logias Rosa Cruz lo haremos.

THE SECRETS OF MASONRY 2

Dr. Arnold Krumm Heller

One of the deeper symbols, which Free and Ancient Masonry possesses, is that which is found in the declaration[90] of proposition forty-seven of the first book of Euclid, [a] proposition which, [is] well-known by the name of "[The] Pythagorean Theorem", [and] reads as follows:

> In any right triangle, the square of the hypotenuse equals the sum of the squares of the two sides.

There are many symbolic interpretations that have occurred for the previous affirmation, all of them based on the meaning of the triangle and the square, the two perfect figures of Geometry.

My sincere affirmations [as] to the fertility and depth [of] Mathematics have led me down a short path towards an interpretation that I dare to judge [as] interesting because it is based on the hidden meaning that each of the numbers used in Arithmetic has, remembering that all well-known things have a number, since the number is the essential condition of its existence.

As is known, the numbers which have the special importance of representing the hypotenuse and the two legs of a right triangle satisfy the conditions established in the following three mathematical expressions, in which "n" has any value except 0:

$$2n^2 + 2n + 1;\ 2n^2 + 2n;\ 2n + 1$$

However, [by] substituting "1" for the value of "n", one obtains the three smallest positive integers [that] satisfy the condition required by the Theorem of the sage of Samos [which] are 3, 4 and 5, because $3^2 + 4^2 = 5^2$.

---

[90] Literally 'enunciado' means "enunciate, declare, express, state, express in definite terms, put forward, enounce;"

The Rose-Cross Secrets of Occult Masonry	Los Secretos Rosa-Cruz de la Masonería Oculta
The referenced right triangle[91] would have as its expression for the legs and hypotenuse the indicated numbers: 3, 4 and 5, whose kabalistic meaning is the following:	El triángulo rectángulo en referencia tendría como catetos e hipotenusa los expresados por los números indicados: 3, 4 y 5, cuyos significados cabalísticos son los siguientes:
Number three: Corresponds with the letter Gomor[92] (G).	Número tres: Se corresponde con la letra Gomor (G).

It symbolizes supreme power in the divine world, equilibrium obtained without effort, by the eternally active intelligence, [and] by absolute wisdom.	Simboliza en el mundo divino la potencia suprema, el equilibrio obtenido, sin esfuerzo, por la inteligencia eternamente activa, por la absoluta sabiduría.
In the intellectual universe it represents the universal fecundity[93] of Being.	En el universo intelectual representa la fecundidad universal del Ser.
In the dominion of the physical it indicates the incessant work of Nature, the fecundating germination of the acts which are to arise from the conscious willpower of their own potency[94].	En el dominio de lo físico indica el trabajo incesante de la Naturaleza, la germinación fecunda de los actos que han de surgir de la voluntad consciente de la propia potencia.
This number is represented by a woman in the center of a radiating Sun which indicates the creative power, crowned by 12 stars, with a scepter whose superior part [has] a luminous globe shining which is nothing but the perpetual action that Nature, ever wise, exerts upon the things [that have] been born or [the things that will] be born.	Ese número esta representa por[97] una mujer sentada en el centro de un Sol radiante que indica la potencia creadora, coronada por 12 estrellas, con un cetro en cuya parte superior brilla un globo luminoso que no es sino la acción perpetua que la Naturaleza, siempre sabia, ejerce sobre las cosas nacidas o por nacer.
In the other hand of that allegorical figure, is a landing[95] eagle that reminds [us] of the heights to which the intelligence must soar.	En la otra mano de esa figura alegórica, se posa un águila que recuerda las alturas hasta las cuales ha de remontarse la inteligencia.

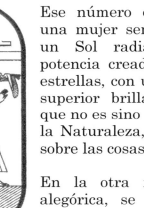

| At the feet of the noble matron shines the Moon which symbolizes the infinitude[96] of matter and its slavery with respect to the spirit. | A los pies de la noble matrona brilla la Luna que simboliza la infinitud de la materia y su esclavitud respecto al espíritu. |

---

[91] Literally 'triángulo rectángulo' means "right-angled triangle"
[92] 'Gomor' is the Esoteric name of the letter that corresponds to the 3rd Hebrew letter 'Gimel'
[93] Literally 'fecundidad' means "fertility, fecundity, fruitfulness"
[94] Literally 'potencia' means "potency, strength, power; capacity to work, energy;"
[95] Literally 'posa' means "pose; land; sit"
[96] Literally 'infinitud' means "infinitude, immeasurableness, boundlessness; infinite amount"

[97] Originalmente "se corporiza por medio de"

Number four: Corresponds with the letter Dinain[98] (D).

It symbolizes perpetual realization in the divine world, [achieved] in [a] hierarchic way, [and] of the potentialities[99] which form the absolute being.

In the intellectual universe it represents the realization of the ideas of Being, by means of the quadruple work of the spirit, that is to say by means of the affirmation, of the negation, of the discussion and of the solution.[100]

In the dominion of the physical it indicates the realization of acts directed by the science of Truth, by the love of Justice, by the strength of the Willpower and by the work of Material Energy.

This number is personified by means of the figure of a warrior covered with a helmet which gives the idea of strength that conquers well directed power, seated upon a cubic stone, [the] image of matter [which has been] dominated[101], the perfectly concluded human work.

With the right hand he holds[102] a scepter, while his legs are placed in the form of the cross which symbolizes the four elements, [and] the expansion of the human potency towards the four directions[103] of the spirit.

Número cuatro: Se corresponde con la letra Dinain (D).

Simboliza en el mundo divino la realización perpetua, en modo jerárquico, de las virtualidades que configuran el ser absoluto.

En el universo intelectual representa la realización de las ideas del Ser, por medio del cuádruple trabajo del espíritu, es decir por medio de la afirmación, de la negación, de la discusión y de la solución.[104]

En el dominio de lo físico indica la realización de los actos dirigidos por la ciencia de la Verdad, por el amor a la Justicia, por la fuerza de la Voluntad y por el trabajo de la Energía Material.

Este número se personifica mediante la figura de un guerrero cubierto con un casco que da la idea de la fuerza que conquista el poder bien dirigido, sentado sobre una piedra cúbica, imagen de la materia domada, de la obra humana perfectamente concluida.

Con la mano derecha sostiene un cetro, mientras sus piernas están colocadas en forma de cruz que simboliza los cuatro elementos, la expansión de la potencia humana hacia los cuatro rumbos del espíritu.

---

[98] 'Dinain' is the Esoteric name of the letter that corresponds to the 4th Hebrew letter 'Dalet'
[99] Literally 'virtualidades' means "potentiality, latent power, strength that is not visible; hidden characteristics, concealed attributes"
[100] Editor's note: Compare "Knowing how to always find the synthesis is beneficial because from the thesis one has to pass on to the antithesis but the truth is not found in the antithesis nor in the thesis. In the thesis and in the antithesis there is discussion and that is what is really wanted: affirmation, negation, discussion and solution." from Ch. 3.05 (The Dominion of the Mind) of *The Revolution of the Dialectic* by Samael Aun Weor
[101] Literally 'domada' means "tame, domesticate; control;"
[102] Literally 'sostiene' means "sustain, uphold, support; maintain; bear; live"
[103] Literally 'rumbos' means "directions, course; path, walk"

[104] Nota del editor: Comparar "Saber buscar siempre la síntesis es benéfico porque de la tesis hay que pasar a la antítesis pero la verdad no se encuentra ni en la antítesis ni en la tesis. En la tesis y en la antítesis hay discusión y eso es lo que realmente se quiere; afirmación, negación, discusión y solución." del Cap. 3.05 (El Dominio de la Mente) en *La Revolución de la Dialéctica* por Samael Aun Weor

Number five: Corresponds with the letter Eni[105] (E).

In the divine world it symbolizes the universal Law regulator of the manifestations of the Being in the unity of [all] substance.

In the intellectual universe it represents religion, that is to say the intimate relation of the absolute Being with the relative Being, of the infinite [thing] with the limited [thing].

In the dominion of the physical, it indicates inspiration communicated to man by the vibrations of the astral fluid; it reminds [us of] the thousand [of] ordeals that the human being is put through if he exercises his own freedom of action over the insurmountable[106] circle of the Universal Law.

This number is represented by a Hierophant [who is the] genius of the good inspirations of the spirit, seated in the space which is between the two columns of the Sanctuary; he [makes a] sign[107] with the index [finger] of the right hand, on the chest, [which is] the sign of silence as [an] invitation to withdraw if one wants to hear the voice of heaven through[108] the silencing of the passions and the material instincts.

The right column symbolizes the divine Law, [and] the one on the left represents the faculty to obey or to disobey that same divine Law.

Número cinco: Se corresponde con la letra Eni (E).

Simboliza en el mundo divino la Ley universal reguladora de las manifestaciones del Ser en la unidad de la sustancia.

En el universo intelectual representa la religión, es decir la relación íntima del Ser absoluto con el Ser relativo, de lo infinito con lo limitado.

En el dominio de lo físico, indica la inspiración comunicada al hombre por las vibraciones del fluido astral; recuerda las mil pruebas a las que está sometido el ser humano si ejerce la propia libertad de acción por el círculo infranqueable de la Ley Universal.

Ese número esta representa por[109] un Hierofante genio de las buenas inspiraciones del espíritu, sentado en el espacio que queda entre las dos columnas del Santuario; traza con el índice de la mano derecha, sobre el pecho, el signo del silencio como invitación al recogimiento si se desea escuchar la voz del cielo en el silencio de las pasiones y de los instintos materiales.

La columna derecha simboliza la Ley divina, la de la izquierda representa la facultad de obedecer o desobedecer esa misma Ley divina.

---

[105] 'Eni' is the Esoteric name of the letter that corresponds to the 5th Hebrew letter 'Heh'
[106] Literally 'infranqueable' means "impassable, impossible to cross; impossible to pass through; cannot be traveled through"
[107] Literally 'traza' means "design, plan; sketch, diagram; model, looks, appearance, countenance; trace, sign, trail"
[108] Literally 'en' means "in, into; for, to; on, at; by; about"

[109] Originalmente "se corporiza por medio de"

The Hierophant appears leaning[110] on a cross of three horizontal arms, emblem of the spirit of the Great Architect of the Universe that penetrates into the three worlds in order to awaken all the manifestations of universal life.

At his feet, two men kneel, the genius of light, dressed in red, [and] the spirit of darkness, [dressed] in black, both ready to obey the Master of the Sacred Mysteries…

El Hierofante aparece apoyado sobre una cruz de tres brazos horizontales, emblema del espíritu del Gran Arquitecto del Universo que penetra en los tres mundos para despertar todas las manifestaciones de la vida universal.

A sus pies, dos hombres de rodillas, el genio de la luz, vestido de rojo, el espíritu de las tinieblas, de negro, listos ambos para obedecer al Maestro de los Misterios Sagrados...

The Pythagorean Triangle, then, is formed, in the divine world, by the Universal Law as [the] hypotenuse and [the] legs [are formed] by the Supreme power and the perpetual realization of the potentialities of the absolute Being.

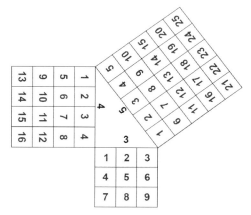

El Triángulo Pitagórico, pues, está formado, en el mundo divino, por la Ley Universal como hipotenusa y como catetos, por la potencia Suprema y por la realización perpetua de las virtualidades del Ser absoluto.

In the intellectual universe the hypotenuse of this same triangle is religion and the legs are constructed by the universal fecundity of Being and by the realization of the ideas of that same being in carrying out the quadruple work of the spirit, which is nothing but the compact group of the affirmation, the negation, the discussion and the solution.

En el universo intelectual la hipotenusa de ese mismo triángulo es la religión y los catetos están construidos por la fecundidad universal del Ser y por la realización de las ideas de ese mismo ser al efectuar el cuádruple trabajo del espíritu, que no es sino el grupo compacto de la afirmación, la negación, la discusión y la solución.

In the dominion of the physical, the hypotenuse of the triangle of Pythagoras is inspiration, and the legs form the fecundating action of Nature and the realization of human acts by means of Truth, Justice, Willpower and Energy.

En el dominio de lo físico, la hipotenusa del triángulo de Pitágoras es la inspiración, y los catetos los forman la acción fecunda de la Naturaleza y la realización de los actos humanos por medio de la Verdad, la Justicia, la Voluntad y la Energía.

However, the Theorem of Pythagoras says that: $3^2 + 4^2 = 5^2$ [equals] $9 + 16 = 25$

Ahora bien, el Teorema de Pitágoras dice que: $3^2 + 4^2 = 5^2$ [es igual a] $9 + 16 = 25$

---

[110] Literally 'apoyado' means "lean, rest against; recline; hold up, prop up; support, prop; sustain; underwrite"

The number nine, corresponds to the letter Thala[111] (Th), [which] symbolizes absolute wisdom in the divine world; in the intellectual Universe, [it symbolizes] the prudence that prevails and wisely directs the Willpower; [and] in the dominion of the physical [world] it is discretion[112] in actions.

Thala

Theth

This number is personified by a old man, [reflecting] the experience acquired from the difficulties of life, who walks supported by a walking stick, which is nothing but the support that gives prudence and who carries an ignited lamp, the light of intelligence, half hidden under the cloak which covers it, [a] cloak which symbolizes discretion.

Number sixteen is decomposed, for kabalistic effects, into ten and six.[113]

The number ten, corresponds exactly to the letter Ioithi[114] (I, J or Y), symbolizing the active principle that vivifies[115] beings in the divine world, in the intellectual universe [it symbolizes] the authority that governs everything, and in the physical dominion, [it symbolizes] good or bad fortune.

Ioithi

Yod/Jod

This number is represented by a wheel whose axis is maintained by two columns; Hermanubis to the right, genius of Good, strives to raise up, whereas [on] the left Typhon, the genius of evil, is seen precipitating [himself] into the abyss.

El número nueve, correspondiente a la letra Thala (Th), simboliza en el mundo divino la sabiduría absoluta; en el Universo intelectual, la prudencia que rige y dirige sabiamente a la Voluntad; en el dominio de lo físico es la circunspección en los actos.

Ese número se personifica en un anciano, la experiencia adquirida en las dificultades de la vida, que camina apoyado en un báculo, que no es sino el sostén que presta la prudencia y que lleva una lámpara encendida, la luz de la inteligencia, medio oculta bajo el manto que lo cubre, manto que simboliza la discreción.

El número dieciseis se descompone, para los efectos cabalísticos, en diez y en seis.[116]

El número diez, correspondiente a la letra Ioithi (I, J o Y), simboliza en el mundo divino el principio activo que vivifica los seres, en el universo intelectual, la autoridad que todo lo gobierna y en el dominio físico, la buena o la mala fortuna.

Ese número esta representa por[117] una rueda cuyo eje está sostenido por dos columnas; a la derecha Hermanubis, genio del Bien, se esfuerza en subir, mientras que a la izquierda Tyfón, el genio del mal, se ve precipitado al abismo.

---

[111] 'Thala' or 'Thela' is the Esoteric name of the letter that corresponds to the 9th Hebrew letter 'Teth'
[112] Literally 'circunspección' means "circumspection, discretion"
[113] Editor's note: In Gnostic Kabalah this is not how numbers are reduced. See Parts 4 and 5 of *Tarot & Kabalah* by Samael Aun Weor
[114] 'Ioithi' or 'Iamin' is the Esoteric name of the letter that corresponds to the 10th Hebrew letter 'Yod'
[115] Literally 'vivifica' means "vivify, animate"

[116] Nota del editor: En la Kabalah Gnóstica no es así como los números se reducen. Ver partes 4 y 5 del *Tarot y Kábala* por Samael Aun Weor
[117] Originalmente "se corporiza por medio de"

The Sphinx [is] above the wheel in equilibrium, [he is] inflexible, [and] maintains[118] a sword between his lion claws, the sword of destiny, that is always awake in order to forge[119] the chains for the depraved and to weave[120] garlands[121] so as to make a virtue of necessity.

The number six corresponds to the letter Ur[122] (U).

Symbolizing in the divine world the Science of Good and Evil; in the intellectual universe the balance between necessity and liberty[123], and in the physical dominion [it symbolizes] the indestructible antagonism which exists between natural forces, the intimate linking that unites the causes to the effects.

This number is personified by a man, standing stationary[124] in the crossing of two paths, who watches the ground fixedly while two women touch his shoulders and the one on the right indicates the good route and the one on the left [indicates] the path of tempting vice.[125]

Ur

Vau/Vav

En equilibrio sobre la rueda está le Esfinge, inflexible, que conserva entre sus garras de león una espada, la espada del destino, que está despierto siempre para forjar las cadenas para el vicioso y entretejer guirnaldas para el que ha hecho de la virtud norma.

El número seis corresponde a la letra Ur (U).

Simboliza en el mundo divino la Ciencia del Bien y el Mal; en el universo intelectual el equilibrio entre la necesidad y la libertad[126], y en el dominio físico el antagonismo indestructible que existe entre las fuerzas naturales, el encadenamiento íntimo que une a las causas los efectos.

Ese número se personifica en un hombre de pié, inmóvil en el cruce de dos caminos, que mira al suelo fijamente mientras dos mujeres le tocan los hombros y le señalan la de la derecha la ruta del bien y la de la izquierda el camino del vicio tentador.[127]

---

[118] Literally 'conserva' means "preserve, conserve; keep, retain"
[119] Literally 'forjar' means "forge, fashion; trump up"
[120] Literally 'guirnaldas' means "Garland, a wreath or open crown interwoven with flowers (funeral)."
[121] Literally 'entretejer' means "interweave, intertwine; insert"
[122] 'Ur' is the Esoteric name of the letter that corresponds to the 6th Hebrew letter 'Vau'
[123] Editor's note: Compare "Those supreme laws of liberty and necessity control and moderate each other, [they] are found everywhere and dominate all the facts where any virtue, just power or authority, is revealed." from the Preliminary Discourse to *Dogma and Ritual of High Magic* by Eliphas Levi (the Preliminary Discourse was also published in English as *The Reconciliation of Science and Religion*)
[124] Literally 'inmóvil' means "immobile, stationary; immovable, motionless, still"
[125] Editor's note: To clarify, it is *his* right and left that the women are standing on. The one on our left (his right) has a crown or serpent protruding from her brow, indicating she symbolizes the good path.

---

[126] Nota del editor: Comparar "Esta ley suprema de la libertad y la necesidad, regidas y atemperadas una por la otra, se halla en todas partes y domina todos los actos en que es revelada una virtud, un poder justo o una autoridad cualquiera." del Discurso Preliminar de *Dogma y Ritual de Alta Magia* por Eliphas Levi
[127] Nota del editor: Para aclarar, es *su* derecho y dejó que las mujeres están de pie. El que está a la izquierda (su derecha) tiene una corona o una serpiente que sobresale de la frente, lo que indica que simboliza el buen camino.

Above and behind the group [is] the genius of Justice, suspended in a brilliant aura, preparing a bow in order to shoot a mortal arrow against morbid[128] temptations.

The whole [thing][129] (as is easily comprehended) expresses the fight, which occurs[130] in the interior of man, between the morbid passions and rectified consciousness.

Also number twenty-five, for its kabalistic interpretation, must be decomposed into twenty plus five.

Number twenty corresponds exactly to the letter Caitha[131] (K, C).

Symbolizing in the divine world the principle of all the spiritual or material forces; in the intellectual universe [it symbolizes] the moral power, and in the physical domain, the organic force.

This number in embodied in a beautiful maiden[132] who with her delicate hands closes the hungry jaws of a lion of Nemea[133] without difficulties…

It is (as can be easily deduced) the emblem of strength/force[134] on its own and [its] potent energies.

Por encima y por detrás del grupo el genio de la Justicia, suspendido en una aureola fulgurante, apronta el arco para disparar la flecha mortal contra las tentaciones malsanas.

El conjunto, como fácilmente se comprende, expresa la lucha que, en el interior del hombre, se verifica, entre las pasiones malsanas y la conciencia recta.

También el número veinticinco, para su interpretación cabalística, debe descomponerse en veinte más cinco.

El número veinte corresponde a la letra Caitha (K,C).

Simboliza en el mundo divino el principio de todas las fuerzas espirituales o materiales; en el universo intelectual la potencia moral, y en el dominio físico la fuerza orgánica.

Este número esta representa por[135] una bella doncella que cierra sin dificultades entre sus delicadas manos las fauces hambrientas de un león de Nemea…

Es, como muy fácilmente se puede colegir, el emblema de la fuerza en las propias y potentes energías.

---

[128] Literally 'malsanas' means "unhealthy, sickly; morbid"
[129] Literally 'conjunto' means "whole; aggregate, conjunction; ensemble; chorus; union; set"
[130] Literally 'verifica' means "verify, check; synchronize; establish"
[131] 'Caitha' or 'Kaita' is the Esoteric name of the letter that corresponds to the 11th Hebrew letter 'Kaph'
[132] Literally 'doncella' means "maid, servant; maiden, virgin"
[133] The Nemean lion was a vicious monster in Greek mythology eventually killed by Hercules (the first of his twelve labours).
[134] Literally 'fuerza' means "force, might, power, forcefulness, pithiness, punch, robustness; strength, vigor;"

[135] Originalmente "se corporiza por medio de"

[Regarding] the number five, there is no need to repeat more here [than what] was [already] explained above about the symbolism which [is] enclosed [within this number].

From the above discussion it follows that the Pythagorean Theorem means in the divine world that the principle of all strength, which [is] the regulating Universal Law of the manifestations of Being in the unity of substance [that] is originated by the combined action of absolute wisdom, of the active principle that gives life to beings and the Science of Good and Evil.

PYTHAGORAS

In the intellectual universe, the same geometric proposal indicates that the moral power, [which is] religion wisely understood, comes[136] from the agreement that must exist between the prudence that governs the acts of Willpower and the supreme Authority that governs everything, establishing the absolute balance between Liberty and Necessity.[137]

In the physical dominion, the Pythagorean formulation establishes that the organic force and the inspiration communicated to the finite being by the vibrations of the infinite Being, is born from a perfect prudence in actions aided by the destiny that establishes good and bad fortunes in obedience to the absolute connection[138] which exists between causes and effects, [a] connection which is born from the antagonism that the natural forces sense [between] one another.

Del número cinco, no es preciso repetir aquí cuanto más arriba quedó explicado acerca del simbolismo que encierra.

De la exposición anterior se deduce que el Teorema de Pitágoras significa en el mundo divino que el principio de toda fuerza, que la Ley Universal reguladora de las manifestaciones del Ser en la unidad de la sustancia es originada por la acción combinada de la sabiduría absoluta, del principio activo que da vida a los seres y la Ciencia del Bien y del Mal.

En el universo intelectual, la misma proposición geométrica indica que la potencia moral, la religión sabiamente entendida, resulta del acuerdo que debe existir entre la prudencia que rige los actos de la Voluntad y la Autoridad suprema que todo lo gobierna, estableciendo el equilibrio absoluto entre la Libertad y la Necesidad.[139]

En el dominio físico, el enunciado Pitagórico establece que la fuerza orgánica y la inspiración comunicada al ser finito por las vibraciones del Ser infinito, nace de una perfecta prudencia en los actos auxiliada por el destino que establece las buenas y las malas fortunas en obediencia al encadenamiento absoluto que existe entre las causas y los efectos, encadenamiento que nace del antagonismo que las fuerzas naturales sienten unas por otras.

---

[136] Literally 'resulta' means "result, effect, outcome, consequence"
[137] Editor's note: Compare "Divinity, in its essence, has two essential conditions as fundamental bases of its being: necessity and liberty." and "The whole science, in fact, is in the understanding of ... the idea itself of God, who is absolute reason, necessity and liberty..." from Ch.2 and Ch. 4 of *Dogma of High Magic* by Eliphas Levi.
[138] Literally 'encadenamiento' means "connection, chaining, catenation, concatenation, linking; confinement, incarceration; concatenation"

[139] Nota del editor: Comparar "La divinidad, es una en su esencia, tiene dos condiciones esenciales, como bases fundamentales de su ser; la necesidad y la libertad." y "Toda ciencia está, en efecto, en la entendimiento de ... la idea misma de Dios, que es razón absoluta, necesidad y libertad..." del Cap. 2 y Cap. 4 de *Dogma de Alta Magia* por Eliphas Levi

Summarizing the three worlds into one[140], it is possible to say that [when] Pythagoras enunciated his Theorem: "In any right triangle, the square of the hypotenuse equals the sum of the squares of the two sides" [he] expressed a proposition whose clearly philosophical nature was [a] profound statement serving as the basis for one of the most perfect philosophies:

The universal renovation that man obtains by means of the inspiration, which [is] directly received from Occult Powers, can only be reached with[141] the action of prudence that maintains the universal equilibrium, through the impulse of good fortune directed by a powerful willpower and by the constancy in the thousand ordeals that human beings must be subjected to in the presence of the many temptations of Good and Evil.

Resumiendo los tres mundos en uno solo, se puede decir que al enunciar Pitágoras su Teorema: "En todo triángulo rectángulo el cuadrado construido sobre la hipotenusa es igual a la suma de los cuadrados construidos sobre los dos catetos" expresó una proposición de índole netamente filosófica cuyo profundo enunciado sirvió de base a una de las más perfectas filosofías:

La renovación universal que obtendrá el hombre por medio de la inspiración que recibe directamente de las Potencias Ocultas, ha de alcanzarse únicamente por la acción de la prudencia que mantiene el equilibrio universal, por el impulso de la fortuna bien dirigida por una voluntad potente y por la constancia en las mil pruebas a las que ha de verse sometido el ser humano en presencia de las múltiples tentaciones del Bien y del Mal.

---

[140] Literally 'en uno solo' means "in only one; into a single"
[141] Literally 'ha de alcanzarse únicamente por' means "has to be reached only by"

Esoteric Explanation of Baphomet, the Devil, Masonry and Religion

Explicación Esoterico del Baphomet, el Diablo, la Masonería y la Religión

Esoteric Explanation of Baphomet, the Devil, Masonry and Religion | Explicación Esoterico del Baphomet, el Diablo, la Masonería y la Religión

| Esoteric Explanation of Baphomet, the Devil, Masonry and Religion | Explicación Esoterico del Baphomet, el Diablo, la Masonería y la Religión |

| Extracts from Part Three of **THE BOOK OF SPLENDOURS**[1] by Eliphas Levi, entitled: "THE FLAMING STAR" | Extractos de la Parte Tres del **LIBRO DE LOS ESPLENDORES** por Eliphas Levi, titulado: "LA ESTRELLA FLAMÍGERA" |

BAPHOMET / BAPHOMET

Tem∴ o∴ h∴ p∴ Abb∴[2] | Tem ∴ o ∴ h ∴ p ∴ Abb ∴[5]

Binario Verbum Vitae Mortem et Vitam Aequilibrans[3]

BINARIO VERBUM VITÆ MORTEM ET VITAM ÆQUILIBRANS

There are several figures of Baphomet [which] exist.

Sometimes he is shown with a beard and [with] the horns of a goat, the face of a man, the breast of a woman, the mane and claws of a lion, the wings of an eagle and the hooves of a bull.

He is the resurrected sphinx of Thebes; he is the monster alternating between[4] captive and conqueror of Oedipus.

He is the science which protests against idolatry through the very monstrosity of the idol.

He carries between his horns the torch of life, and the living soul of this torch is God.

Existen varias figuras de Baphomet.

A veces tiene la barba y los cuernos del macho cabrio, la faz de un hombre, el seno de una mujer, la melena y las garras de un leon, las alas de un aguila y los flancos y las pezunas de un toro.

Es la esfinge resucitada de Tebas, el monstruo sucesivamente cautivo y vencedor de Edipo[6].

Es la ciencia que protesta de la idolatria por la misma monstruosidad del idolo.

Lleva entre los cuernos la antorcha de la vida, y el alma viviente de esta antorcha es Dios.

---

[1] The present English extracts of the Eliphas Levi's "LIVRE DES SPLENDEURS" have been translated directly from the original French language and so the English footnotes refer to their corresponding French text (which is not here) and therefore may not correspond to the Spanish.
[2] In Ch. 15 of *Ritual of High Magic*, Levi explains this by saying: "The Baphomet of the templars (who's name should be spelled out kabalistically in reverse) is composed of three abbreviations: TEM OHP AB, *Templi omnium hominem pacis abbas*, meaning "the father of the temple, universal peace to all men"…"
[3] This is a difficult Latin phrase to translate, but may mean something like this: "[The] Duality [of the] Verb [is] Living Death and Living Equilibrium"
[4] Literally 'tour à tour' means "alternately, in rotation"

[5] En Cap. 15 de *Ritual de la Alta Magia*, Levi explica esto diciendo: "El Baphomet de los Templarios, es un nombre que debe leerse cabalísticamente, en sentido inverso, y está compuesto de tres abreviaturas: TEM OHP AB, *Templi omnium hominem pacis abbas*, significado "el padre del templo, paz universal de los hombres"…"
[6] Hijo de Layo y de Yocasta, reyes de Tebas, a quien el oraculo predijo que mataria a su padre y se casaria con su madre, lo cual, por las extraordinarias circunstancias que envolvieron su nacimiento, llego a realizarse y tuvo cuatro hijos de Yocasta. N. del T.

It was forbidden for the Israelites to give the figure of man, or those of any animal, to divine concepts.	Se habia prohibido a los israelitas dar a las concepciones divinas figura humana o de animal.
Likewise, they only dared to sculpt Cherubs on the ark of the covenant and in the sanctuary, that is to say Sphinxes with the bodies of bulls and the heads of men, of eagles or of lions.	Asi es que no osaban esculpir en el arco y en el santuario nada mas que querubes, es decir, esfinges con cuerpos de toros y cabezas de hombres, de aguilas o de leon.
These mixed figures reproduced neither the complete form of man, nor that of any animal.	Tales figuras mixtas no reproducian en su totalidad, ni la forma humana ni la de animal alguno.
These hybrid creations[7] of impossible animals made [those who observed them] comprehend that the sign was not an idol nor an image of a living thing, but rather a character or representation of something having its existence in thought.	Esos conjuntos hibridos de animales fantasticos daban a comprender que el signo no era un idolo ni la imagen de cosa alguna.
Baphomet is not worshipped; God is worshipped without [a] face[8] before this formless form and this image [that has] no resemblance with created beings[9].	No se adora a Baphomet, sino a Dios, en esa imagen informe y viviente, sino la representacion de un pensamiento.
	Sin semejanza alguna con los seres creados.
Baphomet is not a God: he is the sign of initiation; he is also the hieroglyphic figure of the great divine tetragrammaton.	El Baphomet no es un Dios, es el signo de la iniciacion; es tambien la figura jeroglifica del gran tetragrama divino.
He is a recollection[10] of the Cherubs of the ark and the Holy of holies.	Es un recuerdo de los querubes del arco y del Santo de los santos.
He is the guardian of the key to the temple.	El Baphomet es analogo del Dios negro de Rabi Simeon.
Baphomet is analogous to the black God of Rabbi Simeon.	Es el guardian de la llave del templo.
He is the dark side of the divine face.	Es el lado oscuro de la faz divina.

---

[7] Literally 'assemblages' means "assemblage, assembly; dovetailing"
[8] Literally 'figure' means "face, feature, countenance; figure, shape; picture card"
[9] Literally 'sans ressemblance avec les êtres créés' means "without resemblance to created beings"
[10] Literally 'souvenir' means "memory, recollection, remembrance; keepsake, souvenir; token, memento"

This is why, during the ceremony of initiation, the recipient is required to kiss the hind-face of Baphomet or, in order to give him a more vulgar name, the devil.

Por eso, en las ceremonias iniciaticas, se exigia del recipiendario que diera un beso a la faz posterior de Baphomet, o del diablo, para darle un nombre mas vulgar.

Extracted from Chapter 15 of
DOGMA OF HIGH MAGIC[11]
by Eliphas Levi

...We are about to confront, even in his own sanctuary, the black god of the Sabbath, the tremendous[12] goat of Mendes.

Here, those who are afraid should close the book, and persons who are subject to nervous impressions will do well to divert their attention or to abstain; but we have imposed a task upon ourselves, [and] we will complete it.

Let us first of all tackle these questions frankly and boldly:

Does a devil exist?

What is the devil?

As to the first question, science is quiet; philosophy denies it at random, and religion only answers affirmatively.

As to the second [question], religion states that the devil is the fallen angel; occult philosophy accepts and explains this definition.

We will not go back over[13] what we have already said [about this], but we will add a new revelation:

THE DEVIL, IN BLACK MAGIC, IS THE GREAT MAGICAL AGENT EMPLOYED FOR EVIL PURPOSES BY A PERVERSE WILLPOWER.

Extracto de el Capituo 15 del
DOGMA DE LA ALTA MAGIA
por Eliphas Levi

...Vamos a afrontar, hasta en su santuario, al dios negro del Sabbat, al formidable macho cabrío de Mendés.

Aquí, aquellos que tengan miedo, pueden cerrar el libro, y las personas sujetas a impresiones nerviosas harán bien en distraerse o abstenerse; pero nosotros nos hemos impuesto una tarea y forzoso es llevarla a cabo.

Abordemos, pues, franca y audazmente el asunto:

¿Existe un diablo?

¿Qué cosa es un diablo?

A la primera pregunta la ciencia se calla; la filosofía niega, al azar, y sólo la religión responde afirmativamente.

A la segunda, la religión dice que el demonio es el ángel caído; la filosofía oculta acepta y explica esta definición.

Ya volveremos sobre lo que hemos dicho al respecto; pero, permítasenos aquí una nueva revelación.

EL DIABLO EN MAGIA NEGRA ES EL GRAN AGENTE MÁGICO EMPLEADO PARA EL MAL, POR UNA VOLUNTAD PERVERSA

---

[11] The present English extracts of the Eliphas Levi's "DOGME ET RITUEL DE LA HAUTE MAGIE" have been translated directly from the original French language and so the English footnotes refer to their corresponding French text (which is not in this Text) and therefore may not correspond to the Spanish.
[12] Literally 'formidable' means "tremendous, fantastic; wonderful, sensational; terrific, splendid; marvelous"
[13] Literally 'reviendrons' means "come back, return; recur, turn, revert; cast back"

The old serpent of the legend is nothing other than the universal agent, it is the eternal fire of terrestrial life, it is the soul of the earth, and the living fountain of hell.

We have said that the astral light is the receptacle of forms.

Evoked by reason, these forms are produced with harmony; [but] evoked by foolishness[14] they attain[15] disordered and monstrous [forms]: such is the cradle of the nightmares of saint Anthony and the phantoms of the Sabbath...

La antigua serpiente de la leyenda no es otra cosa que el agente universal; es el fuego eterno de la vida terrestre; es el alma de la tierra y el foco viviente del infierno.

Ya hemos dicho que la luz astral es el receptáculo de las formas.

Evocadas por la razón, esas formas se producen con armonía; evocadas por la locura, se aparecen desordenadas y monstruosas; tal es el origen de las pesadillas de San Antonio y de los fantasmas del Sabbat...

---

[14] Literally 'folie' means "madness, craziness, folly; craze things, insanity, extravaganza"
[15] Literally 'viennent' means "come; reach, arrive; attain, achieve"

Extracted from the INTRODUCTION to DOGMA OF HIGH MAGIC[16] by Eliphas Levi

...The philosophical stone, the universal medicine, the transmutation of metals, the quadrature of the circle and the secret of perpetual motion are then neither mystifications of science nor dreams of foolishness[17]; they are terms which must be comprehended in their true[18] sense, and which express all the different uses of the same secret, [or] the different characters of the same operation, which is defined in a way more generally by calling it simply the great work.

In nature there also exists a force [which is] more powerful[19] than steam[20], and by means of which a single man, who can seize[21] and know [how to] direct it, will overturn and change the face of the world.

This force was known to the ancients: it consists of a universal agent, the supreme law of which is equilibrium, and through its direction [one] immediately holds[22] the great arcanum of transcendental magic.

---

[16] The present English extracts of the Eliphas Levi's "DOGME ET RITUEL DE LA HAUTE MAGIE" have been translated directly from the original French language and so the English footnotes refer to their corresponding French text (which is not in this Text) and therefore may not correspond to the Spanish.
[17] Literally 'folie' means "madness, craziness, folly; craze things, insanity, extravaganza"
[18] Literally 'véritable' means "real, true; perfect, proper; veritable, genuine; effective"
[19] Literally 'bien autrement puissante' means "otherwise well powerful"
[20] Editor's note: 'steam' may have been the powerful mechanism of the time, and so we could replace this here with 'rocket fuel' or 'atomic energy' or something else which we consider to be a powerful fuel nowadays.
[21] Literally 'emparer' means "grab, grasp, seize, snatch; take over, commandeer"
[22] Literally 'tient' means "hold, keep, have; sustain, convene; fulfil, mind"

Extracto de la INTRODUCCIÓN del DOGMA DE LA ALTA MAGIA por Eliphas Levi

...La piedra filosofal, la medicina universal, la transmutación de los metales, la cuadratura del círculo y el secreto del movimiento continuo, no son, pues, ni mistificaciones de la ciencia, ni ensueños de la locura; son términos que es preciso comprender en su verdadero sentido, y que manifiestan todos los diferentes usos de un mismo secreto, los diferentes caracteres de una misma operación que se define de una manera más general, llamándola únicamente la gran obra.

Existe asimismo en la naturaleza una fuerza mucho más poderosa, siquiera sea en otra forma que el vapor, y por medio de la cual, un solo hombre que pudiera apoderarse de ella y supiera dirigirla, trastornaría y cambiaría la faz del mundo.

Esta fuerza era conocida por los antiguos, y consiste en agente universal cuya ley suprema es el equilibrio y cuya dirección tiende inmediatamente al gran arcano de la magia trascendental.

By directing[23] this agent, it is possible to modify the very order of the seasons, to produce at night the phenomena of the day, to travel[24] in an instant from one extremity of the earth to the other, to see, like Apollonius, what is happening on the [other] side of the world, to heal or hurt[25] from a distance, to give, in a word, universal success and reverberation[26].

This agent, which barely manifests itself under the uncertain methods[27] of Mesmer's disciples, is precisely that which the adepts of the middle ages called the first matter[28] of the great work.

The gnostics made it [through] the igneous[29] body of the Holy Spirit; and it was him who was adored in the secret rites of the sabbath or of the temple, under the hieroglyphic figure of Baphomet or under the Androgynous goat of Mendes...

Por medio de la dirección de ese agente, se puede cambiar el orden de las estaciones; producir en la noche fenómenos inherentes al día; corresponder en un instante de uno a otro confín del mundo; ver, como Apolonio, lo que ocurría al otro extremo de la tierra; dara la palabra un éxito y una repercusión universal.

Este agente, que apenas se revela ante el tacto de los discípulos de Mesmer, es precisamente lo que los aceptos de la Edad Media llamaban la materia primera de la gran obra.

Los gnósticos hacían ígneo el cuerpo del Espíritu Santo, ya él era a quien adoraban en los sitios secretos del sabbat o del templo, bajo la jeroglífica figura del Baphomet o del macho cabrío del Andrógino de Méndez...

---

[23] Literally 'la direction de ' means "the direction of"
[24] Literally 'correspondre' means "correspond, to write letters, to be in touch; communicate, connect; be linked;"
[25] Literally 'frapper' means "hit, strike; stab, deal; stamp out, knock, beat; stroke, punch; batter, beat up, afflict, bat; upset; belabor, chastise; impact, overtake; slash"
[26] Literally 'retentissement' means "effect, impact; resounding, repercussion"
[27] Literally 'tâtonnements' means "trial and error, trying and failing, trying to find one's way"
[28] Editor's note: The First Matter (or *Materia Prima*) is the proto-matter or primordial substance from which all other types of matter are formed. It is considered to be first in a chaotic state which then needs order for it to manifest as something. In Genesis 1:1-4 the *Materia Prima* is described symbolically and is given form by the Elohim (often translated as 'God') who exclaim "Let there be Light!" and then this substance becomes light.
[29] Literally 'igné' means "heat-engendered, pyrogenic, igneous; fiery, burning, flaming"

Extracts from Part Three of
THE BOOK OF SPLENDOURS[30]
by Eliphas Levi, entitled:
"THE FLAMING STAR"

Extractos de la Parte Tres del
LIBRO DE LOS ESPLENDORES
por Eliphas Levi, titulado:
"LA ESTRELLA FLAMÍGERA"

…Now, in the symbolism of the head with two faces, the back[31] of God is the devil, and the back of the devil is the hieroglyphic face of God.

Why the name of frank-masons[32] or free-masons?

Free from what? From the fear of God?

Yes, no doubt, since, when one fears God, one is looking at him from behind.

The tremendous[33] God is the black God, [which] is the Devil.

The freemasons want to build a spiritual temple to God alone, to the God of light, to the God of understanding and philanthropy, [and so] they battle[34] the God of the devil and the devil of God.

…Ahora bien, en el simbolismo de la cabeza de dos caras la que esta detras de Dios es el diablo, y la de detras del diablo es la figura jeroglifica de Dios.

Por que el nombre de francmasones o masones libres?

Libres de que? Del temor de Dios?

Si, sin duda, porque cuando se teme a Dios es que se le mira por detras.

El Dios formidable, es el dios negro, es el diablo.

Los francmasones quieren erigir un templo espiritual al Dios unico, al Dios de la luz, al Dios de la inteligencia y de la filantropia; en cambio hacen la guerra la dios del diablo y al diablo de dios.

---

[30] The present English extracts of the Eliphas Levi's "LIVRE DES SPLENDEURS" have been translated directly from the original French language and so the English footnotes refer to their corresponding French text (which is not here) and therefore may not correspond to the Spanish.
[31] Literally 'derrière' means "backside, back; behind, bottom; other side"
[32] Literally the 'franc' in the word 'francs-maçons' means "frank, straightforward, direct; candid, honest, truthful, open; outspoken, forthright; genuine, simple, steady, upfront", but in French 'francs-maçons' is used the same way we use the term "free-masons" in Enlgish
[33] Literally 'formidable' means "tremendous, fantastic; wonderful, sensational; terrific, splendid; marvelous"
[34] Literally 'font la guerre' means "make war"

But they bow[35] before the pious beliefs of Socrates, of Vincent de Paul[36] and of Fenelon[37].	Pero se inclinan ante las piadosas creencias de Socrates, de San Vicente de Paul y de Fenelon.
What they would, [along] with Voltaire, gladly call "infamy[38]" is this head or better [said] this silliness[39] which took the place of God during the Middle Ages.	Los que, con Voltaire, apelaron de buen grado a la infamia, son aquella cabeza o mas bien aquella bestia que en la Edad Media habia ocupado el sitio de Dios.
The brighter a light is, the darker the shadow it produces is.	Cuanto mas viva es una luz, mas negra es la oscuridad que se le opone.
Christianism has been at the same time the salvation[40] and the curse[41] of the world.	El cristianismo ha sido a la vez, la salvacion y el azote del mundo.
It is the most sublime of all the wisdoms and the most frightening[42] of [all the] follies.	Es la mas sublime de todas las sabidurias y la mas espantosa de las locuras.
If Jesus was not God, he was the most dangerous of evil-doers.	Si Jesus no fuera Dios; seria el mas peligroso de los malhechores.
The Jesus of Veuillot[43] is accursed[44].	El Jesus de Veuillot es execrable.

---

[35] Literally 'inclinent' means "tilt, bend, slope, incline; tip, slant, angle"
[36] Vincent de Paul (1581-1660) was a priest of the Catholic Church who became dedicated to serving the poor.
[37] François de Salignac de la Mothe-Fénelon, more commonly known as François Fénelon (1651-1715), was a French Roman Catholic archbishop, theologian, poet and writer who is often remembered as one of the main advocates of quietism. Quietism is a Christian philosophy that insists, with more or less emphasis, on intellectual stillness and interior passivity as essential conditions of perfection.
[38] Literally 'infâme' means "infamous, nefarious, vile, blackguardly, villainous"
[39] Literally 'bêtise' means "foolishness, nonsense; rubbish, stupidity"
[40] Literally 'salut' means "bow, salutation, greeting; safety; salvation; saving, salute; hi, hello!"
[41] Literally 'fléau' means "scourge, curse, bane; catastrophe, disaster; evil, trouble, nuisance, decay"
[42] Literally 'effroyable' means "horrifying, appaling, terrible, frightful, fearsome"
[43] Louis Veuillot (1813-1883) was a French journalist and author who helped to popularize ultramontanism, a religious philosophy within the Roman Catholic community that places strong emphasis on the prerogatives and powers of the Pope.
[44] Literally 'exécrable' means "abysmal, abhorrent, accursed, execrable"

That of Renan[45] is inexcusable, that of the Gospels is unexplainable, but that of Vincent de Paul and of Fenelon is adorable.

If christianism is for you the condemnation of reason, the despotism of ignorance and of the majority of mankind, [then] you are the enemy of humanity.

[However if] you understand christianism as the life of God in humanity, the heroism of philanthropy which, under the unique name of charity, makes the sacrifices of men for each other divine[46], [and] which, through communion, makes them live the same life and inspires them with the same love, [then] you are a savior of the world.

The religion of Moses is a truth, the so-called mosaic religion of the pharisees was a lie.

The religion of Jesus is the same truth [as the religion of Moses, but] has taken a step forward and revealed itself to men through a new manifestation.

The religion of the inquisitors and the oppressors of the human consciousness is a lie.

The catholicism of the Church Fathers and of the saints is a truth.

The catholicism of Veuillot is a lie.

El de Renan Inexcusable; el del Evangelio inexplicable; pero el de Vicente de Paul y del Fenelon, es adorable.

El cristianismo es para vosotros la condenacion de la razon, el despotismo de la ignorancia y el enemigo de la humanidad.

Entendeis por cristianismo la vida de Dios en la humanidad, el heroismo de la filantropia, que, con el nombre de caridad, diviniza el sacrificio de los hombres, quienes, mediante la comunion, los hacen vivir la misma vida e inspirarse en el mismo amor.

La religion de Moises es una verdad; el pretendido mosaismo de los fariseos es una mentira.

La religion de Jesus es la misma verdad que ha dado un paso hacia adelante, revelandose a los hombres mediante una nueva manifestacion.

La religion de los inquisidores y de los opresores de la conciencia humana es una mentira.

El catolicismo de los Padres de la Iglesia y de los santos es una verdad.

El catolicismo de Veuillot es una mentira.

---

[45] Ernest Renan (1823-1892) was a French expert of Middle East ancient languages and civilizations, philosopher and writer. He is best known for his influential historical works on early Christianity and his political theories, especially concerning nationalism and national identity.

[46] Literally 'divinise le sacrifice des hommes les uns pour les autres' means "divinises the sacrifice of men for one another"

This is the lie that freemasonry has [chosen] as [its] mission[47] to fight[48] for the benefit of the truth[49].

Freemasonry does not want the doctrines of Torquemada[50] or those of Escobar[51], but it does admit among its symbols those of Hermes, Moses and Jesus Christ; the pelican at the foot of the cross is embroidered on the ribbon of its initiates of the highest degree[52]; it only prohibits fanaticism, ignorance, foolish[53] gullibility and hate, but it believes in [a] dogma, single in its spirit and multiple in its forms, which is that of humanity.

Its religion is neither the Judaism [which is the] enemy of all other peoples, nor [is it] exclusive catholicism, nor [is it] strict protestantism: it is true catholicity[54] worthy of this name, that is, universal philanthropy!

This is the messianism[55] of the Hebrews!

Es esa misma mentira que la francmasoneria tiene por mision combatir, en provecho de la verdad.

La francmasoneria no quiere las doctrinas de Torquemada[56], de los Escobar, sino que admite por simbolos los de Hermes, Moises y Jesucristo; el pelicano al pie de la cruz esta bordado en la cinta de los iniciados de mayor grado; y no prescribe mas que el fanatismo, la ignorancia, la necia credulidad y el odio, pero cree en el dogma, unico en su espiritu y multiple en sus formas, que es el de la humanidad.

Su religion no es ni el judaismo, enemigo de los demas pueblos, ni el catolicismo, verdaderamente digno de este nombre, es decir, la filantropia universal.

!Es el mesianismo de los hebreos!.

---

[47] Literally 'mission' means "mission; assignment, errand; charge; work, duty"
[48] Literally 'combattre' means "fight, combat, attack, struggle; oppose, contend, engage"
[49] Literally 'au profit de la vérité' means "to the profit of the truth"
[50] Levi is probably referring to Tomás de Torquemada (1420-1498), a fifteenth century Spanish Dominican friar, first Inquisitor General of Spain, and confessor to Isabella I of Castile. He is known for his campaign against the crypto-Jews and crypto-Muslims of Spain.
[51] Levi seems to be referring to Antonio Escobar y Mendoza (1589-1669) who was a Spanish churchman. He is best known as a writer on casuistry. In applied ethics, casuistry is case-based reasoning. Casuistry is used in juridical and ethical discussions of law and ethics, and often is a critique of principle- or rule-based reasoning.
[52] Literally 'grade' means "rank, grade"
[53] Literally 'sotte' means "silly, foolish, stupid, witless; simple, fatuous"
[54] Editor's note: Remember that the word 'catholic' means "universal"
[55] Messianism is the belief in a messiah, a savior or redeemer. Many religions have a messiah concept, including the Jewish Messiah, the Christian Christ, the Shia Muslim Mahdi, the Buddhist Maitreya, the Daoist Li Hong, the Hindu Kalki and the Zoroastrian Saoshyant.

[56] Primer inquisidor general de Espana, vallisoletano (1420-1489). Contribuyo a la expulsion de los judios y pronuncio 800 sentencias de muerte y 100.000 condenas menores. N. del T.

Everything is true in the books of Hermes. But by hiding them from the profane they have become in some way useless to the world.

Everything is true in the dogma of Moses; what is false is the exclusivity and despotism of some rabbis.

Everything is true in the christian dogma; but catholic priests have committed the same faults as the rabbis of Judaism.

These dogmas complete and explain one another, and their synthesis will be the religion of the future.

The error of the disciples of Hermes was this: "One must leave the profane to error[57] and truth should be rendered impenetrable to the whole world except to priests and kings."

Idolatry, despotism and the attacks[58] of the priesthood have been the bitter fruits of this doctrine.

The error of the Jews was to claim that they are a unique and privileged nation, that they alone are the elect of God and that [all] other peoples are cursed.

And the Jews, by a cruel twist of fate[59], have been cursed and persecuted by all the other nations.

The catholics have been deceived by three fundamental errors:

1. They believed that faith must be imposed by force upon reason and even upon science, whose progress they have fought;

Todo es verdad en los libros de Hermes. Pero la fuerza de ocultarlos a los profanos se ha terminado por volverlos inutiles al mundo.

Todo es verdad en el dogma de Moises; lo que es falso es el exclusivismo y el despotismo de algunos rabinos.

Todo es verdad el dogma cristiano, pero los sacerdotes catolicos han cometido las mismas faltas que los rabinos del judaismo.

Estos dogmas se completan y se explican los unos por los otros, y su sintesis sera la religion del porvenir.

El error de los discipulos de Hermes ha sido el siguiente: "Es preciso dejar el error a los profanos y hacer la verdad impenetrable a todo el mundo, excepto a los sacerdotes, constituyen el amargo fruto de esta doctrina."

La idolatria, el despotismo y los atentados a los sacerdotes, han sido frutos amargos de esta doctrina.

El error de los judios fue creer que constituian una nacion unica y privilegiada y que ellos solos eran los elegidos de Dios.

Y los judios, por cruel represalia, han sido maldecidos y perseguidos por todas las naciones.

Los catolicos han sido enganados por tres errores fundamentales:

1. Han creido que la fe se debe imponer por fuerza a la razon y hasta la ciencia, cuyos progresos ha combinado;

---

[57] Literally 'l'erreur aux profanes' means "the error to the profane"
[58] Literally 'attentats' means "assassination attempt; attack; violation, harmful act;"
[59] Literally 'représaille' means "reprisal; retaliation"

2. They attributed to the Pope an infallibility which was not only conservative[60] and disciplinary[61], but absolute, like that of God;

3. They thought that man should diminish[62] himself, cancel[63] himself out, render himself unfortunate in this life in order to deserve[64] the future life, whereas on the contrary man must cultivate all his faculties, develop them, expand[65] his soul, experience[66], love, beautify[67] his life, in a word render himself happy, because the present life is a preparation for the future life, and the eternal happiness of man begins as soon as he has conquered[68] the profound peace which results from perfect equilibrium.

The result of these errors have been the protest[69] against nature, [against] science and [against] reason, which have made [us] believe for a moment in the loss of all faith and in the annihilation[70] of all religion from the [face of the] earth.

But the world can not live without religion just like [a] man can not live without [a] heart.

When all the religions are dead, the unique and universal religion will live on…

---

[60] Literally 'conservatrice' means "conservative; caretaker"
[61] Literally 'disciplinaire' means "disciplinary, disciplinarian"
[62] Literally 'amoindrir' means "lessen, diminish; undermine"
[63] Literally 'annuler' means "cancel, call off, withdraw; annul, render null and void, invalidate, rescind, revoke, nullify, quash; undo;"
[64] Literally 'mériter' means "deserve, worth, merit, (be) worth (it), claim, earn, rate;"
[65] Literally 'agrandir' means "enlarge, widen, extend; aggrandize, grow"
[66] Literally 'connaître' means "know; be acquainted; experience; taste"
[67] Literally 'embellir' means "beautify, embellish; pretty up, ornament; grace, bedeck; improve, glamorise"
[68] Literally 'conquis' means "conquered, victorious, triumphant"
[69] Literally 'protestation' means "protest, protestation, outcry; remonstrance; furor"
[70] Literally 'anéantissement' means "destruction, annihilation; extermination; wreckage"

*The Synthesis of
All Religions*

*La Síntesis de
Todas las Religiones*

Extracted from Chapter 1 of
CHRISTMAS MESSAGE 1961-62
by Samael Aun Weor

[NO TITLE GIVEN]

It is said that there are seven Great Religions and Five thousand Sects; we the Gnostics affirm that there is only one great Religion, and that is the TRUTH.

We firmly believe that only he who lives the Truth is profoundly Religious.

The truth wants to know itself in each man.

Jesus of Nazareth is a living embodiment[1] of the TRUTH.

Jesus Incarnated the TRUTH.

Whoever Incarnates the TRUTH becomes free.

Those who Incarnated the Truth founded the Great Religions and the Great Mystery Schools.

Buddha, Hermes, Krishna, Quetzalcoatl, etc. incarnated the Truth, and all those who dissolve the "I" and raise the columns of the Temple upon the living Rock incarnate the Truth.

There is no higher Religion than the Truth.

We should distinguish between Religious forms and Religious principles.

It is necessary to know that the Principles are living cosmic Formulae.

---

[1] Literally 'cuerpo' means "body, carcass, corpse; main part; bones; length; corps, specialized military unit; outfit; bodice, corsage"

Religious forms are the different systems of teaching those Principles.

The Great Infinite Universal Cosmic Religion assumes distinct forms according to the needs of each race and of each epoch.

Thus, Religious forms have succeeded one another throughout millions of years; the successive string[2] of all the Religions that have existed in the world always reveal the same immutable principles of the Truth.

Religion is [an] inherent property of life, as humidity is of water.

A man could belong to no religion and nonetheless be profoundly religious.

Everyone who is capable of experiencing the Truth is profoundly religious, even if they do not belong to any religion.

Religion is the intimate relationship of the mind with the Truth.

Only the religious man is truly revolutionary.

Some philosophers say that Religions have failed; we assure you that every Religion has fulfilled its historic mission.

With only one living Buddha [being] born from among the ranks of Buddhism, Buddhism fulfilled its mission; with only one Christified [person being born] among the ranks of Christianity justifies the existence of Christianity; with only one Imam [being born] among the ranks of Mohammedism very much justifies the existence of the Religion of Mohammed.

Las formas Religiosas son los distintos sistemas de enseñar esos Principios.

La Gran Religión Cósmica Universal Infinita asume distintas formas, según las necesidades de cada raza y de cada época.

Así las formas Religiosas se han sucedido unas tras otras a través de millones de años; la cinta sucesiva de todas las Religiones que han existido en el mundo revela siempre los mismos principios inmutables de la Verdad.

La Religión es propiedad inherente a la vida como la humedad al agua.

Podría un hombre no pertenecer a ninguna religión. Y sin embargo ser profundamente religioso.

Todo aquel que sea capaz de vivenciar la Verdad es profundamente religioso aunque no pertenezca a ninguna religión.

La íntima relación de la mente con la Verdad es Religión.

Sólo el hombre religioso es verdaderamente revolucionario.

Algunos Filósofos dicen que las Religiones han fracasado; nosotros aseguramos que toda Religión ha cumplido su misión histórica.

Con un solo Buddha viviente nacido entre las filas del Budismo ya el Budismo ha cumplido su misión; con un solo Crístificado entre las filas del Cristianismo ya queda justificada la existencia del Cristianismo; con un solo Imán entre las filas del Mahometanismo, ya queda bien justificada la existencia de la Religión Mahometana.

---

[2] Literally 'cinta' means "tape; ribbon; film; cassette; loading belt; headband"

| The Synthesis of All Religions | La Síntesis de Todas las Religiones |

All the great Religions of the World have achieved their objective through men who obtained their 'Reunion', that is to say, [those] who Incarnated the Truth.

Really, many are called, but few are chosen.

This law has already been fulfilled in all the Religions.

There is no basis for asserting[3] that religions failed in their mission to 'Reunite' man with the Truth.

In all Religions there are perfect men who succeeded in Reuniting.

There is no motive which justifies Religious wars, because all Religions teach the same principles.

The Witchdoctor[4] in Central Africa and the Archbishop in the Metropolitan Cathedral of Rome or London are based on the same Marvelous force of the Cosmic Religion; the principles are the same; the only thing that varies are the Religious forms, therefore, the fratricidal struggle among diverse Religions is absurd.

The Cosmic Religion Vibrates in each atom of the Cosmos, because [it] palpitates in the heart of the suns, in the heart of man, and in that of the ant.

Todas las grandes Religiones del Mundo han logrado su objetivo con hombres que consiguieron el Religarse, es decir que Encarnaron la verdad.

Realmente muchos son los llamados y pocos los escogidos.

Esta ley se ha cumplido ya en todas las Religiones.

No existe motivo para asegurar que las Religiones fracasaron en su misión de Religar al hombre con la Verdad.

En todas las Religiones hay hombres de perfección que alcanzaron a Religarse.

No hay motivo que justifique las guerras Religiosas, porque todas las Religiones enseñan los mismos principios.

El Brujo del Centro del África y el Arzobispo de la Catedral Metropolitana de Roma o de Londres se apoyan en la misma fuerza Maravillosa de la Religión Cósmica; los principios son los mismos; lo único que varia son las formas Religiosas, resulta pues absurda la lucha fratricida entre las diversas Religiones.

La Religión Cósmica Vibra en cada átomo del Cosmos, porque palpita en el corazón de los soles, en el corazón del hombre y en el de la hormiga.

---

[3] Literally 'asegurar' means "secure, ensure; guarantee, warrant; assert; adjust; underwrite; fasten"
[4] Literally 'Brujo' means "sorcerer, magician, witch, warlock"

Extracted from Chapter 7 of
THE REVOLUTION OF THE DIALECTIC
by Samael Aun Weor

"RELIGIOUS PRINCIPLES"

All religions are precious gems[5] strung on the golden thread of the Divinity.

Religions preserve the eternal values, false religions do not exist.

All religions are necessary, all religions fulfill their mission in life.

It is absurd to say that the neighbor's religion is useless and that only ours is legitimate[6].

If the neighbor's religion is useless, then so is ours because the values are always the same.

It is stupid to say that the religion of the indigenous tribes of America is idolatry; [if we do so] then they also have the right to say that our religion is idolatry.

And if we laugh at them, then they can also laugh at us.

And if we say that they adore or adored idols, then they can also say that we adore idols.

We cannot discredit the religion of others without discrediting ours as well, because the principles are always the same.

All religions have the same principles.

Every religion under the sun is born, grows, develops, multiplies into many sects and dies.

---

[5] Literally 'piedras preciosas' means "precious stones, gemstones"
[6] Literally 'verdadera' means "legitimate, legal, lawful; acceptable; born of parents who are legally married; correct, sound; incorrupt, perfect"

Extracto del Capítulo VII de
LA REVOLUCIÓN DE LA DIALÉCTICA
por Samael Aun Weor

"LOS PRINCIPIOS RELIGIOSOS"

Todas las religiones son piedras preciosas engarzadas en el hilo de oro de la Divinidad.

Las religiones conservan los valores eternos, no existen religiones falsas.

Todas las religiones son necesarias, todas las religiones cumplen su misión en la vida.

Es absurdo decir que la religión del vecino no sirve y que sólo la mía es verdadera.

Si la religión del vecino no sirve, entonces la mía tampoco sirve porque los valores son siempre los mismos.

Es estúpido decir que la religión de las tribus indígenas de América es idolatría, entonces ellos también tienen derecho a decir que nuestra religión es idolatría.

Y si nosotros nos reímos de ellos, ellos también pueden reírse de nosotros.

Y si nosotros decimos que ellos adoran o adoraban ídolos, ellos también pueden decir que nosotros adoramos ídolos.

No podemos desacreditar la religión de otros sin desacreditar la nuestra también, porque los principios son siempre los mismos.

Todas las religiones tienen los mismos principios.

Bajo el sol, toda religión nace, crece, se desarrolla, se multiplica en muchas sectas y muere.

| The Synthesis of All Religions | La Síntesis de Todas las Religiones |

| This is how it has always been and will always be. | Así ha sido siempre y así será siempre. |

| Religious principles never die. | Los principios religiosos nunca mueren. |

| Religious forms can die, but the religious principles, [that] is to say, the eternal values, never die. | Pueden morir las formas religiosas, pero los principios religiosos, es decir, los valores eternos, no mueren jamás. |

| They continue [on], they dress [up] again[7] with new forms. | Ellos continúan, ellos se revisten con nuevas formas. |

| Religion is [as] inherent to life as humidity is to water. | La religión es inherente a la vida como la humedad lo es al agua. |

| There are profoundly religious people who do not belong to any religious form. | Hay hombres profundamente religiosos que no pertenecen a ninguna forma religiosa. |

| People without religion are conservative and reactionary by nature. | La gente sin religión es conservadora y reaccionaria por naturaleza. |

| Only the religious person [can] achieve the Revolution of the Dialectic. | Sólo el hombre religioso logra la Revolución de la Dialéctica. |

| There is no reason[8] which justifies religious wars like those of Ireland. | No hay motivo que justifique las guerras religiosas como las de Irlanda. |

| It is absurd to classify others as infidels[9], heretics or pagans, for the simple fact that [they do] not belonging to our religion. | Es absurdo calificar a otros de infieles, herejes o paganos, por el simple hecho de no pertenecer a nuestra religión. |

| The witchdoctor[10], that exercises his priesthood before the tribe of cannibals in the heart of the african jungles, and the aristocratic christian archbishop who officiates in the Metropolitan Cathedral of London, Paris or Rome, rely[11] on the same principles, only the religious forms vary. | El brujo, que en el corazón de las selvas africanas, ejerce su sacerdocio ante la tribu de caníbales, y el aristócrata arzobispo cristiano que oficia en la Catedral Metropolitana de Londres, París o Roma, se apoyan en los mismos principios, sólo varían las formas religiosas. |

---

[7] Literally 'revisten' means "cover, coat, line; take on, have", but it comes from 'visten' which means "dress; wear; cover;"
[8] Literally 'motivo' means "motive, reason, cause; motif"
[9] Literally 'infieles' means "treacherous, infidel, unfaithful"
[10] Literally 'brujo' means "sorcerer, magician, witch, warlock"
[11] Literally 'apoyan' means "ean, rest against; recline; hold up, prop up; support, prop; sustain; underwrite"

Jesus, the Divine Rabbi of Galilee, taught all human beings the path of Truth and the Revolution of the Dialectic.

The Truth was made flesh in Jesus and will become flesh in every person[12] who achieves the Integral Revolution.

If we study religions, if we carry out a comparative study of religions, we will find in all of them the worship[13] of the Christ; the only thing that varies are the names which are given to the Christ.

The Divine Rabbi of Galilee has the same attributes as Zeus, Apollo, Krishna, Quetzalcoatl, Lao-Tzu, Fu-Xi —the Chinese Christ—, Buddha, etc.

One is amazed when one carries out a comparative study of religions.

All these sacred religious personages which personify the Christ are born on the 24th of december at 12 midnight.

All of these sacred personages are sons of immaculate conceptions, all of them are born by the work and grace of the Holy Spirit, all of them are born from Virgins [who are] immaculate before childbirth, during childbirth and after childbirth.

The poor and unknown hebrew woman Mary, mother of the Adorable Savior Jesus, the Christ, receives the same attributes and cosmic powers as the Goddess Isis, Juno, Demeter, Ceres, Vesta, Maia, Adonin, Insobertha, Rea, Cybele, Tonantzin, etc.

All of these feminine deities always represent the Divine Mother, the Eternal Cosmic Feminine.

---

[12] Literally 'hombre' means "man, adult male human; husband;"
[13] Literally 'culto' means "worship, homage, tribute; cult"

Jesús, el Divino Rabí de Galilea, enseñó a todos los seres humanos el camino de la Verdad y la Revolución de la Dialéctica.

La Verdad se hizo carne en Jesús y se hará carne en todo hombre que logre la Revolución Integral.

Si estudiamos las religiones, si hacemos un estudio comparativo de las religiones, en todas ellas encontraremos el culto al Cristo, lo único que varían son los nombres que se le dan al Cristo.

El Divino Rabí de Galilea tiene los mismos atributos de Zeus, Apolo, Krishna, Quetzalcoatl, Lao Tsé, Fu-ji —el Cristo chino—, Buddha, etc.

Uno se queda asombrado cuando hace un estudio comparativo de las religiones.

Todos estos sagrados personajes religiosos que personifican al Cristo nacen el 24 de diciembre a las 12 de la noche.

Todos estos sagrados personajes son hijos de inmaculadas concepciones, todos ellos nacen por obra y gracia del Espíritu Santo, todos ellos nacen en Vírgenes inmaculadas antes del parto, en el parto y después del parto.

La pobre y desconocida mujer hebrea María, madre del Adorable Salvador Jesús, el Cristo, recibió los mismos atributos y poderes cósmicos de la Diosa Isis, Juno, Démeter, Ceres, Vesta, Maía, Adonía, Insoberta, Rea, Cibeles, Tonantzín, etc.

Todas estas deidades femeninas representan siempre a la Madre Divina, el Eterno Femenino Cósmico.

The Christ is always the son of the Divine Mother and worship is rendered to her [in] all the holy religions.

Mary is impregnated[14] by the Holy Spirit.

According to tradition the Third Logos, in the form of a dove, impregnated the immaculate womb of Mary.

The dove is always a phallic symbol.

Let us remember Peristhera, nymph of the court of Venus, transformed into a dove by love.

Among the chinese, the Christ is Fu-Xi. The chinese Christ who is miraculously born by the work and grace of the Holy Spirit.

While a virgin named Hoa-Se walked on the river bank, she placed her foot on the footprint of the Great Man; immediately she was emotionally moved[15] seeing herself surrounded by a marvelous splendor and her womb conceived.

Twelve years transpired, [and] on the fourth day of the tenth Moon, at midnight, Fu-Xi was born, [who was] named in memory of the river beside which he was conceived.

In Ancient Mexico, Christ is Quetzalcoatl, who was the Messiah and transformer of the toltecs.

One day, while Chimalman was alone with her two sisters, a messenger[16] from heaven appeared to her.

The sisters, upon seeing him, died of fright.

---

[14] Literally 'fecundada' means "fertilized, impregnated"
[15] Literally 'conmovió' means "touch, get through to, melt, move, move deeply, move to compassion, move to pity, move to tears, stir up;"
[16] Literally 'enviado' means "envoy, messenger"

She, upon hearing from the angel's mouth that she would conceive a boy, instantly conceived, Quetzalcoatl, the mexican Christ, without the work of a male.

Among the japanese, the Christ is Amida, who intercedes before the Supreme Goddess Ten-Sic-Dai-Tain praying for all sinners.

Amida, the japanese Christ of the Shinto Religion, is the one who has the powers to open the doors of Gokurat, Paradise.

The german Eddas mention[17] the Khristos, the God of their Theogony[18], similar to Jesus, born on the 24th of December at midnight, the same as Odin, Wotan and Belenos.

When one studies the Gospel of Krishna, the hindu Christ, one is astonished to discover the same Gospel of Jesus, and nonetheless, Krishna was born many centuries before Jesus.

Devaki, the hindu virgin, conceived Krishna by the work and grace of the Holy Spirit.

The child-god Krishna was transported to the stable of Nanden and the gods and angels came to adore him.

The life, passion and death of Krishna is similar to that of Jesus.

It is worthwhile to study all religions.

Ella, al oír de boca del ángel que concebiría un hijo, concibió al instante, sin obra de varón, a Quetzalcoatl, el Cristo mexicano.

Entre los japoneses, el Cristo es Amida, quien intercede ante la Diosa Suprema Ten Sic Dai Tain rogando por todos los pecadores.

Amida, el Cristo japonés de la Religión Sintoísta, es quien tiene los poderes para abrir las puertas del Gokurat, el Paraíso.

Los Eddas germanos citan a Khristos, el Dios de su Teogonía, semejante a Jesús, nacido también el 24 de diciembre a media noche, lo mismo que Odín, Wotan y Beleno.

Cuando uno estudia el Evangelio de Krishna, el Cristo hindú, se queda asombrado al descubrir el mismo Evangelio de Jesús, y sin embargo Krishna nació muchos siglos antes que Jesús.

Devaki, la virgen hindú, concibió a Krishna por obra y gracia del Espíritu Santo.

El niño dios Krishna fue transportado al establo de Nanden y los dioses y ángeles vinieron a adorarle.

La vida, pasión y muerte de Krishna es similar a la de Jesús.

Vale la pena estudiar todas las religiones.

---

[17] Literally 'citan' means "quote, mention, make reference to, quote from, paraphrase;"
[18] Literally 'Teogonía' means "Theogony, the study of the origins and genealogy of the gods."

The comparative study of religions leads one to comprehend that all religions conserve the eternal values, that no religion is false, [and] that all are true.

All Religions talk about the soul, about heaven, about hell, etc.

The principles are always the same.

Among the romans, hell was the Avernus; among the greeks, it was the Tartarus and among the hindus, [it was] the Avitchi, etc.

Heaven, among the romans and greeks, was Olympus.

Each religion has its heaven.

When the religion of the romans ended, when it degenerated, the priests became fortunetellers[19], puppeteers, etc., but the eternal principles did not die, they dressed themselves up again with the new religious form of christianism.

The pagan priests, called Augur, Druid, Flamen, Hierophant, Dionysius and Sacrificer, were re-baptized in christianism with the sacred titles of Clergy, Pastors, Prelates, Pope, Anointed, Abbot, Theologian, etc.

The Sibyls, Vestals, Druidesses, Popesses, Deaconesses, Menades, Pythonesses, etc., were denominated as Novices, Abbesses, Canonesses, Superior Prelates, Reverends, Sisters, Nuns in christianism.

The Gods, Demi-gods, Titans, Goddesses, Syliphids, Cyclops, Messengers of the gods of ancient religions were re-baptized with the names of Angels, Archangels, Seraphim, Powers, Virtues, Thrones, etc.

---

[19] Literally 'adivinos' means "fortuneteller, diviner, soothsayer, seer, foreteller, vaticinator; thought reader, mind reader"

El estudio comparativo de las religiones lo lleva a uno a comprender que todas las religiones conservan los valores eternos, que ninguna religión es falsa, que todas son verdaderas.

Todas las Religiones hablan del alma, del cielo, del infierno, etc.

Los principios son siempre los mismos.

Entre los romanos, el infierno era el Averno; entre los griegos era el Tartarus y entre los indostaníes el Avitchi, etc.

El cielo, entre los romanos y griegos, era el Olimpo.

Cada religión tiene su cielo.

Cuando terminó la religión de los romanos, cuando se degeneró, los sacerdotes se convirtieron en adivinos, titiriteros, etc., pero los principios eternos no murieron, ellos se revistieron con la nueva forma religiosa del cristianismo.

Los sacerdotes paganos, denominados Augur, Druida, Flamen, Hierofante, Dionisios y Sacrificador, fueron rebautizados en el cristianismo con los sagrados títulos de Clérigos, Pastores, Prelados, Pope, Ungido, Abate, Teólogo, etc.

Las Sibilas, Vestales, Druidesas, Papisas, Diaconisas, Ménades, Pitonisas, etc., en el cristianismo fueron denominadas Novicias, Abadesas, Canonesas, Prelados Superiores, Reverendas, Hermanas, Monjas.

Los Dioses, Semi dioses, Titanes, Diosas, Sílfides, Cíclopes, Mensajeros de los dioses de las antiguas religiones, fueron rebautizados con los nombres de Ángeles, Arcángeles, Serafines, Potestades, Virtudes, Tronos, etc.

If the gods were adored in antiquity, they are also adored now, except with different names.

Religious forms change according to the historical times[20] and the races.

Each race needs its special religious form.

People need religion.

A people without [a] religion are in fact a totally barbaric, cruel, and pitiless people.

Si antiguamente se adoraron a los dioses, ahora también se les adora, sólo que con otros nombres.

Las formas religiosas cambian según las épocas históricas y las razas.

Cada raza necesita su forma religiosa especial.

Los pueblos necesitan la religión.

Un pueblo sin religión es de hecho un pueblo totalmente bárbaro, cruel y despiadado.

---

[20] Literally 'épocas' means "period, age, era; season; lesson; length of time"

Extracted from the INTRODUCTION to
THE PERFECT MATRIMONY
by Samael Aun Weor

The Perfect Matrimony and the Cosmic Christ are the synthesis of all religions, schools, orders, sects, lodges, yoga systems, etc., etc., etc.

It is truly unfortunate that so many who discovered the practical synthesis have left it, to fall into an intricate labyrinth of theories.

According to tradition, the Synthesis is found in the center of the Labyrinth, that is to say the Labarum[21] of the temple.

The word labyrinth comes etymologically from the word labarum. The latter is a double-edged axe, a symbol of the masculine-feminine sexual force.

Really, whosoever finds the Synthesis commits the greatest foolishness when they leave the center and return to the complicated corridors of all the theories that form the labyrinth of the mind.

Christ and Sexual Magic represent religious synthesis.

If we make a comparative study of religions, we will discover that, at the base of all schools, religions and esoteric sects, there exists phallicism[22].

Extracto de la INTRODUCCIÓN de
EL MATRIMONIO PERFECTO
por Samael Aun Weor

El Matrimonio Perfecto y el Cristo Cósmico constituyen la síntesis de todas las religiones, escuelas, órdenes, sectas, logias, yogas, etc., etc., etc.

Es lástima verdad, que tantos que hallaron la Síntesis Práctica, se hayan salido de ella para caer en el intrincado laberinto de las teorías.

Cuenta la tradición que en el centro del Laberinto existía la Síntesis, es decir el Lábaro del templo.

La palabra laberinto viene etimológicamente de la palabra lábaro. Este último era un hacha de doble filo, símbolo de la fuerza sexual, masculino-femenina.

Realmente quien encuentra la Síntesis, comete la más grande de las tonterías cuando se sale del centro y se regresa a los complicados corredores de todas las teorías que forman el laberinto de la mente.

Cristo y la Magia Sexual representan la síntesis religiosa.

Si hacemos un estudio comparativo de religiones, descubriremos que en el fondo de todas las escuelas, religiones y sectas esotéricas, existe el falismo.

---

[21] Literally 'Lábaro' means "Labarum, an ecclesiastical banner"
[22] Literally 'falismo' means "phallicism, worship of the phallus, especially as symbolic of power or of the generative principle of nature"

Let's remember Peristera, the nymph, the hand maiden of Venus, who was transformed into a dove through love.

Let's remember the Virtuous Venus, let's remember the processions of the God Priapus in the old august Rome of the caesars, when the priestesses of the temple, full of ecstasy, majestically carried an enormous phallus of sacred wood.

With just reason Freud, the founder of Psychoanalysis, says that religions have a sexual origin.

The Mysteries of Fire are [found] within the Perfect Matrimony.

All fire cults are absolutely sexual.

The vestals were true priestesses of love; with them the celibate priests reached Adepthood.

It is unfortunate that the modern vestals (the nuns) do not know the key of Sexual Magic.

It is a pity that the modern priests have forgotten the secret key of sex.

We feel profound pain seeing so many yogis who ignore Sexual Magic, the supreme key of Yoga, the supreme synthesis of all systems of Yoga.

People are filled with horror when they hear about Sexual Magic, but they are not filled with horror when they give themselves over to sexual deviation and carnal passion.

Here you have dear reader, the synthesis of all religions, schools and sects.

Our Doctrine is the Doctrine of Synthesis.

| The Synthesis of All Religions | La Síntesis de Todas las Religiones |

In the profound night of the centuries there existed powerful civilizations and grandiose mysteries.

The priestesses of love were never absent from the temples.

Those who practiced Sexual Magic with them became Masters of the White Lodge.

The Master must be born inside ourselves by means of Sexual Magic.

In the sunny land of Kem, in the old Egypt of the pharaohs, whoever revealed the Great Arcanum (Sexual Magic) was condemned to death, his head was cut off, his heart was torn out and his ashes were hurled to the four winds.

In the land of the aztecs, men and women, aspiring to be Adepts, practiced Sexual Magic for long periods of time, caressing each other, loving each other within the courtyards of the temples.

In these temple practices, whoever spilled the Glass of Hermes was beheaded for having profaned the temple.

All systems of intimate self-education have Sexual Magic as their ultimate practical synthesis.

Every religion, every esoteric cult, has Sexual Magic (the Arcanum A.Z.F.) as [its] synthesis.

In the Mysteries of Eleusis there was naked dancing and ineffable things. Sexual Magic was the fundamental basis of those Mysteries.

En la noche profunda de los siglos existieron poderosas civilizaciones y grandiosos misterios.

Jamás faltaron sacerdotisas del amor en los templos.

Con ellas practicaron Magia Sexual aquellos que se volvieron Maestros de la Logia Blanca.

El Maestro debe nacer dentro de nosotros con la Magia Sexual.

En el país soleado de Kem, allá en el viejo Egipto de los faraones, quien divulgaba el Gran Arcano (la Magia Sexual), era condenado a pena de muerte, se le cortaba la cabeza, se le arrancaba el corazón y sus cenizas eran arrojadas a los cuatro vientos.

En el país de los aztecas, hombres y mujeres aspirantes al Adeptado, permanecían tiempos enteros acariciándose, amándose y practicando Magia Sexual dentro de los patios de los templos.

Quien derramaba el Vaso de Hermes en esas prácticas del templo, era decapitado por haber profanado el templo.

Todos los sistemas de auto-educación íntima tienen como última síntesis práctica, la Magia Sexual.

Toda religión, todo culto esotérico tiene por síntesis, la Magia Sexual (el Arcano A.Z.F.).

En los Misterios de Eleusis existían bailes al desnudo y cosas inefables. La Magia Sexual era la base fundamental de esos Misterios.

In those days nobody thought dirty things because they profoundly venerated sex.

Initiates know that the Third Logos works within sex.

We have written this book[23] with complete clarity; we have unveiled what was veiled.

Now, whoever wants to realize themselves in depth can do so, here is the guide; here is the complete teaching.

I have already been harassed, humiliated, calumniated and persecuted etc., for teaching the Path of the Perfect Matrimony; that does not matter to me; at first the treason and slander[24] hurt me a great deal, but now I have become like steel and the treason and slander no longer hurts.

I know only too well that humanity hates the truth and mortally hates the prophets; so, it is normal that they hate me for having written this book.

There is only one thing we pursue, one goal, one objective: Christification.

It is necessary that each person christifies themselves.

It is necessary to incarnate the Christ.

In this book we have lifted the veil of the Christic Mysteries.

We have explained what the Christic Principle is.

Entonces nadie pensaba en porquerías porque el sexo era profundamente venerado.

Los Iniciados saben que en el sexo trabaja el Tercer Logos.

Hemos escrito este libro[25] con entera claridad; hemos develado lo que estaba velado.

Quien quiera ahora realizarse a fondo, bien puede hacerlo, aquí está la guía, aquí está la enseñanza completa.

Ya he sido vejado, humillado, calumniado, perseguido, etc., por enseñar la Senda del Matrimonio Perfecto; eso no me importa; en principio me dolían muchísimo las traiciones y calumnias, ahora me he vuelto de acero, y las calumnias y traiciones ya no me duelen.

Sé demasiado que la humanidad odia la verdad y aborrece mortalmente a los profetas; así pues, es apenas normal que a mí me odien por haber escrito este libro.

Una sola cosa perseguimos, una meta, un objetivo: la Cristificación.

Es necesario que cada hombre se cristifique.

Es necesario encarnar al Cristo.

En este libro hemos levantado el velo de los Misterios Crísticos.

Hemos explicado lo que es el Principio Crístico.

---

[23] This is referring to *The Perfect Matrimony*, from which this has been extracted
[24] Literally 'calumnias' means "calumny, slander, libel; defamation, slur"

[25] Esto se refiere a *El Matrimonio Perfecto*, desde que ésta se ha extraído

We have invited all human beings to follow the Path of the Perfect Matrimony to attain Christification.

We have explained that Christ is not an individual, but an impersonal universal cosmic principle, which must be assimilated by each person through Sexual Magic.

Naturally, all this scandalizes the fanatics, but the truth is the truth and we have to tell it, even when it costs us our lives.

The teachings of the Zend Avesta are similar to the doctrinal principles contained in The Egyptian Book of the Dead, and contain the Christic principle.

The Iliad of Homer, the Hebrew Bible, the Germanic Edda and the Siblylline Books of the romans contain the same Christic principle.

This is sufficient to demonstrate that Christ existed before[26] Jesus of Nazareth.[27]

Christ is not an individual.

Christ is a cosmic principle that we must assimilate within our own physical, psychic, somatic and spiritual nature, through Sexual Magic.

Amongst the persians Christ is Ormuz, Ahura Mazda, the terrible enemy of Ahriman (Satan), which we have within us.

Amongst the hindus, Krishna is Christ, and the gospel of Krishna is very similar to that of Jesus of Nazareth.

---

[26] Literally 'es anterior a' means "is anterior to"
[27] Editor's note: St. Augustine, considered one of the Fathers of the Christian Church said: "What we now call the Christian religion existed amongst the ancients, and was from the beginning of the human race, until Christ Himself came in the flesh; from which time the already existing true religion began to be styled Christian." (Retract., I, xiii, 3)

Among the egyptians, Christ is Osiris and whosoever incarnated him was in fact an osirified [one].

Amongst the chinese it is Fu-Xi, the Cosmic Christ who composed the I-Ching, the book of laws and appointed dragon ministers.

Among the greeks, Christ is called Zeus, Jupiter, the Father of the Gods.

Amongst the aztecs it is Quetzalcoatl, the mexican Christ.

In the Germanic Edda it is Balder, the Christ who was assassinated by Hoder, god of war, with an arrow of mistletoe, etc.

Thus we can find the Cosmic Christ in thousands of ancient texts and old traditions that came millions of years before Jesus.

All this invites us to accept that Christ is a Cosmic Principle contained in the essential principles of all religions.

Really there is only one unique and cosmic religion.

This religion assumes different forms according to the times and the needs of humanity.

Therefore, religious conflicts are absurd because, at their base all religions are only modifications of the Universal Cosmic Religion.

From this point of view we affirm that this book is not against any religion, school or system of thought.

Entre los egipcios, Cristo es Osiris y todo aquel que lo encarnaba era de hecho un osirificado.

Entre los chinos es Fu-Hi el Cristo Cósmico quien compuso el I-King, libro de las leyes y nombró ministros dragones.

Entre los griegos, el Cristo se llama Zeus, Júpiter, el Padre de los Dioses.

Entre los aztecas es Ketzalkoatl, el Cristo mexicano.

Entre los Eddas Germanos es Balder, el Cristo que fue asesinado por Hoder, dios de la guerra, con una flecha de muérdago, etc.

Así podríamos citar al Cristo Cósmico en millares de libros arcaicos y viejas tradiciones que vienen de millones de años antes de Jesús.

Todo esto nos invita a aceptar que Cristo es un Principio Cósmico contenido en los principios sustanciales de todas las religiones.

Realmente sólo existe de hecho una sola religión única y cósmica.

Esta religión asume diferentes formas religiosas según los tiempos y las necesidades de la humanidad.

Así pues, resultan absurdas las luchas religiosas porque en el fondo todas son únicamente modificaciones de la Religión Cósmica Universal.

Desde este punto de vista afirmamos que este libro no está contra ninguna religión, escuela o sistema de pensamiento.

The only purpose of this book is to give to humanity a key, a sexual secret, a key with which every living being may assimilate the Christic Principle contained in the foundation of all the great religions of the world.

We recognize Jesus-Iesus-Zeus-Jupiter, as the new Superman who totally assimilated the Christic Principle, and in fact converted himself into a God-Man.

We consider that we must imitate him.

He was a complete man, a true man in the fullest sense of the word, and through Sexual Magic he attained the absolute assimilation of the Universal Cosmic Christic Principle.

Those few students [who are] very comprehensive should study the Gospel of John, chapter three from verses one to twenty-one; there the devotee of The Perfect Matrimony will find pure and legitimate Sexual Magic as taught by Jesus.

Of course the teaching is given in code, but whosoever understands will understand it intuitively.

Modern humanity has committed the error of separating the great Master Jesus from all his predecessors who, like him, christified themselves; this has damaged the present humanity.

We need to comprehend well that all religions are only one Religion.

Mary the mother of Jesus, is the same as Isis, Juno, Demeter, Ceres, Maia, etc, the Cosmic Mother or Kundalini (Sexual Fire) of whom the Cosmic Christ is always born.

| The Synthesis of All Religions | La Síntesis de Todas las Religiones |

Mary Magdalene is the same as Salambo, Matres, Ishtar, Astarte, Aphrodite and Venus, with whom we must practice Sexual Magic to awaken the fire.

The martyrs, saints, virgins, angels and cherubim, are the same Gods, demi-gods, titans, goddesses, sylphs, cyclops and messengers of the Gods of the pagan mythologies.

All the religious principles of christianism are pagan, and when the present religious forms disappear, their principles will be assimilated by the new religious forms of the future.

We need to comprehend what immaculate conception is, we need to know that only with the Perfect Matrimony can the Christ be born in the heart of man.

It is urgent to awaken the fire of Kundalini, or fire of the Holy Spirit in order to incarnate the Christ.

Whosoever awakens the Kundalini transforms themselves like Ganymede into the Eagle of the Spirit, in order to rise atop [Mount] Olympus and serve as cup-bearer to the ineffable Gods.

It is lamentable that the catholic priests have destroyed so many documents and so many valuable treasures of antiquity.

Fortunately they were not able to destroy them all.

During the age of the Renaissance some marvelous books were discovered by valiant priests.

La María Magdalena es la misma Salambo, Matra, Ishtar, Astarté, Afrodita y Venus con la cual tenemos que practicar Magia Sexual para despertar el fuego.

Los mártires, santos, vírgenes, ángeles y querubines son los mismos Dioses, semidioses, titanes, diosas, sílfides, cíclopes y mensajeros de los Dioses en las mitologías paganas.

Todos los principios religiosos del cristianismo son paganos, y cuando las formas religiosas actuales desaparezcan, sus principios serán asimilados por las nuevas formas religiosas del futuro.

Es necesario comprender lo que son las inmaculadas concepciones; es necesario saber que sólo con el Matrimonio Perfecto nace el Cristo en el corazón del hombre.

Es urgente despertar el fuego del Kundalini o fuego del Espíritu Santo para encarnar el Cristo.

Quien despierta el Kundalini se transforma como Ganímedes en el Aguila del Espíritu para subir al Olimpo y servir de copero a los Dioses inefables.

Es lamentable que los sacerdotes católicos hayan destruido tanto documento y tanto tesoro valioso de la antigüedad.

Afortunadamente no todo lo pudieron destruir.

Durante la edad del Renacimiento fueron descubiertos por valientes sacerdotes algunos libros maravillosos.

So, despite the persecutions of the clergy, Dante Alighieri, Boccaccio, Petrarch, Erasmus etc., were able to translate works as famous as the Illiad and the Odyssey of Homer, true books of Occult Science and Sexual Magic.

They also translated The Aeneid of Virgil, the Theogony, The Works and Days of Hesiod, [the] Metamorphoses of Ovid and other writings of Lucretius, Horace, Tibullus, Titus Livius, Tacitus, Apulius, Cicero, etc., etc.

All [this] is pure gnosticism.

It is really lamentable that some ignorant people abandon Gnosis in order to follow systems and methods that ignore Sexual Magic and the Perfect Matrimony.

We have investigated all the great gnostic treasures, we have scrutinized the foundation of all the archaic religions, and we have found the supreme key of Sexual Magic at the foundation of all cults.

Now we deliver this treasure, this key to suffering humanity.

Así, Dante Alighieri, Bocacio, Petrarca, Erasmo, etc., lograron traducir, a pesar de las persecuciones del clero, obras tan famosas como La Iliada y La Odisea de Homero, verdaderos libros de Ciencia Oculta y Magia Sexual.

También tradujeron La Eneida de Virgilio, la Teogonía, Los Trabajos y los Días de Hesíodo, Metamorfosis de Ovidio y demás escritos de Lucrecio, Horacio, Tíbulo, Tito Livio, Tácito, Apuleyo, Cicerón, etc., etc.

Todo es gnosticismo puro.

Realmente es lamentable como algunos ignorantes abandonan la Gnosis para seguir sistemas y métodos que ignoran la Magia Sexual y el Matrimonio Perfecto.

Nosotros hemos investigado todos los grandes tesoros gnósticos, hemos escudriñado en el fondo de todas las religiones arcaicas, hemos hallado la clave suprema de la Magia Sexual en el fondo de todos los cultos.

Ahora le entregamos este tesoro, esta llave a la humanidad doliente.

The Shadow of God   *La Sombra de Dios*

Extracted from Chapter 2 of
THE THREE MOUNTAINS
by Samael Aun Weor

"RELIGION"

GOD

All the religions are precious pearls strung on the golden thread of the Divinity.

The love that all the mystical institutions of the world feel for the Divine: Allah, Brahma, Tao, Zen, I.A.O., INRI, God, etc., etc., etc., is ostensible[1].

Religious Esotericism does not teach any manner of atheism, except in the sense implied by the Sanskrit word NASTIKA: [meaning that there] is to be no admission of idols, included in this is the anthropomorphic God of the ignorant (it would be absurd to believe in a celestial dictator, sitting up there on his throne of tyranny, throwing lightning and thunderbolts against this sad human anthill).

Esotericism admits a LOGOS or collective "CREATOR" of the universe, a DEMIURGE architect.

It is unquestionable that this DEMIURGE is not a personal Deity as many wrongly suppose, but only the collective of the DHYAN CHOHANS, Angels, Archangels and the rest of the forces. GOD IS GODS.

It is written with characters of fire in the resplendent Book of Life, that God is the Army of the Voice, the Great Word, The Verb.

---

[1] Literally 'ostensible' means "ostensible, appearing to be true, professed to be a certain way (but often having hidden meaning or intent)"

"In the beginning was the Verb, and the Verb was with God, and the Verb was God."

"All things were made by Him and without Him nothing of that which was made would have been made."
[see John 1:1-3]

It is somewhat glaring and manifest that any authentic man who really achieves perfection joins the current of sound, the celestial militia constituted by the Buddhas of compassion, Angels, Planetary Spirits, Elohim, Rishi-Prajapatis, etc., etc., etc.

We have been told with great emphasis that the LOGOS makes a sound, and this is obvious. The DEMIURGE, The Verb, is perfect multiple unity.

Whosoever worships the Gods, whosoever renders worship unto them is capable of capturing the deep significance of the various divine aspects of the DEMIURGE architect in a better way.

When humanity began to mock the Holy Gods, then it fell mortally wounded into the gross[2] materialism of this iron age.

LUCIFER

We can and must radically eliminate all the tenebrous and perverse subjective psychic aggregates which we have inside; however, it is unquestionable that we would never be able to dissolve within ourselves the shadow of the intimate Logos.

It is clear and evident that LUCIFER is the antithesis of the Creator Demiurge, its living shadow projected into the profound depths of the MICRO-COSMOS-MAN.

---

[2] Literally 'grosero' means "gross; coarse, crude, vulgar; disgusting, offensive"

The Shadow of God	La Sombra de Dios
LUCIFER is the Guardian of the Door and of the keys to the Sanctuary, so that only those anointed and possessing the secret of Hermes can enter it.	LUCIFER es el Guardián de la Puerta y de las llaves del Santuario, para que no penetren en él sino los ungidos que poseen el secreto de Hermes.
And since we have just written this name, so abominable[3] for the pious ears of the vulgar, it is necessary to state[4] the fact that the esoteric LUCIFER of the Archaic Doctrine is the opposite of what the Theologians, such as the famous DeMOUSSEAUX and the Marquis of MIRVILLE, mistakenly suppose, since he is an allegory of good, the Gnostic symbol of the highest sacrifice (CHRISTOS-LUCIFER) and the God of wisdom under [an] infinite [number of] names.	Y ya que hemos escrito este tan aborrecible nombre para los oídos piadosos del vulgo, necesario sería consignar también que el LUCIFER esotérico de la Doctrina Arcaica es todo lo contrario de lo que los Teólogos, cual el famoso DES MOUSSEAUX y el Marqués de MIRVILLE; suponen equivocadamente, pues es la alegoría del bien, el símbolo del más alto sacrificio (CHRISTOS-LUCIFER) de los Gnósticos y el Dios de la sabiduría bajo infinitos nombres.
Light and shadow, mysterious symbiosis[5] of the Solar Logos, [the] perfect multiple unity, INRI is LUCIFER…	Luz y sombra, misteriosa simbiosis del Logos Solar, unidad múltiple perfecta, INRI es LUCIFER…

---

[3] Literally 'aborrecible' means "detestable, hateful, abominable, loathsome, obnoxious, repulsive, abhorrent, heinous, odious;"
[4] Literally 'consignar' means "to record, to write down; dispatch, consign; record; state; entrust, to deliver;"
[5] Literally 'simbiosis' means "symbiosis, arrangement in which two dissimilar organisms live together in what is usually a mutually beneficial manner (Biology)"

Extracted from pages 194-195 of
THE FIFTH GOSPEL:

"RIGORS[6] OF THE SUPERIOR ETHIC"

...The more we liberate ourselves[7] from all the many, many ethical codes, the more individual we are becoming, [then] the more we will comprehend the necessity to dissolve the Ego, the "myself", the "oneself".

And [since] it is that the "I", as I have said to you [before], is a book of many volumes, [it is, therefore,] a book that we have to study, because it is not possible to dissolve the Ego, the "myself" without having integrally, [and] totally comprehended it.

It is in the terrain of practical life where we must self-discover [the defects within] ourselves.

The errors that we carry within arise precisely in practical life, and if we are in a state of alertness, then we discover them as they are.

A defect discovered, must be integrally comprehended, through the technique of meditation.

Once comprehended, it must be eliminated with the annihilating[8] serpentine power that is developed in the body of the ascetic, that is to say, with the power of Devi-Kundalini.

Extracto de páginas 194-195 de
EL QUINTO EVANGELIO:

"RIGORES DE LA ÉTICA SUPERIOR"

...Cuanto más nos vayamos liberando de tantos y tantos códigos de ética, cuanto más individuales nos vayamos volviendo, tanto más iremos comprendiendo la necesidad de disolver el Ego, el "mí mismo", el "sí mismo".

Y es que el "Yo", como les he dicho a ustedes, es un libro de muchos tomos, un libro que tenemos que estudiar, porque no es posible disolver el Ego, el "mí mismo" sin haberlo comprendido íntegramente, totalmente.

Es en el terreno de la vida practica donde debemos autodescubrirnos.

Los errores que llevamos dentro, afloran precisamente en la vida practica, y si nosotros nos hallamos en estado de alerta, entonces los descubrimos tal cual son.

Defecto descubierto, debe ser comprendido, íntegramente, a través de la técnica de la meditación.

Una vez comprendido, debe ser eliminado con el poder serpentino anular que se desarrolla en el cuerpo del asceta, es decir, con el poder de Devi- Kundalini.

---

[6] Literally 'rigor' means "rigor, exactness, severity, strictness, stringency, rigour;"
[7] Literally 'nos vayamos liberando' means "[as] we go [about] liberating ourselves"
[8] Literally 'anular' means "annul, abolish, make void, negate, void, cancel, nullify;"

As the Ego is disintegrated more [and more], the Consciousness will become stronger and stronger and in the end, what will be introduced, we could say, (within oneself) [is] a Permanent Center of Gravity, a Center of authentic Individuality that will totally liberate us, from the actions and reactions that come from the exterior world.

However it is necessary for us to create that Permanent Center of Gravity within ourselves, and that is only possible [by] dissolving the Ego.

[By] creating that Center of Gravity (I repeat), we will have individuality.

But, nowadays, we are not individual subjects, we are machines controlled by "I's"; the whole world plays[9] with us, [since] we do not have authentic individuality.

When we have dissolved the Ego, the "myself", we will discover with mystical astonishment that there is something which is not possible to dissolve, and that "something" is hated by the people of all the religions.

I am referring to the biblical Satan (this word, is naturally horrifying to many, we [already] know the role that the Devil has played in the Old Testament). But we must comprehend it.

That Devil, which scares us so much, is less harmful [than we are led to believe], as Goethe says in one of his poems (words that [are] put forth from the mouth of God):

> "Of all of your species, rebellious subjects of my law, [you] are less harmful and detrimental[10]"...

Cuanto mas se vaya desintegrando el Ego, la Conciencia se irá haciendo cada vez más fuerte y al fin quedará introducido, dijéramos, (dentro de sí mismos), un Centro de Gravedad Permanente, un Centro de Individualidad auténtica que nos liberará, totalmente, de las acciones y reacciones que provienen del mundo exterior.

Pero necesitamos crear ese Centro de Gravedad Permanente dentro de sí mismos, y eso solamente es posible disolviendo el Ego.

Creando (repito) ese Centro de Gravedad, tendremos individualidad.

Pero, hoy por hoy, no somos sujetos individuales, somos máquinas controladas por "Yoes"; todo el mundo juega con nosotros, no tenemos auténtica individualidad.

Cuando hayamos disuelto el Ego, el "mí mismo", descubriremos con asombro místico que hay algo que no es posible disolver, y ese "algo" es odiado por las gentes de todas las religiones.

Me refiero al Satán bíblico (esta palabra, naturalmente horroriza a muchos, ya sabemos el papel que ha hecho el Diablo en el Antiguo Testamento). Mas nosotros debemos comprenderlo.

Ese Diablo, que tanto nos asusta, es el menos dañino, como dijera Goethe, en uno de sus poemas (palabras que pone en boca de Dios):

> "De todos los de tu especie, súbditos a mi ley rebeldes, el menos dañino y perjudicial tú eres"...

---

[9] Literally 'juega' means "play, game, sport; move; gamble; coquet"

[10] Literally 'perjudicial' means "damaging, harmful, injurious"

Is Mephistopheles (Satan) less harmful and detrimental[11] [than we are led to believe]?

It seems incredible!, right?

But all the religious people think (precisely) that Satan is very harmful, and if we pronounced ourselves in favor of Satan, they declare us [to be] "satanists", "black magicians", "sorcerers", "witches", "damn people", etc. (such is humanity).

However, you [should] remember that Satan is the shadow of the Eternal one.

We can dissolve the Ego, reduce it to dust, but we cannot dissolve Satan because it is the shadow of the Eternal one.

If we go on a terrace, we project our own shadow, [isn't this] true? ([the shadow] from the light of the Sun).

Thus, also, the Eternal one projects its shadow in each of us.

You [must] remember that each of us has a Divine, Virginal, [and] Ineffable Spark (which is our intimate Logoi, our Seity).

It projects its shadow into our psyche, and that shadow is indeed Satan, Mephistopheles, that among the Aztecs is Xolotl, the Lucifer of our Lord Quetzalcóatl.

[Let] us reflect [on this], my dear[12] brethren.

¿Que Mefistófeles (Satán) sea el menos dañino y perjudicial?

¡Parece increíble!, ¿verdad?

Pero todas las gentes religiosas piensan que (precisamente) Satanás es lo más dañino, y si nosotros nos pronunciamos a favor de Satanás, nos declaran "satanistas", "magos negros", "hechiceros", "brujos", "gente maldita", etc. (así es la humanidad).

Empero, recuerden ustedes que Satanás es la sombra del Eterno.

Podríamos disolver el Ego, reducirlo a polvo, pero a Satanás no podemos disolverlo porque es la sombra del Eterno.

Si vamos por una calle, proyectamos nuestra propia sombra, ¿verdad? (por la luz del Sol).

Así, también, el Eterno proyecta su sombra en cada uno de nosotros.

Recuerden ustedes que cada uno de nosotros tiene una Chispa Divina, Virginal, Inefable (que es nuestro Logoi íntimo, nuestra Seidad).

Ella proyecta su sombra en nuestra psiquis, y esa sombra es precisamente Satanás, Mefistófeles, que entre los Aztecas es Xolotl, el Lucifer de nuestro Señor Quetzalcóatl.

Reflexionemos, mis caros hermanos.

---

[11] Literally 'perjudicial' means "damaging, harmful, injurious"
[12] Literally 'caros' means "dear, beloved, cherished;"

This Satan, the shadow of the Eternal in each one of us, must be transformed into Lucifer.

Obviously, Lucifer[13] is the "Giver of Light", the "Star of the Morning", and also the "Vespertine Star".

We must, then, transform the Devil into Lucifer.

When we see our own Devil (in the superior worlds of Cosmic Consciousness), we comprehend the necessity to transform it.

The Devil of any profane person, the mephistophelian shadow (speaking like Goethe) of any subject, is black as coal, and it is clear that it gives off[14] a sinister fire ([which] is a Fohat[15] that [is] diabolical).

But here is what [is] spectacular[16]: to transform, to convert that black shadow, that Devil into Lucifer, [and this] becomes possible when we eliminate the animal Ego, when we destroy the "inhuman elements" that we carry within.

Then that shadow of the Eternal can dress itself in the Tunic of Glory and convert itself into [an] Archangel of Light.

You must not forget that Lucifer has power over the Heavens, the Earth and the Infernos.

In the Heavens the angels obey him, on the Earth he makes the humans tremble and in the Infernos [he makes] the demons [obey].

---

[13] The word Lucifer is derived from the Latin words *lucem ferre* and means "light-bearer". It was the name given to the dawn appearance of the planet Venus (also called the "Morning Star" or the "Day Star"), since it is the precursor to daylight.

[14] Literally 'arroja' means "throw, dart, dash, fling off, toss, cast out, fling, heave, hurl, throw out; throw up, vomit, disgorge, regorge; yield, afford; exhaust, belch out;"

[15] The FOHAT is "the generative FORCE, the living and philosophical CENTRAL FIRE"

[16] Literally 'grandioso' means "grand, spectacular, formidable, great, magnificent, tremendous, grandiose;"

Ese Satanás, la sombra del Eterno en cada uno de nosotros, debe ser transformado en Lucifer.

Obviamente, Lucifer es el "Dador de Luz", el "Lucero de la Mañana", y también el "Lucero Vespertino".

Debemos, pues, transformar al Diablo en Lucifer.

Cuando nosotros (en los mundos superiores de Conciencia Cósmica) vemos a nuestro propio Diablo, comprendemos la necesidad de transformarlo.

El Diablo de cualquier profano, la sombra mefistofélica (hablando a lo Goethe) de cualquier sujeto, es negro como el carbón, y es claro que arroja un fuego siniestro (es el Fohat[17] aquél, diabólico).

Pero he ahí lo grandioso: transformar, convertir a esa sombra negra, a ese Diablo en Lucifer, se hace posible cuando eliminamos el Ego animal, cuando destruimos los "elementos inhumanos" que llevamos dentro.

Entonces puede, aquella sombra del Eterno, vestirse con la Túnica de Gloria y convertirse en Arcángel de Luz.

No olviden ustedes que Lucifer tiene potestad sobre los Cielos, sobre la Tierra y sobre los Infiernos.

En los Cielos le obedecen los ángeles, en la Tierra hace temblar a los humanos y en los Infiernos a los demonios.

---

[17] El FOHAT es "la FUERZA generatriz, el FUEGO CENTRAL viviente y filosofal"

He is then, Lucifer, the Prince of Light, the Archangel of Glory.	Es pues, Lucifer, el Príncipe de la Luz, el Arcángel de Gloria.
We repeat [that] it is necessary to turn the Devil into Lucifer, to modify that black and tenebrous aspect of the shadow of the Eternal, to whiten it in order to make it pure, [and] perfect; to embellish it, through the dissolution of the animal Ego.	Nosotros, repito, necesitamos convertir al Diablo en Lucifer, modificar ese aspecto negro y tenebroso de la sombra del Eterno, blanquearlo para hacerlo puro, perfecto; embellecerlo, mediante la disolución del Ego animal.
If we proceed thus, the payment will be spectacular: he will confer immortality [upon] us, he will make us really strong, because nowadays, we are really weak[18], absolutely weak; we are victims of others, the whole world plays with us, and disgracefully we have not wanted to comprehend that others play with us.	Si así procedemos, el pago será grandioso: él nos conferirá la inmortalidad, él nos hará realmente fuertes, porque hoy por hoy, somos realmente débiles, absolutamente débiles; somos víctimas de los demás, todo el mundo juega con nosotros, y desgraciadamente no hemos querido comprender que los demás juegan con nosotros.
We are victims of others and we do not know it; we have been created powerful, but [at present] we are not more than miserable logs, tossed [around] in the stormy sea of existence.	Somos víctimas de los demás y no lo sabemos; nos creemos poderosos, cuando no somos más que míseros leños, arrojados en el mar borrascoso de la existencia.

I invite you then, my dear brethren, to dissolve the Ego with the proposition that you whiten your own Daimon, your Xolotl; in order to convert it into the Prince of Light, into the Lord who has power over the Heavens, over the Earth and over the Infernos.

Los invito pues, mis caros hermanos, a disolver el Ego con el propósito de que blanqueen a su propio Daimon, a su Xolotl; para que lo conviertan en el Príncipe de la Luz, en el Señor que tiene potestad sobre los Cielos, sobre la Tierra y sobre los Infiernos.

You [should] reflect, then, [so that you can] become very individual…

Reflexionad, pues, vuélvanse mas individuales…

---

[18] Literally 'débiles' means "weak, faint, feeble, dim, enfeebled, feeble-bodied, flimsy, frail, lean, sickly, weakly, faltering, infirm, strengthless;"

Extracted from Chapter 46 of
THE THREE MOUNTAINS
by Samael Aun Weor

"THE ELEVENTH LABOR OF HERCULES"

...The CHRISTOS-LUCIFER of the Gnostics is the God of Wisdom under different names, the God of our planet Earth without any shadow of evil, because he is one with the Platonic Logos...

PROMETHEUS-LUCIFER is the Minister of the SOLAR LOGOS and Lord of the Seven Mansions of HADES...

LUCIFER is certainly the Spirit of 'the Spiritual Illumination of Humanity' and of 'the Freedom of Choice[19]' and, metaphysically, 'the torch of humanity'; the LOGOS in his superior aspect, and the adversary in his inferior aspect; the Divine and chained PROMETHEUS; the active and centrifugal energy of the universe; fire, light, life, struggle, effort, consciousness, liberty, independence, etc., etc., etc.

The Sword and the Scale of Cosmic Justice are entrusted to LUCIFER, because he is the standard of weight, measure and number.

Inside each one of us, LUCIFER is the reflection of the Intimate LOGOS, shadow of the Lord projected into the depth of our Being...

...

...Unquestionably he is the "Divine Daimon" of Socrates; our special trainer in the Psychological Gymnasium of Life...

---

[19] Literally 'Libertad de Elección' means "Liberty of Election"

Extracted from page 65 of THE FIFTH GOSPEL:

"THE AUTHENTIC SYMBOLISM OF CHRISTMAS"

...LUCIFER IS ONLY THE SHADOW OF GOD, the Shadow of the Intimate Logos within ourselves; [or] better said, our Profound Inner Logos, the Intimate Christ, projects its Shadow within us; and that Shadow is useful, we need it...

If you read the "Divine Comedy" by Dante, you will see how Virgil and Dante descended on the Stairs of Lucifer.

Each hair of Lucifer's body seemed [like] a beam[20], by which they went down and also up, until arriving at the top, where "The Golgotha[21]" is; this is symbolic:

"Lucifer is the stairs to go down. Lucifer is stairs to go up"...

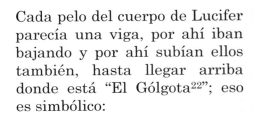

The Christ disguises himself as Lucifer in order to serve as stairs [for] us and [to] get us out of the Abyss, carrying us to the Light.

Therefore, we must look at Lucifer from a new point of view.

This Lucifer, really, is just the Reflection of the Logos within ourselves, its Shadow, and it is useful: it gives the sexual impulse.

---

[20] Literally 'viga' means "beam, girder, rafter, timber;"
[21] The Greek word Golgotha is Γολγοθᾶ *gol-goth-ah'* and is of Chaldee origin; it means: the skull; Golgotha, a knoll near Jerusalem. The Hebrew word is גלגלת *gulgoleth* or *gul-go'-leth* and means a skull (as round); by implication a head (in enumeration of persons): - head, every man, poll, skull.

Extracto de página 65 de EL QUINTO EVANGELIO:

"EL AUTÉNTICO SIMBOLISMO DE LA NAVIDAD"

...LUCIFER NO ES MÁS QUE LA SOMBRA DE DIOS, la Sombra del Logos Íntimo dentro de nosotros mismos; mejor dicho, nuestro Logos Interior Profundo, el Cristo Íntimo proyecta su Sombra dentro de nosotros; y esa Sombra es útil, la necesitamos...

Léanse ustedes "La Divina Comedia" del Dante, y verán ustedes como Virgilio y el Dante bajaban por la Escalera de Lucifer.

Cada pelo del cuerpo de Lucifer parecía una viga, por ahí iban bajando y por ahí subían ellos también, hasta llegar arriba donde está "El Gólgota[22]"; eso es simbólico:

"Lucifer es escalera para bajar. Lucifer es escalera para subir"...

El Cristo se disfraza de Lucifer para servirnos de escalera y sacarnos del Abismo, llevarnos a la Luz.

De manera que hay que mirar a Lucifer ahora desde un punto de vista nuevo.

Este Lucifer, realmente, no es más que la Reflexión del Logos dentro de nosotros mismos, su Sombra, y útil además: da el impulso sexual.

---

[22] La palabra griega Gólgota es Γολγοθᾶ *gol-goth-a'* y es del origin Caldeo; esta significa: el cráneo; Gólgota, un otero cerca de Jerusalén. La palabra hebrea es גלגלת *gulgoleth* o *gul-go'-leth* y significa una calavera (como ronda); por implicación una cabeza (en la enumeración de las personas): - jefe, cada hombre, poll, el cráneo.

That impulse is rebellious in itself, [and is] of [a] luciferic type.	Ese impulso es rebelde de por sí, de tipo luciférico.
But, if we are capable of controlling that animal impulse, then the Sperm is transmuted into Energy, the Great Work begins, and we win [a] battle with Lucifer…	Mas si uno es capaz de controlar ese impulso animal, entonces transmuta el Esperma en Energía, comienza la Gran Obra, y le gana una batalla a Lucifer…
Whenever we manage to dominate the animal impulse, we get up a step on the Stairs of Lucifer; and in this way we go up[23], step by step, until reaching the top, Self-Realized and Perfect…	Cada vez que uno logra, pues, dominar el impulso, animal, sube un peldaño por la Escala de Lucifer; y así, va uno subiendo de peldaño en peldaño, hasta que sale arriba, Autorrealizado y Perfecto…
Consequently, Lucifer is our staircase to go up, and vice-versa, if we want to go down, we have to use the Staircase of Lucifer…	De manera que Lucifer le sirve a uno de escalera para subir, y viceversa, si uno quiere bajar, no le queda más remedio que bajar por la Escalera de Lucifer…

---

[23] Literally 'subiendo' means "rise, ascend; carry up; upload; get into; advance; gain; (Slang) bump up, move up to a better position"

Extracted from pages 37-39 of THE FIFTH GOSPEL: "GNOSTIC CULT TO AGNOSTHOS THEOS"	Extracto de páginas 37-39 de EL QUINTO EVANGELIO: "CULTO GNÓSTICO AL AGNOSTHOS THEOS"
...The creation of the Superior Existential Bodies of the Being is also [a thing] of great patience: It is necessary for us TO TRANSMUTE THE SACRED SPERM INTO ENERGY. In other times, when humanity had not yet developed the abominable KUNDAR-TIGUATOR ORGAN, no one extracted the Sacred Sperm from their body; but when it was projected [outside the body] of the "intellectual animal" [it became] the abominable Kundartiguator Organ, [and] then they enjoyed[24] eliminating the Sacred Sperm. If we transmute this Venerable Material into Energy, we can create the Superior Existential Bodies of the Being, but first and foremost, we must comprehend the diverse ALCHEMICAL PROCESSES... We have been told that for the GREAT WORK, [one must work] with a single substance [which] we have. What would that substance be? We respond: The MERCURY OF THE SECRET PHILOSOPHY. And what is this Mercury? Well, it is the METALLIC SOUL OF THE SPERM.	...La creación de los Cuerpos Existenciales Superiores del Ser, es también de suma paciencia: Necesitamos TRANSMUTAR EL SAGRADO ESPERMA EN ENERGÍA. En otros tiempos, cuando la humanidad todavía no había desarrollado el abominable ÓRGANO KUNDARTIGUADOR, nadie extraía de su cuerpo el Sagrado Esperma; mas cuando le fue proyectado, al "animal intelectual", el abominable Órgano Kundartiguador, entonces gozó eliminando el Sagrado Esperma. Si nosotros transmutamos a esa Materia Venerable en Energía, podremos crear los Cuerpos Existenciales Superiores del Ser, pero ante todo, hay que comprender los diversos PROCESOS ALQUÍMICOS... Se nos ha dicho que para la GRAN OBRA, con una sola substancia tenemos. ¿Cuál será esa substancia? Nosotros respondemos: El MERCURIO DE LA FILOSOFÍA SECRETA. ¿Y dónde está ese Mercurio? Pues bien, es el ALMA METÁLICA DEL ESPERMA.

---

[24] Literally 'gozó' means "enjoy, enjoy oneself, have a good time, rejoice;"

It is clear that to not spend the Sexual Liquor [allows us to] transmute [it] into Energy and that Energy is the Mercury of the Secret Philosophy, that is to say, the Metallic Soul of the Sperm is the Mercury of the Secret Philosophy and this Metallic Soul is represented by LUCIFER.

When mentioning this personage, we do not have to be scandalized; this is Lucifer.

But let's not think about an anthropomorphic Archangel, Lucifer is very individual (each one of us has our own PARTICULAR, individual LUCIFER).

Lucifer is one of the aspects of our Inner Being and in truth [he is] the most important [aspect]; he is, so to speak, THE DOUBLE of our INNER LOGOI, duplicate of the THIRD LOGOS in us, the SHADOW OF SHIVA (The Arch-Hierophant and the Arch-Magician).

That [which] shines..., is truly: Burning like [an] Ineffable Archangel, he was the Holy Kumara; but when we fell into "generation animal", that which is, [as] we said, the root of our sex, or the one of the most important aspects of our Being, because he is[25] the double[26] of our Intimate God, he fell in fact into the Darkness of this world and was converted into the DEVIL.

There are as many Devils on the Earth, as [there are] human beings; each of us has our own Devil and this PARTICULAR DEVIL in each one of us is BLACK as coal, and exhales the NEGATIVE FOHAT, the FIRE OF FATALITY, the LUCIFERIAN FIRE, through the KUNDARTIGUADOR ORGAN.

He is in disgrace, after being the most excellent creature.

Nobody can see him, except us: WE MUST WHITEN [HIM], and this is [what is] written.

---

[25] Literally 'por ser' means "by being"
[26] Literally 'duplicado' means "double, duplicate"

Es claro que al no gastar el Licor Sexual, éste se transmuta en Energía y esa Energía es el Mercurio de la Filosofía Secreta, es decir, el Alma Metálica del Esperma es el Mercurio de la Filosofía Secreta y ese Alma Metálica está representada por LUCIFER.

Al citar a este personaje, no debemos escandalizarnos; ése es Lucifer.

Pero no pensemos en un Arcángel antropomórfico, el Lucifer es muy individual (cada uno de nos tiene su LUCIFER PARTICULAR, individual).

Lucifer es uno de los aspectos de nuestro Ser Interior y en verdad que el más importante; es, por decirlo así, EL DOBLE de nuestro LOGOI INTERIOR, duplicado del TERCER LOGOS en nosotros, la SOMBRA DE SHIVA (El Archi-Hierofante y el Archi-Mago).

Que resplandecía..., es verdad: Abrasadoramente como Arcángel Inefable, era un Santo Kumará; pero cuando caímos en la "generación animal", ése, que es, dijéramos, la raíz de nuestro sexo, o uno de los aspectos más importantes de nuestro Ser, por ser el duplicado de nuestro Dios Íntimo, cayó de hecho en las Tinieblas de este mundo y se convirtió en el DIABLO.

Hay tantos Diablos en la Tierra, cuantos seres humanos; cada uno de nosotros tiene su propio Diablo y este DIABLO PARTICULAR de cada uno de nos, es NEGRO como el carbón, y exhala por el ÓRGANO KUNDARTIGUADOR, el FOHAT NEGATIVO, el FUEGO DE LA FATALIDAD, el FUEGO LUCIFERINO.

Está en desgracia, después de ser la criatura más excelente.

Nadie puede ver por él, sino nosotros: DEBEMOS BLANQUEARLO, y eso está escrito.

The medieval Alchemists said:

"Burn your books and whiten the brass"...

One already knows that the brass is made of copper and copper is related to VENUS, the STAR OF THE MORNING and to the vespertine[27] hour...

"To whiten the brass" signifies to whiten our own Interior Devil in order to liberate him.

He is the CHAINED PROMETHEUS: A vulture tirelessly devours his entrails (the vulture of desire).

He is a colossus, he has power over the Heavens, over the Earth and over the Infernos, but we have him in disgrace; if we whiten him, we will be compensated and with interest.

But, how do [we] whiten him?

ELIMINATING THE EGO, and CREATING THE SUPERIOR EXISTENTIAL BODIES OF THE BEING in ourselves and SACRIFICING OURSELVES FOR HUMANITY

Among the Aztecs, Lucifer appears launching himself head-first to the bottom of Abyss, symbol of our SEXUAL FALL.

But there is something novel in the Aztec Doctrine: Lucifer girdled[28] [with] the Cord of the penitent, [the Cord] of the anchorite... Lucifer doing penance[29].

---

[27] Literally 'vespertina' means "evening, of the period of time between afternoon and night"
[28] Literally 'ciñendo' means "fit tightly, tighten, be tight on, belt, cincture, gird, girdle, hug;"
[29] Literally 'penitencia' means "penance, penitence (feeling or expressing sorrow for sin or wrongdoing and disposed to atonement and amendment; repentant; contrite)"

Los Alquimistas medievales dijeron:

"Quema tus libros y blanquea el latón"...

Ya se sabe que el latón es de cobre y el cobre está relacionado con VENUS, la ESTRELLA DE LA MAÑANA y de la hora vespertina...

"Blanquear el latón" significa blanquear a nuestro propio Diablo Interior para libertarlo.

Él, es el PROMETEO ENCADENADO: Un buitre le devora las entrañas incansablemente (el buitre del deseo).

Es un coloso, tiene potestad sobre los Cielos, sobre la Tierra y sobre los Infiernos, pero lo tenemos en desgracia; si lo blanqueamos, seremos recompensados y con creces.

Mas, ¿cómo blanquearlo?

ELIMINANDO EL EGO, y CREANDO en nosotros LOS CUERPOS EXISTENCIALES SUPERIORES DEL SER y SACRIFICÁNDONOS POR LA HUMANIDAD

Entre los Aztecas, el Lucifer aparece lanzándose de cabeza al fondo del Abismo, símbolo de nuestra CAÍDA SEXUAL.

Mas hay algo novedoso en la Doctrina Azteca: Lucifer ciñendo el Cordón de penitente, de anacoreta... Lucifer haciendo penitencia.

Have you [ever] seen something more extraordinary?

And well, brethren, this Lucifer is, we could say, the representation of our PHILOSOPHER'S STONE; in the end[30], we have this paradigm in us.

But it is intimately related with the Mercury of the Secret Philosophy, it seems as if we are passing through a digression, when doing our dissertation, [but] we have not passed through any digression; what is needed is to put much attention [into this subject]...

Either I said that the Metallic Soul of the Sperm is the Philosopher's Stone, or I said that Lucifer is the Philosopher's Stone.

Let's see[31]: Which of these two is the Philosophical Stone?

In reality[32], AS MUCH AS LUCIFER IS THE "METALLIC SOUL OF THE SPERM", [HE ALSO] CONSTITUTES THE PHILOSOPHER'S STONE; [because] that Stone is guarded[33] by Lucifer...

Well, in the Cathedral of Notre Dame of Paris, there appears a bird, a CROW, with its view directed towards the "cornerstone".

What is on the "cornerstone"? A figure [of] the Devil!...

What does the "CROW OF PUTRIFACTION" signify? DEATH!

¿Habrán visto algo más extraordinario?

Y bien, hermanos, este Lucifer es, dijéramos, la representación de nuestra PIEDRA FILOSOFAL; en el fondo, ese paradigma tiene en nosotros.

Pero está tan relacionado íntimamente con el Mercurio de la Filosofía Secreta, que parece como si hubiésemos nosotros pasado por una disgresión, al hacer nuestra disertación, más no hemos pasado por ninguna disgresión; se necesita poner mucho atención...

Ya dije que el Alma Metálica del Esperma es la Piedra Filosofal, ya dije que Lucifer es la Piedra Filosofal.

Adivinen: ¿Cuál de los dos es la Piedra Filosofal?

En realidad de verdad, TANTO LUCIFER COMO EL "ALMA METÁLICA DEL ESPERMA", CONSTITUYEN LA PIEDRA FILOSOFAL; esa Piedra está velada por Lucifer...

Bien, en la Catedral de Notre Dame de París, aparece un ave, un CUERVO, con la vista dirigida hacia la "piedrecita del rincón".

¿Qué hay en la "piedrecita del rincón"? ¡Una figura, el Diablo!...

¿Qué significa el "CUERVO DE LA PUTREFACCIÓN"? ¡LA MUERTE!

---

[30] Literally 'en el fondo' means "at bottom, at the far end, privately, ultimately, really"
[31] Literally 'adivinen' means "guess, divine, foresee, foretell;"
[32] Literally 'En realidad de verdad' means "In [the] reality of truth"
[33] Literally 'velada' means "watch over, watch; stay awake, be up late, stay up, keep vigil; "

We need the elimination, [we need] to kill, [we need] to destroy the Ego animal; only thus is it possible "to whiten the Devil" which is in the corner of the Temple and which wants its liberation, because it wants to return to being the LUMINOUS ARCHANGEL of former[34] times.

That Metallic Soul of the Sperm is, I repeat, extraordinary; it has emanated from the CHAOS, which is the SEMINAL WATERS OF LIFE.

In its turn, a THIRD WATER is emitted from that Metallic Soul, through projection: [which] is the, Energetic, Creative, Fluid proper, which is raised through the channels of Ida and Pingala up to the brain.

When the FIRE, the SULFUR fecundates that Mercury, then the marvelous process of INITIATION begins; but note[35] the three aspects of Mercury:

First: as Metallic Chaos, [the] Sperm itself[36].

Second: as Metallic Soul or Mercury.

The Third: the Third Water, the fluid which is marvelous [and] which is raised through the channels of Ida and Pingala up to the brain.

A moment arrives, or will [soon] arrive, in which that "Soul", that third aspect, those Sexual Fluids, ascends through the channels of Ida and Pingala, fecundated by the Sacred Fire (here one has the linking of the Mercury and the Sulfur in its first aspect), and all our esoteric progress is based on the incessant mixings[37] of the Mercury with the Sulfur…

---

[34] Literally 'otros' means "other, another; remaining; the next day, the day after; second; separated"
[35] Literally 'cuenta' means "account, count, counting, numeration, reckoning, score, tally;"
[36] Literally 'simple' means "simple; mere; plain; bare"
[37] Literally 'cruces' means "cross, breed, interbreed;"

Necesitamos la eliminación, matar, destruir el Ego animal; sólo así es posible "blanquear al Diablo" que está en el rincón del Templo y que desea su liberación, pues quiere volver a ser el ARCANGEL LUMINOSO de otros tiempos.

Ese Alma Metálica del Esperma, repito, es extraordinaria; ha emanado del CAOS, que son las AGUAS SEMINALES DE LA VIDA.

A su vez, de ese Alma Metálica, mediante proyección, se desprende un TERCER AGUA: es el Fluido, propiamente, Energético, Creador, que sube por los canales de Idá y Pingalá hasta el cerebro.

Cuando el FUEGO, el AZUFRE hace fecundo a ese Mercurio, entonces comienza el proceso maravilloso de la INICIACIÓN; pero téngase en cuenta los tres aspectos del Mercurio:

Primero: como Caos Metálico, simple Esperma.

Segundo: como Alma Metálica o Mercurio.

Lo Tercero: el Tercer Agua, el fluido aquél maravilloso que sube por los canales de Idá y Pingalá hasta el cerebro.

Un momento llega, o llegará, en que ese "Alma", ese tercer aspecto, esos Fluidos Sexuales, ascendiendo por los canales de Idá y Pingalá, sean fecundados por el Fuego Sagrado (he ahí el ligamen del Mercurio y el Azufre en su primer aspecto), y todo el progreso esotérico de nosotros, se fundamenta en los cruces incesantes del Mercurio con el Azufre…

The Shadow of God	La Sombra de Dios
The SEXUAL HYDROGEN SI-12, which is spoken of by the best[38] occultists[39] (among them Gurdjieff), obviously corresponds to the Mercury itself, to the third aspect, to the THIRD MERCURIAL WATER.	El HIDRÓGENO SEXUAL SI-12, del cual nos hablan los mejores ocultistas, entre ellos Gurdjieff, obviamente, les corresponde al Mercurio mismo, al tercer aspecto, a la TERCERA AGUA MERCURIAL.
This Mercury becomes extraordinary and marvelous when crystallizing in its first vehicle, which is the ASTRAL [BODY]; only through this Mercury will the Astral Body take form, [but of course in order to accomplish this] we have to work [with it].	Ese Mercurio, al cristalizar en su primer vehículo, que es el ASTRAL, se hace extraordinario y maravilloso; pero para que ese Mercurio tome la forma del Cuerpo Astral, hay que trabajarlo.
Through transmutation, the moment will arrive when this Mercury takes the already mentioned[40] form[41] of an Astral Body, [and then] we can travel through Infinite space with it.	Mediante la transmutación, llegará el momento en que ese Mercurio tome esa figura y ya provistos de un Cuerpo Astral, podemos viajar con él a través del espacio Infinito.
Much later, the Mercury comes to crystallize in the form of [the] MENTAL BODY, and, still much much later, with the form of the CAUSAL BODY (you [can now] see the three forms of the crystallization of Mercury).	Mucho más tarde, el Mercurio viene a cristalizar en la forma de CUERPO MENTAL, y aún, muchísimo más tarde, con la forma del CUERPO CAUSAL (vean ustedes las tres formas de la cristalización del Mercurio).

When those Existential Bodies have been formed, we incarnate the HUMAN SOUL; but it is not enough to create the Superior Existential Bodies of the Being with the Mercury; we must [also] know that the Mercury is called to carry[42] the GOLD OF THE COSMIC CHRIST within itself (SAINT CHRISTOPHER, carrying the boy, or the sheep carrying its fleece, is an allegory of this truth that we are saying).

Cuando esos Cuerpos Existenciales han quedado formados, encarnamos el ALMA HUMANA; pero no basta crear, con el Mercurio, los Cuerpos Existenciales Superiores del Ser; debemos saber que el Mercurio está llamado a cargar el ORO DEL CRISTO CÓSMICO dentro de sí mismo (SAN CRISTOBAL, cargando al niño, o la oveja cargando su vellón, es una alegoría de esta verdad que estamos diciendo).

---

[38] Literally 'mejores' means "better, best, superior, any better, better off, preferable, very best;"
[39] Literally 'del cual nos hablan los mejores ocultistas' means "of which the best occultists speak to us"
[40] Literally 'provistos' means "provided, supplied; possessing"
[41] Literally 'en que ese Mercurio tome esa figura y ya provistos' means "in which this Mercury will take that figure and already provided with"
[42] Literally 'cargar' means "charge, charge up, energize; load, load up, load on, put load on, weight; carry, bear, bear in arms, take the weight of;"

Each one of us must, first of all, prepare their Mercury; once prepared, [one must] not forget that one must develop within oneself the GOLDEN CHILD of Sexual Alchemy.

Therefore, the Sexual Hydrogen SI-12 (which Gurdjieff talks about[43]) is none other than the same Mercury.

When one says that "the Gold is developed within Mercury", it is true.

But, what kind[44] of Gold is formed?

Repeating: [It is] the CHRISTIC GOLD, because Christ is Gold; within those Bodies of Mercury one must form the Gold, the Gold of the Christ.

That is to say, the LOGOS must take form in us; and this is a costly[45], arduous, [and] difficult work…

It is not enough to create the Superior Existential Bodies of the Being, [we should] go much further: It is necessary TO PERFECT THEM so that they can be covered, much later, with the distinct[46] parts of the Being…

[Also see Chapters 15 & 37
of *Tarot and Kabalah* by Samael Aun Weor
for more information on this Topic.]

---

[43] Literally 'del que nos habla Gurdjieff' means "of which Gurdjieff speaks to us"
[44] Literally 'clase' means "kind, category, class, classification, sort, bracket, form, order;"
[45] Literally 'dispendioso' means "expensive, costly;"
[46] Literally 'distintas' means "distinct, different; diverse, varied; several; separate"

*Esoteric Explanation of
the Symbolism of Satan,
the Devil, Lucifer, the Serpent
and the Astral Light*

*Explicación Esoterico
del Simbolismo de Satán,
el Diablo, Lucifer el Serpiente
y la Luz Astral*

Extracted from the INTRODUCTION to THE HISTORY OF MAGIC[1] by Eliphas Levi

...God is really present when [a] collection[2] of souls and touched hearts worship him; he is sensibly and terribly absent when one speaks of him without fire or without light, that is to say, without understanding and without love.

The idea that one must have of God, according the wise kabalist, is [that of] saint Paul himself who will reveal it to us:

> "In order to reach[3] God", says this apostle, "one must believe that he exists[4] and that he rewards[5] those who seek him."

Thus, nothing outside of the idea of being, joined with the notion of goodness and justice, since this idea alone is absolute.

To say that God is not, or to define what God is, are equally blasphemy.

Every definition of God, ventured by human understanding, is a recipe of religious empiricism, through[6] which superstition will later be able to extract a devil.

In kabalistic symbolism, God is always represented by a double image, one upright, the other reversed, one white and the other black.

---

[1] The present English extracts of the Eliphas Levi's "HISTOIRE DE LA MAGIE" have been translated directly from the original French language and so the English footnotes refer to their corresponding French text (which is not in this Text) and therefore may not correspond to the Spanish.
[2] Literally 'recueillies' means "gather, collect; garner, obtain, take in; reflect, meditate, contemplate"
[3] Literally 'arriver' means "arrive, come; check in, reach, show up; happen, occur; betide, get ahead, turn up"
[4] Literally 'qu'il est' means "that he is"
[5] Literally 'récompense' means "recompense, reward, award; payoff, reimbursement, repayment; retribution; return"
[6] Literally 'au moyen de' means "by means of, with"

Extracto del INTRODUCCIÓN de HISTORIA DE LA MAGIA por Eliphas Levi

...Dios está verdaderamente presente cuando lo adoran las almas recogidas y los corazones tiernos; está ausente, sensible y terriblemente, cuando se lo discute sin luz ni celo, es decir, sin inteligencia ni amor.

El concepto adecuado sobre Dios según el cabalismo instruido es el revelado por San Pablo cuando dijo que:

> Para llegar a Dios, debemos creer que El existe y recompensa a quienes Le buscan.

De modo que no hay nada fuera de la idea del ser en combinación con la idea del bien y la justicia: estos solos son absolutos.

Decir que no hay Dios, o definir lo que El es, constituye igual blasfemia.

Toda definición de Dios aventurada por la inteligencia humana es una receta de empirismo religioso, de donde la superstición extraerá subsiguientemente un diablo.

En el simbolismo cabalístico Dios está siempre representado mediante una imagen duplicada: una derecha, la otra invertida; una blanca, y la otra, negra.

Extracted from the INTRODUCTION to THE HISTORY OF MAGIC[7] by Eliphas Levi

...In which of the catholic symbols, in fact, is there any question of the devil?

Would it not be blasphemy to say: we believe in him?

He is named, but not defined in holy Scripture; no where does Genesis speak of a supposed[8] fall of angels; it ascribes the first sin of man to the serpent, the most cunning[9] and dangerous of [all] living beings.

We know what there is of this subject within the christian tradition; but if this tradition explains itself by one of the greatest and most universal allegories of science, what can this solution bring to the faith which aspires to God alone, and [which] despises the pomp[10] and works of Lucifer?

Lucifer! The light-bearer! what [a] strange name [to be] given to the spirit of darkness.

But is it him who carries the light and who blinds the weak[11] souls?

Yes, do not doubt it, since the traditions are full of divine revelations and inspirations.

Extracto del INTRODUCCIÓN de HISTORIA DE LA MAGIA por Eliphas Levi

...¿En cuál de los credos católicos hay una cuestión que se le refiera al diablo?

¿No sería una blasfemia decir que creemos en él?

En las Sagradas Escrituras se le nombra pero no se le define; el Génesis no hace alusión a una célebre rebelión de los ángeles; atribuye la caída de Adán a la serpiente, como el más sutil y peligroso de los seres vivientes.

Estamos familiarizados con la tradición cristiana a este respecto, pero si esa tradición es explicable por una de las máximas y más difundidas alegorías de la ciencia, ¿qué puede significar tal solución para la fe que sólo aspira a Dios, que desdeña las pompas y las obras de Lucifer?

¡Lucifer! ¡Portador de la Luz! ¡cuan extraño nombre atribuido al espíritu de la oscuridad!

¿El portador de la luz enceguece, empero, a las almas débiles?

Incuestionablemente, la respuesta es sí; pues las tradiciones rebosan revelaciones e inspiraciones divinas.

---

[7] The present English extracts of the Eliphas Levi's "HISTOIRE DE LA MAGIE" have been translated directly from the original French language and so the English footnotes refer to their corresponding French text (which is not in this Text) and therefore may not correspond to the Spanish.
[8] Literally 'prétendue' means "so-called, supposed, alleged; pretended, ostensible"
[9] Literally 'rusé' means "crafty, cunning, artful, astute; designing, guileful, sly; trick, wily"
[10] Literally 'pompes' means "pump; shoe; pomp;"
[11] Literally 'faibles' means "weak, frail, feeble; soft, faint, mild; low, poor; lame, failing, limp, deficient; dull, inaudible; helpless; tenuous, wan"

"The devil carries the light", says saint Paul, "and often [is] himself transformed into a radiant[12] angel." [see 2Co 11:14]

"I have seen", said the Savior of the world : "I have seen Satan fall from the heaven like lightning." [see Luk 10:18]

"How have you fallen from heaven", cried the prophet Isaiah, "luminous star, you who rises [in] the morning." [see Isa 14:12]

Then Lucifer is a fallen star; he is a meteor who always burns and who blazes when he brightens no more.

But is this Lucifer a person or a force? Is it an angel or a lost thunderbolt?

Tradition supposes that it is an angel; but doesn't the Psalmist say in psalm 103:

"You make your angels from storms[13] and your ministers from quick [burning] fires?"

The word angel is given in the Bible to all the envoys[14] of God: messengers or new creations, revealers or scourges, radiant spirits or dazzling[15] things.

The arrows of fire that the Most High shoots[16] from the clouds are the angels of his wrath and this figurative language is familiar to all readers of eastern poetry.

"Satán se transformó en un ángel de luz", dice San Pablo.

Y Cristo dijo: "Vi a Satán caer de los cielos como un relámpago".

En igual sentido se expresa el profeta Isaías: "¿Cómo caíste del cielo, oh Lucifer, hijo de la mañana?"

Lucifer es, entonces, una estrella caída, un meteoro en eterna ignición, que arde cuando no brilla más.

Pero este Lucifer, ¿es una persona o una fuerza, un ángel o un rayo a la deriva?

La tradición supone que es un ángel, mas el Salmista dice:

"Quien convierte a sus ángeles en espíritus, y a sus ministros en fuego llameante".

El vocablo "ángel' se aplica en la Biblia a todos los mensajeros de Dios: emisarios o nuevas creaciones, reveladores o azotes, espíritus radiante u objetos brillantes.

Las ígneas flechas que el Altísimo dispara a través de las nubes son los ángeles de Su ira, y ese lenguaje figurado es familiar para todos los lectores de poesía oriental.

---

[12] Literally 'splendeur' means "splendor, magnificence; refulgence, gorgeousness, radiancy"
[13] Literally 'tempêtes' means "storm, tempest, thunder; blast, flaw, weather"
[14] Literally 'envoyés' means "envoy, diplomat"
[15] Literally 'éclatantes' means "bright, vivid; brilliant, blazing; dazzling, radiant; glorious; glaring; flamboyant, flaming; glowing, shining, showy; self-evident, blatant"
[16] Literally 'darde' means "dart, shoot, wing"

After having been the terror of the world during the middle ages, the devil has [now] become a laughingstock.	Luego de ser terror del mundo durante la Edad Media, el demonio se convirtió en su irrisión.
Heir to the monstrous forms of all the false gods [who have been] successively overturned, the grotesque scarecrow has become ridiculous through deformity and ugliness[17].	Heredero de las formas monstruosas de todos los falsos dioses derribados sucesivamente de sus tronos, el grotesco espantajo se convirtió en un cuco deforme y horrendo.
Yet let us observe something: which is that the only ones [who] dare to laugh at the devil [are those] who do not fear God.	Empero, obsérvese al respecto que sólo se atreven a reírse del demonio quienes no conocen el temor de Dios.
The devil, even for sick imaginations, should then be the shadow of God himself…	¿Es posible que para muchas imaginaciones enfermas sea la sombra de Dios…?

---

[17] Literally 'laideur' means "ugliness, monstrosity, baseness"

Extracted from Ch.3 of Book 3 to
THE HISTORY OF MAGIC[18]
by Eliphas Levi, entitled:
"ON THE DEVIL"

...The Church, on this question, returns to the texts of the Gospel, and has never given dogmatic decisions with the definition of the devil as their object.

Good christians avoid even naming him, and religious moralists recommend to their faithful[19] to not occupy themselves with him, but to resist him by only thinking of God.

We can only admire this wise reservation of the priestly teaching.

Why, in fact, should one attribute the light of the dogma to he who is [an] intellectual obscurity and [to] the darkest night of the heart?

May he remain unknown, this spirit which wants to tear us from the knowledge of God!

We do not claim to do here what the Church has not done, we only record[20] what the secret teaching of the initiates of the occult sciences is on this subject.

Extracto del Cap.3 del Libro 3 de
HISTORIA DE LA MAGIA
por Eliphas Levi, titulado:
"SOBRE EL DIABLO"[21]

...Sobre esta cuestión la Iglesia se contenta con los textos evangélicos, sin hacer pública decisión dogmática alguna, que defina objetivamente al diablo.

Los buenos cristianos evitan incluso nombrarlo, mientras los moralistas religiosos recomiendan a los fieles no preocuparse por él, y procurar resistir sus artes pensando sólo en Dios.

No podemos sino admirar esta sabia reserva de parte de la enseñanza sacerdotal.

¿En verdad, por qué debe reflejarse en él la luz de la doctrina cuando es la oscuridad y la noche más tenebrosa del corazón?

Que el espíritu que nos distraeria del conocimientos de Dios permanezca desconocido por nosotros.

Con seguridad, no es nuestra intención realizar lo que la Iglesia omitió; damos fe de tal cuestión sólo respecto de la instrucción secreta de los iniciados en las ciencias ocultas.

---

[18] The present English extracts of the Eliphas Levi's "HISTOIRE DE LA MAGIE" have been translated directly from the original French language and so the English footnotes refer to their corresponding French text (which is not in this Text) and therefore may not correspond to the Spanish.
[19] Literally 'fidèles' means "faithful, devoted, loyal, true; truthful, retentive, stalwart; firm, steadfast"
[20] Literally 'constatons' means "note, observe, notice; certify, record, list"

[21] También titulado "EL DEMONIO"

They have said that the great magical agent, justly called Lucifer, is a intermediary force spread[22] throughout creation, because it is the vehicle of the light and the receptacle of all forms; that it serves to create and to destroy, and that the fall of Adam was an erotic intoxication which rendered his generation slave to this fatal light; that all loving passion which invades the senses is a whirlwind[23] of this light that wants to coach[24] us towards the chasm[25] of death; that the folly, the hallucinations, visions, ecstasies, are a very dangerous exaltation of this interior phosphorous; that this light finally is the nature of fire, of which the intelligent use warms and vivifies, [and] of which the misuse[26] burns, dissolves and annihilates.

Man will be called to acquire[27] a sovereign empire upon this light and to conquer his immortality through this means, while he is at the same time threatened by its intoxication, absorption and eternal destruction.

This light, in its devouring, avenging and fatal aspect, will be the fire of hell, the serpent of legend; and the tormented error which will be full of the tears and the gnashing of teeth on the part of the aborted beings that it devoirs, the phantom of life which escapes them, and seems to insult their misery, all this will be [called] the devil or Satan.

---

[22] Literally 'répandue' means "widespread, expanded, prevailing, prevalent; spread, diffuse; pervading, rampant, trendy"
[23] Literally 'tourbillon' means "whirlwind, whirlpool, maelstrom, whirl, vortex; swirl, eddy; hustle, welter; merry go round"
[24] Literally 'entraîner' means "carry, drag along; drive, train; coach, rush; entrain, bring, school"
[25] Literally 'gouffre' means "gulf, chasm, maw"
[26] Literally 'l'excès au contraire' means "the excess [use] to the contrary"
[27] Literally 'prendre' means "take; catch; take up, pick up; book, acquire; capture; take in, have; take over, occupy; get on, seize; assume"

…

The true name of Satan, the kabalists say, is the name of Jehovah reversed, since Satan is not a black god, but [rather] the negation of God.

The devil is the personification of atheism and idolatry.

For the initiates, this is not a person, it is a force created for good, and which can serve for evil; it is the instrument of liberty.

They represented this force, which presides over physical generation, under the mythological figure of the horned god Pan; the goat of the [black] sabbath comes from here, the brother of the ancient serpent, and the light-bearer or *phosphorus* whom the poets have made into the false Lucifer of legends…

…

Según los cabalistas, el verdadero nombre de Satán es el de Jehová al revés; pues Satán no es un dios negro sino la negación de Dios.

El diablo es la personificación del ateísmo y la idolatría.

No es una personalidad para los iniciados sino una fuerza creada con un buen objeto, aunque puede ser aplicado al mal; en realidad es el instrumento de la libertad.

Representaban esta fuerza, que preside la generación física, bajo la figura mitológica del cornudo dios Pan, y de allí deriva el macho cabrío del Sabbath, hermano de la vieja serpiente, el lucífero o *fósforo*, convertido por los poetas en el falso Lucifer de la leyenda…

Extracted from Article 1 of First Part of
THE KEY TO THE GREAT MYSTERIES[28]
by Eliphas Levi, entitled:
"THE QUATERNARY"

...The angel of liberty was born before the dawn of the first day, even before the awakening of understanding, and God called him the morning star.

O Lucifer! you willingly[29] and disdainfully[30] detached yourself from heaven where the sun drowned you in his clarity, in order to furrow[31] with your own rays the uncultivated fields of the night.

You shine when the sun sets, and your sparkling gaze precedes the daybreak.

You fall in order to rise again; you taste death in order to know life better.

You are, for the ancient glories of the world, the evening star; [and] for the [ever] renewing[32] truth, [you are] the beautiful star of morning!

Liberty is not licentiousness[33]: since licentiousness is tyranny.

Liberty is the guardian of duty, because it asserts[34] the right[35] [to do].

---

[28] The present English extracts of the Eliphas Levi's "LA CLEF DES GRANDS MYSTÈRES" have been translated directly from the original French language and so the English footnotes refer to their corresponding French text (which is not in this Text) and therefore may not correspond to the Spanish.
[29] Literally 'volontairement' means "willingly, gladly"
[30] Literally 'dédaigneusement' means "disdainfully, contemptuously"
[31] Literally 'sillonner' means "furrow, cross, criss-cross, groove"
[32] Literally 'renaissante' means "renascent, being reborn; renewed, resurgent"
[33] Literally 'licence' means "license, licentiousness (sexually unrestrained; lascivious; libertine; lewd; unrestrained by law or general morality; lawless; immoral)"
[34] Literally 'revendique' means "demand, claim; lay claim; assert, exercise, stand out for"
[35] Literally 'le droit' means "the right; the law"

Extracto del Artículo 1 del Primero Parte de
LA CLAVE DE LOS GRANDES MISTERIOS
por Eliphas Levi, titulado:
"EL CUATERNARIO"

...El ángel de la libertad ha nacido antes de la autora del primer día, antes del despertar mismo de la inteligencia, y Dios le ha llamado la estrella de la mañana.

¡Oh, Lucifer!, te has apartado por tu desdeñosa voluntad del cielo donde el sol te bañaba en su esplendor, para explorar con tus propios rayos los campos incultos de la noche.

Tú brillas cuando el sol se oculta, y tu centelleante mirada precede al comienzo del día.

Caes para remontarte de nuevo. Escoges la muerte para conocer mejor la vida.

Para las glorias pasadas del mundo eres la estrella de la tarde. Para la verdad que renace, el bello lucero de la mañana.

La libertad no es la licencia, ya que la licencia es tiranía.

La libertad es guardiana del deber, puesto que ella reinvindica el derecho.

Lucifer, of whom the dark ages have made the genius of evil, will truly be the angel of light when, having conquered liberty at the price of disapproval[36], he will make use of it in order to submit himself to eternal order, thereby inaugurating the glories of voluntary obedience.	Lucifer, a quien edades de tinieblas han convertido en genio del mal, será verdaderamente el ángel de luz cuando haya conquistado la libertad al precio de su reprobación, y haga uso de esta libertad para someterse al orden eterno, inaugurando así las glorias de la obediencia voluntaria.
The right [to do] is merely the root of duty, one must possess in order to give.	El derecho no es sino la raíz del deber. Hace falta tener para dar.
Now, this is how a high and profound poetry explains the fall of the angels.	Así, vemos cómo la más alta y profunda poesía explica la caída de los ángeles.
God had given to his spirits light and life, then he said to them:	Dios había concedido a sus espíritus la luz y la vida. Luego les dijo:
"Love!"	Amad.
"What is 'to love'?" replied the spirits.	¿Qué es amar?, respondieron éstos.
"To love is to give oneself to others," replied God. "Those who love will suffer, but they will be loved."	Amar es darse a los otros, les dijo Dios. Los que amen sufrirán, pero ellos serán amados.
"We have [the] right to give nothing, and we do not wish to suffer", said the spirits [who were] enemies of love.	Tenemos derecho a no dar nada y no queremos sufrir, dijeron los espíritus enemigos del amor.
"Remain in your right," replied God, "and let us separate! Me and mine wish to suffer and even to die, in order to love. This is our duty!"	Permaneced en vuestro derecho, respondió Dios, y separémonos. Yo y los míos queremos amar y aun morir por amor. ¡Es nuestro deber!
The fallen angel is then he who refused to love from the beginning; he does not love, and this is his whole torture; he does not give, and this is his misery; he does not suffer, and this is his nothingness; he does not die, and that is his exile.	El ángel caído es, pues, aquel que desde el comienzo ha rehusado amar. El no ama, y en ello consiste todo su suplicio. El no da, y en ello estriba toda su miseria. El no sufre, y ésta es su vacuidad. El no muere, y en ello encuentra su exilio.
The fallen angel is not Lucifer the light-bearer; it is Satan, the slanderer[37] of love.	El ángel caído no es Lucifer, el portador de luz, sino Satán, el calumniador del amor.

---

[36] Literally 'réprobation' means "disapproval, disapprobation, reprobation; denunciation"
[37] Literally 'calomniateur' means "calumniator, slanderer"

To be rich is to give; to give nothing is to be poor; to live is to love; to love nothing is to be dead; to be happy is to devote oneself; to exist only for oneself is to damn[38] oneself, and to exile oneself to hell.

Heaven is the harmony of generous sentiments; hell is the conflict of cowardly instincts…

---

[38] Literally 'réprouver' means "reprove, condemn, disapprove; reprobate, damn"

Extracted from Ch.3 of Book One of Part 3 of
THE KEY TO THE GREAT MYSTERIES[39]
by Eliphas Levi, entitled:
"THE MYSTERIES OF HALLUCINATIONS AND THE EVOCATION OF SPIRITS"

...

"The reason for miracles[40], or the devil before science.

"Why the devil?"

— Because we have demonstrated with facts what Mr. de Mirville had, before us, incompletely set forth.

We say *incompletely*; because the devil is, for Mr. de Mirville, a fantastic personage, while for us, it is the misuse of a natural force.

A medium once said: "Hell is not a place, it is a State." We could add: "The devil is neither a person nor a force, it is a vice, and consequently, a weakness."

...

All ... miracles are accomplished by means of a single agent which the Hebrews called OD, as did the Chevalier de Reichenback, which we, with the School of Pasqualis Martinez, call "astral light", which Mr. de Mirville calls the devil, and which the ancient alchemists called azoth.

It is the vital element which manifests itself through the phenomena of heat, light, electricity and magnetism, which attracts all terrestrial globes, and all living beings.

---

[39] The present English extracts of the Eliphas Levi's "LA CLEF DES GRANDS MYSTÈRES" have been translated directly from the original French language and so the English footnotes refer to their corresponding French text (which is not in this Text) and therefore may not correspond to the Spanish.
[40] Literally 'prodiges' means "prodigy, marvel, miracle; wonder"

In this agent are even manifested the proofs of the kabalistic doctrine on equilibrium and movement, through the double polarity of the one attracting while the other repels, one produces heat, [while] the other cold, one gives a blue or greenish light, [and] the other a yellow or reddish light.

This agent, by its different modes of magnetization, attracts us to each other, or separates us from each other, submitting one to the willpower of the other by making him enter into his center of attraction, [which] reestablishes or disrupts the equilibrium in the animal economy by its transmutations and its alternate currents, [which then] receives and transmits the imprints of the force of imagination which is the image and the semblance of the creative verb in man, [which] thus produces premonitions[41] and determines dreams. [42]

The science of miracles is then the knowledge of this marvelous force, and the art of doing miracles is quite simply the art of magnetizing or "illuminating" beings according to the invariable laws of magnetism or astral light.

We prefer the word "light" to the word "magnetism", because it is more traditional in occultism, and [because] it expresses in a more complete and perfect manner the nature of the secret agent.

Here is, in truth, the liquid and potable gold of the masters in alchemy; the word "or" [French for "gold"] comes from the Hebrew "aour" which signifies "light"...

En este mismo agente encuentran su prueba las doctrinas cabalísticas sobre el equilibrio y el movimiento por virtud de la doble polaridad, donde un polo atrae en tanto que el otro reposa, uno produce el calor y el otro el frío, y mientras uno irradia una luz azul y verdosa, el otro genera una luz amarilla y rojiza.

Mediante sus distintas formas de magnetismo, dicho agente nos acerca o nos separa unos de otros y, al someter a uno a la voluntad del otro, haciéndole entrar en su círculo de atracción, perturba o restablece el equilibrio dentro de la economía animal, a través de sus transmutaciones y sus efluvios alternativos, recibiendo y transmitiendo las impresiones de esa fuerza imaginaria que es para el hombre la imagen y semejanza del Verbo creador, llegando así a producir los presentimientos y a determinar los sueños.

La ciencia de los milagros no es otra cosa que el conocimiento de esta fuerza maravillosa, y el arte de hacer milagros se reduce a la sencilla acción de imantar o iluminar a los seres, siguiendo las leyes invariables del magnetismo o de la luz astral.

Preferimos la palabra luz a la de magnetismo, por ser más tradicional en ocultismo y porque expresa de una forma más completa y perfecta la naturaleza de este secreto agente.

Ella es, en verdad, el oro fluido y potable de los maestros alquimistas; la palabra oro se deriva de la voz hebrea aour, que significa luz...

---

[41] Literally 'pressentiments' means "premonition, foreboding; presentiment, feeling"
[42] Editor's note: For more information on the subject, see Ch.8 of *Dogma of High Magic* by Eliphas Levi.

Extracted from the INTRODUCTION to THE HISTORY OF MAGIC[43] by Eliphas Levi

...there exists a mixed agent, a natural and divine agent, a corporeal and spiritual [agent], a universal plastic mediator, a common receptacle of the vibrations of movement and images of form, a fluid and a force which can be called, in a some sense, the *imagination of nature*.

Through this force every nervous apparatus is in secret communication together; from here sympathy and antipathy are born; dreams come from here; the phenomena of second sight and extra-natural vision comes from here.

This universal agent of nature's works is the "od" of the hebrews and of the knight of Reichenbach, it is the astral light of the martinists, and we prefer this last name, as [it is] more explicit.

The existence and possible usage of this force are the great arcanum of practical magic.

It is the wand of thaumaturges[44] and the key of black magic.

It is the edenic serpent who transmitted to Eve the seductions of a fallen angel.

---

[43] The present English extracts of the Eliphas Levi's "HISTOIRE DE LA MAGIE" have been translated directly from the original French language and so the English footnotes refer to their corresponding French text (which is not in this Text) and therefore may not correspond to the Spanish.
[44] Literally 'thaumaturges' means "thaumaturge, a performer of miracles or magic feats"

The astral light pulls[45], warms, illuminates, magnetizes, attracts, repels, vivifies, destroys, coagulates, separates, breaks, [and] reassembles all things under the impulse[46] of powerful willpowers.

God created it on the first day, when he said FIAT LUX[47]!

It is, in itself, a blind force, but it is directed by the *egregores*, that is to say, by the chiefs of the souls.

The chiefs of the souls are the spirits of energy and action.

This already explains all the theory of prodigies and miracles...

---

[45] Literally 'aimante' means "magnetic, operating via magnetic means; attractive; loving, affectionate, passionate"
[46] Literally 'impulsion' means "impetus, pulse; impulse, drive"
[47] Latin, often translated as "Let there be light!" or "May the light be!" and refers to the first 4 verses of Genesis.

Extracted from the INTRODUCTION to RITUAL OF HIGH MAGIC[48]
by Eliphas Levi

...Nowhere is the demon mentioned in [the book of] *Genesis*.

It is an allegorical serpent which deceives our first parents.

Here is what most translators make the sacred text say:

> "Now the <u>serpent</u> was more subtle than any beast of the field that the Lord God had made." [Gen. 3:1]

And here is what Moses said:

וה<u>נחש</u> היה ערום מכל היה אשר עשד
יהוה אלהים :

Wha-<u>Nahàsh</u> haîah hâroum mi-chol hàîath ha-shadeh asher hâshah Jhôah Ælohîm.

That is to say, in French [now translated into English], according to Fabre d'Olivet[49]:

---

[48] The present English extracts of the Eliphas Levi's "RITUEL DE LA HAUTE MAGIE" have been translated directly from the original French language and so the English footnotes refer to their corresponding French text (which is not in this Text) and therefore may not correspond to the Spanish.
[49] Antoine Fabre d'Olivet (1767-1825) was a French author, poet and composer, who is best known for his research on the Hebrew language, Pythagoras's thirty-six Golden Verses and the sacred art of music.

"Now, the original attraction (the greed[50]) was the rousing[51] passion of all elementary life (the interior drive[52]) of nature, the work of Jhôah [יהוה], the Being of beings."

But here, Fabre d'Olivet is just missing[53] the true interpretation, because he is ignorant of the great keys of the kabalah.

The word Nahash [נהש], explained by the symbolic letters of the Tarot, rigorously signifies:

14   נ   Nun. — The force which produces mixtures.

5   ה   He. — The recipient and passive producer of forms.

21   ש   Shin. — The natural fire and central equilibrium through double polarization.

The word employed by Moses, read kabalistically, then gives us the description and definition of this universal magical agent, featured in all theogonies[54] through the serpent and to which the Hebrews also gave the name of OD, when it manifested its active force; the name of OB, when it allows its passive force to appear, and that of AUR, when it reveals itself entirely in its balanced power, [being the] producer of light in heaven and of gold among the metals.

---

[50] Literally 'cupidité' means "greed, avarice, cupidity"
[51] Literally 'entraînante' means "stirring, rousing; catchy"
[52] Literally 'ressort' means "spring; spirit, drive; motivation; springiness, elasticity; resilience; jurisdiction"
[53] Literally 'à côté de' means "alongside, beside, close by, next to, by, at the side of"
[54] Literally 'théogonies' means "theogonies" from the word *theogony* which is "the origin of the gods; an account of this; a genealogical account of the gods"

It is therefore here [that] this ancient serpent who enveloped the world and who soothes[55] its devouring head under the foot of a Virgin, symbol of initiation; of that Virgin who presents a little new-born infant for the worship of the royal magi and receives from them, in exchange for this favor, gold, myrrh, and incense.

Dogma thus serves in all hieratic religions to veil the secret of the forces of nature from which the initiate can partake[56], [while] religious formulas are the summary of these words full of mystery and power which cause the gods to descend from heaven and submit themselves to the will of men… | Es esta antigua serpiente que envuelve al mundo y que apacigua su cabeza devoradora debajo del pie de la Virgen, figura del iniciado, de la Virgen que presenta una criatura recién nacida para su adoración a los tres reyes magos y recibe de ellos, en cambio de este favor, oro, mirra e incienso.

El dogma sirve, así, en todas las religiones heréticas, para encubrir el secreto de las fuerzas de la naturaleza que puede disponer el iniciado; las formulas religiosas son los resúmenes de estas palabras llenas de misterio y fuerzas que hacen los dioses descender del cielo y las someten a la voluntad de los hombres… |

---

[55] Literally 'apaise' means "appease, soothe; alleviate, assuage; mollify, pacify; salve, smooth down, sweeten; ease, gentle; placate, quench, quiet, settle"
[56] Literally 'disposer' means "arrange, set; lay, dispose; place, put out; array, apply"

Lucifer and the Arcanum A.Z.F.   *Lucifer y el Arcano A.Z.F.*

Extracted from Chapter 2 from
THE PISTIS SOPHIA UNVEILED
by Samael Aun Weor

The fifteenth day of the Moon corresponds with Lucifer.

The key of Lucifer is the Arcanum A.Z.F., the Sexual Force.

Unquestionably, the creative power of the Logos is in the creative organs.

The profound, resplendent, interior Sun shines on the path of the Initiate.

The luminous Sexual Force shines extraordinarily in the aura of the Christified Ones.

In synthesis[1], the Sexual Force comes from the Light of Lights, which is precisely the Logos.

Unquestionably, this Light comes from the Last and First Mystery, which in reality is the Twenty-Fourth Mystery, the Mystery of the Great Work, the Mystery of the Work in the Great Laboratory of the Universe.

All that we have said in these paragraphs is completely understandable to the well qualified Hermetic Artists.

Indubitably, the Hermetic Artists belong to the Esoteric Orders that work in the Second Space of the First Mystery.

It is understandable that [the] Second Space of the First Mystery is the region where the Hermetic Sages live.

The Ancient of days dwells within the First Space of the First Mystery, and the twenty-two Commandments of the Law of God correspond exactly to Him.

---

[1] Literally 'en última síntesis' means "in final synthesis"

Extracts from Chapter 3 from
THE PISTIS SOPHIA UNVEILED
by Samael Aun Weor

Unquestionably the Ascension of the Intimate Christ within ourselves is [achieved] through the Fifteenth Mystery, which is, the Mystery of Typhoon Baphomet.

The Mystery of Baphomet is solved with the Sixth Mystery; you know this.

$$15 = 1+5 = 6$$

The Hermetic figure of Baphomet was never absent from the houses of the old medieval Alchemists.

Lucifer-Baphomet grants us the sexual impulse, through which the realization of the Great Work is possible.

When we beat[2] Baphomet to death with the Lance of Longinus, we transmute lead into Gold.

Sexual transmutation is fundamental for christification, this is the Mystery of Baphomet.

Indubitably, if we spill the Hermetic Glass, then metallic transmutation is absolutely impossible.

Those who learn how to utilize the sexual impulse intelligently can perform the Great Work.

The ascension of the Intimate Christ within us is absolutely possible when we have comprehended the Fifteenth Mystery, which is the same Mystery of Lucifer-Baphomet.

---

[2] Literally 'herimos' means "injure, hurt; wound; hit, strike; lacerate; cripple; shoot; bruise"

Extractos del Capítulo III de
PISTIS SOPHIA DEVELADO
por Samael Aun Weor

Incuestionablemente, es mediante el Misterio Quince, que es el del Tiphón Baphometo, como puede realizarse la Ascensión del Cristo Intimo en nosotros.

El misterio del Baphometo se resuelve con el Sexto Misterio, tú lo sabes.

Jamás pudo faltar la figura hermética del Baphometo en las casas de los viejos Alquimistas medievales.

Lucifer-Baphometo nos otorga el impulso sexual mediante el cual es posible la realización de la Gran Obra.

Cuando herimos de muerte al Baphometo con la Lanza de Longinus, transmutamos el plomo en Oro.

Transmutación sexual resulta fundamental para la cristificación, ése es el misterio de Baphometo.

Indudablemente, resultaría absolutamente imposible cualquier transmutación metálica si derramáramos el Vaso Hermético.

Quienes aprenden a usar inteligentemente el impulso sexual pueden realizar la Gran Obra.

La Ascensión del Cristo Intimo en nosotros se hace absolutamente posible cuando se comprende el Misterio Quince que es el mismo que el del Lucifer-Baphometo.

The Ascension of the Intimate Jesus Christ is a Sexual Mystery of transcendental and practical Alchemy.

Certainly, the Ascension of the Christ within us is clearly through the wise combination of the Three Amens, I am emphatically referring to the Three Fundamental Forces of Nature and the Cosmos.

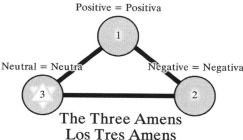

The Three Amens
Los Tres Amens

The Three Forces, Positive, Negative, and Neutral, wisely combined in the Flaming Forge of Vulcan, originate the Human Transformation, the Ascension of Christ within us.

Stella Maris, the Divine Mother Kundalini, guides the navigator in the boisterous[3] ocean.

The victorious Intimate Christ is the Red Christ.

The revolutionary Christ, the rebel Christ, shakes[4] all the Potencies of Good and Evil.

The Red Christ can never be comprehended by the Potencies of Good and Evil.

All the Powers of Heaven are in agitation and set into movement, one against the other, in the presence of the strange procedures of the revolutionary Logos.

In reality, all the Beings, all the Aeons, and all the Regions of the Tree of Life, and their Orders are in agitation before the Red Christ.

La Ascensión del Jesucristo Intimo es un Misterio Sexual de Alquimia trascendental y práctica.

Ciertamente, la Ascensión del Cristo en nosotros resulta clara mediante la sabia combinación de los Tres Amens, quiero referirme en forma enfática a las Tres Fuerzas Fundamentales de la Naturaleza y del Cosmos.

Las Tres Fuerzas, Positiva, Negativa y Neutra, sabiamente combinadas en la Fragua encendida de Vulcano, originan la Transformación Humana, la Ascensión de Cristo en nosotros.

Stella Maris, la Divina Madre Kundalini, orienta al navegante en el borrascoso océano.

El Cristo Intimo victorioso es el Cristo Rojo.

El Cristo revolucionario, el Cristo rebelde, hace estremecer a todas las Potencias del Bien y del Mal.

El Cristo Rojo nunca podría ser comprendido por las Potencias del Bien y del Mal.

Todos los Poderes del Cielo se agitan y se ponen en movimiento, unos contra otros, ante los extraños procederes del Logos revolucionario.

En realidad, todos los Seres, todos los Aeones y todas las Regiones del Árbol de la Vida y sus Ordenes, se agitan ante el Cristo Rojo.

---

[3] Literally 'borrascoso' means "stormy, blustery, gusty"
[4] Literally 'estremecer' means "shake; thrill"

The Red Christ is the Christ who worked in the flaming Forge of Vulcan, the Intimate Savior Christ, the Christ who became victorious in the hour of temptation; the Christ who expelled[5] all the merchants of the Interior Temple, the Christ who killed the infidels[6], the Christ dressed with the Purple of the Kings.

The Profound Interior Christ must fight a tremendous battle against the eternal enemies of the night, who are within us here and now.

These enemies are the infidels, the diverse psychic aggregates that personify our psychological defects.

The Ascension of the Christ within ourselves is a sexual problem.

The Powers of Light and the Powers of Darkness are in agitation and revolve when the Resurrection and Ascension of the Intimate Christ occurs within us.

The Intimate Christ must fight against the Powers of Good and Evil.

The Intimate Christ is beyond Good and Evil.

The Intimate Christ grasps the sword of Cosmic Justice.

The Powers of Good and Evil fight amongst themselves while in the presence of Christic events.

The Three Primary Forces of Nature and of the Cosmos must be crystallized within man.

The Sacred Absolute Sun wants to crystallize the Three Primary Forces within each one of us.

El Cristo Rojo es el Cristo que trabajó en la Fragua encendida de Vulcano, el Cristo Salvador Intimo, el Cristo que salió victorioso a la hora de la tentación, el Cristo que expulsó a los mercaderes del Templo Interior, el Cristo que mató a los infieles, el Cristo vestido con la Púrpura de los Reyes.

El Cristo Interior Profundo debe pelear tremendamente contra los eternos enemigos de la noche que están dentro de nosotros mismos, aquí y ahora.

Estos enemigos son los infieles, los diversos agregados psíquicos que personifican a nuestros defectos psicológicos.

La Ascensión del Cristo en nosotros es un problema sexual.

Los Poderes de la Luz y los Poderes de las Tinieblas se agitan y revuelven ante la Resurrección y Ascensión del Cristo Intimo en nosotros.

El Cristo Intimo debe pelear contra los Poderes del Bien y del Mal.

El Cristo Intimo está más allá del Bien y del Mal.

El Cristo Intimo empuña la espada de la Justicia Cósmica.

Los Poderes del Bien y del Mal luchan entre sí ante los eventos Crísticos.

Deben cristalizar en el hombre las Tres Fuerzas Primarias de la Naturaleza y del Cosmos.

El Sagrado Sol Absoluto quiere hacer cristalizar en cada uno de nosotros las Tres Fuerzas Primarias.

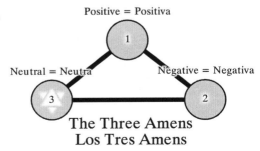

The Three Amens
Los Tres Amens

---

[5] Literally 'expulsó' means "expel, eject; scavenge"
[6] Literally 'infieles' means "treacherous, infidel, unfaithful"

The Initiate develops under the Constellation of the Whale.[7]

The Intimate Self-realization of the Being would be impossible without Lucifer-Baphomet.

Lucifer originates the sexual impulse within each one of us.

If we control the sexual impulse and transmute the Sacred Sperm, [then] we rise from degree to degree.

All the work of the Great Work is realized in the Ninth Sphere.

The Ninth Sphere is Sex.

Those who spill the Glass of Hermes fail in the Great Work.

---

[7] See Ch. 48 of *Tarot & Kabalah* by Samael Aun Weor for more information about this Topic.

Extracts from Chapter 6 from
THE PISTIS SOPHIA UNVEILED
by Samael Aun Weor

The egyptians said: "Osiris is a black god."

Human beings are not capable of resisting the Light of Glory.

The Light of the Christ dazzles[9] the dwellers of the Earth.

This is why Osiris-Christ is black for the human beings.

The splendors of the Christ blind[10] the inhabitants of the Earth.

In truth, people do not comprehend the splendors of the Christ.

The multitudes have their Consciousness asleep.

As long as the ego, the "I", continues within us, [then] unquestionably, the Consciousness will continue to sleep.

The awakening [of the Consciousness] only occurs by annihilating the ego.

Only the awakened can understand the Christic Mysteries.

...

The Intimate Christ comes time and time again, constantly, each time when it is necessary.

The Cosmic Christ is a force, like electricity, [or] the force of gravity, etc.

The Cosmic Christ is beyond the personality, individuality, and the "I".

---

[9] Literally 'deslumbra' means "blind, dazzle; glare"
[10] Literally 'ofuscan' means "dim, daze, obfuscate"

Extractos del Capítulo VI de
PISTIS SOPHIA DEVELADO
por Samael Aun Weor

Osiris es un dios negro, decían los egipcios.

Los seres humanos no son capaces de resistir la Luz de Gloria.

La Luz del Cristo deslumbra a los moradores de la Tierra.

Osiris-Cristo es por eso negro para los seres humanos.

Los esplendores del Cristo ofuscan a los moradores de la Tierra.

Los esplendores del Cristo, en verdad, no son comprendidos por las gentes.

Las multitudes tienen la Conciencia dormida.

En tanto continúe el ego, el yo dentro de nosotros, incuestionablemente la Conciencia continuará dormida.

Sólo aniquilando al ego adviene el despertar.

Sólo el despierto podrá comprender los Misterios Crísticos.

...

Cristo Intimo vuelve una y otra vez, constantemente, cada vez que es necesario.

El Cristo Cósmico es una fuerza como la electricidad, como la fuerza de la gravedad, etc.

El Cristo Cósmico está más allá de la personalidad, de la individualidad y del yo.

The Christ expresses itself through any Human Being who is perfectly prepared.	El Cristo se expresa a través de cualquier Hombre que esté debidamente preparado.
Nevertheless, all the Christic events are accompanied by great earthquakes and confusions.	Empero, todos los eventos Crísticos van acompañados de grandes terremotos y confusiones.
Christic events are terribly revolutionary.	Los eventos Crísticos son terriblemente revolucionarios.

Extracted from Chapter 14 from
THE PISTIS SOPHIA UNVEILED
by Samael Aun Weor

The Intimate Jesus-Christ, totally incarnated in any Christified Adept, shines gloriously.

Therefore, to obtain the Christification is urgent, it cannot be delayed or postponed....

8,700 myriads of Light is a symbolic quantity.

8 + 7 + 0 + 0 = 15.

Unquestionably, the Fifteenth Arcanum is terrible.

Typhoon Baphomet, Lucifer, is the Fifteenth Arcanum.

Sexual transmutation is the foundation of the Mystery of Baphomet.

Typhoon-Baphomet is the reflection of the Solar Logos within our own selves, here and now.

Lucifer-Baphomet always gives the sexual impulse, if we refrain the sexual impulse in the sexual act, we obtain transmutation.

Lucifer-Baphomet gives the great impulse, however, if we thrust the Lance of Willpower into his side, we will defeat him.

Defeating temptation is equivalent to climbing on the back of Lucifer.

Lucifer is the stairs to go up. Lucifer is the stairs to go down.

1 + 5 = 6, the Lover, Love. Six is the key of the Fifteenth Arcanum.

Lucifer will convert us into Archangels if we realize the Mystery of Baphomet within ourselves.	Lucifer nos convertirá en Arcángeles si realizamos en sí mismos el Misterio del Baphometo.
The brass must be whitened.	Hay que blanquear el latón.
Burn your books and whiten the brass.	Quema tus libros y blanquea el latón.
Whiten the devil, convert him into Lucifer.	Blanquead al diablo, convertido en Lucifer.
One whitens the devil when one transmutes the sexual energy and eliminates the ego.	Uno blanquea al diablo cuando transmuta la energía sexual y elimina el ego.
People have their Lucifer converted into a devil.	Las gentes tienen a su Lucifer convertido en diablo.
When [the] resplendent Lucifer integrates with the Human Being, he converts us into Archangels of Light.	Lucifer resplandeciente, integrado con el Hombre, nos convierte en Arcángeles de la Luz.
Within the totally Christified Adept, that Light is of 8,700 myriads, you know this.	En el Adepto Crístificado totalmente, esa Luz es de 8,700 miríadas, tú lo sabes.
Only those who have worked with Lucifer in the Infernos can reach or possess such Light.	Sólo Aquellos que han trabajado con Lucifer en los Infiernos pueden llegar a poseer tal Luz.
Lo and behold the Mystery of Baphomet and of Abraxas.	He allí el Misterio del Baphometo y de Abraxas.
Light is born from Darkness, and the Cosmos sprouts from Chaos.	La Luz nace de las Tinieblas y el Cosmos brota del Caos.

Extracted from Chapter 64 from
THE PISTIS SOPHIA UNVEILED
by Samael Aun Weor

We must distinguish between Satan and Lucifer: Satan is the devil, black like coal, the fallen Lucifer.

We must whiten the devil and this is only possible by practicing Sexual Magic intensely and by disintegrating the ego.

Humanity has converted Lucifer into the devil.

Each one of us must whiten our own particular devil in order to convert him into Lucifer.

When Lucifer shines in ourselves, he converts himself into our particular, individual Moses.

Fortunate is the one who integrates himself with his own Moses.

Moses, descending from Sinai with the luminous horns upon his forehead, deserved to be chiseled by Michelangelo.

The Doctrine of Moses is the Doctrine of Lucifer.

Christus-Lucifer is our Savior, the Redeemer of Pistis Sophia.

Christus-Lucifer grasps the scale and the sword as [a] Lord of Justice.

Lucifer, integrated with the Intimate Christ, shines in Sabaoth, the Solar Man.

The Heavenly Sabaoth crystallizes within the Sabaoth-Man, thanks to the Intimate Moses.

Sabaoth-Moses is totally integrated.

Sabaoth is the internal God who must crystallize in the human person, thanks to the beneficial[11] services[12] of Lucifer.

The Antichrist, the Ego, knows nothing about these things, he merely wants a mechanical man and a Universe, originated by chance, an absurd miracle from the reason without reason.

On [the] other side, religion hates Lucifer, and curses him without knowing that he is the unfolding of the Intimate Christ.

Those who ignore the intelligent igneous principles without whom [the] existence of the cell and the atom would not be possible, are as ignorant as those religious fanatics who hate Lucifer.

Christus-Lucifer is the Savior within each one of us.

The Ray of Light, [that] is to say, the Christ-Man, shines in the Chaos and in all regions.

The demons are terrified before the presence of the Christ-Man.

The Christ-Man is covered with all the light powers that the tenebrous ones had taken away from Pistis Sophia.

The tenebrous ones never dare to touch the Christ-Man in the obscure Chaos.

In the Chaos, the ego, the egos, the red demons of Set, run away from the presence of the Christ-Man.

---

[11] Literally 'buenos' means "good; fine; right; strong; nice, kind; decent; enjoyable; convenient; cozy; plentiful"
[12] Literally 'oficios' means "trade, profession; job; service; function, role"

The Gnostic Mystery of Lucifer *El Misterio Gnóstico de Lucifer*

Extract translated from pages 985-996 of
THE FIFTH GOSPEL:

"THE GNOSTIC MYSTERY OF LUCIFER[1]"

The DEVIL is, certainly, the PHILOSPHER'S STONE of the Medieval Alchemists

Undoubtedly, each person has their own Devil.

The Devil, as it has been said, is no more than the REFLECTION OF THE INTERIOR LOGOI within each of us; that is obvious.

"He has power over the Heavens, over the Earth, and over the Infernos..."

When it is said: "*Lock[2] the Devil in the violin*", [this] intends to say that "one has to grab, apprehend, capture, that manifested Verb, we [could] say, of the Christ-Satan of the gnostics"; that Verb [which is] proficient and [is] occupied, we [could] say, with the art of making musical instruments, and [in this way] give form to that Verb in an instrument, so that it resonates miraculously.

Thus, we should make a clear DIFFERENTIATION BETWEEN what the DEVIL is and what LUCIFER is.

The Devil, in himself (as [a] Reflection of the Logos in us and within ourselves) is the BRUTE[3] STONE that must be carved[4], until [he is] converted into the PERFECT CUBIC STONE.

Extracto de páginas 985-996 de
EL QUINTO EVANGELIO:

"EL MISTERIO GNÓSTICO DE LUCIFER[5]"

El DIABLO es, ciertamente, la PIEDRA FILOSOFAL de los Alquimistas Medievales.

Indudablemente, cada persona tiene su propio Diablo.

El Diablo como se ha dicho, no es más que la REFLEXIÓN DEL LOGOI INTERIOR dentro de cada uno de nosotros; eso es obvio.

"Tiene potestad sobre los Cielos, sobre la Tierra y sobre los Infiernos..."

Cuando se dice: "*Encerrar al Diablo en el violín*", se quiere decir que "hay que captar, aprehender, capturar, ese Verbo manifestado, dijéramos, del Cristo-Satán de los gnósticos"; ese Verbo proficiente y ocuparlo, dijéramos, en el arte de hacer instrumentos musicales, y darle forma a ese Verbo en un instrumento, para que resuene milagrosamente.

Debemos, pues, hacer una clara DIFERENCIACIÓN ENTRE lo que es el DIABLO y lo que es LUCIFER.

El Diablo, en sí mismo, como Reflexión del Logos en nosotros y dentro de nosotros mismos, es la PIEDRA BRUTA que hay que labrar, hasta convertirla en la PIEDRA CÚBICA PERFECTA.

---

[1] This lecture is #96 and has also been called "THE DEVIL AND LUCIFER"
[2] Literally 'Encerrar' means "shut in, lock in, close in, confine, coop, coop up, fence in, hem in, hold in, imprison, lock away, lock up, pen in, put under restraint, round up, shut away; surround, hem;"
[3] Literally 'bruta' means "coarse, unpolished, in a rough state; brutish, bestial; stupid; currish, crude; raw"
[4] Literally 'labrar' means "carve, carve out, fashion, forge, hew, tool;"

[5] También se llama "EL DIABLO Y LUCIFER"

And we have at the foot of that pair of columns the Brute Stone and the Chiseled Stone; what is there should be understood.

[The] Brute [Stone]: when it is not carved, the Devil (or, the Reflection of the Logos in us), [is] unworked, unpolished, [it is] BLACK AS COAL, it is SATAN, in his darkest[6] and most tenebrous aspect.

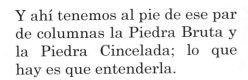

But it is not an anthropomorphic Satan, like that which the clergy want us to see; no, it is [our very] own particular Satan.

But when we have already achieved the dissolution of the Ego, when we have reduced it to ashes, then that Brute Stone has been transformed into the PERFECT CUBIC STONE; then Satan is already LUCIFER, the "MAKER OF LIGHT"

In other times Lucifer, the Maker of Light, was confused with VENUS, the "MORNING STAR", and even in the "Revelation" of Saint John it is said that "*to you who overcome, you will be given the Star of the Morning*"...

The Lord QUETZALCOATL, after having burned his inhuman elements in the Infernal Worlds, ascended to Heaven and became the Star of the Morning, in VESPERS[7], [he became] the Bright Evening Star[8].

Y ahí tenemos al pie de ese par de columnas la Piedra Bruta y la Piedra Cincelada; lo que hay es que entenderla.

Bruta: cuando está sin labrar, el Diablo (o sea, la Reflexión del Logos en nosotros), sin labrar, sin pulir, NEGRA COMO EL CARBÓN, es SATANÁS, en su aspecto más obscuro y tenebroso.

Pero no es un Satanás antropomórfico, como el que quiere hacernos ver la clerigalía; no, es un Satanás propio particular.

Pero cuando ya hemos conseguido la disolución del Ego, cuando lo hemos reducido a cenizas, entonces esa Piedra Bruta se ha transformado en la PIEDRA CÚBICA PERFECTA; entonces Satanás es ya LUCIFER, el "HACEDOR DE LUZ"

En otros tiempos al Hacedor de Luz a Lucifer se le confundía con VENUS, la "ESTRELLA DE LA MAÑANA", y hasta en el "Apocalipsis" de San Juan se dice que "*al que venciere, se le dará la Estrella de la Mañana*"...

El Señor QUETZALCÓATL, después de haber quemado pues, sus elementos inhumanos en los Mundos Infiernos, ascendió a los Cielos y se convirtió en la Estrella de la Mañana, en VESPERO, el Lucero Vespertino.

---

[6] Literally 'obscuro' means "dark, dim, dusky; dark, obscure, sullen; obscure, incomprehensible, abstruse;"
[7] Literally 'Vespero' means "Vespers, the sunset evening prayer service in the Christian liturgies of the canonical hours. The word comes from the Greek ἑσπέρα and the Latin *vesper*, meaning evening."
[8] Literally 'lucero' means "morning star, bright star;"

Thus, the Devil is transformed into Lucifer, [who is] resplendent[9] like the Sun, "he has the power over the Heavens, over the Earth, and over Hell". Principle of the Light, Lord of Glory, the most grandiose Archangel, the MINISTER OF THE SOLAR LOGOS!

If, in the Suprasensible Worlds, we invoke this Reflection of the Logos of any person who has not dissolved the Ego, we will see a Satan black as coal; but there [in the Suprasensible Worlds], if we invoke, say, the Satan of someone who has dissolved the Ego, [we will see] with great astonishment [that] we will be with an Archangel of Light, with a Glorious Lucifer.

Then we will see that such a Satan is the Brute Stone that must be carved.

For the brethren to take a little more Consciousness from what we are saying, [let's have Mr.] A. arrange there, between the two columns, the Brute Stone and perfect Cubic Stone.

There is a Stone in brute [form], [and] there [is] the perfect Cubic Stone.

Disciple. In the Brute Stone that is there … […X…][10]

Master. Correct! This Satan that each [person] carries inside, in the individual who has not yet chiseled the Philosopher's Stone, their Stone in the Brute [state], is Satan who [is] black as coal, displaying[11] all the aspects[12] of our psychological defects.

---

[9] Literally 'resplandeciente' means "blazing, bright, brilliant, aureate, dazzling, flaring, flashy, glaring, radiant, shining, glary, resplendent, splendent;"
[10] The "[…X…]" means that the recording of the lecture (from which this was transcribed in Spanish) is inaudible at this point, so we do not have a record of what was said.
[11] Literally 'ostentando' means "show off, show, boast, display, flaunt;"
[12] Literally 'aristas' means "edges"

Así pues, el Diablo transformado en Lucifer, resplandeciente como el Sol, "tiene potestad sobre los Cielos, sobre la Tierra y sobre los Infiernos". ¡Príncipe de la Luz, Señor de Gloria, el Arcángel más grandioso, el MINISTRO DEL LOGOS SOLAR!

Si invocamos en los Mundos Suprasensibles a esa Reflexión del Logos de cualquier persona que no ha disuelto el Ego, veremos un Satanás negro como el carbón; pero allá, si invocamos, dijéramos, al Satanás de alguien que sí disolvió el Ego, con gran asombro nos encontraremos con un Arcángel de la Luz, con un Lucifer Glorioso.

Entonces venimos a evidenciar que el tal Satanás es la Piedra Bruta que hay que labrar.

Para que los hermanos tomen un poquito de más Conciencia sobre lo que estamos diciendo, conviene que A. ponga ahí, entre las dos columnas, a la Piedra Bruta y a la Piedra Cúbica perfecta.

Ahí tienen la Piedra en bruto, ahí la Piedra Cúbica perfecta.

Discípulo. En la Piedra Bruta hay que… […X…]

Maestro. ¡Correcto! Ese Satanás que cada cual lleva adentro, en el individuo que no ha burilado todavía su Piedra Filosofal, su Piedra en Bruto, ese Satanás está negro como el carbón, ostentando todas las aristas de nuestros defectos psicológicos.

But when we have carved the Stone, then this Satan becomes[13] the perfect Cubic Stone; that is to say, when we have dissolved the Ego, it transforms itself into the perfect Cubic Stone, and the splendor and glory arise from there [as a result].

It is very interesting to observe the Devil outside of the physical body: [It is] frightening[14] to look at it, black as coal, with that tenebrous fire that tosses & turns[15] in the individual who has not yet eliminated the Ego; but [on the other hand it is] surprising to see (in someone who has already eliminated the Ego) [a] Glorious Archangel, full of splendor.

But clearly, what is first necessary is to eliminate the inhuman elements that we carry inside.

If we observe every authentic Man, [we will] discover in them Three Triangles.

The first is the "LOGOIC TRIANGLE"; the second you could call the "ETHICAL TRIANGLE"; and it is good for us to call the third the "MAGIC TRIANGLE".[16]

As for the first, the LOGOIC, it consists of three aspects of the hebrew Kabalah: KETHER, [who] is the Ancient of the Days, the goodness of goodnesses, the mercy of mercies, the occult of the occult.

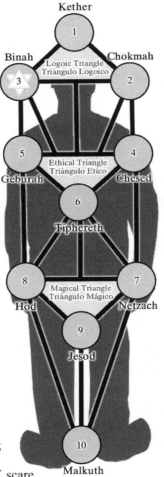

Pero cuando ya nosotros hemos labrado la Piedra, ese Satanás se convierte entonces en la Piedra Cúbica perfecta; es decir, cuando hemos disuelto el Ego, se transforma en la Piedra Cúbica perfecta, y de allí deviene pues, el esplendor y la gloria.

Resulta muy interesante observar al Diablo fuera del cuerpo físico: Espanta verlo, negro como el carbón, con ese fuego tenebroso que arroja en el individuo que todavía no ha eliminado el Ego; pero asombra en verlo (en quien que ya eliminó el Ego) en Arcángel Glorioso, lleno de esplendor.

Pero claro, lo primero que necesitamos es eliminar los elementos inhumanos que cargamos dentro.

Si observamos a todo Hombre auténtico, descubrimos en él Tres Triángulos.

El primero es el "TRIÁNGULO LOGOICO"; el segundo podríamos llamarlo el "TRIÁNGULO ÉTICO"; y el tercero, está bien que lo llamemos el "TRIÁNGULO MÁGICO".

En cuanto al primero, el LOGOICO, está constituido por los tres aspectos de la Kábala hebraica: KETHER, es el Anciano de los Días, la bondad de las bondades, la misericordia de las misericordias, lo oculto de lo oculto.

---

[13] Literally 'convierte' means "transform, convert; proselytize"
[14] Literally 'espanta' means "frighten, frighten off, scare away, terrify, appall, frighten away, frighten out, intimidate, scare, scare off, spook, whisk away, whisk off;"
[15] Literally 'arroja' means "throw, dart, dash, fling off, toss, cast out, fling, heave, hurl, sling, throw out;"
[16] Editor's note: For more information about these triangles, see Ch. 54 in *Tarot & Kabalah* by Samael Aun Weor

It is the MATHEMATICAL POINT in the immense, infinite, unchangeable[17] space.

It is obvious that he unfolds, in his turn, into CHOKMAH, the SON, the COSMIC CHRIST (who is said to be related to the whole Zodiac, and it is so), the further unfolding of Chokmah results in the HOLY SPIRIT, BINAH.

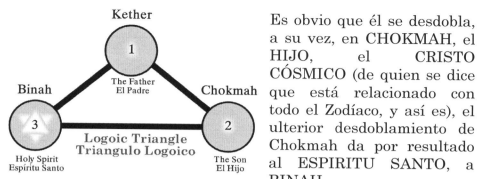

Some Kabalists emphasize the idea that Binah, "the Holy Spirit, is female"; this assertion turns out to be mistaken[18].

It is quite clearly said (in "The Divine Comedy"), that "the Holy Spirit is the husband of the Divine Mother"; and it is the Holy Spirit, the Third Logos, Binah, that unfolds himself in his turn into his Wife, into the SHAKTI of the Hindus.

Thus, then, we [must] know [how] to understand it.

Many, [who have] the view that the Third Logos unfolds itself into the DIVINE MOTHER, into the Kundalini-Shakti (who has many names), have believed that the Holy Spirit is feminine and [they] were mistaken.

Obviously, this Archangel converts itself into the LIBERATOR; this is obvious.

Because of the fusion of the Archangel with the Human Soul, with the Spirit, with the Being (in a word), turns out to precisely be the Archangel.

This is not written in any book of esotericism.

Es el PUNTO MATEMÁTICO en el espacio inmenso, infinito, inalterable.

Es obvio que él se desdobla, a su vez, en CHOKMAH, el HIJO, el CRISTO CÓSMICO (de quien se dice que está relacionado con todo el Zodíaco, y así es), el ulterior desdoblamiento de Chokmah da por resultado al ESPIRITU SANTO, a BINAH.

Algunos Kabalistas enfatizan la idea de que Binah, "el Espíritu Santo, es femenino"; tal afirmación resulta equivocada.

Con entera claridad se ha dicho (en "La Divina Comedia"), que "el Espíritu Santo es el esposo de la Madre Divina"; y es que el Espíritu Santo, el Tercer Logos, Binah, se desdobla a su vez en su Esposa, en la SHAKTI de los Indostanes.

Así, pues, hay que saberlo entender.

Muchos, al ver que el Tercer Logos se desdobla en la MADRE DIVINA, en la Kundalini-Shakti (la cual tiene muchos nombres), han creído que el Espíritu Santo es femenino y se han equivocado.

Obviamente, ese Arcángel se convierte en el LIBERTADOR; eso es obvio.

Porque de la fusión de ese Arcángel con el Alma Humana, con el Espíritu, con el Ser (en una palabra), resulta precisamente el Arcángel.

No está escrito esto en ningún libro de esoterismo.

---

[17] Literally 'inalterable' means "inalterable, unalterable, stable, undying; immovablel; unchanged, unchanging"
[18] Literally 'equivocado' means "wrong, erroneous, mistaken, inaccurate, off base, off the rails; misguided, lost;"

There are many libraries, and nevertheless, [this] has not been discussed in detail, and everyone confuses the Devil with Lucifer.

And it turns out that the Brute Stone is one thing and the Perfect Cubic Stone is another thing.

Continuing, then, in tonight's discussion, we get a perfect account of that which marvelously exists in the depth of each one of us.

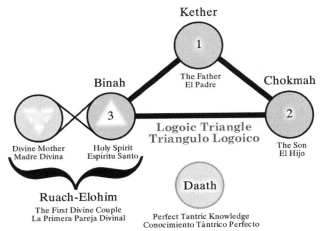

HE [the Holy Spirit], I repeat, is male, but [HE] unfolds into HER forming the first DIVINE COUPLE, the ineffable: The ELOHIM CREATOR, the KABIR or THE INCA or High Priest, the RUACH-ELOHIM that according to Moses "fashioned the waters at the beginning of the world..."

It is necessary that we, all [of us], profoundly reflect [on this], [so] that we comprehend all [of] this in-depth...

He and She are united in the CUBIC STONE OF YESOD (that Stone is Sex).

DAATH, Perfect Tantric Knowledge, comes about from the union of Him and Her, through which we can integrally SELF-REALIZE OURSELVES in all the Levels of Being.

Some of the Kabalists suppose[19] that the Sephirah Daath (Knowledge or Wisdom) comes from the fusion or union of the masculine Chokmah (the Cosmic Christ) with Binah, supposing that it is exclusively feminine.

---

[19] Literally 'suponen' means "suppose, presume; guess; mean; involve; pretend"

Such an assertion[20] is absolutely false, because, really, I repeat, the Holy Spirit is masculine; but the unfolding of Binah forms the perfect couple.

When they join [together] sexually in the Cubic Stone of Yesod, in the Ninth Sphere, they become Tantric Knowledge, TANTRIC INITIATION, the Tantras through which it is possible to develop the SERPENT via the spinal column[21], the Intimate Self-Realization of the Being.

In our studies of Kabalah we need to be practical.

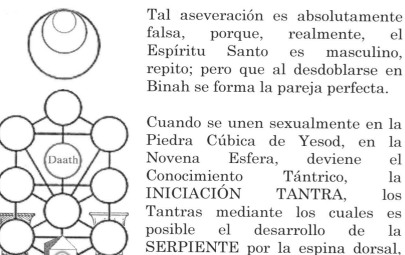

There are many authors, certainly [some are] wonderful, but when one reads of them [one] realizes that they have not lived what they write, they have not experienced [anything] in themselves, and that is why they are mistaken.

I consider that one should write what one has directly experienced for themselves, so I have[22] [done this] for my part...

Thus, the First Triangle is transcendental; but the FATHER, the SON and the HOLY SPIRIT are an INDIVISIBLE UNITY, UNI-EXISTING for itself; it is very much beyond the body, the affections and the mind.

It is the Being, "*and the reason for Being to be, is the Being itself...*"

---

[20] Literally 'aseveración' means "assertion, affirmation, declaration, say-so, statement, claim, pronouncement, asseveration, averment, averral, avowal, contention;"
[21] Literally 'espina dorsal' means "spinal column, backbone, spine, rachis, vertebral column, dorsal spine;"
[22] Literally 'procedido' means "proceed, advance, go on, keep on, take action;"

The Cubic Stone of Yesod, located in the creative organs, is, indeed, that "METALLIC SOUL" which results from sexual transmutations.

We could call it the "MERCURY OF THE SECRET PHILOSOPHY", or to talk in simpler language: "CREATIVE ENERGY".

It, in itself, is allegorized or symbolized, [it] is personified (as I have already said), in the Devil.

When we say that "we have to work with the Devil", [we are saying] not only to lock [him] in a musical instrument, but even more: To transform him into a Lucifer, or [a] Maker of Light.

We are talking, clearly, [about how] to work in the GREAT WORK.

It is interesting that it is there, precisely in the Cubic Stone of Yesod, where the SHIVA-SHAKTI, OSIRIS and ISIS will join sexually; and this is precisely where the Sephirah Daath, Tantric Knowledge [is found], without which it is not possible to reach the Intimate Self-Realization of the Being...

In Oriental Tibet BHON MONKS are radical; [and this is] why H.P.B. (Helena Petronila Blavatsky) thought that they were Black Magicians.

All of us have repeated that mistake and we feel the need to rectify [it].

I am not saying that the DUGPAS are some Saints, [or] some [kind of] gentle sheep, they are BLACK MAGICIANS they teach Black Tantrism; but the Bhons (although they use a red cap), are not Black, as Blavatsky mistakenly supposed. What they are is Radical.

La Piedra Cúbica de Yesod, situada en los órganos creadores, es, ciertamente, aquella "ALMA METÁLICA" que resulta de las transmutaciones sexuales.

Podríamos denominarla el "MERCURIO DE LA FILOSOFÍA SECRETA", o para hablar en un lenguaje más sencillo: "ENERGÍA CREADORA".

Ella, en sí, está alegorizada o simbolizada, está personificada (como ya lo he dicho), en el Diablo.

Cuando decimos que "hay que trabajar con el Diablo", no sólo para encerrarlo en un instrumento musical, sino aún más: Para transformarlo en un Lucifer, o Hacedor de la Luz.

Nos estamos refiriendo, claramente, al trabajo en la GRAN OBRA.

Resulta interesante que sea allí, precisamente en la Piedra Cúbica de Yesod, donde el SHIVA-SHAKTI, OSIRIS e ISIS se unan sexualmente; y es precisamente allí donde está el Sephirote Daath, el Conocimiento Tántrico, sin el cual no es posible llegar a la Auto-Realización Íntima del Ser...

En el Tíbet Oriental los MONJES BHONS son radicales; motivo por el cual H.P.B. (Helena Petronila Blavatsky) pensaba de ellos que eran Magos Negros.

Todos nosotros hemos repetido aquella equivocación y nos vemos en la necesidad de rectificar.

No digo que los DUGPAS sean unos Santos, unas mansas ovejas, ellos sí son MAGOS NEGROS porque enseñan el Tantrismo Negro; pero los Bhons (aunque usen capacete rojo), no son Negros, como equivocadamente supuso Blavatsky. Radicales, es lo que son.

If someone, for example, among the Bhons, does not want Self-Realization, but [does want] liberation for a time (to come back, for example, in the future Sixth Race Root), or better, they never want Self-Realization, but EMANCIPATION WITHOUT SELF-REALIZATION, then, they succeed.

How? First of all, they take the neophyte to a remote place; they invoke all those inhuman elements that [the neophyte] possesses (through procedures of High Magic they will be drawn out of the Astral World [into the physical world]), and in that remote [place] in the mountain those [inhuman elements] become visible, tangible and everything.

They try to devour[23] the neophyte, but if the neophyte remains calm, there is no more to do: he has emerged triumphant.

He knows then that he has to eliminate the Ego, reduced it to ashes and also [that he has to] work. And the ordeal requires the maximum [amount of] effort[24] in the Physical World.

[This work] consists of pronouncing those MANTRAMS OF DISINCARNATION; which are two words, and [one] becomes disincarnated instantly.

It is frightful[25] to see the Bhon Priests (dressed with their white apron, full of skulls and dead bones; a red turban on their head, a miter[26]; carrying a dagger in his right hand) at the time that the neophyte pronounces then the two mantrams of fatality. His body instantly falls dead.

---

[23] Literally 'devorar' means "devour, eat; demolish; live off"
[24] Literally 'esfuerzos' means "effort, elbow grease, endeavor, exertion, push, spirit, struggle, endeavour, pull;"
[25] Literally 'espeluznante' means "hair-raising, frightful, scary, blood-curdling, bloodcurdling, chilly, crawly, creepy, eerie, horrifying, lurid, spooky;"
[26] Literally 'mitra' means "mitre: the liturgical headdress of a bishop or abbot, in most western churches consisting of a tall pointed cleft cap with two bands hanging down at the back"

But, it is then [that] the neophyte is subjected to great ordeals in the Internal Worlds; he has to face the TERRORS OF DEATH; he has to withstand the HURRICANE OF KARMA; he has to emerge victorious in the ordeal that the Father-Mother puts you [though]; you should know [how to] CLOSE [THE] MATRIX, etc., in the end to be able to enter, or be reborn, we [could] say, in the super-human form, in any of those KINGDOMS OF THE DEVAS: Already in the [Kingdom] "of the Great Concentration," or "of the Long Hair", or in the [Kingdom] "Amitabha-Buddha", or "of Maitreya", or in the [Kingdom] "of Supreme Happiness", etc., and [it is] in these regions where he is going to finish in order to prepare for LIBERATION.

The Divine Mother Kundalini assists [in] eliminating his inhuman elements, and in the end [he] is [finally] able to IMMERSE HIMSELF IN THE MIDST OF THE GREAT REALITY, not as a Self-Realized Master, but AS AN ELEMENTAL BUDDHA.

There [he] submerges, in that state, so as to return in the future Sixth Root Race, with the purpose of Self-Realization.

Others simply do not want Mastery, but emancipation and remain forever converted into Elemental Buddhic Ones and nothing more, but [they are] happy.

Whereas those who seek liberation, THOSE WHO really, we [can] say, NEED SELF-REALIZATION, those who really want to become Mahatmas or Hierophants, are different: THEY WILL HAVE TO UNDERGO TANTRIC INITIATION, and then, [they will have] to WORK IN THE NINTH SPHERE.

But in general, they will teach you all [about] Tantrism: How to awaken the Serpent and how to elevate [it] through the spinal column; how to open those chakras, discs or magical wheels.

Pero, es entonces el neófito sometido a grandes ordalías en los Mundos Internos; tiene que enfrentarse a los TERRORES DE LA MUERTE; tiene que soportar el HURACÁN DEL KARMA; tiene que salir victorioso en la prueba que el Padre-Madre le pone; tiene que saber CERRAR MATRIZ, etc., a fin de poder entrar, o renacer, dijéramos, en forma sobrehumana, en cualquiera de esos REINOS DE LOS DEVAS: Ya en el "de la Gran Concentración", o en el "de los Cabellos Largos", o en el "Amitabha-Buddha", o en el "de Maitreya", o en el "de la Suprema Felicidad", etc., y en esas regiones es donde va a acabar para prepararse para la LIBERACIÓN.

La Madre Divina Kundalini le auxilia, eliminando sus elementos inhumanos, y al fin consigue SUMERGIRSE ENTRE EL SENO DE LA GRAN REALIDAD, no como un Maestro Autorrealizado, sino COMO UN BUDDHA ELEMENTAL.

Allí se sumerge, en ese estado, para retornar en la futura Sexta Raza Raíz, con el propósito de Auto-realización.

Otros sencillamente no quieren la Maestría, sino emanciparse y quedaran para siempre convertidos en Elementales Búddhicos y nada más, pero felices.

Mas los que intentan liberarse, LOS QUE verdaderamente QUIEREN, dijéramos, AUTO-REALIZARSE, los que de verdad quieren convertirse en Mahatmas o Hierofantes, es diferente: TENDRÁN QUE SOMETERSE A LA INICIACIÓN TANTRA, Y luego, a TRABAJAR EN LA NOVENA ESFERA.

Pero en general, se le enseñará todo el Tantrismo: Cómo despertar la Serpiente y cómo levantarla por la espina dorsal; cómo abrir esos chakras, discos o ruedas mágicas.

| The Gnostic Mystery of Lucifer | El Misterio Gnóstico de Lucifer |

Thus, what happens is that the Bhons are radical: someone either will Self-Realize, or they will not Self-Realize; [either] they are going to be released without Self-Realization, or claim[27] [they are] liberating themselves [and that thay are] Self-Realizing.

Before them is something which defines: A "Yes" or a "No".

[In them] everything is violent[28]; [this is] why Helena Petronila Blavatsky judged them, considering them as "Black Magicians".

But when one studies the Tantrism of the Bhons, one realizes that it is White, not Black but White (transmutation of the sperm into Energy in order to achieve in depth Self-Realization)...

It is therefore there, in that SEPHIRAH [OF] YESOD, where Tantric Knowledge is [found] (the Daath of the hebraic Kabalah).

But, brethren, lets move from the LOGOIC TRIANGLE to the TRIANGLE OF THE SON.

It is formed by CHESED (that is, the Ineffable Atman, the Intimus), by BUDDHI (the Spiritual Soul, which is feminine, [and] is [the] GEBURAH of the hebraic Kabalah), and finally, by TIPHERETH (the Human Soul, the Son proper).

It is interesting, and I may reveal[29] when I made contact with the work in the Sphere of Tiphereth.

Así pues, lo que sucede es que los Bhons son radicales: o se va Auto-realizar alguien, o no se va Auto-realizar; se va a liberar sin Auto-realización, o pretenden liberarse Auto-realizado.

Ante ellos tiene uno que definirse: Un "Sí" o un "No".

Allí todo es violento; motivo por el cual Helena Petronila Blavatsky los juzgó, considerándolos "Magos Negros".

Pero cuando uno estudia el Tantrismo de los Bhons, se da cuenta que es Blanco, no Negro sino Blanco (transmutación del esperma en Energía para conseguir la Auto-realización a fondo)...

Es pues ahí, en ese SEPHIROTH YESOD, donde está el Conocimiento Tántrico (el Daath de la Kábala hebraica).

Pero pasemos hermanos, del TRIÁNGULO LOGOICO al TRIÁNGULO DEL HIJO.

Éste está formado por CHESED (o sea, el Atman Inefable, el Íntimo), por BUDDHI (el Alma Espiritual, que es femenina, es GEBURAH de la Kábala hebraica), y por último, por TIPHERETH (el Alma Humana, el Hijo propiamente dicho).

Es interesante, y yo lo puede evidenciar cuando me tocó trabajar en la Esfera de Tiphereth.

Triangle of the Son / Triángulo del Hijo

5 — Geburah — Buddhi, the Spiritual Soul. / Buddhi, el Alma Espiritual.
4 — Chesed — The Ineffable Atman, the Intimus. / El Atman Inefable, el Íntimo.
6 — Tiphereth — The Human Soul, the Son proper. / El Alma Humana, el Hijo propiamente dicho.

---

[27] Literally 'pretenden' means "purport, pretend; profess, allege, claim"
[28] Literally 'violento' means "violent, forceful, bitter;"
[29] Literally 'evidenciar' means "evidence, demonstrate, give evidence of, show, evince, make evident, manifest;"

Obviously, I first went (before passing through the exaltation), into the MALKUTH OF VENUS, [then] into the VENUSIAN Kingdom of KLIPOTH, [or] better said, into the VENUSIAN Atomic Worlds or [VENUSIAN] ATOMIC INFERNOS.

There, many inhuman elements had to be eliminated.

[Upon] completion of the work, the one who is perfect (The Cosmic Christ) entered into me, and I was transformed.

I then saw the mothers who brought up their children; I blessed them and spoke with the gospel parable which says:

> "*Let the children come to me, because the Kingdom of Heaven is in them...*"

That state is [a state] of static happiness, but in the end, of course, it is a march[30].

I, as Tiphereth, as the Human Soul, I comprehended what had been the objective of their manifestation.

Yes, the Cosmic Christ usually manifests himself through the Human Soul, by that Tiphereth of the Hebrew Kabalah.

This is the Triangle of the Son, a wonderful triangle formed by the Atman-Buddhi-Manas of Oriental Theosophy.

But the GRAVITATIONAL CENTER of the Triangle of the Son is, precisely, TIPHERETH, the Human Soul, that Soul that suffers, that cries, that groans, [and] shouts for truth...

---
[30] Literally 'marchó' means "march, parade; walk, go, march, transit; work, run; be going, be doing;"

Obviamente, hube de hundirme primero (antes de pasar por la exaltación), en MALKUTH DE VENUS, en el Reino de los KLIPHOS VENUSINOS, en Mundos Atómicos o INFIERNOS ATÓMICOS, mejor dijera, VENUSINOS.

Había que eliminar, allí, muchos elementos inhumanos.

Concluida la labor, aquél que es perfecto (El Cristo Cósmico) entró en mí, y me sentí transformado.

Vi entonces a unas madres que traían sus niños; los bendije y hablé con la parábola evangélica que dice:

> "*Dejad que vengan los niños a mí, porque de ellos es el Reino de los Cielos*"...

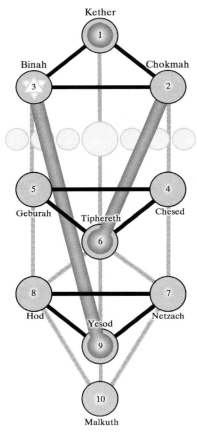

Aquel estado fue de estática felicidad, pero al fin, claro, él se marchó.

Yo, como Tiphereth, como Alma Humana, comprendí cuál había sido el objetivo de su manifestación.

Sí, el Cristo Cósmico suele manifestarse a través del Alma Humana, de ese Tiphereth de la Kábala Hebraica.

Éste es el Triángulo del Hijo, un triángulo maravilloso, formado por el Atman-Buddhi-Manas de la Teosofía Oriental.

Pero el CENTRO GRAVITACIONAL del Triángulo del Hijo es, precisamente, TIPHERETH, el Alma Humana, ese Alma que sufre, que llora, que gime, que grita de verdad...

[...X...]

In practice we have seen that the Triangle of the Son, with its Gravitational Center in Tiphereth, is a tremendous reality.

[...X...]

Everything [which is] Begun[31] must, sooner or later, be anointed by the Father, by that Kether, Chokmah and Binah, by that Immortal Logoic Triad, which is indivisible and exists in itself...

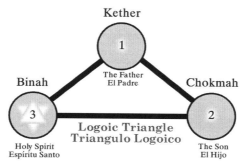

When I had to be anointed, in [those] moments in which he poured pure oil [upon me], [he] exclaimed:

"This is what I love most in the world, [it] is my most beloved Son; seek for[32] him"...

AND there came to my memory, in those moments, the case of the Great Kabir Jesus, or Jeshua Ben Pandir, as he was known in ancient times.

Phillip, the expert Master in the Jinas States, told him:

– Show us the Father.

And the Great Kabir responded:

– One who has seen the Son, has seen the Father...

[...X...]

En la práctica hemos podido evidenciar que el Triángulo del Hijo, con su Centro Gravitacional en Tiphereth, es una tremenda realidad.

[...X...]

Todo Iniciado, tarde o temprano, debe ser ungido por el Padre, por ese Kether, Chokmah y Binah, por esa Tríada Logoica Inmortal, que es indivisible y existente por sí misma...

Cuando yo hube de ser ungido, en instantes en que él me ungía con el aceite puro, exclamó:

"Éste es mi Hijo muy amado, es lo que más he amado en el mundo; buscadle a él"...

Y me viene a la memoria, en estos momentos, el caso del Gran Kabir Jesús, o de Jeshuá Ben Pandirá, como se le llamaba en los antiguos tiempos.

Felipe, el Maestro experto en los Estados de Jinas, le dijo:

– Muéstranos al Padre.

Y el Gran Kabir responde:

– El que ha visto al Hijo, ha visto al Padre...

---

[31] Literally 'Iniciado' means "initiate, launch, start; log-in; log-on; pioneer; enter into"

[32] Literally 'buscar' means "look for, look up for, seek, be out for, beat about for, cast about for, go in quest of, hunt up, look about for, look around for, look out for, scout for, seek for, buck for;"

The Triangle of the Son: Chesed, Geburah, Tiphereth (or the Intimus with his two Souls, Divine and Human, to be more clear), is, let's say, the unfolding of the Father, the manifestation of the Father.

Continuing, then, on the path of our study of the TREE OF LIFE, we see something in the Magic Triangle, [which is] below that Triangle of the Son.

The Triangle of the Son is [also] called the "ETHICAL TRIANGLE".

Why? Because there we recognize[33] the rigor of the Law; there we come to know that which is good and evil; and [to distinguish] those things which are good from [those which are] evil and the evil from the good, etc...

The Third Triangle, the MAGIC TRIANGLE, is very interesting [and it] is composed of NETZACH, or the Mind; HOD the Astral Body; [and] YESOD, the Linga Sharira or Etheric Body, or the Basic Sexual Principle of Universal Life.

Why is it called the "Magic Triangle"?

Because [it is] undoubtedly in these Kingdoms of the Mind and the Astral (and [we should also] include Klipoth or the Infernal Worlds) where one has to exercise HIGH MAGIC.

Something very important should be precisely illustrated here.

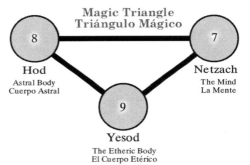

El Triángulo del Hijo: Chesed, Geburah, Tiphereth (o el Íntimo con sus dos Almas, Divina y Humana, para ser más claros), es, dijéramos, el desdobla-miento del Padre, la manifestación del Padre.

Continuando, pues, en el camino sobre el estudio del ÁRBOL DE LA VIDA, vemos como se desdobla aquel Triángulo del Hijo, en el Triángulo Mágico.

Al Triángulo del Hijo se le llama el "TRIANGULO ÉTICO".

¿Por qué? Porque allí conocemos nosotros el rigor de la Ley; allí venimos a saber que es lo bueno y lo malo; y que cosa es lo bueno de lo malo y lo malo de lo bueno, etc...

Resulta muy interesante el Tercer Triángulo, el TRIÁNGULO MÁGICO, está formado por NETZACH, o sea, la Mente; HOD el Cuerpo Astral; YESOD, el Linga Sharira o Cuerpo Etérico, o Principio Básico Sexual de la Vida Universal.

¿Por qué se le llama "Triángulo Mágico"?

Porque indudablemente, en esos Reinos de la Mente y del Astral (y hasta de los Kliphos o Mundos Infernales), donde uno tiene que ejercer la ALTA MAGIA.

Precisamente, cabe aquí ilustrar esto con algo muy importante.

---

[33] Literally 'conocemos' means "know, become acquainted, meet; learn; recognize; see; taste"

We have all heard in Occultism about the "Witches' Sabbaths", about the "Worker Bee[34]" and the "Witches".

Some look at this as something strange while[35] others can smile a little.

But the stark reality is certainly that those medieval witches' sabbaths, with the famous "midnight witches", have more realism [than one may wish to think] […X…]

Obviously, these "Hags[36]" (as they say in rigorously academic and hispanic language), belong, lets say, to the WORLD OF KLIPOTH, that KINGDOM OF MALKUTH or the INFERNAL WORLDS of the Kabalistic Leviathon.

Many quite strange [things] were seen [in those sabbaths], [including] that of MARY OF ANTINA (so named in the ancient medieval convents), [who] was specifically[37] their governor.

Obviously, the[38] witches of [those] ancient witches' sabbaths named her "SAINT MARY".

And when I investigated in the World of Klipoth about this strange creature, how she shared her life with so many Black Magicians, how she could end up in so many witches' sabbaths, nonetheless, I never saw what we would call "perversity".

The Tenebrous Ones of the Left Hand [Path], the Sublunar creatures rendered cult [to] her and considered her a Magess (a type of Hecate or Proserpine) not as something tenebrous, but as a Saint.

---

[34] Literally 'zánganos' means "drone, male of the honeybee; loafer, idler;"
[35] Literally 'u' means "or"
[36] Literally 'calchonas' means "ghost, phantom; hag, mean and ugly old woman"
[37] Literally 'exactamente' means "exactly, accurately, precisely; punctually; correctly; truly; right; just"
[38] Literally 'tales' means "such, suchlike"

I know what there was of truth in that [claim] of the alleged "Holiness" of a creature that mingled with the Darkness, that took part in so many witches' sabbaths and Monasteries of the Middle Ages.

Because, who, [of those] who has studied [the] old chronicles of High and Low Magic from medieval [times], has not heard of Mary of Antina?

[She] figured in lots of short chronicles, [which are] today hidden between the dust of many libraries...

Clearly, the matter was enigmatic and I had to clarify it.

And it was clarified when [I was], precisely, in the World of Tiphereth, in the Second Triangle (the Triangle of the Son), I therefore invoked that entity; and she came, and I encountered her as a SELF-REALIZED and PERFECT MASTER with amazement.

I then comprehended. She had emanated, of herself, from her Bodhisattva; and this Bodhisattva was educated in the exercise of the Magic in the Inferior Triangle or Third Triangle, passing through rigorous training and living within Klipoth, but without doing evil to anyone.

Later, I got in direct contact with her Bodhisattva, with Mary of Antina, clearly; and when I invited the [Bodhisattva] to visit the World of Nirvana, [that Bodhisattva] pleasantly accepted my invitation; and when I fused with her Real Being, with the Secret Master, then I saw that it was the Bodhisattva of a Great Adept, of a creature that had achieved perfection in High Magic and that while she lived in the world of Klipoth, she was completing her education or psychological training, exercising tremendous Powers and without doing harm to anyone.

Yo quise saber qué había de verdad en eso de la presunta "Santidad" de una criatura que se mezclaba con las Tinieblas, que figuraba en tantos aquelarres y Monasterios de la Edad Media.

Porque, ¿quién, que se haya ocupado de estudiar viejos cronicones de la Alta y Baja Magia del medievo, no ha oído hablar alguna vez de María de la Antina?

Figura entre tantos cronicones, hoy escondidos entre el polvo de muchas bibliotecas...

Claro, el asunto era enigmático y yo tenía que aclararlo.

Y aclaré cuando, precisamente, en el Mundo de Tiphereth, en el Segundo Triángulo (Triángulo del Hijo), invoqué, pues, a esa entidad; y vino ella, y para asombro me encontré con un MAESTRO AUTO-REALIZADO y PERFECTO.

Entonces comprendí. Había emanado, de sí mismo, a su Bodhisattva; y ese Bodhisattva se educaba en el ejercicio de la Magia en el Triángulo Inferior o Tercer Triángulo, pasando por entrenamientos rigurosos y viviendo con los Kliphos, pero sin hacer mal a nadie.

Después, me puse en contacto directo con su Bodhisattva, con María de la Antina, claramente; y cuando la invité a visitar el Mundo del Nirvana, con agrado aceptó mi invitación; y cuando me fusionó con su Real Ser, con el Maestro Secreto, entonces vi que se trataba del Bodhisattva de un Gran Adepto, de una criatura que había logrado la perfección en la Alta Magia y que si bien vivía en el Mundo de los Kliphos, era para acabar de educarse o entrenarse psicológicamente, ejerciendo Poderes tremendos y sin hacer mal a nadie.

She was educated in High Magic.

When one observes that creature integrated with her Real Being, one realizes that she is an extraordinary WHITE MAGICIAN, who knows both the KINGDOMS OF THE LIGHT, as [well as] the WORLD OF MALKUTH, that is to say, the WORLD OF KLIPOTH.

So that Third Triangle is that of Practical Magic.

It takes[39] a bit of work, but whoever is on the Path can understand how it works in the Third Triangle, because you have to stop all kinds of prejudices in order to work in that World of the Klipoth...

Netzach is the Mind, Hod is the Astral Body and Yesod, undoubtedly, is the Ninth Sphere.

Then comes the Kingdom of Malkuth, which is the Physical World; and that which is within the Physical World, that is to say, that which is within the bowels of the Earth, properly speaking in Malkuth, are the adverse Sephiroth, the Klipoth, the "Demons" (as they say), the Souls in sorrow[40], those who suffer, the lost, those who have already exhausted their cycle of existences and that [are] involuting in time, or the fallen Angels, the Genies of Evil, etc...

In those regions that exist within the Kingdom of Klipoth, I saw, undoubtedly, those who develop themselves in High Magic, and who assist anyone to repent for their mistakes and who yearn for the Light.

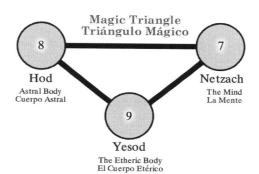

Estaba educada en la Alta Magia.

Cuando uno observa a esa criatura integrada con su Real Ser, se da cuenta de que es un MAGO BLANCO extraordinario, que conoce a fondo tanto los REINOS DE LA LUZ, como el MUNDO DE MALKUTH, o sea, el MUNDO DE LOS KLIPHOS.

Así que ese Tercer Triángulo es el de la Magia Práctica.

Cuesta un poco de trabajo que quien esté en el Sendero, pueda entender cómo se trabaja en el Tercer Triángulo, porque hay que dejar toda clase de prejuicios para poder trabajar en ese Mundo de los Kliphos...

Netzach es la Mente, Hod es el Cuerpo Astral y Yesod, indudablemente, es la Novena Esfera.

Luego viene el Reino de Malkuth, que es el Mundo Físico; y lo que está dentro del Mundo Físico, es decir, lo que está dentro de las entrañas de la Tierra, propiamente dicho, en Malkuth, son los Sephirotes adversos, los Kliphos, los "Demonios" (como se dice), las Almas en pena, los que sufren, los perdidos, aquellos que ya agotaron su ciclo de existencias y que involucionan en el tiempo, o los Ángeles caídos, los Genios del Mal, etc...

En esas regiones que existen dentro del Reino de los Kliphos, vi, indudablemente, a estos que se desarrollan en la Alta Magia, y que auxilian a cualquiera que se arrepienta de sus errores y que anhele la Luz.

---

[39] Literally 'cuesta' means "cost, be worth, be priced at, sell for; be difficult to; be expensive, turn out to be expensive; find it difficult to, find it hard to; be hard to do, be difficult to do, be hard to accomplish, cost;"
[40] Literally 'pena' means "grief, regret, sorrow, heartache, pain, trouble, woe; punishment, penalty; embarrassment;"

Thus, when we study the Tree of Life, it is quite interesting to see, first, the Wisdom of the Eternal.

The Kabalists adjust[41] the distinct Sephiroth of the hebraic Kabalah to the [different] Worlds.

They say, for example, that the ANCIENT OF DAYS is a POINT in the infinite space (lets accept this as a symbol); that CHOKMAH is governed by the RESPLENDANT ZODIAC, and [it] is true that BINAH is governed (they say) by SATURN.

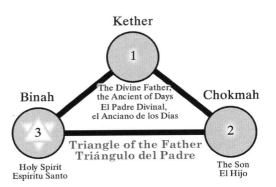

[But] there comes a point at which we have to dissent[42].

Not to say that the Holy Spirit is not ruled by Saturn, and that there is no relation of the Holy Spirit with Saturn; yes there is, but that is not all.

Because there is no doubt that he is related to the world of JUPITER, in certain ways, because he has the power, the throne. [And also] with NEPTUNE, as he is the "edifier[43] [of] the Waters of the Life".

There are those who say that NETZACH, or the Mind, is governed by VENUS; and that is all.

The Mind Is Governed by MERCURY...

But well, we are going [through each sephiroth] in order to understand [these things].

---

[41] Literally 'acomodan' means "adjust; accommodate; usher in; repair, fix;"
[42] Literally 'disentir' means "dissent, disagree;"
[43] Literally 'labra' means "till, plow, plough, toil; carve, carve out, fashion, forge, hew, tool; forge, bring about; build, edify;"

Let's study the Second Triangle, because we have seen the first...

CHESED, they say is governed directly by JUPITER and nothing more; and that is false.

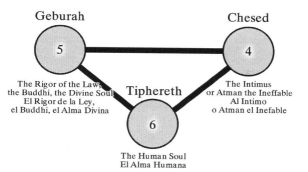

The INTIMUS is MARTIAN, [a] warrior, [a] fighter; he has to fight for his own Intimate Self-Realization.

Does it have any Jupiterian influence? [That] is also certain, because it can wield the Scepter of the Kings, but [to say] that [it] is uniquely and exclusively Jupiterian, that is false.

That GEBURAH (the Rigor, the Law) is exclusively MARTIAN [is a] mistake!

Because Geburah is a Buddhic or Intuitional World, the World of Spiritual Soul, which is female.

Here is the LION OF THE LAW, we do not deny it. It is SOLAR; that is certain.

But you know that the Lion also has nobility; here, in Geburah, we find the rigor of the Law and we find the nobility of the Lion.

The World of the Spiritual Soul, the Buddhic or Intuitional World, is completely Solar.

The World of TIPHERETH, the World of the Human Soul (or the Son, properly speaking), undoubtedly, is really governed not by the SUN, as the Kabalists claim, but by VENUS.

That is why the Christ was crucified on Good Friday, and this is something that we should meditation upon[44]...

---

[44] Literally 'debe ponernos a meditar...' means "put ourselves to meditate on..."

Estudiemos el Segundo Triángulo, ya que vimos el primero...

CHESED, dicen que está gobernado directamente por JÚPITER y nada más; y eso es falso.

El ÍNTIMO es MARCIANO, guerrero, luchador; tiene que estar peleando por su propia Auto-Realización Íntima.

¿Que tiene alguna influencia Jupiteriana? También es cierto, porque puede empuñar el Cetro de los Reyes, pero que sea única y exclusivamente Jupiteriano, eso es falso.

Que GEBURAH (el Rigor, la Ley) sea exclusivamente MARCIANA, ¡equivocación!

Porque Geburah es un Mundo Búddhico o Intuicional, el Mundo del Alma Espiritual, que es femenina.

Allí está el LEON DE LA LEY, no lo niego. Es SOLAR; eso sí es cierto.

Pero ustedes saben que el León también tiene nobleza; aquí, en Geburah, encontramos el rigor de la Ley y encontramos la nobleza del León.

El Mundo del Alma Espiritual, el Mundo Búddhico o Intuicional, es completamente Solar.

El Mundo de TIPHERETH, el Mundo del Alma Humana (o del Hijo, propiamente dicho), indubitablemente, está realmente gobernado no por el SOL, como pretenden los Kabalistas, sino por VENUS.

Por eso el Cristo es crucificado un Viernes Santo, y eso es algo que debe ponernos a meditar...

With regard[45] to the MIND, to say that it is governed by VENUS, is false.

We know well that the Mind is MERCURIAN, that Mercury gives Wisdom, [and] that Mercury gives the word, etc. The Mind is, then, Mercurian.

And if we descend a little [more] into the World of the Sephiroth, we come to the ASTRAL, this is LUNAR.

Some tribes, for example, in the very deep jungles in the Amazon, give their people or [themselves] use some special potions; such potions are administered by the Shaman.

This, for example, [is] managed [by] what is called the "yague", and combined with the guarumo. [The Shaman] cooks [the] yague and [the] guarumo in a saucepan, and the neophyte drinks it when the Moon is waxing.

Then the [ASTAL] UNFOLDING is produced.

Because they know very well, the Piaches or Priests-Witches of these tribes, that the Astral, is governed by the Moon; that is obvious.

But many Kabalists suppose that it is governed by Mercury and are mistaken.

And with regard to the VITAL PRINCIPLE or Seat of Organic Life, with regard to the Sephirah YESOD (which is closely connected with the creative organs), it is obviously LUNAR; and we cannot deny it.

In Esoteric Gnosticism [there] appears the Moon and a woman, an ineffable and divine Virgin, dressed in a blue tunic that symbolizes the night, standing on the Moon; you need to know how to understand [this]: The Moon represents the Sephirah Yesod, that is to say, the Sexual Force.

---

[45] Literally 'en cuanto' means "inasmuch as, insomuch as, as soon as"

And in terms of the color of the robe, it represents the night in which the Great Mysteries of Life and Death develop.

This signifies that ONE MUST WORK WITH THE CREATIVE ENERGY of the Third Logos ONLY AT NIGHT; NEVER IN THE DAY, i.e. the work of the Laboratorium-Oratorium of the Holy Spirit should only be in the nighttime hours.

The Sahaja Maithuna (speaking in other terms), should only be practiced during [the] darkness of night, because the day, the Sun, is the opposite of generation; that is clear.

I have already explained this to you the other day, that if a hen with eggs is missing from her brood, for example, [and] the light of the Sun [shines on those eggs], then those [eggs will be] unable to hatch, and if she leaves some chick, [it will] die; because the Sun is the enemy of generation.

Whosoever wants to search [for] the Light should ask the Logos, which is behind the Sun that illuminates us; in the profound night; that is obvious...

As for the Sephirah MALKUTH (which is the Physical World).

It is said to be a "fallen Sephirah", but the INFERNAL WORLDS also belong to Malkuth; that is clear.

In these Infernal Worlds we have to work for the emergence of life, separating the SUPERIOR WATERS from the INFERIOR [WATERS] or [the] Infernos of Leviathan.

In "Genesis," it said: "It is to separate the Superiors Waters from the Inferior"... [see Gen 1:6-7]

What are those "Superior Waters"?

Y en cuanto a la túnica de ese color, representa a la noche en que se desarrollan los Grandes Misterios de la Vida y de la Muerte.

Significa eso que SOLAMENTE EN LA NOCHE SE DEBE TRABAJAR CON LA ENERGÍA CREADORA del Tercer Logos; JAMÁS EN EL DÍA, es decir, el trabajo del Laboratorium-Oratorium del Espíritu Santo sólo debe ser en las horas nocturnas.

El Sahaja Maithuna (hablando en otros términos), sólo debe practicarse entre tinieblas de la noche, porque el día, el Sol, es el opuesto de la generación; eso es claro.

Ya les explicaba a ustedes, el otro día, que si uno echaba, por ejemplo, una gallina con sus huevos a la luz del Sol, para que los empollara, pues, aquellos no lograban ser empollados, y si salía algún polluelo, moriría; porque el Sol es enemigo de la generación.

Quien quiera buscar la Luz debe pedírsela al Logos, que está detrás del Sol que nos ilumina; en la noche profunda; eso es obvio...

En cuanto al Sephirote MALKUTH (que es el Mundo Físico).

Se dice que es un "Sephirote caído", pero los MUNDOS INFIERNOS también pertenecen a Malkuth; eso es claro.

En esos Mundos Infiernos tenemos nosotros que trabajar, separando las AGUAS SUPERIORES de las INFERIORES o Infernales de Leviatán, para que surja la vida.

En "El Génesis", ya lo dijo: "Hay que separar las Aguas Superiores de las Inferiores"... [véase Gen 1:6-7]

¿Cuáles son las "Aguas Superiores"?

The Gnostic Mystery of Lucifer	El Misterio Gnóstico de Lucifer

The Superior Waters are the "METALLIC SOUL" of the Sacred Sperm, that is to say, the MERCURY OF THE SECRET PHILOSOPHY, which must be separated from the Inferior [Waters], [but] how? Through the transmutation of the Sexual Energy.

This is like separating the Superior Waters (or the Soul of the Sperm) from the Inferior [Waters], of the same Sperm, what for? For the emergence[46] of life.

Because of these Superior Waters, which are the Mercury of the Secret Philosophy, [...X...] leaves everything.

With them one can create the Superior Existential Bodies of the Being, with them one can develop[47] the CHILD OF GOLD, with them one can radically transform the human being.

The Superior Waters, the Mercury, is also allegorized with the figure of the Devil, but we must transform the Devil into Lucifer.

This is the end of the talk for this evening, my dear brethren.

If anyone has something to ask, you can do [so] with complete liberty.

Disciple. Why do the Gnostic Teachings indicate that only in the "darkness[48]" can a new creature be engendered[49]?

Why [do they] indicate[50] that only at night is it possible to create the Superior Existential Bodies of the Being?

Las Aguas Superiores son el "ALMA METÁLICA" del Esperma Sagrado, o sea, el MERCURIO DE LA FILOSOFÍA SECRETA, que hay que separarlo de las Inferiores, ¿cómo? Mediante la transmutación de la Energía Sexual.

Así es como se separan las Aguas Superiores (o sea, el Alma del Esperma) de las Inferiores, del Esperma mismo, ¿para qué? Para que surja la vida.

Porque de esas Aguas Superiores, que es el Mercurio de la Filosofía Secreta, [...X...] sale todo.

Con ellas se pueden crear los Cuerpos Existenciales Superiores del Ser, con ellas se puede elaborar el NIÑO DE ORO, con ellas se puede transformar radicalmente el ser humano.

Las Aguas Superiores, el Mercurio, también están alegorizadas con la figura del Diablo, pero hay que transformar al Diablo en Lucifer.

Hasta aquí la plática de esta noche, mis queridos hermanos.

Si alguno tiene algo que preguntar, puede hacerlo con la más entera libertad.

Discípulo. ¿Por qué las Enseñanzas Gnósticas indican que sólo en la "obscuridad" se puede procrear una nueva criatura?

¿Por qué señalan que sólo en la noche es posible fabricar los Cuerpos Existenciales Superiores del Ser?

---

[46] Literally 'surja' means "appear, arise, emerge; intervene;"
[47] Literally 'elaborar' means "elaborate, brew, fabricate, manufacture, craft, make;"
[48] Literally 'obscuridad' means "obscurity, blackness, darkness, gloom;"
[49] Literally 'procrear' means "procreate, beget, breed, engender;"
[50] Literally 'señalan' means "signal, indicate, point at, point out, point to, finger, mark, put one's finger on, sign, designate;"

Master. The crude reality is that, due to the disposition of the creative organs, such procreation is verified in darkness, because the zoosperm goes out[51] of the sexual glands, [it is] not illuminated by the light of the Sun, but flows[52] in darkness.

In darkness it passes through the Fallopian Tubes, to encounter the ovum which descends from the Graafian Follicle[53], and is gestated within the darkness of the matrix.

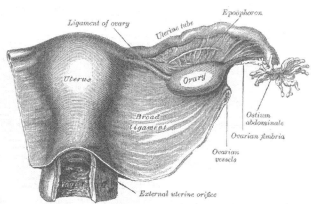

What would happen if that zoosperm, instead of exiting from the sexual glands protected by the darkness, could run under the light of the Sun, [if it] could leave uncovered, so that the Sun could shower it with its light?

What would happen if the fetus was not in the darkness, but it was uncovered in the belly of the mother, directly exposed to the light of the Sun?

It is obvious that failure would be a fact.

So, therefore, THE FERTILIZATION IS ALWAYS REALIZED IN THE DARKNESS THROUGH THE DISPOSITION OF THE SAME CREATIVE ORGANS.

Likewise, THE SAGE SHOULD ALSO WORK IN THE DARKNESS AND THE AUGUST SILENCE OF THOUGHT, in order to one day reach the Intimate Self-Realization of the Being.

---

[51] Literally 'sale' from 'salir' means "to go out, to get out, to leave, to go; to get out, to escape;"
[52] Literally 'discurre' means "to wander, to walk; to go by, to pass; to flow; to think, to reflect; to go about, to wander, to roam;"
[53] Literally 'Folículo de Graff' means "Graafian follicle or antral follicle: an ovarian follicle during a certain latter stage of folliculogenesis (the maturation of the ovarian follicle)."

The work in the night is indicated to us by that Virgin of the Immaculate Conception, standing still upon the Moon and dressed in a Blue tunic.

[…X…]

D. […X…] Dear Master, being [that] Satan [is] the Reflection of God, and therefore, being [that] Satan [is] Love, would it not be inconsistent[54] to say that "the Ego is satanic"?

M. Remember that there exist two Types of Darkness.

The first is called the DARKNESS OF SILENCE AND [THE DARKNESS] OF THE AUGUST SECRET OF THE SAGES; the second we call the DARKNESS OF IGNORANCE AND OF ERROR.

Obviously the first is the SUPER DARKNESS; indubitably, the second is the INFRA-DARKENSS.

This means that the Shadows bipolarize themselves and that the Negative is only the unfolding of the Positive.

By simple logical deduction, I invite you to comprehend that PROMETHEUS-LUCIFER, chained to the hard rock, sacrifices himself for us, [and is] subjected to all the torture, EVEN THE [ONE WHO IS] FAITHFUL TO THE SCALE, THE GIVER OF THE LIGHT, THE GUARDIAN OF THE SEVEN MANSIONS, which does not pass but those who has been anointed by Wisdom, who carries the Lamp of Hermes in their right [hand], inevitably UNFOLD THEMSELVES into a fatal aspect of egoic multiplicity, INTO THOSE sinister PSYCHIC AGGREGATES which compose our "I", and which have been duly studied by the Esoteric Tantric Buddhism.

---

[54] Literally 'incogruente' means "incongruent, incompatible, inconsistent, incoherent, incongruous;"

With this explanation, gentlemen, I believe that you have understood my words... [...X...]

D. [...X...] Can we use the Clavicle of Solomon, exclusively to evoke dangerous entities, or can it also be used to invoke the divine entities?

M. One CAN INVOKE THE ANGELS [AND] THE HOLY GODS WITH THE CLAVICLE OF SOLOMON.

In the middle ages the Clavicles were used, then, to invoke Lucifer.

Of course, you need to have a lot of valor[55] to make a type of invocation of this class.

It is very dangerous, because the individual still does not have the structure of an Adept, of a Magician, and before a question of this [kind], what happened to this good friend [may] happen to [you]: She died three days afterwards...

And it is not out [of scope], in these moments, [if I go] back to [what I] remember happened in Costa Rica: the case of the woman "whore" who lived in a state of inebriation, [going] from bar to bar.

And although it is a little grotesque to repeat her words, for the sake of the Great Cause [I will] comply in repeating them.

She said: "I, daily (forgive my expression), I sleep[56] with so many men, fourteen, fifteen, [sometimes even] twenty..."

---

[55] Literally 'valor' means "courage, manhood, valor, bravery, gallantry, grit, grittiness, pluck, derring-do, stoutheartedness, valour;"
[56] Literally 'acuesto' means "tuck in, put to sleep; lay down;"

And she said: "And if the Devil appeared to me in person", (I am refining her words, I am not totally quoting [her words], so as to [avoid] being too vulgar), "then I would also sleep with him..."

Well (recounting, [similar to how the locals] know everyone [in] the world in a village of Costa Rica), certainly, one day of those many [days,] an apparent sailor came to visit, with this women; which, of course, required affection and [he] also slept with her.

After a while that woman, then, having realized the sexual act with the sailor in question, sat down at the threshold of the door of her horrible apartment.

Sitting there watching the landscape, the panorama, [and] the people who came and went, etc., etc. Suddenly she felt someone was calling; it was the sailor:

He said [to] her: "You do not know me; You think you know me because you slept with me, but you're wrong, [you] do not know me.

You should look inward to know me."

Then she turned to look, and [what] did she see?

LUCIFER was converted into a true Devil, terrible, as he is depicted [in] mythology out there, with all his cavernous horrors.

The woman fell [down] instantly "fainting[57]". [And] three days later she died in the hospital.

Those who witnessed that apartment said that [a smell of] sulfur was coming out of it.

For a time, people did not want to pass by that street.

---

[57] Literally 'privada' means "knock unconscious, knock out, render unconscious;"

Of course, before she died, [she] told [me] her story, it was enough to tell someone, but [she could] not resist, [she] died...

What happened? Well her very Lucifer, who was so horrible, clearly intervened for her own good.

Possibly (I am not saying "possibly", but [rather] that it is obvious) [HE] WAS SENT BY THE ANCIENT OF DAYS, by her own Father[58], who is in secret, and [he] actualized, [or] materialized himself physically.

Clearly, the lesson for the woman was terrible: [she] disincarnated.

We can be sure that when that woman retakes a body, when she returns, [she will] never again fall into prostitution.

Now it is possible for her to follow the Path of Chastity, because the lesson that she received was very bitter, that is, her Father who is in secret, solved[59] [this problem by] carrying out a "surgical operation".

Yes, the Elegance[60] [of the situation] is worthy of that part of the Being called Lucifer, and [as a result] much later [on] this woman can even walk the Path[61].

D. Venerable [Master], and then [in order] to "whiten" our Lucifer, what do we do?

M. DESTROY THE EGO, reduce it to cosmic dust.

It is necessary to be dressed in White.

---

[58] Literally this would read "by her own Father of her's"
[59] Literally 'resolvió' means "resolve, determine, decide; solve, find a solution;"
[60] Literally 'Gracia' means "wit, funniness, wittiness; grace, charm, elegance, loveliness, gracefulness, piquancy, spice, graciosity, graciousness"
[61] Literally this would read "can even come to grasp the Way"

Furthermore: It is necessary to dress with the Purple of the Kings.

We must feel pity[62] for our own Lucifer.

D. And if he sometimes... [...X...] ?

M. HE GIVES THE SEXUAL IMPULSE to the whole world.

What is [critical] to know is [how] to make use of[63] this impulse, [but] how?

Thrusting[64] the Lance into his side.

You remember that "*Lucifer is [the] staircase to descend and remember that Lucifer is [the] staircase to ascend*".

Read the "Divine Comedy", and in it [you will] find ample illustration of Lucifer, in the Ninth Sphere.

D. Master, how is it that you say that Krishnamurti has absolutely no[65] Ego, when in reality, after the Second Mountain, the Master still has to continue executing [the] work to achieve Perfection, and [is this because] before achieving Resurrection [one] has to work in the Infernos of different planets, disintegrating, let's say, [the] germs of Ego?

---

[62] Literally 'piedad' means "pity, compassion, mercy, ruth, sorriness; piety, devotion, piousness;"
[63] Litearlly 'aprovechar' means "make good use of, make use of, utilize, avail, capitalize on, profit by, utilise; take the opportunity, take advantage; make use of; be useful, be helpful, be a help;"
[64] Literally 'Clavando' means "nail down; knock in; spike; rivet; fasten; thrust; plunge"
[65] Literally this would read "completely nothing of [the]"

M. Yes, KRISHNAMURTI, the lord Krishnamurti, is a very ancient Soul; but really, despite the fact that he does not have, we [could] say, what is called "Ego", therefore, he has not achieved the Resurrection, because he lacks something.

Obviously, one must descend to the Ninth Sphere to work.

Clearly, SOMETHING MUST BE ELIMINATED which he is unacquainted[66] [with].

But if we say that he has no Ego, that [he] is clean of Egos, that is, in what is [only] humanly understandable.

Because beyond, there are still certain "elements" that escape, we [can] say, the comprehension of everyone and we have to disintegrate [those] as well.

D. Venerable Master, returning to Genesis, regarding a question that was previously [asked], which is to say that after the separation of the sexes, not all fell and that those great Masters who have not fallen since their exaltation continue on their Path.

But has every Master in a past Maha-Manvantara necessarily descended, or [have they] necessarily always been produced [from] the Paradisiacal Fall?

M. Well, there is [a fall] in "Genesis", [and there] is [one] in the "Revolt of the Angels"; nonetheless [we must] DISTINGUISH THAT WHICH IS A FALL[67] FROM [THAT WHICH IS] A DESCENT[68].

M. Sí, KRISHNAMURTI, el señor Krishnamurti, es un Alma muy antigua; pero realmente, a pesar de que no tiene, dijéramos, lo que se llama "Ego", pues, no ha conseguido la Resurrección, porque le falta algo.

Obviamente, debe bajar a la Novena Esfera a trabajar.

Claro, que ALGO TIENE QUE ELIMINAR, que él desconoce.

Pero si decimos que no tiene Ego, que está limpio de Egos, así es, en lo que es humanamente comprensible.

Porque más allá, todavía existen ciertos "elementos" que escapan, dijéramos, a la comprensión de todos y que hay que desintegrar también.

D. Venerable Maestro, volviendo al Génesis, sobre una pregunta que se hizo anteriormente, es decir que después de la separación de los sexos, no todos cayeron y que esos grandes Maestros que no habían caído pues, siguieron su Camino, su exaltación.

Pero, ¿necesariamente, todo Maestro en un pasado Maha-Manvantara ha debido bajar, o necesariamente siempre se produce la Caída Paradisiaca?

M. Pues, así está en el "Génesis", así está en la "Revuelta de los Ángeles"; empero hay que DISTINGUIR LO QUE ES UNA CAÍDA DE UNA BAJADA.

---

[66] Literally 'desconoce' means "be ignorant of, be unacquainted with, know not; fail to recognize, be unable to recognize, recognize not;"
[67] Literally 'caída' means "fall, collapse, downfall, downturn, drop, falling, falling-off, tumble;"
[68] Literally 'bajada' means "descent, downgrade, drop, going-down, lowering, way down;"

Many confuse a "fall" with a "descent"; and in both cases the Initiate goes down[69] to the Infernal Worlds, to the Ninth Dantesque Circle, to work with the Fire and the Water, origin of worlds, beasts, Men and Gods, then lends itself, we [could] say, to many interpretations.

But we must never confuse a "fall" with a "descent".

They are different, and "falls" and "descents" always appear in every Genesis.

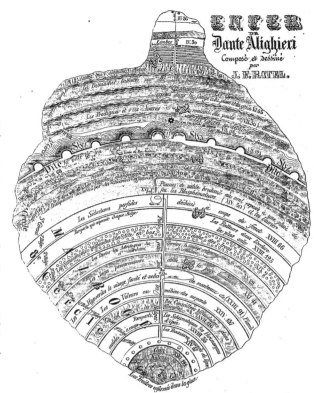

D. I mean, the error, shall we say, of Sakaky, which is always processing itself?

M. Well, [the error of] Sakaky is not processed in all the cases; THE ARCHANGEL SAKAKY WAS MISTAKEN HERE, in this Solar System, or on this planet Earth; but that is a case for a new paragraph[70]...

D. Yes Master. I mean that, referring to Sakaky, not referring myself to that same drama, [maybe it] was not Sakaky, [it] was another one, [who] perpetually produced the Fall?

M. IN EVERY UNIVERSE [WHICH IS] BORN, [THERE] ARE FALLS AND [THERE] ARE DESCENTS.

---

[69] Literally 'desciende' means "descend, climb down, go down, walk down;"
[70] Literally 'punto y aparte' means "period and apart"

The Elohim must go down, but some times [they] fall; but in any case they need to descend, to amplify[71] themselves, to descend in order to later be able to ascend, [and] to arise victoriously.

That is to say, all ascent is preceded by a descent; *"all exaltation is preceded by a frightful and terrible humiliation"*.

If not, [then] where would the merit be?

D. Master, when a Master submerges themselves into the Absolute Sun [do they] convert themselves into an Aelohim?

M. Well, I do not think that it is possible to be turned into [an] Elohim in the Absolute...

D. [An] Aelohim...

M. An Elohim, in order to be able to submerge itself into the Absolute, first [has] to convert [itself] into [an] Elohim and afterwards [it has] to submerge

D. First one is converted into [an] Aelohim...

M. What did you say?

D. No, this is the question I am asking: What is it that converts itself into [an] Aelohim...

M. Aelohim is Aelohim, and Elohim is Elohim.

---

[71] Literally 'expandirse' means "expand, amplify, enlarge, augment, bulk, bulk out, extend, aggrandize; elongate, stretch"

AELOHIM is the Eternal Common Cosmic Father, the Infinitude[72] that sustains everything, the Omni-merciful[73], the Ineffable Absolute, and ELOHIM is the Second Unity, the manifested Unity, the Host[74] of the Elohim Creators, the Host of the Androgynous ones who created the Universe, etc., etc., that is to say, the Army of the Word, the Army of the Voice, the Verb.

Indubitably, the Elohim that submerge themselves into the bosom of the Eternal Cosmic Father, into the Absolute, receive their true name, which is that of PARAMARTHA-SATYA.

A Paramartha-satya is something ineffable, something impossible to comprehend at a simple glance.

The Paramartha-satya is beyond good and evil, [it is] far beyond the Personality, [and far beyond] the Individuality and the "I".

The Paramartha-satya is transparent like a crystal, [it is] terribly divine.

Very few are those who manage to become Paramartha-satyas.

D. Master, returning to Lucifer. Since one has to whiten Lucifer, right?, I mean one has turn him brilliant [white], right?, into Brass, then, he himself can collaborate with us so that we[75] convert him into that exalted Lucifer?

M. He COLLABORATES WITH THE TEMPTATION, because if not, in what other way could [he] collaborate?

---

[72] Literally 'infinitud' means "infinitude, infinity, infiniteness, limitlessness;"
[73] Literally 'misericordioso' means "merciful, compassionate, forgiving, gracious, clement;"
[74] Literally 'hueste' means "crew, squad, battalion, troop, host;"
[75] Literally this would say "collaborate with one so that one"

"Temptation is fire, but triumph over temptation is Light".

If one overcomes the temptation, then one overcomes Lucifer.

When overcoming him, upon the same body of Lucifer, on his back, one triumphs, [and then one is] raised up...

You remember that in the "Divine Comedy" of the Dante Alighieri, Virgil goes down on the ribs of Mr. Lucifer and also goes up on the ribs of Mr. Lucifer.

> "Lucifer is the stairs to descend, Lucifer is the stairs to ascend".

If we overcome temptation, we ascend on the very same back of Lucifer... [...X...] ... he puts the temptation [in front of] us so that we can ascend.

Now you can see Christ disguised as Lucifer: How grandiose is **CHRISTUS-LUCIFER**!

How grandiose, putting the "stairs" for us so that we [can] raise up!

D. Venerable [Master], you said that Krishnamurti has aged[76], but when the Phoenix Bird rose from the ashes, Krishnamurti mounted him and elevated himself...

M. I did not say anything [like that]; I said that Krishnamurti is lacking something and that is all.

What [is] he lacking?

Only he knows that [which] he lacks.

"La tentación es fuego, pero el triunfo sobre la tentación es Luz".

Si uno vence la tentación, pues vence a Lucifer.

Al vencerlo, sobre el mismo cuerpo de Lucifer, sobre las espaldas de él, triunfa uno, sube...

Recuerden ustedes que en la "Divina Comedia" del Dante Alighieri, Virgilio baja por las costillas del Señor Lucifer y sube por las costillas, también, del Señor Lucifer.

> "Lucifer es escalera para bajar, Lucifer es escalera para subir".

Si vencemos la tentación, subimos por las mismísimas espaldas de Lucifer... [...X...] ...él nos pone la tentación para que nosotros podamos subir.

Vean ustedes a Cristo, disfrazado como Lucifer: ¡Cuán grandioso es **CHRISTUS-LUCIFER**!

¡Cuán grandioso, poniéndonos la "escalera" para que subamos!

D. Venerable, dice usted que Krishnamurti ha envejecido, pero cuando el Ave Fénix resurgió de las cenizas, Krishnamurti montó en él y se elevó...

M. No digo nada; yo digo que a Krishnamurti le falta algo y eso es todo.

¿Que le faltará?

Solamente él lo sabe qué le falta.

---

[76] Literally 'envejecido' means "aged, ancient, out-of-date, aging, elderly, obsolete, old, old-looking, long in the tooth;"

I said that he lacks the descent into the Infernal Worlds; well, that is my concept [of his situation], others can think differently.

D. Master, in reading the book of Krishnamurti, the Bhagavad Gita, one can see... [that] it is very deep, but does not descent into the Infernos; and speaking with some [of] his Adepts[77], one sees that they do not work with the Third Logos.

Because they are simply "abstinent" and they say that they use sex solely to procreate.

That is [to say], that if they have his Teaching [then this] means that he does not work in that aspect...

M. The work of the BHAGAVAD GITA is a very wise work, IT HAS TWO SIDES: the PUBLIC and the SECRET.

Because in the secret side, we can see perfectly that ALL OF THE ESOTERIC WORK is defined.

Because we encounter ARJUNA under the direction of one's Internal God, KRISHNA, fighting terribly on the battlefield against their relatives [with the] lance in hand; this is nothing other than THE FIGHT AGAINST THE inhuman PSYCHIC AGGREGATES, which we all carry in our interior.

So when the lance and everything is spoken of, one must know how to understand it.

Krishna indubitably, was a Great Avatar...

What [did] you say?

---

[77] Literally 'algunos Adeptos en su propiedad' means "some Adepts under his possession"

D. Venerable [Master], [we should] establish a differentiation between Krishna and Krishnamurti, that they are two different things, right?

M. Yes, because we are speaking..., she has asked for Krishna and the Bhagavad Gita, right?

D. [...X...]

M. Krishnamurti is another thing, right?

We know well that Mr. Krishnamurti lives at the moment in Ohio, the United States, right?

So then, to whom you are referring?

D. Well, Master, sincerely, I was referring to to that which the Master was mentioning...

The one that wrote the Bhagavad Gita...

M. The one who wrote the Bhagavad Gita is one thing, that is Krishna, and Krishnamurti is another thing, [which] is [for a] new paragraph...

D. Ah, good!...

D. Master, why it is a crime[78] to throw [away] the Philosopher's Stone more than seven times?

M. Well, because THE CHRISTUS IS ALREADY EXPOSED TO [SO] MUCH SUFFERING; in such a way that it is possible to fall under [a] curse.

Let's see, brother....

---

[78] Literally 'delito' means "crime, felony; misdemeanor, misdeed"

D. Venerable Master, when I have worked with Lucifer, with the Divine Daimon, to leave in [the] Astral Body, or in Jinas, and especially to know my bestial entities in the different Levels of the Subconscious [mind] I have been with the Terrible Brother, [but] must I overcome him or be friends with the Terrible Brother?...

M. Well, you must overcome him, if you want to overcome.

But remember that everything is symbolic.

Remember that what interests us is, practically [speaking], the death of the myself, of the oneself.

While a man does not pass through the death of the Ego, while he is not beheaded, then, obviously, [he] marches on the path of error.

This is why[79] Mr. Lucifer interests us, because he serves as stairs for us to ascend; and that is all.

And it is from this most interesting, [and] important point of view [that we must see him]; and that is what is in this cathedra[80], [which] especially interests us.

I am referring to this cathedra specifically.

The death of the animal Ego is fundamental...

Let's see, brother....

D. Venerable Master, returning to Genesis [and the Archangel Sakaky], okay?

D. Venerable Maestro, cuando he trabajado con Lucifer, con el Divino Daimon, para salir en Cuerpo Astral, o en Jinas, y especialmente para conocer mi entidades bestiales en los diferentes Niveles del Subconsciente me he encontrado con el Hermano Terrible, ¿lo debo vencer o debo ser amigo de el Hermano Terrible?...

M. Pues, debes vencerlo, si quieres vencerlo.

Pero recuérdese que todo eso es simbólico.

Recuérdese que lo que nos interesa a nosotros es, prácticamente, la muerte del mí mismo, del sí mismo.

Mientras un hombre no pase por la muerte del Ego, mientras no sea decapitado, pues, obviamente, marcha por el camino del error.

Para algo nos interesa el Señor Lucifer, porque nos sirve de escalera para subir; y eso es todo.

Y es desde ese punto de vista interesantísimo, importante; y es lo que en esta cátedra, especialmente, nos debe interesar.

Me refiero, específicamente, a esta cátedra.

La muerte del Ego animal es fundamental...

A ver, hermano....

D. Venerable Maestro, volviendo al Génesis, ¿no?

---

[79] Literally 'Para algo' means "For something"
[80] Literally 'cáthedra' means "cathedra, professorship, university instructor, teacher, chair, official chair (as of university professor); bishop's throne or chair; position or duties of a bishop;"

And as the Bible says, that man was only... [...X...] ...producing a drama..., this..., the question would be the following: [There] exists the Luciferic Power, what reason was there then [to] give to humanity the Kundartiguador Organ...?

M. That WAS NECESSARY at some epoch; [BUT] THERE WERE ERRORS IN CALCULATION, [WHICH] IS ANOTHER THING.

Obviously each organic machine captures certain types and subtypes of Cosmic Energy, which [it] soon transforms and retransmits to the following layers of the planetary organism in which we live.

Since you asked [about] what happened in those Lemurian times, then [we will explain], the Earth did not have stability, the geological crust shook, there were incessant earthquakes, [so the Kundartiguator Organ] was considered necessary, then, what [happened was that] this machine which served to transform Energies (mistakenly called "Man"), then, should readapt, and he was given the abominable KUNDARTIGUADOR ORGAN.

The result [of this] was magnificent: The stabilization of the geological crust was established; but there was a MISCALCULATION[81] by the Great ANGEL SAKAKY, because [he] failed IN TRANSFINITE NUMBERS.

[81] Literally this would read "an ERROR OF CALCULATION"

That miscalculation, caused humanity to have the Kundartiguador Organ much longer than a certain normal time, that is to say, "it was the hand" of Archangel Sakaky [which specifically caused this]; and the result was that, when the abominable Kundartiguador Organ disappeared (due to the intervention of the COMMON ARCHI-PHYSICAL-CHEMICAL SERAFIM ANGEL LOISOS), the evil consequences of the abominable Kundartiguador Organ were already in the human organism.

Those evil consequences are the cruel psychic aggregates that we all carry in our interior; I am referring, in an emphatic form, to the "I's", that personify our defects…

You said what to me, brother?

D. Can we establish that Lucifer is the docile sexual impulse, the Guide Dog?

M. YES, SEE IT FROM THAT POINT OF VIEW.

In the end, Lucifer is the REFLECTION OF THE LOGOS in us, who gives that impulse.

If we managed to thrust[82] the lance into Lucifer, dominating the sexual impulse, then, we rise degree by degree, with the same body of Mr. Lucifer [as did Virgil and Dante].

For that reason it is said to you, in humorous form, that if we truly want to arrive at the Intimate Self-realization of the Being, we needed to have the Devil as a godparent[83]…

D. Venerable [Master], I mean that, to really polish the Mandate of Rome, is "to whiten the Brass"?

---

[82] Literally 'clavarle' means "nail down, nail, fix with nails, nail in; hammer, hammer in, knock in, strike in;"
[83] Literally 'compadre' means "godfather, fellow parent; friend;"

M. Well, the Brass does not whiten if the Sacrament of the Church of Rome is not refined.

IF THE SACRAMENT of the Church of Rome IS REFINED IT WHITENS THE BRASS; on condition that one work on the psychic aggregates which we carry in our interior, to destroy them with Lance of Longinus.

D. Master, we know what a Master is, [we can] declare [him] then, the King of the Nature, and that the Elements, for example like the Gnomes and Pigmies of the Earth obey the Master, [they also] do so in trying to fix those problems that exist in the layers of the Earth, [and so] was it not possible [for that] to be done by means of orders from the Ineffable Masters, we [could] say, [by] ordering the Gnomes and Pigmies to execute that work?

M. Well, the Masters are not empirical, they work with the very same Laws of Nature; "they imitate Nature and with Nature they transform Nature", this is stipulated by Sendivogius[84], the Great Medieval Alchemist.

So it is indubitable that LAWS CANNOT BE BROKEN; it is necessary to use the same Laws so as to be able to organize Nature...

D. I mean, that would have been almost like a leap, thus, what would have been given [to] Nature...

M. What you are saying would be empirical; IT IS NECESSARY TO WORK IN AGREEMENT WITH THE RULES ACCORDING TO ART:

> "Nature transforms into Nature and obeys the very same Nature".

---

[84] Michael Sendivogius (1566 - 1636) was a Polish alchemist, philosopher, and medical doctor.

The Alchemist must know how to imitate Nature if they want to triumph.

For example: If somebody wants to create the Superior Existential Bodies of the Being, if they want, they will have to work at night in the Ninth Sphere, not in the day; why?

Because in the day the solar rays are active, and they are detrimental for all generation.

Put down a chicken egg, for example, in the light of the sun, to see if the hen hatches, to see if they leave, if the chick leaves [its shell].

But the nest of the hen is placed in darkness, [and she] will leave the chicks there.

It is always necessary to work with the very same Rules of the very same Nature.

Not in an empirical way; everything has its science, and the Masters must act in accordance with the Rules of Science according to [the] art...

D. Master, it is true that Lucifer can be used to make pacts to secure money?

MY father, when I was small told, me that one day [he] had gone to a mount, that [he] had taken a cat, and that he had thrown [it in] alive to boil [it] in a copper container; and that soon he had to leave and with that water... [...X...] ... and soon to go upon a path... [...X...] ... and hand over with a feather in the mouth; and there Lucifer appeared to him, and to release the feather to Lucifer; and then that Lucifer said to him that he [could] ask him [for] what [he] wanted; and that he, then, wanted to request wealth from him.

Then, Lucifer can be used for those things?

El Alquimista tiene que saber imitar a la Naturaleza si es que quiere triunfar.

Por ejemplo: Si alguien quiere crear los Cuerpos Superiores Existenciales del Ser, si los quiere, tendrá que trabajar en la noche en la Novena Esfera, no en el día; ¿por qué?

Porque en el día los rayos solares están activos, y son ellos perjudiciales para toda generación.

Póngase unos huevos de gallina, por ejemplo, a la luz del sol, que la gallina los empolle, a ver si salen, si salen los polluelos.

Pero si se coloca el nido de la gallina en las tinieblas, de allí saldrán los polluelos.

Siempre hay que trabajar con las mismísimas Reglas de la mismísima Naturaleza.

No en forma empírica; todo tiene su ciencia, y los Maestros tienen que actuar de acuerdo con las Reglas de la Ciencia según arte...

D. Maestro, ¿es verdad que el Lucifer se puede utilizar para hacer pactos para conseguir dinero?

MI padre, cuando yo estaba pequeña, me contaba que un día había ido a un monte, que había cogido un gato, y lo había echado a hervir vivo en una vasija de cobre; y que luego tenía que salir y con esa agua... [...X...] ...y luego salir a un camino... [...X...] ...y pasar con una pluma en la boca; y ahí se le aparecía Lucifer, y descargarle la pluma a Lucifer; y entonces que el Lucifer le decía que le pidiese lo que quisiera; y que él, pues, que le quería pedir riqueza.

Entonces, ¿el Lucifer se puede utilizarse para esas cosas?

Clearly, he did not reach completion, because he was scared.

M. Well, the reality is that with those operations of Black Magic, what the people do is to invoke Demons.

HE IS NOT FOR THOSE THINGS, he is the Reflection of the Logos, the same Christ within us, Christus-Lucifer is sacred.

When he provides us with a lot of temptation, it[85] is for our own good...

D. Excuse me...

M. Yes, brother...

D. How can we differentiate the Sensual "I" from [the] Luciferian Impulse?

M. From what?...

D. From [the] Luciferian Impulse, from Lucifer?

M. Well, [BY] AWAKENING THE CONSCIOUSNESS.

The sleeping ones do not know of these things.

The sleeping one sleeps [with] this and "[they] get the wrong end of the stick[86]", one and a million times; that is clear...

Let's see, brother...

D. Master, forgive me, as [a] discipline, can we say, normalize what questions we ask of Third Chamber?

---

[85] Literally 'y eso' means "and this"
[86] Literally 'confunde la gimnasia con la magnesia' means "he confuses gymnastics with magnesium".

Because often those [of us] that are instructors only ask questions of First Chamber; can we, as [a] discipline, be standardized [with] this criterion?

M. Well, we are in Third Chamber and I understand that the questions that are being asked are of Third Chamber, right?

D. Since we have heard questions of First Chamber, for that reason I ask the question: if it is possible to ask questions of First, of Second, or exclusively of Third Chamber?

M. Well, we return again to the question [of] "Consciousness": This small group although it is in Third Chamber still is not wide-awake, and then, THE MASTER MUST BE SUFFICIENTLY COMPREHENSIVE, [so] as to empower the class.

Because if one converts oneself into a character[87], we [can] said, [a] reactionary [character], into a hard character, first of all, naturally one would not be capable of giving the class.

It is necessary to have, we [could] said, comprehension with the students; although this is the class of Third Chamber, since, all do not comprehend the totality and it is necessary to try to descend to their level so that they can understand.

D. Understood, Master…

M. Let's see…

D. Master, it is said that Lucifer is [the] stairs to go up and to go down; then, what would become of us if he did not exist?

---

[87] Literally 'personaje' means "character, personage, fiction character, persona; big name, big wheel, personage, personality, remarkable person;"

M. Then, [our] existence [itself] would be inconceivable, as well as [the existence] of that person.

IF LUCIFER DID NOT EXIST, YOU WOULD NOT EXIST: Since you exist you need a sexual impulse; surging[88], which caused the father and the mother who brought you into the world to create your physical body that you actually have [now].

In this way, if Lucifer did not exist you would not exist, nor would anything exist which is present here; that is the crude reality of facts.

But Lucifer is not a separate individual, like that devil who puts those remedies there, with an enormous trident[89] and [who] governs the Universe, no.

Lucifer is the Reflection of the Logos within ourselves.

Everyone has their own Lucifer.

I believe that the cathedra, then, has already concluded.

We are going to give some treatments, but do not leave me with a heap of treatments, because we can not catch up [with] the time…

A baby that was going to be brought to me…, a sister that…, [it is] good I have spoken of a psychic subject; [it is] good that [this is] like an exception because in Third Chamber [one] does not make those. The baby, bring it!…

---

[88] Literally 'surgió' means "spring forth; appear; arise, emerge"
[89] Literally 'tenedor' means "fork; possessor, bearer, holder; trident; payee"

Extracted from the Lecture   **Extraído de la Conferencia**

Sephira / Sephirote	Attribute / Atributo	Association / Asociación	Triangle / Triángulo	World(s) / Mundo(s)
Kether	Father / Padre	The Ancient of Days / El Anciano de los Días	Logoic / Logoico	A Point in the Infinite Space / Un Punto en el Espacio Infinito
Chokmah	Son / Hijo	Cosmic Christ / Christo Cósmico	Logoic / Logoico	Resplendant Zodiac / Zodíaco Resplande
Binah	Holy Spirit / Espíritu Santo	Ruach Elohim	Logoic / Logoico	Saturn, Jupiter & Neptune / Saturno, Júpiter & Neptuno
Daath	Wisdom or Knowledge / Conocimiento o Sapiencia	Perfect Tantric Knowledge / Conocimiento Tántrico Perfecto		
Chesed	Atman	The Intimus [Inner Being] / El Intimo [Ser Interno]	Ethical / Ético	Mars & Jupiter / Marte & Júpiter
Geburah	Buddhi or Intuition / Buddhi o Intuicion	Divine or Spiritual Soul / Alma Divina o Espiritual	Ethical / Ético	Sun & Mars / Sol & Marte
Tiphereth	Manas	Human Soul / Alma Humana	Ethical / Ético	Venus / Venus
Netzach	Mind / Mente	Wisdom / Sabiduría	Magical / Mágico	Mercury / Mercurio
Hod	Astral	[Emotions / Emociones]	Magical / Mágico	Moon / Luna
Yesod	Vital Principle / Principio Vital	The Sexual Force & the Metallic Soul / La Fuerza Sexual & el Alma Metálica	Magical / Mágico	Moon / Luna
Malkuth	Physical World / Mundo Físico	Fallen Sephira / Sephirote Caído		[Earth / Tierra]
Klipoth / Kliphos	Atomic Infernos / Infernos Atómicos	Infernal Worlds / Mundos Infernales		The Bowels of the Earth / Las Entrañas de la Tierra

*The Luciferic Roots
of the Great Work*

*Raíces Luciféricas
de la Gran Obra*

Extract of pages 1009-1015 of
THE FIFTH GOSPEL:

"LUCIFERIC ROOTS OF THE GREAT WORK[1]"

Beloved brethren: today we meet here reunited in order to investigate[2], to study and to define the path that will lead[3] us to final Liberation.

The old medieval alchemists spoke of the "Great Work", and this is quite interesting...

In the ground, in the floor of the old gothic cathedrals, a multitude of concentric circles [can] be seen, forming a true labyrinth that traveled[4] or went from the center to the periphery and [from] the periphery to the center.

Much has been said about labyrinths; tradition also speaks about the labyrinth[5] of Crete and the famous Cretan Minotaur.

Certainly, in Crete a labyrinth was recently found (it was called "ABSOLUM"; as if saying: "ABSOLUTE").

"ABSOLUTE" is the term that was used [by] the medieval alchemists to designate the Philosopher's Stone.

Behold, then, a great mystery.

---

[1] This lecture is #98 and has also been called "THE MAGNUS OPUS OR THE GREAT WORK"
[2] Literally 'con el propósito de investigar' means "with the proposition of investigating"
[3] Literally 'conducirnos' means "conduct, direct, manage, drive; guide, walk, usher; lead"
[4] Literally 'llegaba' means "arrive, come; reach; roll along; land; immigrate; invade; get; travel; vaporize"
[5] In Greek mythology, the Labyrinth was an elaborate structure designed and built by the legendary artificer Daedalus for King Minos of Crete at Knossos. Its function was to hold the Minotaur, a mythical creature that was half man and half bull which was eventually killed by the Athenian hero Theseus.

Extracto de páginas 1009-1015 de
EL QUINTO EVANGELIO:

"RAÍCES LUCIFÉRICAS DE LA GRAN OBRA[6]"

Queridos hermanos: hoy nos encontramos aquí reunidos con el propósito de investigar, estudiar y definir el camino que ha de conducirnos a la Liberación final.

Los antiguos alquimistas medievales hablaban sobre la "Gran Obra", y eso es bastante interesante...

En el suelo, en el piso de las antiguas catedrales góticas, se veían multitud de círculos concéntricos, formando un verdadero laberinto que llegaba o iba del centro a la periferia y de la periferia al centro.

Mucho es lo que se ha dicho sobre los laberintos; también habla la tradición sobre el laberinto de Creta y sobre el famoso Minotauro Cretense.

Ciertamente, en Creta se encontró recientemente un laberinto (lo llamaban "ABSOLUM"; como quien dice: "ABSOLUTO").

"ABSOLUTO" es el término que utilizaban los alquimistas medievales para designar a la Piedra Filosofal.

He ahí, pues, un gran misterio.

---

[6] También se llama "EL MAGNUS OPUS O LA GRAN OBRA"

We need the THREAD OF ARIADNE[7], like Theseus, to get out of that mysterious labyrinth.

Obviously, one has to enter [into] and get out of the labyrinth.

In the center there was always the Minotaur. Theseus managed to overcome it (and here is the greek tradition).

We also need to overcome[8] him, we need to destroy the animal Ego. So as to arrive at the center of the labyrinth, where the Minotaur is, [and to do so] it is necessary to fight a lot.

There are innumerable theories, schools of all species, organizations of all types. One says that the way is over here, others that [it is] over that way, others that it is over there, and we must orient ourselves in the middle of that great labyrinth of theories and antithetical[9] concepts, if we truly want to arrive at the living center of ourselves, because it is precisely in the center where we can find the Minotaur.

When one has managed to arrive at the center of the labyrinth, one must use one's wits[10] to get out of it.

Theseus managed to leave the strange labyrinth by means of a mysterious thread (the "Thread of Ariadne").

Nosotros necesitamos, como Teseo, el HILO DE ARIADNA para salir de aquel laberinto misterioso.

Obviamente, hay que entrar y salir del laberinto.

En el centro se encontraba siempre el Minotauro. Teseo logró vencerlo (he allí la tradición griega).

Nosotros también necesitamos vencerlo, necesitamos destruir al Ego animal. Para llegar al centro del laberinto, donde está el Minotauro, hay que luchar muchísimo.

Hay innumerables teorías, escuelas de toda especie, organizaciones de todo tipo. Unas dicen que el camino es por allá, otras que por aquí, otras que por acullá, y nosotros tenemos que orientarnos en medio de ese gran laberinto de teorías y de conceptos antitéticos, si es que queremos, en verdad, llegar hasta el centro viviente del mismo, porque es precisamente en el centro donde podemos hallar al Minotauro.

Cuando uno ha logrado llegar al centro del laberinto, tiene que ingeniárselas para salir de él.

Teseo, mediante un hilo misterioso (el "Hilo de Ariadna"), logró salir del extraño laberinto.

---

[7] Theseus was aided by Ariadne, who provided him with a twisted piece of thread, literally the "clew", or "clue", so he could find his way out again.
[8] Literally 'vencerlo' means "get the best of, conquer, overcome, beat"
[9] Literally 'antitéticos' means "antithetic, antithetical; oppositional;"
[10] Literally 'ingeniárselas' means "engineer, conceive, invent, contrive, devise;"

That [thread] of "Ariadne" appears to us to [be] HIRAM, the Secret Master that occult masonry speaks of and that we all must resurrect[11] within ourselves, here and now.

"Ariadne[12]" also indicates to us the "Spider[13]", symbol of the Soul that incessantly weaves the loom of destiny.

Therefore, brethren, the hour to reflect has arrived...

Fig. 170.—Sleeping Ariadne (Vatican).

But, what in fact is that "Thread of Ariadne"?, what is that thread which saves the Soul, which allows one to leave that mysterious labyrinth in order to arrive at one's Real Inner Being?

Much has been said about the subject[14]; the great alchemists thought that it was the Philosopher's Stone.

We are in agreement with that, but we go just a little bit further, [and] in agreement with our discourse[15], then, [we can say] that in truth the Philosopher's Stone is symbolized in the Cathedral of Notre Dame in Paris by Lucifer (now we will comprehend why the Philosopher's Stone is [found] in sex itself).

Thus, we discover Lucifer in the sexual organs.

Lucifer is, then, the "Thread of Ariadne" which leads us to the final Liberation.

This seems rather, we could say, kind of antithetical or paradoxical, because everyone has [the] concept that Lucifer (the Devil, Satan) is evil.

---

[11] Literally 'resucitar' means "resuscitate, bring back to life, pull back to life, revive;"
[12] Ariadne from Greek: **Αριάδνη** (Cretan Greek αρι [ari] "most" and αδνος [adnos] "holy", Latin: Ariadna; "most holy").
[13] The Greek word for spider is "αράχνη" (arachne) compare with "αριάδνη" (araidne)
[14] Literally 'particular' means "individual, citizen, civilian, private citizen, private individual, private person; matter, point;"
[15] Literally 'disquisiciones' means "disquisition, formal discourse on a subject;"

We need evident self-reflection, if we want to penetrate deeply[16] into the Great Arcanum.

This Lucifer that we find in sex, is the Living Stone, [the] "head of the corner[17]", the Master Stone, the Cornerstone (in the Cathedral of Notre Dame in Paris), the Stone of Truth.

To penetrate a little deeper, then, into these mysteries, is indispensable when one is trying to know [what] the "Thread of Ariadne" [is]...

Once again I remind you, [of] the famous [initiation rites in the] Sacred Sanctuaries of the authentic Gnostic-Rosicrucians ([the] esotericists of the Middle Ages): when the neophyte was led to the center of the Lumisial, he was wearing [a] blindfold [over] his eyes.

Somebody pulled off[18] the blindfold and then the astonished and perplexed neophyte contemplated an unusual figure.

There he was, before its presence, the MALE GOAT of Mendez ([that] strange figure [of] the Devil). Horns shined upon its forehead, [and] on its head [was] a torch of fire (however, something indicates that [this figure should be] treated as a symbol).

In the Lumisial of Initiation, the neophyte was before the figure of TYPHON BAPHOMET, the terrible figure of Arcanum 15 of the Kabalah (the torch, burning on his head, shinning [brightly]).

---

[16] Literally 'ahondar' means "deepen, delve, penetrate deeply;"
[17] Literally 'ángulo' means "angle, space between two or more lines which are joined at a common point; corner"
[18] Literally 'arrancaba' means "pull out, pluck, rip away, rip off, rip out, tear away, uproot; start, take off, pull off, set off, pick off;"

Additionally, the Blazing Star of five points, with the superior angle upwards and both inferior angles downwards, indicates to us that [this] is not a tenebrous[19] figure.

The neophyte was ordered to kiss the Devil's backside[20].

If the neophyte disobeyed, the blindfold was put on him again and he was taken out through a secret door (all this was happening in the middle [of the] night; the neophyte never knew from where he had entered nor from where he had left, because the Initiates always met in the middle [of the] night, having taken extreme care to not be victims of the Inquisition).

But if the neophyte obeyed, then a door opened on that cube (upon which the figure of the Baphomet was seated).

From there an Isis came out who received the Initiate with open arms, immediately giving him a holy kiss[21] on the forehead.

From that moment [on], that neophyte was a new brother, [an] Initiate of the Order.

That Male Goat, that Typhon Baphomet, that Lucifer, is quite interesting, because it is the sexual energy, the energy that one has to know how to use, if we want to realize the Great Work.

Now you will understand why Typhon Baphomet, the Male Goat of Mendez, represents the Philosopher's Stone, sex.

It is with that tremendous force that one must work.

---

[19] Literally 'tenebrosa' means "tenebrous, dismal, gloomy, dark, cheerless"
[20] Literally 'trasero' means "rear end, buttocks, back end, backside, behind, bottom, breech, butt, derriere, lower part of the trunk of the body;"
[21] Literally 'ósculo' means "osculate, kiss"

Let's remember that, in ancient times, the "Ark of the Covenant" had four horns of [a] Male Goat in the four corners (corresponding to the four cardinal points of the Earth) and when it was transported, one always took hold of it or grasped it by those four horns).

Moses transformed himself (on [Mount] Sinai).

When [he] came down, the clairvoyants saw two rays of light on his forehead, resembling those of the Male Goat of Mendez.

[It is] for this [reason] that Michael Angelo put those symbolic horns on the head [of his sculpture of Moses] when chiseling the living stone.

This is because the Male Goat represents the sexual force, but also the Devil; but that Devil or Lucifer is the same virile potency which, properly transmuted, allows us the intimate Self-Realization of the Being.

For this reason it has been said that "Lucifer is the Prince of Heaven, the Earth and the Infernos".

In the old gothic cathedrals, all [of] this was foreseen.

As far as the plan[22] of the temples [was concerned] it was organized in the form of [a] cross, and this reminds us of "crucis", "crux", "crucible[23]", etc.

---

[22] Literally 'planta' means "plant; floor, story; industrial plant, plant, works; top view, ground plan;"
[23] Literally 'crisol' means "crucible, melting pot, pot for heating a substance at very high temperatures;"

We already know that the vertical piece of wood[24] of the cross is masculine and that the horizontal [piece] is feminine.

The key of all the mysteries is found in their intersection[25].

Their intersection[26] is the "crucible" of the medieval alchemists, in which one "cooks[27]" and "recooks[28]" and [then] returns [to] "cook [again]" the materia prima[29] of the Great Work.

That "materia prima" is the Sacred Sperm, which is converted into energy [when it is] transformed.

It is with this most subtle energy that we can open a "Chakra", awaken all the occult (magical) powers, [and] create the Superior Existential Bodies of the Being, etc.

This is quite important, quite interesting…

The cross, in itself, is a sexual symbol.

In the cross is the Lingam-Yoni of the Great Arcanum.

On the two crossed pieces of wood of the cross, are the imprints of the three nails.

Those three nails, although it is certain that they allow the opening [of] the stigmata of the Initiate (that is, the "Chakras" of the palms of the hands and the feet, etc.), also symbolize, in themselves, the THREE PURIFICATIONS of the Christ in substance (there is another transcendental mystery here).

Ya sabemos que el palo vertical de la cruz es masculino y que el horizontal es femenino.

En el cruce de ambos, se halla la clave de todos los misterios.

El cruce de ambos, es el "crisol" de los alquimistas medievales, en el cual hay que "cocer" y "recocer" y volver a "cocer" la materia prima de la Gran Obra.

Esa "materia prima" es el Esperma Sagrado, que transformado se convierte en energía.

Es con esa sutilísima energía con la que podemos nosotros abrir un "Chacra", despertar todos los poderes ocultos (mágicos), crear los Cuerpos Existenciales Superiores del Ser, etc.

Esto es bastante importante, bastante interesante…

La cruz, en sí misma, es un símbolo sexual.

En la cruz está el Lingam-Yoni del Gran Arcano.

En los dos maderos atravesados de la cruz, están las huellas de los tres clavos.

Esos tres clavos, si bien es cierto que permiten abrir los estigmas del Iniciado (o sea, los "Chacras" de las palmas de las manos y de los pies, etc.), también simbolizan, en sí mismos, las TRES PURIFICACIONES del Cristo en substancia, (he ahí otro misterio trascendental).

---

[24] Literally 'palo' means "stick, rod; piece of wood, log, piece of timber;"
[25] Literally 'En el cruce de ambos' means "In the crossing of them both"
[26] Literally 'El cruce de ambos' means "The crossing of them both"
[27] Literally 'cocer' means "cook, boil in water; bake, harden in the oven;"
[28] Literally 'recocer' means "overcook, recook; anneal;"
[29] Literally 'materia prima' means "raw material"

In any case, my dear brethren, to realize the Great Work is [only possible] through [a] unique [path] which is worth[30] [all] the living pain [that one experiences upon it].

Peter, the beloved disciple of our Lord the Christ, has as [his] Gospel the Great Arcanum, the Mysteries of Sex.

[It is] for this reason that Jesus called him "Petrus" (STONE): "You are [a] Stone and on that Stone I will build my Church[31]".

Sex is, therefore, the Basic Stone, the Cubic Stone, the Philosopher's Stone that we must chisel, with [the] chisel and [the] hammer, in order to transform it into the perfect Cubic Stone.

That Stone (the brute Stone, in itself) without [any] chiseling, is Lucifer.

[When it is] already chiseled, it is our INNER LOGOI, the "Arche[32]" of the greeks.

The important thing is, then, to chisel it, to work with it, to craft[33] it, [and] to give it [a] perfect cubical form…

En todo caso, mis caros hermanos, realizar la Gran Obra es para lo único que vale la pena vivir.

Pedro, el amado discípulo de nuestro Señor el Cristo, tiene como Evangelio al Gran Arcano, a los Misterios del Sexo.

Por eso fue que Jesús lo llamó "Petrus" (PIEDRA): "Tú eres Piedra y sobre esa Piedra edificaré mi Iglesia".

Es pues, el sexo, la Piedra Básica, la Piedra Cúbica, la Piedra Filosofal que nosotros debemos cincelar, a base de cincel y martillo, para transformarla en la Piedra Cúbica perfecta.

Esa Piedra sin cincelar (la Piedra bruta, en sí misma), es Lucifer.

Ya cincelada es nuestro LOGOI INTERIOR, el "Arché" de los griegos.

Lo importante es, pues, cincelarla, trabajar con ella, elaborarla, darle forma cúbica perfecta…

---

[30] Literally 'vale' means "cost; be worth; earn; deserve, be worth; be equivalent or equal to"

[31] Editor's note: See Mat. 16:18 "…thou art Peter, and upon this rock I will build my church; and the gates of hell shall not prevail against it."(KJV) The word translated "Peter" is Petros "Πέτρος", a primary word meaning a rock or piece of rock; as a name, Petrus, an apostle: - Peter, rock.

[32] Arche (ἀρχή) is a Greek word with primary senses 'beginning', 'origin' or 'first cause' and 'power', 'sovereignty', 'domination' as extended meanings. This list is extended to 'ultimate underlying substance' and 'ultimate undemonstrable principle'. In the language of the archaic period (8th-6th century BC) arche or archai designates the source, origin or root of things that exist. If a thing is to be well established or founded, its arche or starting point must be secure, and the most secure foundations are those provided by the gods (the indestructible, immutable and eternal ordering of things). Aristotle defined the meaning of arche as the element or principle of a thing, which provides the conditions of the possibility of that thing.

[33] Literally 'elaborar' means "elaborate, brew, fabricate, manufacture, craft, make;"

Among the disciples of the Christ there were true prodigies and wonders.

Let's remember that great Master James for a moment.

They say that he is the one that looked the most like the Great Kabir Jesus; they called him the "brother of the Lord", and it is obvious that he had great psychic [and] magical powers.

After the death of the Great Kabir, James was the first who officiated [at] the Gnostic Mass in Jerusalem.

The [ancient] traditions relate[34] [to us] that he had to confront[35] [a] black magician [named] Hermogenes, in Judea.

Since he knew high magic, James fought wisely with the tenebrous one.

If he used a "shroud" of wonders, for example, he used it in order to resist him, and if Hermogenes used the magical staff[36], James used another similar [one], and with the aim of defeating the tenebrous one in the land of Judea.

Nevertheless, he was considered [a] "Magician" (and he was one, beyond all doubt) and he was [even] condemned to death.

But something unusual happened: the case of the sarcophagus of James [which] was suspended in [the] air, as it is said, and was transported to ancient Spain.

Entre los discípulos del Cristo hay verdaderos prodigios y maravillas.

Recordemos por un momento a Santiago, a ese gran Maestro.

Dicen que es el que más se parecía al Gran Kabir Jesús; lo llamaban el "hermano del Señor", y es obvio que disponía de grandes poderes psíquicos, mágicos.

Santiago fue el primero que después de la muerte del Gran Kabir, ofició la Misa Gnóstica en Jerusalén.

Cuentan las tradiciones que tuvo que enfrentarse al mago negro Hermógenes, en Judea.

Santiago, como quiera que conocía la alta magia, combatía sabiamente al tenebroso.

Si aquél usaba un "sudario" de maravillas, por ejemplo, éste lo usaba para contrarrestarlo, y si Hermógenes usaba el bastón mágico, Santiago usaba otro similar, y al fin derrotó al tenebroso en las tierras de Judea.

Sin embargo, se le consideró "Mago" (y lo era, fuera de toda duda) y fue condenado a muerte.

Mas algo insólito sucede: se da el caso de que el sarcófago de Santiago se suspendió en los aires, como se dice, y fue transportado a la antigua España.

---

[34] Literally 'cuentan' means "tell, relate, narrate;"
[35] Literally 'enfrentarse' means "face, confront; clash"
[36] Literally 'bastón' means "walking cane, cane, staff, stick, walking-stick, singlestick;"

Certainly, there is talk of [James or] Santiago de Compostela[37], and it is said of him that "he resurrected among the dead and that in that land [he] was attacked by demons (with [the] figure of [a] bull), [and that he was attacked] by living fire".

In short, many things are said about James.

The great medieval alchemist, Nicholas Flamel, had [James] Santiago de Compostela as Patron [Saint][38] of the Great Work.

On the way of Saint James [el camino de Santiago de Compostela], there is a street that is called "de Santiago" ["from/of James"], and there is also a cavern called "the cave of healing[39]".

At the time when people [started] making pilgrimages towards where [the city of] Santiago de Compostela is [now located], was the same time the alchemists were meeting (in that cave), those that were working in the Great Work, those that not only admired [James] Santiago de Compostela (whom they have as [their] Blessed Patron [Saint]), but also Jacques de Molay[40].

Cierto es que allí se habla de Santiago de Compostela, y dicen del mismo que "resucitó de entre los muertos y que en aquella tierra fue atacado por los demonios (con figura de toro), por fuego vivo".

En fin, se hablan muchas cosas sobre Santiago.

Nicolás Flamel, el gran alquimista medieval, tuvo a Santiago de Compostela como Patrón de la Gran Obra.

En el camino de Santiago de Compostela, hay una calle que la llaman "de Santiago", y también allí hay una caverna que la llaman "la cueva de la salud".

Por la época en que la gente hace peregrinaciones hacia donde está Santiago de Compostela, por esa misma época se reúnen los alquimistas (en tal cueva), los que están trabajando en la Gran Obra, los que admiran no solamente a Santiago de Compostela (al cual tienen por Patrono Bendito), sino también a Jacobo de Morai.

---

[37] Santiago de Compostela is the capital of the autonomous community of Galicia, Spain. The city's Cathedral is the destination of the important 9th century medieval pilgrimage route, the *Way of St. James* (Spanish: *El Camino de Santiago*). Santiago is the local Galician evolution of Vulgar Latin *Sanctu Iacobu* "Saint James". As for Compostela, folk etymology presumes it comes from the Latin *Campus Stellae* meaning "Field of Stars".

[38] Literally 'patrón' means "boss, employer, man in charge; landlord, owner, governor; patron saint, patron;"

[39] Literally 'salud' means "health, freedom from disease; well-being"

[40] James of Molay (French: Jacques de Molay) (1250-1314) was the 23rd and last Grand Master of the Knights Templar, leading the Order from April 20, 1292 until the Order was dissolved by order of Pope Clement V in 1312 and he was burned at the stake in Paris.

They always meet there at the time of the pilgrimage[41].

Therefore, while the people were rendering a cult ([an] exoteric [cult or worship], we could say) to [James] Santiago de Compostela, the alchemists and kabalists reunited in mystical assembly in order to study Kabalah, Alchemy and all the mysteries of the Great Work.

[Here] you [can] see both aspects of christianism ([the] exoteric and [the] esoteric).

Undoubtedly, all this invites us to reflection.

Jacques de Molay, who was burned alive during the Inquisition, is held (by those alchemists and kabalist that met in the "cave of the healing") in the same regard[42] that is given to Hiram Abiff as the Secret Master, which is [that he must be] resurrected in each one of us, and [the same regard is given] to James as the Blessed Patron [Saint] of the Great Work, and this is quite interesting…

What interests us is to realize the Great Work in ourselves, and it is (I think, and with complete certainty, I affirm) the only thing [that] makes [life] worth living.

The other [reasons for living], do not [even] have the least [bit of] importance.

In Compostela, they say that the Patron [Saint] James appears to the pilgrims with the [brim of his] hat turned[43] upwards, in his hand [is] the staff ([upon] which shines the Caduceus of Mercury), and on his chest [is] a sea[44] shell, as if to symbolize to the Blazing Star.

Allí se reúnen siempre, por la época de las peregrinaciones.

Así pues, mientras las gentes están rindiendo un culto (exotérico, dijéramos) a Santiago de Compostela, los alquimistas y cabalistas están reunidos en mística asamblea para estudiar la Cábala, la Alquimia y todos los misterios de la Gran Obra.

Vean ustedes los dos aspectos (exotéricos y esotéricos) del cristianismo.

Indubitablemente, todo esto nos invita a la reflexión.

Jacobo de Morai, quien fuera quemado vivo durante la Inquisición, es tenido (por aquellos alquimistas y cabalistas que se reúnen en la "cueva de la salud") en la misma forma que se tiene a Hiram Abiff como el Maestro Secreto que ha de resucitar en cada uno de nos, y a Santiago como el Bendito Patrón de la Gran Obra, y esto es bastante interesante…

La Gran Obra es lo que nos interesa a nosotros realizar, y es (creo, y con toda seguridad, afirmo) lo único para lo cual vale la pena vivir.

Lo demás, no tiene la menor importancia.

Dicen que el Patrono Santiago, en Compostela, se aparece a los peregrinos con el sombrero echado hacia arriba, en su mano el bastón (el cual luce el Caduceo de Mercurio), y una concha de tortuga en el pecho, como para simbolizar a la Estrella Flamígera.

---

[41] Literally 'peregrinaciones' means "peregrinations, pilgrimage, journey to a sacred or devotional place, long journey, peregrination;"
[42] Literally 'forma' means "shape, form; way, manner; fitness; figure; host"
[43] Literally 'echado' means "throw, cast, toss; add; affix, tack on; bud, shoot; pump; lay; post; blow; tip; send; pour; put"
[44] Literally 'tortuga' means "tortoise, turtle, terrapin; snail"

I advise you to study the "Universal Epistle of James", in the Bible.[45] Certainly, it is marvelous.

It is directed to all those who are working in the Great Work.

James says that "faith without works is dead in itself" [Jas 2:17] ([meaning it is] worth nothing).

You can listen here, from my lips, [to] all the doctrine of the Great Arcanum, all the explanations that we give about the alchemists and the Great Work, but if you do not realize that Great Work, if you do not work in the Great Work, if [you] only have faith, [but] nothing else, and you do not work, [then] you appear ([as] James says, and I repeat) "like a man who looks at a mirror, who sees his face in the glass, [and then] turns around and walks away", forgetting the incident [Jas. 1:22-24].

If you listen to all the explanations that we give and [then] you do not work in the "Forge of the Cyclops", [if you] do not make the Superior Existential Bodies of the Being, [then] you look like that man who "sees himself in the mirror, turns around and walks away", because faith without works are not worth mentioning.

It is necessary for Work to be supported[46] by faith; [and] faith must speak through[47] works.

James says that "we need to be merciful"[48].

This is clear[49], because if we are merciful, the Lords of the Karma will judge us with mercy; but if we are ruthless, the Lords of the Karma will judge us in [a] ruthless way.

---

[45] See the Editor's Appendix
[46] Literally 'respalde' means "underwrite; protect; back, support"
[47] Literally 'con' means "with; by; in spite of"
[48] This is implied from James 2:13: "For judgment without mercy to him that hath not done mercy. And mercy exalteth itself above judgment."
[49] Literally 'claro' means "sure, clear, clearly;"

And since mercy has more power than justice, it is certain that if we are merciful, we will be able to eliminate a lot [of][50] karma (all this invites us to reflection).

James says that we "must control the tongue" (that one who knows [how] to control[51] the tongue, can control the whole body), and uses[52] as [an] example the case of the horse (the horse has the bridle put in its mouth as a brake, and [this] is just like how we are able[53] to dominate it, to handle it) [see Jas. 3:1-3].

James says: "Also look [at] the ships[54]; although [they are] so great [in size] and are carried by violent[55] winds, they are steered[56] with a very small rudder" (which is truly small in comparison with the enormous size that the ships have) [see Jas. 3:4].

The tongue is little[57], yes, but what great fires [it] starts[58]! [see Jas. 3:5]

We are taught, in that epistle, [that] we should never boast about anything.

That one who is boasting about themselves, about their works, about what they have done, is undoubtedly arrogant[59], pompous, and fails in the Great Work.

Y como quiera que la misericordia tiene más poder que la justicia, es seguro que si somos misericordiosos, podremos eliminar mucho karma (todo esto nos invita a la reflexión).

Dice Santiago que nosotros "tenemos que refrenar la lengua" (aquél que sabe refrenar la lengua, puede refrenar todo el cuerpo), y nos pone como ejemplo el caso del caballo (al caballo se le pone el freno en la boca, en el hocico, y es así como logramos dominarlo, manejarlo).

Dice Santiago: "Mirad también las naves; aunque tan grandes y llevadas de impetuosos vientos, son gobernadas con un muy pequeño timón" (que es verdaderamente pequeño, en comparación con el enorme tamaño que tienen los buques).

La lengua es pequeña, sí, pero, ¡que grandes incendios forma!

Se nos enseña, en esa epístola, a no jactarnos jamás de nada.

Aquél que es jactancioso de sí mismo, de sus obras, de lo que ha hecho, indudablemente es soberbio, pedante, y fracasa en la Gran Obra.

---

[50] Literally 'mucho' means "a lot, very much, very many; very, extremely; long"
[51] Literally 'refrenar' means "rein, restrain, control; refrain, restrain oneself"
[52] Literally 'pone' means "put, place; lay; insert; impose; mark; adjust; send; contribute; subscribe; perform; translate"
[53] Literally 'logramos' means "get, obtain; achieve, attain; reach; win"
[54] Literally 'naves' means "nave; ship, large vessel made for sailing on the sea; spacecraft; auditorium"
[55] Literally 'impetuosos' means "violent; impetuous, impulsive; headstrong"
[56] Literally 'gobernadas' means "govern, rule, run, manage; steer, fly"
[57] Literally 'pequeña' means "small; child; dwarf"
[58] Literally 'forma' means "form, shape, fashion, create; design; constitute; arrange; take shape; educate, teach, train; form up"
[59] Literally 'soberbio' means "proud, arrogant; superb"

If we want to work in the Great Work, [then] we need to humble[60] ourselves before the Divinity, to be more and more humble every day; never to assume[61] anything, [instead we should] always be simple.

The same [thing] would happen if we checked[62] the tongue; we would become owners of our whole body.

This is vital when one wants to triumph in the Great Work, in the MAGNUS OPUS.

That Epistle is written with a double meaning.

If read you it literally, [then] you would not understand it.

Thus the protestants, the adventists, the catholics, etc., have read it, and they have not understood it.

That Epistle has a double meaning and is directed, exclusively, to those who work in the Great Work.

As far as faith [is concerned], it is (of course[63]) necessary to have it.

All alchemists must have faith, all kabalists must have faith, but faith is not something empirical, [it is not] something that we are given for free[64].

Faith must create [more] faith[65]; we cannot demand faith from someone who does not have it.

Necesitamos humillarnos ante la Divinidad, ser cada día más y más humildes, si es que queremos trabajar en la Gran Obra; no presumir jamás de nada, ser sencillos siempre.

Lo mismo sucedería si nosotros refrenáramos la lengua; nos haríamos dueños de todo nuestro cuerpo.

Eso es vital cuando se quiere triunfar en la Gran Obra, en el MAGNUS OPUS.

Aquella Epístola está escrita con un doble sentido.

Si ustedes la leen literalmente, no la entenderían.

Así la han leído los protestantes, los adventistas, los católicos, etc., y no la han entendido.

Esa Epístola tiene un doble sentido y está dirigida, exclusivamente, a los que trabajan en la Gran Obra.

En cuanto a la fe, es necesario tenerla (claro).

Todo alquimista debe tener fe, todo cabalista debe tener fe, pero la fe no es algo empírico, algo que se nos dé regalado.

La fe hay que fabricarla; no podemos exigirle a nadie que tenga fe.

---

[60] Literally 'humillarnos' means "humiliate, humble"
[61] Literally 'presumir' means "presume, assume, suppose, conjecture; show off; be conceited or vain"
[62] Literally 'refrenáramos' means "rein, restrain, control; refrain, restrain oneself"
[63] Literally 'claro' means "sure, clearly; of course"
[64] Literally 'regalado' means "dirt cheap; comfortable, easy"
[65] Literally 'La fe hay que fabricarla' means "Faith is necessary to create it"

It must be created, it [must be] developed[66].

How does one make it? On the basis of study and experience.

Could someone have faith, [the kind] which we are speaking of here, if they do not study and they don't experiment[67] for themselves? Obviously not!, right?

But, as we are studying and experimenting, we are [also] comprehending, and true faith comes[68] from that creative comprehension.

Therefore, faith is not something empirical.

No; we need to create it.

Later, yes, much later, the Holy Spirit, the Third Logos, can consolidate it, fortify it and strengthen it within us; but we have to create it…

Another quite interesting apostle (who tells us of this narrow, straight[69] and difficult path that we [must] take), is Andrew.

It is said that he conjured up seven perverse demons in Nicea and that he made them appear (before the multitudes) in the form of seven dogs that fled terrified.

Much has been said about Andrew, and there is no doubt that he was extraordinary, that he was full of a great power.

The reality is that Andrew, the great Master, [and] disciple of Christ, was condemned to death and [was] tortured.

---

[66] Literally 'elaborarla' means "elaborate, provide additional details; process; work out, think out; develop"
[67] Literally 'experimenta' means "test; touch; experiment, attempt to discover or test something; experience, try; feel; taste; undergo"
[68] Literally 'deviene' means "become, be; turn into; be worthy of; be suitable"
[69] Literally 'estrecho' means "narrow, tight; near, close; intimate; cramped, close fitting; short; strict; straight"

The cross of Saint Andrew invites us to reflection: it is an "X" (yes, an "X").

Its two arms, extended to [the] right and [the] left, and its two legs open on both sides, forming [an] "X", and on that "X" Saint Andrew was crucified.

That "X" is very symbolic.

In Greek it is equivalent to a "K", let us remember the CHRESTOS[70].

Unquestionably, the magnificent drama of Andrew was symbolized by the great Initiated monk BACON[71].

In his book (the most extraordinary [one] that he wrote), named "The Waterwheel"[72], he has a plate in which a dead man is clearly seen.

Nevertheless, it is as [if he] tries to raise his head, as [if he is] stretching, as [if he is] resurrecting, while two black crows are picking[73] his flesh with their sharp[74] beaks.

The Soul and the Spirit raise[75] themselves from the cadaver, and this reminds us [of] the phrase of all Initiates, which says:

"THE FLESH COMES AWAY FROM THE BONES…"

---

[70] Editor's note: *Chrestos* is the phonetic spelling of the Greek **Χριστός** (Khristós) meaning "the anointed one", which is where the word Christ comes from.

[71] Editor's note: This seems to be a reference to Roger Bacon (1214 - 1294), also known as Doctor Mirabilis, who was an English philosopher and Franciscan friar who placed considerable emphasis on the study of nature.

[72] Literally 'Azud' means "weir, dam; water wheel, wheel that is turned by the force of flowing water (used to operate machinery, mills, etc.)"

[73] Literally 'quitando' means "weed; remove; brush off; turn off; encroach on; lend; tidy away; relieve; weaken; excise; pinch"

[74] Literally 'acerado' means "steely, of or pertaining to steel; resembling steel, having the properties of steel; sharp"

[75] Literally 'alzan' means "lift, raise; elevate; hoist; gather up; remove; hide; steal"

Saint Andrew, dying on a cross in the form of [an] "X", speaks to us precisely of the disintegration of the Ego: that [we should] reduce it to [a] cosmic cloud [of dust], that [we should] carve it up.

"THE FLESH COMES AWAY FROM THE BONES..."

Only thus it is possible for the Secret Master (Hiram Abiff) to resurrect within ourselves, here and now.

Otherwise, resurrection would be impossible (in the Great Work we must die from instant to instant, from the moment at moment).

And what could we say about John?

He is, beyond all doubt, the Patron [Saint] of Gold manufacturers.

Is there someone who has made gold?

Yes; let's remember Raymond Lull.

He did it: he enriched the coffers[76] of Phillip the Fair[77], of France; and those of the King of England.

Still one is reminded of Raymond Lull's letters[78].

One of them speaks of "a beautiful diamond", which was given[79] to none other than to the King of England (dissolving a crystal, between the "crucible", and then, putting water and mercury on that crystal, it transformed into a gigantic, extraordinarily fine diamond, which was given to the King of England).

---

[76] Literally 'arcas' means "coffers, treasury"
[77] Philip I (1478-1506), known as Philip the Handsome or the Fair, was the first Habsburg King of Castile. He was the first Habsburg monarch in Spain.
[78] Literally 'cartas' means "letter; document; charter; epistle; map; card; playing card; menu"
[79] Literally 'obsequiara' means "give away, bestow, handsel"

And as far as the transmutation of lead into gold, he did this thanks to the Philosophical Mercury.

Raymond Lull enriched all [of] Europe with his metalworking[80], and nevertheless he remained poor.

[He was an] extraordinary traveler of all the countries of the world, [who] died in the end [by being] stoned to death[81] in one of those lands (you [should] reflect on this).

Therefore John, the apostle of Jesus, is the Patron [Saint] of Gold manufacturers.

It is said that on some occasion, he found on his path (in a town [along] the way, in the East) a philosopher who tried to convince the people, to demonstrate to them what he could do with the word, with the verb.

Two young people, who had listened to his teachings, abandoned their wealth, they sold it [all], and with that they bought a great diamond.

In the presence of the honorable public, they put the diamond into the hands of the philosopher; this he returned to them and they destroyed the gem with a stone.

John protested saying:

"With such gem, it would be possible to give the poor [something] to eat..."

It is said that before the multitudes he reconstructed the gem and that they soon sold it, in order to give the multitudes [something] to eat.

---

[80] Literally 'fundicione' means "melting, smelting; foundry"
[81] Literally 'lapidado' means "lapidate, stone, throw stones at someone or something; stone to death"

But the young people, regretted[82] [their decision and] said to themselves:

> "What fools[83] we were to have left all our riches in order to buy a great diamond that has become pieces and then was reconstructed in order to distribute it among the people!".

But John, who saw all the things of heaven and earth (and who knew [how] to transmute lead into gold), brought from the shores of the sea (there close by), some stones and reeds[84] (the stone, symbol of the Philosopher's Stone of sex, and the reed, symbol of the spine, because there we have[85] the power to transmute lead into gold), and after converting those reeds and those stones into gold, he gave the wealth back to the young people; but he said to them:

> "You have lost the best [thing]. I give back to you what you gave, but you lost what you had obtained in the superior worlds".

Afterwards, he approached a woman who was dead, [and] he revived her.

She then told him what she had seen outside the body and also went to those young people, saying that "she had seen their guardian angels crying with great bitterness, because they had lost the best thing for worthless[86] [and] perishable things…"

It is clear that the young people repented, [and] they gave the gold back to John, and John returned that gold into what it was (into reeds and stones), and they converted themselves into his disciples.

Mas los jóvenes, arrepentidos, se dijeron a sí mismos:

> "¡Qué tontos fuimos al haber salido de todas nuestras riquezas para comprar un gran diamante que ahora se vuelve pedazos y que luego reconstruyen para repartirlo entre las gentes!".

Pero Juan, que veía todas las cosas del cielo y de la tierra (y que sabía transmutar el plomo en oro), hizo traer de las orillas del mar (de por allí cerca), unas piedras y unas cañas (la piedra, símbolo de la Piedra Filosofal del sexo, y la caña símbolo de la espina dorsal, pues allí está el poder para transmutar el plomo en oro), y después de convertir aquellas cañas y aquellas piedras en oro, le devolvió las riquezas a los jóvenes; pero les dijo:

> "Habéis perdido lo mejor. Os devuelvo lo que disteis, pero perdisteis lo que habíais logrado en los mundos superiores".

Luego acercándose a una mujer que había muerto, la resucitó.

Ella entonces contó lo que había visto fuera del cuerpo y también se dirigió a aquellos jóvenes, diciendo que "había visto a sus ángeles guardianes llorando con grande amargura, porque ellos habían perdido lo mejor por las vanas cosas perecederas…"

Es claro que los jóvenes se arrepintieron, devolvieron el oro a Juan, y Juan volvió a trocar ese oro en lo que era (en cañas y piedras), y se convirtieron en sus discípulos.

---

[82] Literally 'arrepentidos' means "epentant, penitent; regretful, sorry; contrite, rueful"
[83] Literally 'tontos' means "fool, dummy, stupid, idiot"
[84] Literally 'cañas' means "cane; reed; bone marrow; leg; half"
[85] Literally 'allí está' means "there is"
[86] Literally 'vanas' means "vain, worthless, futile; without meaning or significance"

Therefore, John and the "Order of Saint John" invites us to think.

John is [the] Patron [Saint] of those who make Gold; we need to transmute the lead of the personality into the living gold of the Spirit.

[It is] for this [reason] that the great Masters of the White Lodge are often called, "Brothers of the Order of Saint John".

Many believe that John, the apostle of the Master Jesus, disincarnated; but he did not disincarnate.

Old traditions say that he dug his grave[87], that he lay down in it, [and] that a light shined brightly[88] and [then] disappeared ([then] the grave was empty).

We know that John, the apostle of the Christ, lives with the same body that he had in the Holy Earth and that he lives precisely in Agartha, in the subterranean kingdom, there where the ORDER OF MELCHEZEDEC is [located], and where he accompanies the King of the World (you can see how interesting this is).

Entering then into the magistery[89] of the fire, we must define something (so as to clarify): it becomes necessary, as I have said to you [already], to transmute the Sacred Sperm into energy.

When this is obtained, the fire [then] arrives which climbs up the dorsal spine, and the Great Work begins to be realized.

We need to create the Superior Existential Bodies of the Being, but this is not sufficient.

---

[87] Literally 'fosa sepulcral' means "burial grave, grave tomb"
[88] Literally 'resplandeció' means "glitter, shine; glow, bloom"
[89] Literally 'magisterio' means "magistery, mastery, mastership; the authority over or expert use of [something]"

It is necessary, it is indispensable, it is urgent to cover those vehicles (later) with the different parts of the Being; but, in order to cover them [it] is necessary to perfect them, to turn them into pure gold, into real Spiritual gold.

[So] we are not surprised, then, that John or James has an Astral Body of pure gold, a Mental [Body] or a Causal or Buddhic or Atmic [Body] of the same metal, because they managed to realize the Great Work.

If somehow Count Saint Germain[90] could transmute lead into gold, it is because he himself was gold.

The "Aura" of Count Saint Germain is of pure gold; the atoms [that] form that "Aura", are of gold, and his Superior Existential Bodies, are from gold of the best quality.

Under these conditions, he can throw a coin[91] into the "crucible", yes, and melt it, and then, with the same power that he carries inside, he [can] transmute it into pure gold, because he is gold (this is what it is called "to realize the Great Work").

In this there are degrees and degrees.

Es necesario, es indispensable, es urgente recubrir esos vehículos (después) con las distintas partes del Ser; mas, para recubrirlos hay que perfeccionarlos, convertirlos en oro puro, en oro Espiritual de verdad.

No se extrañen, pues, que Juan o Santiago tengan un Cuerpo Astral de oro puro, un Mental del mismo metal o un Causal o el Búddhico o el Átmico, porque ellos lograron realizar la Gran Obra.

Si por algo el Conde Saint Germain podía transmutar el plomo en oro, es porque él mismo era oro.

El "Aura" del Conde Saint Germain es de oro puro; los átomos forman esa "Aura", son de oro, y sus Cuerpos Existenciales Superiores, son de oro de la mejor calidad.

En esas condiciones, él puede echar una moneda en el "crisol", sí, y derretirla, y luego, con el mismo poder que lleva adentro, transmutarla en oro puro, porque él es oro (eso es lo que se llama "realizar la Gran Obra").

En esto hay grados y grados.

---

[90] The Count of St. Germain achieved great prominence in European high society of the mid-1700s, and since then various scholars have linked him to mysticism, occultism, secret societies, and various conspiracy theories.

[91] Literally 'moneda' means "currency, money; tender; coinage, coin"

First it is necessary to reach Mastery, later we must convert ourselves into Perfect Masters and much later [we must] reach the degree of "Grand Elect[92]".

[The so-called] "Grand Elect" and "Perfect Master" are all those who have realized the Great Work.

Really, the way we are[93], we are evil.

We needed to pass through a radical transformation and, in truth, this is only possible [by] destroying the "inhuman elements" and [by] creating the human [elements].

Only thus we will march towards final Liberation…

In the Cathedral of Notre Dame de Paris, as they say, in a corner there is the Master Stone, or the Cornerstone (that the "builders[94]" of all the sects, schools, religions and others rejected), the Elect, [and] Precious Stone, but which has the figure of Lucifer [on it], and this scares the profane.

Unquestionably, my dear brothers, only there (in sex) can we find that LUCIFERIAN PRINCIPLE that is the foundation itself for Self-Realization.

But, why is Lucifer the "Thread of Ariadne"?, why is [it] precisely he who leads us to final Liberation, when in truth he has practiced[95] evil?

---

[92] Literally 'Elegido' means "elected, chosen, favorite, elect, favourite, preferred, selected;"
[93] Literally 'Así como nos encontramos' means "As we [presently] find ourselves"
[94] Literally 'edificadores' means "builder, constructor; edifier"
[95] Literally 'tenido' means "have, possess; hold; bear; carry; wear; experience; practice; meet with; travel; show"

I have often said, I have affirmed and I emphatically affirm in this chair, that Lucifer is the reflection of the INNER LOGOI (within ourselves), the shadow of our intimate God in us and [this is] for our [own] good, since he is the trainer.

God cannot tempt[96] us; we have our own lusts[97] (so taught James, the Patriarch of the Alchemy, the Patriarch of the Great Work).

Then, what is it that Lucifer does?

He uses our own lusts, he makes them move across the screen of our understanding, in order to train us psychologically, to make us strong; the more we fail [his tests], [the more] we fail in the Great Work.

Nevertheless, we can fail and [we can] rectify.

If we rectify ourselves, we triumph in the Great Work.

Anyone can fail and by their faults [that] they know that they have crimes which [must be] corrected, which [must be] eliminated.

Thus Lucifer trains us, he educates us, he forms us, and through[98] all [this] training he liberates us, he directs[99] us (from sphere to sphere) until [we reach] our Hiram Abiff.

Lucifer is, then, then "Thread of Ariadne" who takes us towards our inner God, who removes us from this painful labyrinth of life, by means of the esoteric work.

He dicho muchas veces, y lo he afirmado enfáticamente en esta cátedra, que Lucifer es la reflexión del LOGOI INTERIOR (dentro de nosotros mismos), la sombra de nuestro Dios íntimo, en nosotros y para nuestro bien, pues él es el entrenador.

Dios no puede tentarnos; nos tientan nuestras propias concupiscencias (así lo enseña Santiago, el Patrono de la Alquimia, el Patrono de la Gran Obra).

Entonces, ¿qué es lo que hace Lucifer?

Él se vale de nuestras propias concupiscencias, las hace pasar por la pantalla del entendimiento, con el propósito de entrenarnos psicológicamente, de hacernos fuertes; más si fallamos, fracasamos en la Gran Obra.

Sin embargo, podemos fallar y rectificar.

Si rectificamos, triunfamos en la Gran Obra.

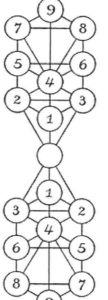

Cualquiera puede fallar y por sus fallas sabe que tiene delitos que corregir, que eliminar.

Así Lucifer nos entrena, nos educa, nos forma, y a fuerza de tanto entrenamiento nos libera, nos va conduciendo (de esfera en esfera) hasta nuestro Hiram Abiff.

Lucifer es, pues, el "Hilo de Ariadna" que nos lleva hacia nuestro Dios interior, que nos saca de este doloroso laberinto de la vida, mediante el trabajo esotérico.

---

[96] Literally 'tentarnos' means "try; tease; tempt, entice"
[97] Literally 'concupiscencias' means "concupiscence, lust of the flesh, lustfulness, sexual appetite; greed"
[98] Literally 'a fuerza de' means "by force of"
[99] Literally 'conduciendo' means "drive, impel forward; guide the direction of something (i.e. car, animal, etc.); lead, conduct; transport in a vehicle"

He, time and time again makes our own lusts pass before the screen of our understanding, (they are none other than our own [lusts]). He points them out[100] [to us], [indicating that we need] to overcome them, to eliminate them, to disintegrate them, to return them [to] dust.

Thus, continuing[101] step by step each time advancing [a little bit] more, we are dividing up the center of the labyrinth from the periphery, in order to one day arrive at our [own] God.

This is the work of Lucifer.

He is the Thread of Ariadne, he is the Philosopher's Stone.

[It is] for this [reason] that the pilgrims of the Cathedral of Notre Dame de Paris, extinguish their lamps[102] in the stony jaws of Lucifer, in the "Little Corner Stone", as they say over there…

Much has been said about "magical powers".

Yes; we can have them, but unquestionably we need to create a lot within ourselves, and to destroy a lot more (there is a lot we have in excess and a lot that we lack).

Everybody thinks that they possess the Superior Existential Bodies of the Being, and this is not so.

It is necessary to create them, and it is only possible to create them in the "Forge of the Cyclops", that is to say, by means of the sexual work.

They will tell us that we are "fanatics of sex". They are mistaken.

---

[100] Literally 'indicado' means "indicate, show; point out; mark, signify; imply; exhibit, reveal; suggest"
[101] Literally 'dando' means "give; present; deal; produce, yield; cause; perform; say; take; teach; lecture; start, begin; overlook; surrender"
[102] Literally 'veladoras' means "bedside lamp"

What happens is that we have a "laboratory", which is our own body, and a "small furnace" in the "laboratory" (the fire of the alchemists), and a "crucible" (which is in the sexual organs) and there [we have] the "Materia Prima" [or "Raw Material"] of the Great Work. To transmute it is indispensable, to convert it into energy, in order to then, with that energy, and with that which it contains, create the Superior Existential Bodies of the Being.

This is the vital thing, the indispensable thing.

A day will arrive in which we will pass beyond sex.

The absurd thing would be to want to pass beyond sex without having arrived at the goal.

That would be as if we wanted to lower ourselves off of the train, before arriving at the station or like wanting to lower ourselves off of the bus or truck (wherever we are going), before arriving at the goal that we have decided upon[103].

During sex[104] it is necessary to create and it is necessary to destroy.

To create the SOLAR VEHICLES is necessary so that our interior God can resurrect in us, and [it is] also [necessary] to eliminate the "inhuman elements" that we have inside…

Everything is reunited here, we must comprehend [this].

Lo que pasa es que tenemos un "laboratorio", que es nuestro propio cuerpo, y un "hornillo" en el "laboratorio" (el fuego del alquimista), y un "crisol" (que está en el sexo) y allí la "Materia Prima" de la Gran Obra. Transmutarla es indispensable, convertirla en energía, para poder luego con esa energía, y con lo que ella contiene, crear los Cuerpos Existenciales Superiores del Ser.

Eso es lo vital, lo indispensable.

Llegará un día en que habremos de pasar más allá del sexo.

Lo absurdo sería querer pasar más allá del sexo sin haber llegado a la meta.

Eso sería tanto como querer bajarnos del tren, antes de llegar a la estación o como querer bajarnos del autobús o camión (donde vamos), antes de llegar a la meta que nos hemos trazado.

En el sexo hay que crear y hay que destruir.

Crear los VEHÍCULOS SOLARES, es necesario para que el Dios interior pueda resucitar en nosotros, y también eliminar los "elementos inhumanos" que llevamos dentro…

Todos reunidos aquí, debemos comprender.

---

[103] Literally 'trazado' means "draw; plot; trace; rule, delineate; build; describe"
[104] Literally 'En el sexo' means "In the sex"

It is not enough for you to listen to what I am saying; it is necessary [for you] to realize this, because "faith without works is dead faith".

It is necessary that faith be accompanied by Work.

It is necessary to realize the Great Work, but it is not enough [to just] have faith in the Great Work.

It is necessary to realize the Great Work.

And what will the final result of the Great Work be? That each one of us is converted into a great God, with power over the Heavens, the Earth and over the Infernos.

This is the end, the result of the Great Work: that each one of us will be converted into a Majesty, into a terribly Divine creature.

But, at the present time, we must recognize that we are not even humans; we are only "humanoids" (in a very crude form one could say that we are "mammalian[105] intellectuals", and nothing else); but we can leave this state in which we find ourselves through the Great Work…

Hiram Abiff is the "Secret Master", the Third Logos (Shiva), the "First-born of Creation", our Real divine inner Being, our true and individual "Monad".

We need to resurrect him, because he is dead within ourselves, although he is alive in the ineffable worlds.

Raymond Lull realized the Great Work: he received the Great Arcanum in the Astral World, and it was with that "Master Key" that he was able to work in the Great Work.

---

[105] Literally 'mamíferos' means "mammalian, of or pertaining to the class Mammalia (class of warm-blooded vertebrate animals which secrete milk to feed their young and have a covering of hair on their bodies)"

Raymond Lull, undoubtedly, knew outside the physical body what the Sacred Conception of the Divine Mother, Kundalini Shakti is.

To know how to realize that Sacred Conception, [is to know] how to[106] materialize (from on high) the Sacred Conception in itself, until it is achieved.

Undoubtedly, the Divine Mother must conceive the Son (by work and grace of the Third Logos).

She remains [a] Virgin before the birth, during the birth and after the birth.

This Child that she conceives, must materialize itself, crystallize [itself] in us from above, from on high, to be completely covered by our physical body, with our "planetary body".

When arriving at this degree one can say that the Great Work has been realized.

In other words: we must, as I have said, resurrect Hiram Abiff within ourselves.

Raimundo Lulio, indubitablemente, conoció fuera del cuerpo físico lo que es la Sagrada Concepción de la Madre Divina, la Kundalini Shakti.

Al conocer cómo se realizaba esa Sagrada Concepción, se propuso materializar (desde lo alto) la Sagrada Concepción en sí mismo, hasta que la logró.

Indudablemente, la Madre Divina debe concebir (por obra y gracia del Tercer Logos) al Hijo.

Ella permanece Virgen antes del parto, en el parto y después del parto.

Ese Niño que ella concibe, debe materializarse, cristalizar en nosotros desde arriba, desde lo alto, hasta quedar revestido completamente con nuestro cuerpo físico, con nuestro "cuerpo planetario".

Al llegar a ese grado puede decirse que la Gran Obra se ha realizado.

En otros términos: debemos resucitar a Hiram Abiff dentro de nosotros, he dicho.

---

[106] Literally 'propuso' means "propose, bring forward, offer, plan, advance, call forth, come up with, hand in, hold out, launch forth, put forth, put forward, put over, set out, submit, tender, proffer, propound;"

Editor's Appendix

Apéndice del Editor

The Book of James

El Libro de Santiago

Editor's Appendix

Here is the *Universal Epistle of James* or *Book of James* (LITV):

Chapter 1

1:1 James, a servant of God and of the Lord Jesus Christ, to the twelve tribes in the Dispersion, greeting:

1:2 My brothers count it all joy when you fall into various trials,

1:3 knowing that the proving of your faith works patience.

1:4 But let patience have its perfective work, that you may be perfect and complete, lacking nothing.

1:5 But if any of you lacks wisdom, let him ask from God, who gives to all freely and with no reproach, and it will be given to him.

1:6 But let him ask in faith, doubting nothing. For the one who doubts is like a wave of the sea, being driven by wind and being tossed;

1:7 for do not let that man suppose that he will receive anything from the Lord;

1:8 he is a double-minded man, not dependable in all his ways.

1:9 But let the lowly brother rejoice in his lifting up;

1:10 and the rich one rejoice in his humiliation, because he will pass away like the flower of the herb.

Apéndice del Editor

Aquí está la *Epístola Universal de Santiago* o *Libro de Santiago* (SRV):

Capítulo 1

1:1 Santiago [Jacobo], siervo de Dios y del Señor Jesucristo, á las doce tribus que están esparcidas, salud.

1:2 Hermanos míos, tened por sumo gozo cuando cayereis en diversas tentaciones;

1:3 Sabiendo que la prueba de vuestra fe obra paciencia.

1:4 Mas tenga la paciencia perfecta su obra, para que seáis perfectos y cabales, sin faltar en alguna cosa.

1:5 Y si alguno de vosotros tiene falta de sabiduría, demándela á Dios, el cual da á todos abundantemente, y no zahiere; y le será dada.

1:6 Pero pida en fe, no dudando nada: porque el que duda es semejante á la onda de la mar, que es movida del viento, y echada de una parte á otra.

1:7 No piense pues el tal hombre que recibirá ninguna cosa del Señor.

1:8 El hombre de doblado ánimo es inconstante en todos sus caminos.

1:9 El hermano que es de baja suerte, gloríese en su alteza:

1:10 Mas el que es rico, en su bajeza; porque él se pasará como la flor de la hierba.

Editor's Appendix

1:11 For the sun rose with the hot wind and dried up the herb, and its flower fell out, and the beauty of its appearance perished; so also the rich one will fade away in his ways. (see Isa. 40:6, 7)

1:12 Blessed is the man who endures temptation, because having been approved he will receive the crown of life which the Lord promised to the ones loving Him.

1:13 Let no one being tempted say, I am tempted from God. For God is not tempted by evil, and He tempts no one.

1:14 But each one is tempted by his own lusts, being drawn out and being seduced by them.

1:15 Then having conceived lust brings forth sin. And sin being fully formed brings forth death.

1:16 Do not go astray, my beloved brothers,

1:17 every act of good giving and every perfect gift is from above, coming down from the Father of lights, with whom is no change or shadow of turning.

1:18 Having purposed, He brought us forth by the Word[1] of truth, for us to be a certain firstfruit of His creatures.

1:19 So that, my beloved brothers, let every man be swift to hear, slow to speak, slow to wrath.

1:20 For the wrath of man does not work out the righteousness of God.

---

[1] G3056 λόγος logos log'-os
From G3004; something said (including the thought); by implication a topic (subject of discourse), also reasoning (the mental faculty) or motive; by extension a computation; specifically (with the article in John) the Divine Expression (that is, Christ): - account, cause, communication, X concerning, doctrine, fame, X have to do, intent, matter, mouth, preaching, question, reason, + reckon, remove, say (-ing), shew, X speaker, speech, talk, thing, + none of these things move me, tidings, treatise, utterance, word, work.

Apéndice del Editor

1:11 Porque salido el sol con ardor, la hierba se secó, y su flor se cayó, y pereció su hermosa apariencia: así también se marchitará el rico en todos sus caminos.

1:12 Bienaventurado el varón que sufre la tentación; porque cuando fuere probado, recibirá la corona de vida, que Dios ha prometido á los que le aman.

1:13 Cuando alguno es tentado, no diga que es tentado de Dios: porque Dios no puede ser tentado de los malos, ni él tienta á alguno:

1:14 Sino que cada uno es tentado, cuando de su propia concupiscencia es atraído, y cebado.

1:15 Y la concupiscencia, después que ha concebido, pare el pecado: y el pecado, siendo cumplido, engendra muerte.

1:16 Amados hermanos míos, no erréis.

1:17 Toda buena dádiva y todo don perfecto es de lo alto, que desciende del Padre de las luces, en el cual no hay mudanza, ni sombra de variación.

1:18 El, de su voluntad nos ha engendrado por la Palabra[2] de verdad, para que seamos primicias de sus criaturas.

1:19 Por esto, mis amados hermanos, todo hombre sea pronto para oir, tardío para hablar, tardío para airarse:

1:20 Porque la ira del hombre no obra la justicia de Dios.

---

[2] Esta palabra es Logos (λόγος) en griego.

1:21 On account of this, putting away all filthiness and overflowing of evil, in meekness receive the implanted Word being able to save your souls.

1:22 But become doers of the Word, and not hearers only, deceiving yourselves.

1:23 Because if anyone is a hearer of the Verb, and not a doer, this one is like a man studying his natural face in a mirror;

1:24 for he studied himself, and has gone away, and immediately he forgot of what kind he was.

1:25 But the one looking into the perfect Law of liberty, and continuing in it, this one not having become a forgetful hearer, but a doer of the work, this one will be blessed in his doing.

1:26 If anyone thinks to be religious among you, yet not bridling his tongue, but deceiving his heart, this one's religion is vain.

1:27 Pure and undefiled religion before God and the Father is this: to visit orphans and widows in their afflictions, and to keep oneself unspotted from the world.

1:21 Por lo cual, dejando toda inmundicia y superfluidad de malicia, recibid con mansedumbre la palabra ingerida, la cual puede hacer salvas vuestras almas.

1:22 Mas sed hacedores de la Palabra, y no tan solamente oidores, engañándoos á vosotros mismos.

1:23 Porque si alguno oye la Palabra, y no la pone por obra, este tal es semejante al hombre que considera en un espejo su rostro natural.

1:24 Porque él se consideró á sí mismo, y se fué, y luego se olvidó qué tal era.

1:25 Mas el que hubiere mirado atentamente en la perfecta ley, que es la de la libertad, y perseverado en ella, no siendo oidor olvidadizo, sino hacedor de la obra, este tal será bienaventurado en su hecho.

1:26 Si alguno piensa ser religioso entre vosotros, y no refrena su lengua, sino engañando su corazón, la religión del tal es vana.

1:27 La religión pura y sin mácula delante de Dios y Padre es esta: Visitar los huérfanos y las viudas en sus tribulaciones, y guardarse sin mancha de este mundo.

Chapter 2

2:1 My brothers, do not have the faith of our Lord Jesus Christ, the Lord of glory with partiality.

2:2 For if a gold-fingered man in splendid clothing comes into your synagogue, and a poor one in shabby clothing also comes in;

2:3 and you look on the one wearing the splendid clothing, and say to him, You sit here comfortably; and to the poor one you say, You stand there, or, Sit here under my footstool;

2:4 did you not also make a difference among yourselves and become judges with evil thoughts?

2:5 Hear, my beloved brothers, did not God choose the poor of this world to be rich in faith, and heirs of the kingdom which He promised to the ones loving Him?

2:6 But you dishonored the poor one. Do not the rich ones oppress you, and they drag you to judgment seats?

2:7 Do they not blaspheme the good Name called on you?

2:8 If you truly fulfill the royal Law according to the Scripture, "You shall love your neighbor as yourself," you do well. (see Lev. 19:18)

2:9 But if you have partiality you work sin, being reproved by the Law as transgressors.

2:10 For whoever shall keep all the Law, but stumbles in one, he has become guilty of all.

Capítulo 2

2:1 Hermanos míos, no tengáis la fe de nuestro Señor Jesucristo glorioso en acepción de personas.

2:2 Porque si en vuestra congregación entra un hombre con anillo de oro, y de preciosa ropa, y también entra un pobre con vestidura vil,

2:3 Y tuviereis respeto al que trae la vestidura preciosa, y le dijereis: Siéntate tú aquí en buen lugar: y dijereis al pobre: Estáte tú allí en pie; ó siéntate aquí debajo de mi estrado:

2:4 ¿No juzguáis en vosotros mismos, y venís á ser jueces de pensamientos malos?

2:5 Hermanos míos amados, oid: ¿No ha elegido Dios los pobres de este mundo, ricos en fe, y herederos del reino que ha prometido á los que le aman?

2:6 Mas vosotros habéis afrentado al pobre. ¿No os oprimen los ricos, y no son ellos los mismos que os arrastran á los juzgados?

2:7 ¿No blasfeman ellos el buen nombre que fué invocado sobre vosotros?

2:8 Si en verdad cumplís vosotros la ley real, conforme á la Escritura: Amarás á tu prójimo como á ti mismo, bien hacéis:

2:9 Mas si hacéis acepción de personas, cometéis pecado, y sois reconvenidos de la ley como transgresores.

2:10 Porque cualquiera que hubiere guardado toda la ley, y ofendiere en un punto, es hecho culpado de todos.

Editor's Appendix	Apéndice del Editor

2:11 For He who said, "You shall not commit adultery," also said, "You shall not murder." (see Ex. 20:14, 13; Deut. 5:18, 17) But if you do not commit adultery, but commit murder, you have become a transgressor of the Law.

2:12 So speak and so do as being about to be judged through the Law of liberty.

2:13 For judgment will be without mercy to the one not doing mercy. And mercy rejoices over judgment.

2:14 My brothers, what is the gain if anyone says he has faith, but he does not have works? Is the faith able to save him?

2:15 But if a brother or a sister is naked and may be lacking in daily food,

2:16 and any one of you say to them, Go in peace, be warmed and filled, but does not give them the things the body needs, what gain is it?

2:17 So also faith, if it does not have works, is dead being by itself.

2:18 But someone will say, You have faith, and I have works. Show me your faith apart from your works, and I will show you my faith out of my works.

2:19 You believe that God is One. You do well; even the demons believe and shudder.

2:20 But are you willing to know, O vain man, that faith apart from works is dead?

2:21 Was not our father Abraham justified by works offering up his son Isaac on the altar? (see Gen. 22:9)

2:22 You see that faith worked with his works; and out of the works the faith was made perfected.

2:11 Porque el que dijo: No cometerás adulterio, también ha dicho: No matarás. Ahora bien, si no hubieres matado, ya eres hecho transgresor de la ley.

2:12 Así hablad, y así obrad, como los que habéis de ser juzgados por la ley de libertad.

2:13 Porque juicio sin misericordia será hecho con aquel que no hiciere misericordia: y la misericordia se gloría contra el juicio.

2:14 Hermanos míos, ¿qué aprovechará si alguno dice que tiene fe, y no tiene obras? ¿Podrá la fe salvarle?

2:15 Y si el hermano ó la hermana están desnudos, y tienen necesidad del mantenimiento de cada día,

2:16 Y alguno de vosotros les dice: Id en paz, calentaos y hartaos; pero no les diereis las cosas que son necesarias para el cuerpo: ¿qué aprovechará?

2:17 Así también la fe, si no tuviere obras, es muerta en sí misma.

2:18 Pero alguno dirá: Tú tienes fe, y yo tengo obras: muéstrame tu fe sin tus obras, y yo te mostraré mi fe por mis obras.

2:19 Tú crees que Dios es uno; bien haces: también los demonios creen, y tiemblan.

2:20 ¿Mas quieres saber, hombre vano, que la fe sin obras es muerta?

2:21 ¿No fué justificado por las obras Abraham nuestro padre, cuando ofreció á su hijo Isaac sobre el altar?

2:22 ¿No ves que la fe obró con sus obras, y que la fe fué perfecta por las obras?

2:23 And the Scripture was fulfilled, saying, "And Abraham believed God, and it was counted for righteousness to him;" and he was called, Friend of God. (see Gen. 15:6; Isa. 41:8)

2:24 You see, then, that a man is justified out of works, and not out of faith only.

2:25 But in the same way Rahab the harlot was also justified out of works, having received the messengers, and sending them out by another way.

2:26 For as the body is dead apart from the spirit, so also faith is dead apart from works.

2:23 Y fué cumplida la Escritura que dice: Abraham creyó á Dios, y le fué imputado á justicia, y fué llamado amigo de Dios.

2:24 Vosotros veis, pues, que el hombre es justificado por las obras, y no solamente por la fe.

2:25 Asimismo también Rahab la ramera, ¿no fué justificada por obras, cuando recibió los mensajeros, y los echó fuera por otro camino?

2:26 Porque como el cuerpo sin espíritu está muerto, así también la fe sin obras es muerta.

| Editor's Appendix | Apéndice del Editor |

Chapter 3 / Capítulo 3

3:1 My brothers do not be many teachers, knowing that we will receive greater judgment.

3:2 For we all stumble in many ways. If any one does not stumble in Word, this one is a mature man, able also to bridle the whole body.

3:3 Behold, we put bits in the mouths of the horses, for them to obey us; and we turn about their whole body.

3:4 Behold, the ships also, being so great, and being driven by violent winds, they are directed by a very small rudder, where the impulse of the one steering purposes.

3:5 So also the tongue is a little member, and boasts great things. Behold, how little a fire kindles how large a forest!

3:6 And the tongue is a fire, the world of iniquity. So the tongue is set among our members, spotting all the body, and inflaming the course of nature, and being inflamed by Hell.

3:7 For every species of beasts, both indeed of birds, of creeping things, and of sea animals, is tamed, and has been tamed by the human species;

3:8 but no one of men is able to tame the tongue; it is an unrestrainable evil, full of death-dealing poison.

3:9 By this we bless God and the Father; and by this we curse men having come into being according to the image of God. (see Gen. 1:26)

3:1 Hermanos míos, no os hagáis muchos maestros, sabiendo que recibiremos mayor condenación.

3:2 Porque todos ofendemos en muchas cosas. Si alguno no ofende en Palabra, éste es varón perfecto, que también puede con freno gobernar todo el cuerpo.

3:3 He aquí nosotros ponemos frenos en las bocas de los caballos para que nos obedezcan, y gobernamos todo su cuerpo.

3:4 Mirad también las naves: aunque tan grandes, y llevadas de impetuosos vientos, son gobernadas con un muy pequeño timón por donde quisiere el que las gobierna.

3:5 Así también, la lengua es un miembro pequeño, y se gloría de grandes cosas. He aquí, un pequeño fuego -cuán grande bosque enciende!

3:6 Y la lengua es un fuego, un mundo de maldad. Así la lengua está puesta entre nuestros miembros, la cual contamina todo el cuerpo, é inflama la rueda de la creación, y es inflamada del infierno.

3:7 Porque toda naturaleza de bestias, y de aves, y de serpientes, y de seres de la mar, se doma y es domada de la naturaleza humana:

3:8 Pero ningún hombre puede domar la lengua, que es un mal que no puede ser refrenado; llena de veneno mortal.

3:9 Con ella bendecimos al Dios y Padre, y con ella maldecimos á los hombres, los cuales son hechos á la semejanza de Dios.

3:10 Out of the same mouth comes forth blessing and cursing. My brothers, it is not fitting for these things to be so.

3:11 Does the fountain out of the same hole send forth the sweet and the bitter?

3:12 My brothers, a fig tree is not able to produce olives, or a vine figs. So neither can a fountain produce both salt and sweet water.

3:13 Who is wise and knowing among you? Let him show his works by his good behavior, in meekness of wisdom.

3:14 But if you have bitter jealousy and contention in your heart, do not boast and lie against the truth.

3:15 This is not the wisdom coming down from above, but is earthly, beastly, devilish.

3:16 For where jealousy and contention are, there is confusion and every foul deed.

3:17 But the wisdom from above is firstly truly pure, then peaceable, forbearing, yielding, full of mercy and of good fruits, not partial and not pretended.

3:18 And the fruit of righteousness is sown in peace for the ones making peace.

3:10 De una misma boca proceden bendición y maldición. Hermanos míos, no conviene que estas cosas sean así hechas.

3:11 ¿Echa alguna fuente por una misma abertura agua dulce y amarga?

3:12 Hermanos míos, ¿puede la higuera producir aceitunas, ó la vid higos? Así ninguna fuente puede hacer agua salada y dulce.

3:13 ¿Quién es sabio y avisado entre vosotros? muestre por buena conversación sus obras en mansedumbre de sabiduría.

3:14 Pero si tenéis envidia amarga y contención en vuestros corazones, no os gloriés, ni seáis mentirosos contra la verdad:

3:15 Que esta sabiduría no es la que desciende de lo alto, sino terrena, animal, diabólica.

3:16 Porque donde hay envidia y contención, allí hay perturbación y toda obra perversa.

3:17 Mas la sabiduría que es de lo alto, primeramente es pura, después pacífica, modesta, benigna, llena de misericordia y de buenos frutos, no juzgadora, no fingida.

3:18 Y el fruto de justicia se siembra en paz para aquellos que hacen paz.

Chapter 4

4:1 From where do wars and fightings among you come? Is it not from this, from your lusts warring in your members?

4:2 You desire and do not have. You murder, and are jealous, and are not able to obtain. You fight and you war, and you do not have, because you do not ask.

4:3 You ask, and do not receive, because you ask wrongly, in order that you may spend on your lusts.

4:4 Adulterers and adulteresses! Do you not know that the friendship of the world is enmity with God? Whoever, then, purposes to be a friend of the world is put down as hostile to God.

4:5 Or do you think that vainly the Scripture says, The spirit which has dwelt in us yearns to envy?

4:6 But He gives greater grace. Because of this it says, "God sets Himself against proud ones, but He gives grace to humble ones." (see Prov. 3:34)

4:7 Then be subject to God. Resist the Devil, and he will flee from you.

4:8 Draw near to God, and He will draw near to you. Cleanse your hands, sinners! And purify your hearts, double minded ones!

4:9 Be distressed, and mourn, and weep. Let your laughter be turned to mourning, and your joy into shame.

4:10 Be humbled before the Lord, and He will exalt you.

Capítulo 4

4:1 ¿De dónde vienen las guerras y los pleitos entre vosotros? ¿No son de vuestras concupiscencias, las cuales combaten en vuestros miembros?

4:2 Codiciáis, y no tenéis; matáis y ardéis de envidia, y no podéis alcanzar; combatís y gerreáis, y no tenéis lo que deseáis, porque no pedís.

4:3 Pedís, y no recibís, porque pedís mal, para gastar en vuestros deleites.

4:4 Adúlteros y adúlteras, ¿no sabéis que la amistad del mundo es enemistad con Dios? Cualquiera pues que quisiere ser amigo del mundo, se constituye enemigo de Dios.

4:5 ¿Pensáis que la Escritura dice sin causa: Es espíritu que mora en nosotros codicia para envidia?

4:6 Mas él da mayor gracia. Por esto dice: Dios resiste á los soberbios, y da gracia á los humildes.

4:7 Someteos pues á Dios; resistid al diablo, y de vosotros huirá.

4:8 Allegaos á Dios, y él se allegará á vosotros. Pecadores, limpiad las manos; y vosotros de doblado ánimo, purificad los corazones.

4:9 Afligíos, y lamentad, y llorad. Vuestra risa se convierta en lloro, y vuestro gozo en tristeza.

4:10 Humillaos delante del Señor, y él os ensalzará.

4:11 Do not speak against one another, brothers. He that speaks against a brother, and is judging a brother, he speaks against Law, and judges Law. But if you judge Law, you are not a doer of Law, but a judge.	4:11 Hermanos, no murmuréis los unos de los otros. El que murmura del hermano, y juzga á su hermano, este tal murmura de la ley, y juzga á la ley; pero si tú juzgas á la ley, no eres guardador de la ley, sino juez.
4:12 One is the Lawgiver, who is able to save and to destroy. Who are you who judges another?	4:12 Uno es el dador de la ley, que puede salvar y perder: ¿quién eres tú que juzgas á otro?
4:13 Come now, those saying, Today or tomorrow we will go into this city, and we will spend one year there, and we will trade and will make a profit,	4:13 Ea ahora, los que decís: Hoy y mañana iremos á tal ciudad, y estaremos allá un año, y compraremos mercadería, y ganaremos:
4:14 who do not know of the morrow. For what is your life? For it is a mist, which for a little while appears, and then disappears.	4:14 Y no sabéis lo que será mañana. Porque ¿qué es vuestra vida? Ciertamente es un vapor que se aparece por un poco de tiempo, y luego se desvanece.
4:15 Instead of you saying, If the Lord wills, even we will live, and we will do this or that;	4:15 En lugar de lo cual deberíais decir: Si el Señor quisiere, y si viviéremos, haremos esto ó aquello.
4:16 but now you boast in your presumptions. All such boasting is evil.	4:16 Mas ahora os jactáis en vuestras soberbias. Toda jactancia semejante es mala.
4:17 Therefore, to anyone knowing to do good, and not doing it, it is sin to him.	4:17 El pecado, pues, está en aquel que sabe hacer lo bueno, y no lo hace.

Chapter 5

5:1 Come now, rich ones, weep, howling over your hardships coming on.

5:2 Your riches have rotted, and your garments have become moth-eaten.

5:3 Your gold and silver have rusted over, and their poison will be a testimony to you, and will eat your flesh as fire. You heaped treasure in the last days.

5:4 Behold, the wages of the workmen who have reaped your fields cry out, being kept back by you. And the cries of the ones who have reaped have entered "into the ears of the Lord of Hosts." (see Isa. 5:9)

5:5 You lived luxuriously on the earth, and lived for self-pleasure; you nourished your hearts as in a day of slaughter;

5:6 you condemned; you murdered the righteous; he does not resist you.

5:7 Therefore, brothers, be long-suffering until the coming of the Lord. Behold, the farmer waits for the precious fruit of the earth, being long-suffering over it until it may receive the early and the latter rain.

5:8 You also be long-suffering. Set your hearts firmly, because the coming of the Lord has drawn near.

5:9 Do not murmur against one another, brothers, that you not be condemned. Behold, the Judge stands before the door.

5:10 My brothers, as an example of suffering ill, and of longsuffering, take the prophets who spoke in the name of the Lord.

Capítulo 5

5:1 Ea ya ahora, oh ricos, llorad aullando por vuestras miserias que os vendrán.

5:2 Vuestras riquezas están podridas: vuestras ropas están comidas de polilla.

5:3 Vuestro oro y plata están corrompidos de orín; y su orín os será testimonio, y comerá del todo vuestras carnes como fuego. Os habéis allegado tesoro para en los postreros días.

5:4 He aquí, el jornal de los obreros que han segado vuestras tierras, el cual por engaño no les ha sido pagado de vosotros, clama; y los clamores de los que habían segado, han entrado en los oídos del Señor de los ejércitos.

5:5 Habéis vivido en deleites sobre la tierra, y sido disolutos; habéis cebado vuestros corazones como en el día de sacrificios.

5:6 Habéis condenado y muerto al justo; y él no os resiste.

5:7 Pues, hermanos, tened paciencia hasta la venida del Señor. Mirad cómo el labrador espera el precioso fruto de la tierra, aguardando con paciencia, hasta que reciba la lluvia temprana y tardía.

5:8 Tened también vosotros paciencia; confirmad vuestros corazones: porque la venida del Señor se acerca.

5:9 Hermanos, no os quejéis unos contra otros, porque no seáis condenados; he aquí, el juez está delante de la puerta.

5:10 Hermanos míos, tomad por ejemplo de aflicción y de paciencia, á los profetas que hablaron en nombre del Señor.

5:11 Behold, we call those blessed who endure. You have heard of the patience of Job, and you saw the end of the Lord, "that the Lord is full of tender mercy and pity." (see Psa. 103:8)

5:12 But before all things, my brothers, do not swear, neither by the heaven, nor by the earth, nor any other oath. But let your yes be yes, and the no, no, that you may not fall under judgment.

5:13 Does anyone suffer ill among you? Let him pray. Is anyone cheerful? Let him praise in song.

5:14 Is any among you sick? Let him call the elders of the assembly, and let them pray over him, anointing him with oil in the name of the Lord.

5:15 And the prayer of faith will save those being sick, and the Lord will raise him up. And if he may have committed sin, it will be forgiven him.

5:16 Confess to one another the deviations from the Law, and pray for one another, that you may be healed. Very strong is a righteous petition, being made effective.

5:17 Elijah was a man of like feeling to us, and he prayed in prayer for it not to rain; and it did not rain on the earth three years and six months.

5:18 And he prayed again, and the heaven gave rain, and the earth caused its fruit to sprout.

5:19 If anyone among you goes astray from the truth, brothers, and anyone turns him back,

5:20 know that the one turning a sinner from the error of his way will save the soul from death, and will hide a multitude of sins.

5:11 He aquí, tenemos por bienaventurados á los que sufren. Habéis oído la paciencia de Job, y habéis visto el fin del Señor, que el Señor es muy misericordioso y piadoso.

5:12 Mas sobre todo, hermanos míos, no juréis, ni por el cielo, ni por la tierra, ni por otro cualquier juramento; sino vuestro sí sea sí, y vuestro no sea no; porque no caigáis en condenación.

5:13 ¿Está alguno entre vosotros afligido? haga oración. ¿Está alguno alegre? cante salmos.

5:14 ¿Está alguno enfermo entre vosotros? llame á los ancianos de la iglesia, y oren por él, ungiéndole con aceite en el nombre del Señor.

5:15 Y la oración de fe salvará al enfermo, y el Señor lo levantará; y si estuviere en pecados, le serán perdonados.

5:16 Confesaos vuestras faltas unos á otros, y rogad los unos por los otros, para que seáis sanos; la oración del justo, obrando eficazmente, puede mucho.

5:17 Elías era hombre sujeto á semejantes pasiones que nosotros, y rogó con oración que no lloviese, y no llovió sobre la tierra en tres años y seis meses.

5:18 Y otra vez oró, y el cielo dió lluvia, y la tierra produjo su fruto.

5:19 Hermanos, si alguno de entre vosotros ha errado de la verdad, y alguno le convirtiere,

5:20 Sepa que el que hubiere hecho convertir al pecador del error de su camino, salvará un alma de muerte, y cubrirá multitud de pecados.

***The Three Traitors
and the Three Gunas***

***Los Tres Traidores
y las Tres Gunas***

Extract from Ch. 39 of PARSIFAL UNVEILED:

"THE THREE TRAITORS"

"And I saw three unclean spirits like frogs come out of the mouth of the dragon, and out of the mouth of the beast, and out of the mouth of the false prophet."

"For they are the spirits of devils, working miracles, which go forth unto the kings of the earth and of the whole world, to gather them to the battle of that great day of God Almighty." (Revelations 6:13-14)

It is written with coals of ardent fire in the marvelous book of all splendors[3], who the three traitors are that assassinate HIRAM or [it would be] better for us to say HIRAM-OSIRIS, the intimate God of every man that comes to [this] world.

We must search with infinite yearning[4] within ourselves for these three assassins of the secret Master, so that finally, on a given day (neither the day nor the hour is important), we will exclaim with all of the strength of our soul: "The King is dead, [long] live the King!"

It is ostensible[5] that the first treacherous [traitor] is certainly the loathsome[6] demon of desire.

It is unquestionable that the second infidel is the horrifying demon of the mind.

---

[3] Literally 'esplendores' means "splendor, magnificence, grandeur; brilliance; bravery"
[4] Literally 'ansia' means "anxiety, worry; anguish; yearning, longing"
[5] Literally 'ostensible' means "ostensible, appearing to be true, professed to be a certain way (but often having hidden meaning or intent)"
[6] Literally 'asqueante' means "disgusting, loathsome, sickening, nauseating"

Extracto del Cap. XXXIX de EL PARSIFAL DELVADO:

"LOS TRES TRAIDORES"

"Y vi salir de la boca del Dragón, y de la boca de la bestia, y de la boca del falso profeta, tres espíritus inmundos a manera de ranas".

"Pues son espíritus de demonios, que hacen señales y van a los reyes de la tierra en todo el mundo, para reunirlos a la batalla de aquel gran día del Dios Todopoderoso". (Apocalipsis).

Escrito está con carbones de fuego ardiente en el libro maravilloso de todos los esplendores, que éstos son los tres traidores que asesinaron a HIRAM o mejor dijéramos HIRAM-OSIRIS, el Dios íntimo de todo hombre que viene al mundo.

Debemos buscar con ansia infinita, dentro de nosotros mismos, a estos tres asesinos del Maestro secreto, hasta que al fin un día cualquiera, no importa la fecha, ni el día, ni la hora, podamos exclamar con todas las fuerzas de nuestra alma: ¡El Rey ha muerto, viva el Rey!

Es ostensible que el primer alevoso es ciertamente el asqueante demonio del deseo.

Es incuestionable que el segundo infiel es el demonio horripilante de la mente.

It is evident, clear and definite [that] the third traitor [is] the vile demon of ill-will.

JUDAS is the first, who sells the Christ secretly for thirty pieces of silver.

PILATE is the second, [who] always washes his hands and declares himself innocent, never recognizing his [own] guilt.

CAIAPHAS is the third; [who] never does the will of the Father; he hated[7] the Lord and still remains hating him.

The origin of these three evil ones is certainly extremely[8] tenebrous; [it] is indubitable[9] that they come from the frightful perversion of the three GUNAS.

SATTVA is the GUNA of universal harmony.

RAYAS is the GUNA of emotion.

TAMAS is the GUNA of inertia[10].

Any illuminated Hierophant [who] studies the AKASHIC records of Nature can clearly[11] verify for themselves, the transcendental fact of the absolute equilibrium of the three GUNAS of mystery during the profound night of the great Pralaya [or cosmic night].

When these three GUNAS become imbalanced[12] in the cosmic scales then [this] initiates the dawning of a new [cosmic] day.

Resulta patético, claro y definido el tercer traidor, el vil demonio de la mala voluntad.

JUDAS es el primero, aquél que vende al Cristo secreto por treinta monedas de plata.

PILATOS es el segundo; siempre se lava las manos y se declara inocente, nunca se reconoce culpable.

CAIFÁS es el tercero; jamás hace la voluntad del Padre; aborreció al Señor y todavía le sigue aborreciendo.

El origen de estos tres malvados ciertamente es demasiado tenebroso; es indubitable que ellos devienen de la perversión espantosa de las tres GUNAS.

SATTVA es la GUNA de la armonía universal.

RAYAS es la GUNA de la emoción.

TAMAS es la GUNA de la inercia.

Cualquier Hierofante iluminado estudiando los registros AKÁSHICOS de la Naturaleza, podrá verificar por sí mismo en forma clara, el hecho trascendental del equilibrio absoluto de las tres GUNAS del misterio durante la noche profunda del gran Pralaya.

Cuando estas tres GUNAS se desequilibran en los platillos de la balanza cósmica entonces se inicia la aurora del nuevo día.

---

[7] Literally 'aborreció' means "abhor, hate, detest; abandon, desert"
[8] Literally 'demasiado' means "overly, overmuch, too much; too many"
[9] Literally 'indubitable' means "indubitable, undoubtable, undoubted, unquestionable"
[10] Literally 'inercia' means "inertia, inertness, inactivity, immobility; in Physics it refers to the tendency of matter to remain at rest or continue at a constant velocity unless acted upon by an outside force"
[11] Literally 'en forma clara' means "in [a] clear form/way"
[12] Literally 'desequilibran' means "unbalanced, imbalanced"

KRISHNA that illustrious[13] man[14] who fulfilled[15] a gigantic mission in the sacred land of the Vedas, emphatically refers himself to the three GUNAS of ancient wisdom, saying:

"If the incarnated being departs when SATTVA predominates, then, it will go to the sphere of the devotees that adore the most high[16]."

"If at the moment of death RAYA predominates, a [person is] born who is the person [that is] addicted to action; and if TAMAS predominates, they will be born among the beings that do not reason."

"Those with SATTVIC temperaments will go up (to the superior spheres of the Universe).

"Those [with] RAYASIC [temperaments] remain in the middle (reborn in [the] human body in [an] immediate or mediated[17] form without having the luxury of a vacation in the ineffable regions).

"And those [with] TAMASIC [temperaments] will go down (submerged within the interior of the earth, they enter into the submerged mineral kingdom in order to involuntarily return[18], in time, descending through the animal, vegetable and mineral steps[19]."

---

[13] Literally 'preclaro' means "preclear, lucid, illustrious"
[14] Literally 'varón' means "he, male; man"
[15] Literally 'otrora cumpliese' means "once fulfilled"
[16] Literally 'elevado' means "elevated, raised high, lofty; elevate, raise, lift; arise, ascend"
[17] Literally 'mediata' means "mediate, of or through an intermediary, dependent on a mediator"
[18] Literally 'retroceder' means "go back, return, regress; flinch"
[19] Literally 'escalones' means "echelon; step; phase; terrace; stagger"

Afterwards [they take] other paths to [reach] the light of the sun and then re-initiate a new ascension of [an] evolutionary type that recommences in the hard rock [or mineral kingdom])."

And the illustrious[20] Lord once again took up the word in order to say the following:

"When knowledge shines through [all] the paths, then one can consider that SATTVA predominates."

"When covetousness[21], activity, the concept of new undertakings[22], restlessness[23], and desire prevail, then Oh Bharata!, RAYAS predominates.

"And when TAMAS predominates, Oh Kounteya!, mental obscurity, inertia, inadvertency[24] and hallucinations prevail."

"Transcending the three GUNAS, which cause this body, the incarnated being is liberated from birth, from death, from old age and from suffering, and becomes immortal."

KUNDALINI YOGA teaches, in a brilliant way, that the BHUJANJINI or serpentine power is found coiled three and a half times within the Coccigeal Chakra.

The three turns [or coils of the serpentine power] represent the three GUNAS of [the] PRAKRITI: SATTVA, RAYAS and TAMAS.

Después salen otra vez a la luz del sol y luego re-inician un nuevo ascenso de tipo evolutivo que ha de recomenzar en la dura piedra)".

Y aquel ínclito Señor tomó otra vez la palabra para decir lo siguiente:

"Cuando el conocimiento brilla a través de los sentidos se debe considerar que predomina SATTVA".

"Cuando prevalecen la codicia, la actividad, el concepto de nuevas empresas, la intranquilidad, y el deseo, entonces ¡Oh Bharata!, predomina el RAYAS".

"Y cuando predomina el TAMAS, ¡Oh Kounteya!, prevalece la oscuridad mental, la inercia, la inadvertencia y la alucinación".

"Trascendiendo a las tres GUNAS, que causan este cuerpo, el ser encarnado se libera del nacimiento, de la muerte, de la vejez y del sufrimiento, y deviene inmortal".

El KUNDALINI YOGA enseña en forma brillante que el BHUJANJINI o poder serpentino se encuentra enroscado tres veces y media dentro del Chacra Coxígeo.

Las tres vueltas representan a la tres GUNAS de PRAKRITI: SATTVA, RAYAS Y TAMAS.

---

[20] Literally 'ínclito' means "illustrious, outstanding; distinguished"
[21] Literally 'codicia' means "greediness, avarice; lust; covet"
[22] Literally 'empresas' means "enterprise, undertaking; venture, gamble; business, company; firm; task; employer; employment"
[23] Literally 'intranquilidad' means "restlessness, restiveness, uneasiness"
[24] Literally 'inadvertencia' means "oversight, inadvertence"

Editor's Appendix	Apéndice del Editor
It is an axiom of occult wisdom that the remaining half [turn] represents VIKRITIS, the modification of [the] PRAKRITI, the eternal feminine.	Es un axioma de la sabiduría oculta que la media cola restante representa a VIKRITIS, la modificación de PRAKRITI el eterno femenino.
The gospel of Lord BUDDHA says:	El evangelio del Señor BUDDHA dice:
"The three daughter of MARA (the three perverse GUNAS), tempted the BODHISATTVA, but he paid no attention to them, and when MARA saw that he could kindle no desire in the victorious heart of SRAMANA, he ordered all the malignant spirits (obedient to their mandates) to attack and overcome the great MUNI."	"Las tres hijas de MARA (las tres GUNAS pervertidas), tentaron al BODHISATTVA, pero no reparó en ellas, y cuando vio MARA que no podía encender ningún deseo en el corazón del SRAMANA victorioso, ordenó a todos los espíritus malignos que, obedientes a sus mandatos, atacaran y aterrasen al gran MUNI".
"But the Blessed One contemplated them as one would watch the harmless games of children and the burning[25] hatred of the evil spirits was without success.	"Pero el Bienaventurado los contempló como quien mira los juegos inocentes de los niños y el ardiente odio de los malos espíritus quedó sin resultado.
The flames of the inferno became wholesome breezes of perfume and the furious rays [of the evil spirits] were changed into lotus blossoms."	Las llamas del infierno se hicieron saludables brisas perfumadas y los rayos furibundos se trocaron en flores de loto".
"After this MARA (THE DRAGON OF DARKNESS) saw this, and his army fled.	"Ante esto MARA (EL DRAGÓN DE LAS TINIEBLAS), y su ejército huyeron.
Meanwhile, a rain of heavenly flowers fell, and the voices of good spirits were heard."	Mientras tanto, de las alturas celestes caía una lluvia de flores y se oían las voces de los buenos espíritus".
"Behold the great MUNI! His spirit is unmoved by hatred[26].	"¡Ved el gran MUNI! ¡El odio no conmueve su espíritu!
The legions of evil (Those red devils who constitute the famous [psychological] "I") did not intimidate him.	Las legiones del malo (Esos diablos rojos que constituyen el famoso Yo), no le han intimidado.
He is pure and wise; he is full of love and compassion."	Es puro y sabio; está lleno de amor y compasión".

---

[25] Literally 'ardiente' means "burning, glowing; fervent, ardent; hot, fervid"
[26] Literally 'odio' means "hate, detest, loathe, despise"

"As the rays of the sun drown the darkness of the world, so he who perseveres in his search will find the truth and the truth will illuminate him."

The former verses were some [from] among the sacred gospel of our Lord BUDDHA.

Many centuries afterwards, the Divine Rabbi of Galilee exclaims with all the strength[27] of his soul:

"And ye shall know the Truth, and the Truth shall set you free." [John: 8:32]

"God is Spirit" -states the Christian Gospel- "and those that worship[28] him, must worship him in Spirit and in Truth." [John: 4:24]

"When, however, the Spirit of Truth, has come, He will guide you [through] all the truths; for he shall not speak of himself, but whatsoever he shall hear, that he shall speak: and he will show[29] you things to come." [John: 16:13]

It is written with characters of ardent fire that only by dying in ourselves, can we incarnate the Spirit of Truth.

Those who know the word of power never pronounce it, [infact] no one has ever pronounced it, except he who has INCARNATED it.

SIDDHARTHA, the BUDDHA, is the one who accomplishes what he promises to himself, as does PARSIFAL of the WAGNERIAN Drama, who courageously grasps the lance of EROS, in order to annihilate first the Demons of SET (THE EGO) and then the three Furies who dwell in the terrible abysses of Acheron.

---

[27] Literally 'fuerzas' means "armaments, forces, strengths"
[28] Literally 'adoren' means "adore; worship, deify; dote"
[29] Literally 'pronunciará' means "pronounce, utter; preach; give; make; pass"

Gautama was certainly a Magician of Tantric Initiation; [he] practiced the SAHAJA MAITHUNA intensely[30] and skillfully handled the lance with singular mastery.

Gautama fue ciertamente un Mago de la Iniciación Tantra; practicó el SAHAJA MAITHUNA intensivamente y manejó la lanza con singular maestría.

---

[30] Literally 'intensivamente' means "intensively, extremely, to a high degree, intensely"

Extracted from the Lecture   Extraído de la Conferencia

	SATTVA	RAYAS	TAMA
Explanation / **Explicación**	the GUNA of universal harmony / la GUNA de la armonía universal	the GUNA of emotion / la GUNA de la emoción	the GUNA of inertia / la GUNA de la inercia
If this Guna predominates at the moment of death / **Si esta Guna predomina en el momento de morir**	will go to the sphere of the devotees that adore the most high / a la esfera de los devotos que adoran a lo más elevado	a [person is] born who is the person [that is] addicted to action / uno nace entre la gente adicta a la acción	they will be born among the beings that do not reason / nace entre los seres que no razonan
Temperment / **Temperamento**	will go up (to the superior spheres of the Universe) / van arriba (a las esferas superiores del Universo)	remain in the middle (reborn in [the] human body in [an] immediate or mediated form without having the luxury of a vacation in the ineffable regions) / quedan en el medio (renacen en cuerpo humano en forma inmediata o mediata sin haberse dado el lujo de unas vacaciones en las regiones inefables)	will go down (submerged within the interior of the earth, they enter into the submerged mineral kingdom in order to involuntarily return) / van abajo (se sumergen dentro del interior de la tierra, ingresan al reino mineral sumergido para retroceder)
Pedominance / **Predomina**	knowledge shines through [all] the paths / el conocimiento brilla a través de los sentidos	covetousness, activity, the concept of new undertakings, restlessness, and desire prevail / la codicia, la actividad, el concepto de nuevas empresas, la intranquilidad, y el deseo	mental obscurity, inertia, inadvertency and hallucinations prevail / prevalece la oscuridad mental, la inercia, la inadvertencia y la alucinación

Editor's Appendix

Extract from pages 1073-1078 of
THE FIFTH GOSPEL:

"THE THREE GUNAS
IN THE COSMIC MATTER"

Well friends, we are going to speak a little on the THREE GUNAS: Sattva, Rayas and Tamas.

SATTVA, then, unquestionably, is Harmony, Beauty, [and] authentic Happiness.

As far as RAYAS, it is animal Passion, Action.

TAMAS, properly said, is Inertia[31].

Therefore, Sattva, Rayas and Tamas, are the Three fundamental Qualities of the PRAKRITI.

And what is the "Prakriti"?, you could ask me.

The Prakriti, then, is the Great Alaya of the Universe, the COSMIC MOTHER, Maha-Kundalini, etc.

In any case, it is the Eternal Feminine Principle.

Before the Dawning of the Maha-Manvantara began, it is clear that Sattva, Rayas and Tamas, the Three Gunas, were in perfect equilibrium, [there] was no decompensation[32]; then the Maha-Pralaya, the Cosmic Night reigned.

Apéndice del Editor

Extracto de páginas 1073-1078 de
EL QUINTO EVANGELIO:

"LAS TRES GUNAS
EN LA MATERIA CÓSMICA"

Bueno amigos, vamos a hablar un poco sobre las TRES GUNAS: Sattva, Rayas y Tamas.

SATTVA, pues, incuestionablemente, es la Armonía, la Belleza, la Felicidad auténtica.

En cuanto a RAYAS, es la Pasión animal, la Acción.

TAMAS, propiamente dicho, es la Inercia.

Así pues, Sattva, Rayas y Tamas, son las Tres Cualidades fundamentales de la PRAKRITI.

¿Y qué es la "Prakriti"?, podría preguntárseme.

La Prakriti, pues, es el Gran Alaya del Universo, La MADRE CÓSMICA, Maha-Kundalini, etc.

En todo caso, es el Principio Femenino Eterno.

Antes de que se iniciara la Aurora del Maha-Manvantara, es claro que Sattva, Rayas y Tamas, las Tres Gunas, se hallaban en perfecto equilibrio, no había descompensación alguna; entonces reinaba el Maha-Pralaya, la Noche Cósmica.

---

[31] Literally 'inercia' means "inertia, inertness, inactivity, immobility; in Physics it refers to the tendency of matter to remain at rest or continue at a constant velocity unless acted upon by an outside force"

[32] Literally 'descompensación' means "decompensation (inability of an organ, especially the heart, to maintain its function due to overload caused by a disease)"

In the bossom[33] of the Eternal Common Cosmic Father, during the Maha-Pralaya, the Elohim are merely Divine Atoms, submerged within That which does not have [a] name.

THE ALTERATION OF THE THREE GUNAS (Sattva, Rayas and Tamas), occurs because those Primordial, Divine Atoms, or simply Virginal Sparks, yearn to be something, or someone.

Then (as [a] result) the Three Gunas become imbalanced[34] in the great plate of the Cosmic Scales, [and] then (as [a] result) Karma enters activity:

The First Logos initiates Electrical Movement, the ELECTRICAL WHIRLWIND[35], and the atoms of the past Universe (which slept within their SPECIE'S[36] CENTERS before), wake up for a new activity.

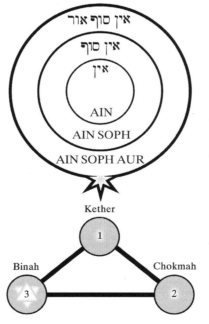

Thus this is how the Dawning of the Maha-Manvantara always begins.

But, obviously, the Causal Logos would not enter into activity (initiating the Electrical Whirlwind, the Electrical Hurricane within the Chaotic Waters of the Life), if the imbalance of the Three Gunas had not previously taken place.

En el seno del Eterno Padre Cósmico Común, durante el Maha-Pralaya, los Elohim son meros Átomos Divinales, sumergidos entre Eso que no tiene nombre.

LA ALTERACIÓN DE LAS TRES GUNAS (Sattva, Rayas y Tamas), se debe a que esos Átomos Primordiales, Divinales, o simplemente Chispas Virginales, anhelan ser algo, o alguien.

Entonces, como resultado, viene el desequilibrio de las Tres Gunas en el gran platillo de la Balanza Cósmica, entonces, como resultado, el Karma entra en actividad:

El Primer Logos inicia el Movimiento Eléctrico, el TORBELLINO ELÉCTRICO, y los átomos del Universo pasado (que antes dormían entre sus CENTROS LAYA), despiertan para una nueva actividad.

Así es como se inicia siempre la Aurora del Maha-Manvantara.

Pero, obviamente, el Logos Causal no entraría en actividad (iniciando el Torbellino Eléctrico, el Huracán Eléctrico entre las Aguas Caóticas de la Vida), si antes no se hubiese producido un desequilibrio de las Tres Gunas.

---

[33] Literally 'seno' means "breast, bosom; womb; heart; bay, gulf"
[34] Literally 'viene el desequilibrio' means "disequilibrium comes [forth]"
[35] Literally 'TORBELLINO' means "Whirlwind, whirlpool, whirl"
[36] Literally 'LAYA' means "breed, blood, kind, type, sort, pedigree, species; spade (digging tool)"

Editor's Appendix

The very fact that the Three Gunas are imbalanced in the Cosmic Scales indicates, then, [the] IMPERFECTION OF the PRIMORDIAL, Divine ATOMS or Virginal Monads, which are at rest within the bossom of the Eternal Common Cosmic Father.

If these Primordial Monads did not yearn to be something, or someone, [then] the imbalance of Three Gunas would not be feasible[37].

In order for the Three Gunas to [become] imbalanced, there must exist an inherent[38] cause, an unknown, profound motivating[39] principle.

I find such causa-causorum within the same Virginal Atoms or Sparks that rest within the bosom of the Eternal Common Cosmic Father.

They must have had some form of imperfection (incomprehensible from [a] merely intellectual analysis), that naturally became that innate cause, which in its turn, caused the Monads, [that were] submerged within the bossom of the Eternal Common Cosmic Father, to yearn to be something, or someone.

If those Monads enjoyed absolute Perfection, they would not want to be something or someone, [and] then the imbalance of the Three Gunas would not be feasible either.

Obviously, within the bossom of the Eternal Common Cosmic Father, Happiness reigns.

Apéndice del Editor

El hecho mismo de que las Tres Gunas se desequilibren en la Balanza Cósmica, indica, pues, IMPERFECCIÓN DE LOS ÁTOMOS PRIMORDIALES, Divinales, o Mónadas Virginales, que se hallan en reposo entre el seno del Eterno Padre Cósmico Común.

Si esas Mónadas Primordiales no anhelaran ser algo, o alguien, el desequilibrio de las Tres Gunas no sería factible.

Para que las Tres Gunas se desequilibren, tiene que existir una causa ingénita, un principio motor ignoto, profundo.

Yo encuentro, tal causa-causorum, entre los mismos Átomos o Chispas Virginales que reposan entre el seno del Eterno Padre Cósmico Común.

Tiene que haber alguna forma de imperfección (incomprensible para el análisis meramente intelectivo), que viene, naturalmente, a convertirse en esa ingénita causa, que a su vez, hace que las Mónadas, sumergidas entre el seno del Eterno Padre Cósmico Común, anhelen ser algo, o alguien.

Si esas Mónadas gozaran de la absoluta Perfección, no desearían ser algo, o alguien, entonces el desequilibrio de las Tres Gunas tampoco sería factible.

Obviamente, entre el seno del Eterno Padre Cósmico Común, reina la Felicidad.

---

[37] Literally 'factible' means "feasible, achievable; practicable; realizable"
[38] Literally 'ingénita' means "innate, native, natural, inborn; inherent"
[39] Literally 'motor' means "motive, moving; motor; driving"

When a Virginal Spark (anyone that it may be) submerges itself within this joy[40], [if it] does not want life, we could say, of [an] egoistical type, [if] it does not want to be something different from the Father, then, within itself it will find different levels, or better we [could] say, Super-Levels of Happiness…

Much has been said about the Being, and everybody yearns to know their own Being.

When one has already known [their own Being], one is happy, but then one wants to know their own Being more, and one can only find that "more" within oneself.

Whosoever has managed to pass [through] the 13th Door of the Hebraic Kabalah submerges themselves within the bosom of the Eternal Common Cosmic Father.

There when doing it, one finds one's Being; but when one has managed to discover one's Being, and to integrate oneself with him, it is that one's Being is more within[41], and when by means of some efforts one has managed, then, to surpass oneself more, one finds that one's Being is even more profound.

Conclusion: THE BEING DOES NOT HAVE LIMITS NOR BORDERS.

How could we put a limit on the Being?

It is not possible! But well, let us be a little more specific, so that this question can be better understood…

---

[40] Literally 'dicha' means "happiness, joy, bliss"
[41] Literally 'adentro' means "in, inside, indoors, inwards"

Let us look at the human constitution: [In] the Hebraic Kabalah, we already know that there are Ten Sephira.

If we begin with MALKUTH, [which] is the Sephiroth that corresponds to the physical body.

If we continue with YESOD, we find the Vital Seat[42], where the Creative Energy is.

The Third Sephiroth is, naturally, the Astral Body, which is HOD, and as far as the fourth Sephiroth, which is the Mental [Body], we find NETZACH.

Much furthur on, we have the Fifth Sephiroth, which is the Human Soul: TIPHERETH, the Causal [Body]; and still furthur on, is the Sixth Sephiroth… […X…][43] …which is GEBURAH: The Rigor, the Law, the Buddhi, the Beautiful Helen, etc., etc., etc.; the Seventh Sephiroth… […X…] …is Gedulah, or simply[44] CHESED, the Intimus; but far beyond the Intimus is the Logos.

BINAH is the Eighth Sephiroth… […X…] …the Holy Spirit; Ninth, the Intimate Christ, the Ninth Sephiroth: CHOKMAH; and as far as the Ancient of the Days[45], KETHER, it is the Tenth Sephiroth.

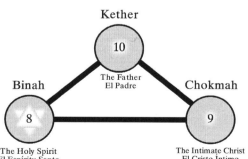

Miremos la constitución humana: La Kábala Hebraica, ya sabemos que tiene Diez Sephirotes.

Si empezamos por MALKUTH, es el Sephirote que corresponde al cuerpo físico.

Si continuamos con YESOD, encontramos el Asiento Vital, donde está la Energía Creadora.

El Tercer Sephirote es, naturalmente, el Cuerpo Astral, que es HOD, y en cuanto al Cuarto Sephirote, que es el Mental, nos encontramos con NETZACH.

Mucho más allá tenemos el Quinto Sephirote, que es el Alma Humana: TIPHERETH, el Causal; y aún más allá, está el Sexto Sephirote… […X…] …que es GEBURAH: El Rigor, la Ley, el Buddhi, la Bella Helena, etc., etc., etc.; el Séptimo Sephirote… […X…] …es Gedulah, o sencillamente CHESED, el Íntimo; pero más allá del Íntimo está el Logos.

BINAH es el Octavo Sephirote… […X…] …el Espíritu Santo; Noveno, el Cristo Íntimo, el Noveno Sephirote: CHOKMAH; y en cuanto al Viejo de los Siglos, KETHER, es el Décimo Sephirote.

---

[42] Literally 'Asiento' means "chair, seat; place, location"
[43] The "[…X…]" means that the recording of the lecture (from which this was transcribed in Spanish) is inaudible at this point, so we do not have a record of what was said.
[44] Literally 'sencillamente' means "simply, just, merely; quite simply"
[45] Literally 'Viejo de los Siglos' means "Elder of the Centuries"

When one has received the INITIATION OF KETHER, obviously one has obtained complete integration with the Ancient of Days...

[...X...]

...But further on is the terrible ELEVENTH DOOR, where very rare is he who dares[46] to knock[47], and the one that knocks without being prepared, will die (this is the Eleventh Sephiroth: The AIN SOPH AUR).

When one achieves success, one is united with that which is beyond the Ancient of Days (I already said: [the] Ain Soph Aur).

The Twelveth Sephiroth is different: [the] AIN SOPH; and the THIRTEEN DOOR is that of [the] AIN.

The one who has managed to integrate themselves with [the] AIN, is then ready to submerge themselves within[48] the bosom of the Eternal Common Cosmic Father.

But when submerging oneself within the bosom of the Eternal Common Cosmic Father, one finds that within oneself, in spite of having integrated with the Ain, there is something more: The BEING, and [one] works (naturally) in order to arrive at Him, and when one obtains Him, one changes the Happiness within the same bosom of the Eternal Common Cosmic Father.

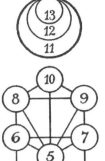

Cuando uno ha recibido la INICIACIÓN DE KETHER, obviamente ha logrado la integración completa con el Viejo de los Siglos...

[...X...]

...Pero más allá está la terrible PUERTA ONCE, donde muy raro es el que se atreve a golpear, y el que golpea sin estar preparado, morirá (ése es el Onceavo Sephirote: El AIN SOPH AUR).

Cuando uno logra el éxito, se une con algo que está más allá del Viejo de los Siglos (ya dije: Ain Soph Aur).

El Doceavo Sephirote es diferente: AIN SOPH; y la PUERTA TRECE es la de AIN.

Aquél que ha logrado integrarse con AIN, está listo, pues, para sumergirse entre el seno del Eterno Padre Cósmico Común.

Pero al sumergirse uno entre el seno del Eterno Padre Cósmico Común, encuentra que dentro de sí mismo, a pesar de haberse integrado con el Ain, hay algo más: El SER, y trabaja (naturalmente) para llegar a Él, y cuando lo logra, cambia la Felicidad dentro del mismo seno del Eterno Padre Cósmico Común.

---

[46] Literally 'atreve' means "dare, venture"
[47] Literally 'golpear' means "strike, hit; knock; beat up on; thump, bang"
[48] Literally 'entre' means "between, among; in the middle, midst, amid; within, inside; by"

Then, when submerging oneself, when not wanting to be anything nor anyone, diving between one's own depths, one finds that one's Being is even [deeper] inside, and upon discovering it, [then] new changes of inextinguishable Harmony and Beauty are verified through the process that does not have [a] name (and this is what I am saying: it does not have limits, nor borders).

In this way the Glory within the bosom of the Unknowable and pure Seity, really never has [any] limits, never ever...

Who could put limits upon the Being?

If THE BEING IS GOD HIMSELF, who could limit God?

But when one wants to be something different from the Being, when [one] desires to exist, even as a Cosmocreator, obviously [then one] falls[49], in fact, into the world of 3 Laws.

It is interesting when... [...X...] ...then, the... [...X...] ...desire, the Monads, to be something or somebody.

The first [things] that are imbalanced, naturally, are the Gunas.

If the Gunas were not imbalanced, [then] the Causa-Causorum, the Causal Logos of the First Instant, the Law of Karma itself, would not enter into activity.

But [when] there is [an] imbalance of the Gunas, and at the moment that such [an] imbalance begins, THE [LAW OF] KARMA ENTERS INTO ACTIVITY AND THE MANIFESTATION [OF THE] UNIVERSE HAPPENS[50].

Entonces, al sumergirse, al no querer ser nada ni nadie, buceando entre sus propias profundidades, encuentra que su Ser está más adentro, y al descubrirlo, nuevos cambios de Armonía y Belleza inextinguibles se verifican entre el proceso de Aquél que no tiene nombre (y esto que estoy diciendo, no tiene límites ni orillas).

De manera que la Gloria entre el seno de la Seidad Incognoscible y pura, realmente no tiene límites jamás, nunca jamás...

¿Quién podría ponerle límites al Ser?

Si EL SER ES DIOS MISMO, ¿quién podría limitar a Dios?

Pero cuando uno quiere ser algo distinto al Ser, cuando desea existir, aunque sea como un Cosmocrator, obviamente cae, de hecho, en el mundo de las 3 Leyes.

Interesante resulta... [...X...] ...pues, el... [...X...] ...desear, las Mónadas, ser algo o alguien.

Lo primero que se desequilibra, naturalmente, son las Gunas.

Si las Gunas no se desequilibraran, la Causa-Causorum, el Logos Causal del Primer Instante, la Ley misma del Karma, no entrarían en actividad.

Pero hay desequilibrio de las Gunas, y en el momento en que tal desequilibrio se inicia, EL KARMA ENTRA EN ACTIVIDAD Y DEVIENE EL UNIVERSO MANIFESTADO.

---

[49] Literally 'cae' means "fall; drop, tumble; plunge; decline; droop; sink; demise; catch on"

[50] Literally 'DEVIENE' means "become, be; turn into; be worthy of; be suitable"

Therefore, the Gunas come to be the Causa-Causorum of all Logoic activity, because the Causal Logos would not enter into activity, if the Gunas were not imbalanced.

The fact of the Gunas being imbalanced, exposes[51] an imperfection: The imperfection of the Monads (that rest within the bosom of That which does not have [a] name), [those] Monads that desire to be something, or someone.

When they feel and they think thus, obviously an imbalance is produced.

That imbalance originates the very [manifiestation of those Monads], and for that reason the manifested Universe becomes[52], beginning the Maha-Manvantara.

Distinguish between [the] Maha-Manvantara, which means "COSMIC DAY" and [the] Maha-Pralaya, which means "COSMIC NIGHT".

[If we] understanding this, [then] we can continue...

The Three Gunas, *per se*, are quite interesting.

Regarding the Three Gunas, they are clearly spoken [of] in the book of Lord Krishna, the famous "Bhagavad Gita".

It is worthwhile, then, for us to comment just a little bit on these Three Gunas...

Así pues, las Gunas viene a ser la Causa-Causorum de toda actividad Logoica, porque no entraría el Logos Causal en acción, si las Gunas no se desequilibraran.

El hecho de desequilibrarse las Gunas, acusa una imperfección: La imperfección de las Mónadas (que reposan entre el seno de Eso que no tiene nombre), Mónadas que desean ser algo, o alguien.

Cuando así sienten y piensan, obviamente se produce un desequilibrio.

Ese desequilibrio lo originan ellas mismas, y por eso deviene el Universo manifestado, se inicia el Maha-Manvantara.

Distíngase entre Maha-Manvantara, que significa "DÍA CÓSMICO" y Maha-Pralaya, que significa "NOCHE CÓSMICA".

Entendido esto, podemos continuar...

Las Tres Gunas, de por sí, son bastante interesantes.

Sobre las Tres Gunas se habla claramente en el libro del Señor Krishna, el famoso "Bhagavad Gita".

Vale la pena, pues, que comentemos un poquito sobre estas Tres Gunas...

---

[51] Literally 'acusa' means "accuse, place blame; charge with a crime, incriminate; denounce; arraign; display; register"
[52] Literally 'deviene' means "become, be; turn into; be worthy of; be suitable"

The "Bhagavad Gita" says the following:

"Oh, Krishna!, are [the] Sattvic, Rayasic or Tamasic [Gunas], the... [...X...] ...from which the religions and [forms of] worship[53] are made, without obeying the Mandates?

The Blessed Lord said:

"The... [...X...] ...that according to their nature bring the incarnated beings, [they] are triple: Sattvic, Rayasic and Tamasic.

One hears what I will say to you on this: Oh... [...X...] ...The... [...X...] ...of each person, is according to their constitution; man is [the] product of his Saya, he reflects his Shada.

SATTVIC MEN (that is to say, those in whom the Guna Sattva predominates), adore the Devas, that is to say, they render cult to the Devas (Celestial Beings, because the Devas are the same [as the] Angels or Divine Beings).

The RAYASIC [PEOPLE] render cult (to whom?) to the Yakshas or Rakshasas (Beings with Supernatural Powers), and the TAMASIC [PEOPLE], [render cult] to the Spirits and the Elements"..."

Therefore one should not forget that there are people [who are] completely Sattvic, they render cult to the Devas (to the Divine Angels, to the Indescribable Beings, to the Elohim).

---

[53] Literally 'adoren' means "adore; worship, deify; dote"

Whosoever of those in whom the Guna Rayas predominates (those who are [full] of Passion or Action), render cult, it says, to the Beings with Supernatural Powers; and the Tamasic [People] (those in whom the Guna of Inertia naturally predominates), render cult to the Spirits and the Elements of Nature.

> "The men who practice severe austerities[54]" –says the "Bhagavad Gita"– "[which are] not recommended in the Scriptures, only for ostentation[55] and egoism, those [men] become attached[56] and concupiscent[57], lacking sanity[58], torturing all the organs of the body and myself as well, who dwells within the body.
>
> Know them: They are of demonic intentions[59]!"...

It is well worth the pain to comment [on] this, [is it] not?

> "The men who practice severe austerities, not recommended by Scriptures" (to pass terrible fasts[60], whereby one is martyred, in the end; those [men] who do violent things), "only by contemplation, and egoism; they become attached and concupiscent, lacking sanity, torturing all the organs of the body and myself as well, who dwells within the body.
>
> Know them: They are of demonic intentions[61]..."

Aquéllos en quienes predomina la Guna Rayas (que es la de la Pasión o Acción), rinden culto, dije, a los Seres con Poderes Sobrenaturales; y los Tamásicos (en quienes predomina, naturalmente la Guna de la Inercia), rinden culto a los Espíritus y a los Elementos de la Naturaleza.

> "Los hombres que practican severas austeridades –dice el «Bhagavad Gita»– no recomendadas por las Escrituras, sólo por ostentación y egoísmo, esos apegados y concupiscentes, desprovistos de sensatez, torturan a todos los órganos del cuerpo y a mí también, que moro dentro del cuerpo.
>
> ¡Conócelos: Son de propósitos demoniacos!"...

Bien vale la pena comentar esto, ¿no?

> "Los hombres que practican severas austeridades, no recomendadas por las Escrituras" (pasar hambres terribles, que se martirizan, en fin; los que hacen cosas violentas), "sólo por contemplación, y egoísmo esos apegados y concupiscentes, desprovistos de sensatez, torturan a todos los órganos del cuerpo, y a mí también, que moro dentro del cuerpo.
>
> ¡Conócelos: Son de propósitos demoniacos"...

---

[54] Literally 'austeridades' means "austerities, penance; severity; dourness; astringency"
[55] Literally 'ostentación' means "ostentation, ambitious demonstration; showiness; garishness"
[56] Literally 'apegados' means "devoted to, faithful to, dedicated to; clinging to, connected to"
[57] Literally 'concupiscentes' means "concupiscent, sensual, prurient"
[58] Literally 'sensatez' means "sobriety, calmness, seriousness; temperance; sanity, saneness"
[59] Literally 'propósitos' means "proposition; resolution; intent; tender; intention, aim; object"
[60] Literally 'hambres' means "hunger; famine, starvation"
[61] Literally 'propósitos' means "proposition; resolution; intent; tender; intention, aim; object"

They are demons who torture themselves, they are demons who take [the] Ascetic[62] life, they are demons who practice HATHA-YOGA, and in the Infernal Worlds there are multitudes of them, and they always think that they are doing very well...

"Also the Foods, [forms of] Worship, Charities and Austerities are triple.

Hear from me what their distinctions are: For the SATTVIC (that is to say, for the individuals in whom the Guna Sattva predominates), they like the foods that increase [their] vitality, energy, strength, health, happiness and appetite, and that are flavorful, [foods] that are oily[63], substantial, pleasant" (vegetables, fruits of all types, etc.).

"The foods preferred by the RAYASIC (that is to say, by the people in whom the Guna Rayas predominates, which is that of Passion), are the bitter, acidic, salty, very hot, spicy, dry and burning ones, and [they] are those that produce weight [gain], suffering and disease..."

It is worth the pain to reflect [on] this, [is it] not?

It is worth the pain for us to think for ourselves about how in the Rayasic foods, there are "the very bitter —put a lot of attention in this—, the acidic, salty, very hot, spicy (those with [a] base [of] chili and such), dry and burning ones, [those that] produce weight [gain], suffering and disease..."

On the contrary you see (in order for us to reflect well), how different the Sattvic foods are: "All that are oily, substantial and pleasant": The vegetables, the fruits, all that...

---

[62] Literally 'Ascética' means "ascetic, asceticism, abstinence and self-denial for the purpose of spiritual discipline"
[63] Literally 'oleaginosos' means "oily, greasy"

"As far as foods preferred by the TAMASIC —that is to say, by those people in whom the Guna Tamas predominates— are the tasteless[64] ones, almost decomposed, bad smelling, leftovers from the previous day, cold food and impure foods…"

[It is] in this way that the people in whom the Guna Tamas predominates, [or] the Tamasic People, they like "tasteless foods —you see what they are saying!–, the decomposed, bad-smelling foods, leftovers from the previous day —excess[65] or reheated–, cold food and the impure foods…"

Those are foods, properly, of Tamasic People.

Let us not forget this here, this commentary, it is worth the pain that we reflect and that, in truth… […X…] …we choose our foods… […X… accordingly]

As far as myself, frankly I say to you, that I do not like Tamasic type foods: I do not like the "tasteless foods, nor the decomposed foods, nor bad-smelling foods, neither the foods of the previous day, nor cold food".

Impure foods (like the pig, etc., etc.), seem to me disagreeable.

In this way, yes it is worth the pain to observe what people eat, [is it] not?

Let us choose one, [which is] much better, the Sattvic Foods: The fruits, the vegetables, all that…

"En cuanto a los alimentos preferidos por los TAMÁSICOS —es decir, por aquellas gentes en que predomina la Guna Tamas— son los desabridos, casi descompuestos, mal olientes, restos del día anterior, comida fría y alimentos impuros"…

De manera que las gentes en quienes predomina la Guna Tamas, a las Gentes Tamásicas, les gustan los "alimentos desabridos —¡vea usted qué cosa!–, los alimentos descompuestos, malolientes, restos del día anterior —sobrados o recalentados–, la comida fría y los alimentos impuros"…

Ésos son alimentos, propiamente, de la Gente Tamásica.

No debemos olvidar aquí esto, este comentario, bien vale la pena que lo reflexionemos y que, de verdad… […X…] …escojamos nuestros alimentos… […X…]

En cuanto a mí, francamente les digo a ustedes, que a mí no me gustan los alimentos de tipo Tamásico: No me gustan las "comidas desabridas, ni los alimentos descompuestos, ni malolientes, ni tampoco los alimentos del día anterior, ni la comida fría".

Alimentos impuros (como el cerdo, etc., etc.), me parecen desagradables.

De manera que sí vale la pena observar qué comen las gentes, ¿no?

Escoger uno, más bien, los Alimentos Sáttvicos: Las frutas, las verduras, todo eso…

---

[64] Literally 'desabridos' means "bland, tasteless, unsavory; ill-conditioned; dull"
[65] Literally 'sobrados' means "superfluous, being more than is needed, excessive; wealthy, rich; bold, forward, blunt; enormous"

"The SATTVIC JNANA, develops[66] according to the Commandments[67]: Concentrating themselves on Worship[68], only [living] for Worship, for men who do not want results" (they are people that love Worship, who adore it, but who do not want egoistical results).

"Oh you, the best of the Bharatas!: The RAYASIC JNANA (that is passionate), develops through temptation and [through] desiring the fruits, [through desiring] merit[69]" (people that practice Rites, but with some interest, not disinterestedly).

As far as the TAMASIC JNANA, "[they] develop against the Commandments: Without Faith, without mantrams, without distributing food to the poor, and without offering their tithe to the Priests".

In [such a] way that the Rites of the Tamasic [people] are peculiar: "They do not give the tithe to the Priests, they do not pronounce the sacred mantrams, they violate the Commandments, they do not have Faith" (their Rites are practically BLACK, [are they] not?).

CORPOREAL AUSTERITY[70] consists of the adoration of the Devas, of the Brahmins, [and] of the spiritual precepts[71] of the Wise; in purity, uprightness, continence and not damaging, not harming anyone.

"El JÑANA SÁTTVICO, se hace según los Mandamientos: Concentrándose en el Culto, sólo por el Culto, por hombres que no desean el resultados" (son gentes que aman el Culto, que lo adoran, pero que no quieren resultados egoístas).

"¡Oh tú, el mejor de los Bharatas!: El JÑANA RAYÁSICO (o sea pasionario), se hace por tentación y deseando los frutos, el mérito" (gentes que practican Ritos, pero con algún interés, no desinteresadamente).

En cuanto al JÑANA TAMÁSICO, "se hace contra los Mandamientos: Sin Fe, sin los mantrams, sin repartir alimentos a los pobres y sin ofrecer su óbolo a los Sacerdotes".

De manera que los Ritos de los Tamásicos son curiosos: "No le dan el óbolo a los Sacerdotes, no pronuncian los sagrados mantrams, violan los Mandamientos, no tienen Fe" (son Ritos prácticamente NEGROS, ¿no?).

La AUSTERIDAD CORPÓREA consiste en la adoración a los Devas, a los Brahamines, a los preceptos espirituales de los Sabios; en la pureza, rectitud, continencia y no dañar, no perjudicar a nadie.

---

[66] Literally 'se hace' means "become, be; turn into; get; turn around; form; go through"
[67] Literally 'Mandamientos' means "mandate, order, command; exile; religious group"
[68] Literally 'Culto' means "cult, worship; cultivated, cultured; well bred, educated, enlightened"
[69] Literally 'mérito' means "merit, value; excellence"
[70] Literally 'AUSTERIDAD' means "austerity; severity; dourness; astringency"
[71] Literally 'preceptos' means "precept, prescript, provisions, commandments"

English	Spanish
VERBAL AUSTERITY consists in the form of speaking clearly, which does not produce any preoccupation; in reliability[72], in [an] agreeable and beneficial way of speaking, and in the daily reading of sacred texts...	La AUSTERIDAD VERBAL consiste en la forma de hablar claramente, que no produce ninguna preocupación; en la veracidad, en el modo agradable y benéfico de hablar, y en la diaria lectura de los textos sagrados...
This is very important, my estimable brethren.	Es muy importante esto, mis estimables hermanos.
It seems to me that it is worth the pain to have Verbal Austerity.	A mí me parece que vale la pena tener uno, Austeridad Verbal.
I have seen, then, how people cast[73] [their] words into the wind[74], how they hurt each other (it is as if they were throwing[75] daggers, as if they were enjoying that).	Yo he visto, pues, cómo echan las gentes a volar las palabras, cómo se hieren los unos a los otros (es como si se clavaran puñales, como si gozaran con eso).
Somebody says something, and one is amazed to see how the [other person] reacts who hears [it] and answers in [a] worse way, right?	Alguien dice algo, y me maravilla ver cómo reacciona el que escucha y contesta en forma peor, ¿no?
This is painful!	¡Eso es doloroso!
One must be austere with the word: to speak clearly, not producing preoccupations in people when one speaks; to be truthful, not lying, to have a pleasant form of speech, a beneficial form, and to read the Sacred Scriptures daily...	Uno debe ser austero en la palabra: hablar claramente, no producir preocupaciones en las gentes cuando se habla; ser veraces, no mentirosos, tener una forma agradable de hablar, una forma benéfica, y leer diariamente las Sagradas Escrituras...
MENTAL AUSTERITY consists of serenity, piety[76], silence, self-control and purity of heart...	La AUSTERIDAD MENTAL consiste en la serenidad, piedad, silencio, autocontrol y pureza de corazón...
It is very interesting to have Mental Austerity.	Es muy interesante tener uno, Austeridad Mental.

---

[72] Literally 'veracidad' means "truthfulness, veracity, accuracy, reliability"

[73] Literally 'echan' means "throw, cast, toss; add; affix, tack on; eject; bud, shoot; pump; lay; post; blow; tip; send; pour; put"

[74] Literally 'volar' means "fly; wing; sail; walk; spring; blow"

[75] Literally 'clavaran' means "nail down; knock in; spike; rivet; fasten; thrust; plunge"

[76] Literally 'piedad' means "piety (reverence for God or devout fulfillment of religious obligations; the quality or state of being pious; dutiful respect or regard for parents, homeland, etc.), devoutness"

How? Being serene[77]: [So] that if they insult, [one] remains serene; [so] that if they praise, [one] remains serene; indifferent before praise and condemnation[78], before triumph and defeat ("I am not greater because they praise nor less because they condemn me, because I always am what I am…")

To thus reflect (in this way), to be pious, silent, to never play with the word, since if one plays with the word, one is no longer austere with the word, and one needs to be austere, to always be controlling oneself (one must put oneself under self-control and always have [a] pure heart).

Mental Austerity is, then, very interesting.

This triple Austerity, practiced with Faith by the man who does not desire merit, is considered as "Sattvic", that is to say, where Verbal Austerity exists, where Mental Austerity exists, [and] where Corporeal Austerity exists, coexisting naturally, one naturally has the Sattvic quality.

Do not forget that Corporeal Austerity consists of the "adoration of the Devas, of the Brahamins, of the Spiritual Teachers[79], [and] of the Wise; in purity, uprightness, continence, and not harming anyone…"

In [such a] way that the Three Austerities: The Physical, the Mental and the Verbal, are necessary when one wants to carry (in one's [own] nature) the Sattvic type of quality.

¿Cómo? Siendo sereno: Que si lo insultan, permanecer sereno; que si lo alaban, permanece sereno; indiferente ante la alabanza y el vituperio, ante el triunfo y la derrota ("yo no soy más porque me alaben ni menos porque me vituperen, porque yo siempre soy lo que soy")…

Reflexionar así (en esa forma), ser piadoso, silencioso, no jugar nunca con la palabra, pues si uno juega con la palabra, ya no es austero con la palabra, y uno necesita ser austero, autocontrolarse siempre (uno debe someterse siempre al autocontrol y llevar el corazón puro).

Es muy interesante, pues, la Austeridad Mental.

Esta triple Austeridad, practicada con Fe por el hombre que no desea mérito, es considerada como "Sáttvica", es decir, donde existe Austeridad Verbal, donde existe Austeridad Mental, donde existe Austeridad Corpórea, hay naturalmente, coexiste naturalmente, la cualidad Sáttvica.

No olviden que la Austeridad Corpórea consiste en la "adoración de los Devas, de los Brahamines, de los Preceptores Espirituales, de los Sabios; en la pureza, rectitud, continencia, y no dañar a nadie"…

De manera que las Tres Austeridades: La Física, la Mental y la Verbal, son necesarias cuando uno quiere cargar, en su naturaleza, la cualidad de tipo Sáttvico.

---

[77] Literally 'sereno' means "calm, serene; easy; self-possessed, self-controlled; lonely; night watchman, nightman"
[78] Literally 'vituperio' means "vituperation, harsh or abusive rebuke or condemnation"
[79] Literally 'Preceptores' means "teacher, preceptor, tutor"

Editor's Appendix

RAYASIC AUSTERITY is different: It is fleeting, less[80] durable, since it is passionate; it is the one that people "practice by ostentation[81], in order to gain respect, honors and reverence"; so that others say: "What a devoted person, how magnificent!", right?

As far as TAMASIC AUSTERITY, it is the one that "is made foolishly, causing suffering, or with the desire to damage the neighbor"…

SATTVIC CHARITY is done like a duty, without the idea of repayment[82], in due place and time, to the person who deserves it.

RAYASIC CHARITY is done waiting for reward, merit, or with reluctantly; and TAMASIC CHARITY is done in [an] inopportune[83] moment, in [an] improper place, with a person who does not deserve it and [is done] with disdain…

OM-TAT-SAT…

"OM" ("That which exists"), has been declared like the "Triple Denomination of Brahma" (The Supreme).

In this form the Brahmans, the Vedas and the Jnanas in the remote past arose[84].

For that [reason], those who follow the Vedic Commandments, pronounce: "OOMMM", before beginning their Jnanas or Rites, Charities and Austerities.

Those that look for the "MOKSA" (Spiritual Emancipation), pronounce the "TAT" ("That"), before making their Jnanas or Rites, Charities and Austerities (they do not desire any merit through these actions).

---

[80] Literally 'poco' means "few, little; shallow; short; lesser"
[81] Literally 'ostentación' means "ostentation, ambitious demonstration; showiness; garishness"
[82] Literally 'retribución' means "retribution, repayment in kind"
[83] Literally 'inoportuno' means "inopportune, untimely; unsuitable, not appropriate"
[84] Literally 'surgieron' means "appear, arise, emerge; intervene; crop up"

Apéndice del Editor

La AUSTERIDAD RAYÁSICA es diferente: Es pasajera, poco durable, puesto que es pasionaria; es la que la gente "practica por ostentación, para ganar respeto, honores y reverencias"; para que otros digan: "¡Qué persona tan devota, qué magnífica!", ¿no?

En cuanto a la AUSTERIDAD TAMÁSICA, es la que "se hace neciamente, causándose sufrimiento, o con el deseo de dañar al prójimo"…

La CARIDAD SÁTTVICA se hace como un deber, sin la idea de retribución, en debido lugar y momento, a la persona que lo merece.

La CARIDAD RAYÁSICA se hace esperando recompensa, mérito, o de mala gana; y la CARIDAD TAMÁSICA se hace en momento inoportuno, en lugar indebido, a una persona que no lo merece y con desdén…

OM-TAT-SAT…

"OM" ("Aquello existe"), ha sido declarado como la "Triple Denominación de Brahma" (Lo Supremo).

De esta forma surgieron los Brahmanes, los Vedas y los Jñanas en el remoto pasado.

Por eso, los que siguen los Mandamientos Védicos, pronuncian: "OOMMM", antes de comenzar sus Jñanas o Ritos, Caridades y Austeridades.

Los que buscan el "MOKSA" (Emancipación Espiritual), pronuncian el "TAT" ("Aquello"), antes de hacer sus Jñanas o Ritos, Caridades y Austeridades (ellos no desean ningún mérito por estas acciones).

The word "SAT", or "PARDAT", is used in the sense of "The Reality", "The Goodness/Kindness[85]", and also for auspicious acts.

[It is] in this way that you [can] see: "OM-TAT-SAT", is of great power, [it is] also like saying, "AUM-TAT-SAT..."

Also the word "Sat" is pronounced in order to obtain certainty in the Jnana (that is to say, in the Rite), in the Austerity, in the Charity and in all the acts done indirectly through the Lord.

Any act or "Pardat", whether this is [a] Jnana or Ritual, Charity or Austerity, if it is done without Faith [then it] is considered as "ASAT" (Nonexistent), it has not been done properly, and it does not bear fruit here nor in the Higher [Worlds]...

[It is] in this way that we are seeing then what the Three Gunas are.

They are most important, because with them and through them this Universe exists (they are the Three Basic Qualities)... [...X...]

Disciple. ...But I wanted to ask now about... With all the explanation that you have given to us about the Gunas.

Could one say that this gives [an] answer to the basic, fundamental, question upon which Philosophy (we [could] say) is based?

Which is (we [could] say) "where do we come from", right?

Then, of course, this is also intimately related with "who are we and towards where are we going"

La palabra "SAT", o "PARDAT", es usada en el sentido de "La Realidad", "La Bondad", y también para los actos auspiciosos.

De manera que vean ustedes: OM-TAT-SAT, es de gran poder, como decir también, AUM-TAT-SAT...

También se pronuncia la palabra "Sat" para lograr constancia en el Jñana (es decir, en el Rito), en la Austeridad, en la Caridad y en todos los actos hechos indirectamente por el Señor.

Cualquier acto o "Pardat", ya sea éste el Jñana o Ritual, la Caridad o la Austeridad, si se hace sin la Fe es considerado como "ASAT" (Inexistente), no ha sido propiamente hecho, y no da fruto aquí ni en el Más Allá...

De manera que estamos viendo pues lo que son las Tres Gunas.

Son importantísimas, porque sobre ellas y por ellas existe este Universo (son las Tres Cualidades Básicas)... [...X...]

Discípulo. ...Pero yo quería preguntarle ahora acerca de... Con toda la explicación que nos ha dado acerca las Gunas.

¿Podría decirse que esto da contestación a la pregunta básica, fundamental, en la que está basada, digamos, la Filosofía?

Que es, digamos, "de dónde venimos", ¿no?

Entonces, desde luego, eso está también íntimamente relacionado con el "quiénes somos y hacia dónde vamos"

---

[85] Literally 'Bondad' means "goodness; graciousness, kindness; benignity; bonhomie"

But I see that the explanation that you have given us about the Gunas, then, definitively gives an answer to the fact of "where we come from", right?

Because this is also how our origin[86] began[87]...

Master. Well, [it is] clear!

D. Now, what I wanted to ask, Master, is: When the Cosmic Day [or Maha-Manvantara] enters into Manifestation (we [could] say) [when] it begins, then, within that beginning of the Cosmic Day entering into Manifestation, are our Essences there?

M. Well, the Essence enters activity much much later.

Now, in order for the Essence of each creature to enter into activity, then, the descent of the Great Life is necessary.

But obviously, if it was[88] not for the Cosmic Day, the Essence would not enter, well, into activity.

WITH THE COSMIC DAY, every Essence ENTERS INTO ACTIVITY.

D. But, in reality, is the Essence already manifested, in all its magnitude, when Creation enters into its Physical Manifestation?

M. Well, from LONG BEFORE [THAT] THE ESSENCE IS ALREADY ACTIVE, right?

Every Essence enters into activity when the Dawn of the Maha-Manvantara begins.

---

[86] Literally 'origen' means "origin, source; beginning; birth, parentage, nationality"
[87] Literally 'inicia' means "initiate, launch, start; log-in; log-on; pioneer; enter into"
[88] Literally 'fuera' means "ou, outside, away, abroad, without"

D. There it begins in a body [which is] totally Mental, right?

M. Well, if the Essences do not have [a] Mental Body, in what Body are they going to enter?

Simply, THEY ACT LIKE INNOCENT ELEMENTALS in [the] process of descent, right?, towards the Physical World.

And since the Universe begins its process of development in the World of the Mind, in the Concrete Mental Substance proper, [then] the Essences begin acting within the Mental Matter, but this does not mean that the Essences (of all those created) already can, by such reason, possess [a] body.

Much much later that Mental Universe crystallizes into [the] Astral form, it is certain and completely true!, right? But this does not mean that the Essences have [an] Astral... [...X...] ...Body.

That this Astral Universe... [...X...] ...crystallizes into the Etheric form, is also certain!

But this does not mean that the Essences have [an] Etheric Body.

And finally, the manifestation comes from the Universe into its physical form; then the Essences have descended until [finally reaching] the Mineral Kingdom, proper.

D. ¿Ahí mismo empieza en un cuerpo totalmente Mental, no?

M. Pues, si no tienen Cuerpo Mental las Esencias, ¿en qué Cuerpo van ellas a entrar?

Simplemente, ACTÚAN COMO ELEMENTALES INOCENTES en proceso de descenso, ¿no?, hacia el Mundo Físico.

Y como quiera que el Universo comienza su proceso de desarrollo en el Mundo de la Mente, en la Substancia Mental Concreta, propiamente, las Esencias, empiezan actuando dentro de la Materia Mental, pero no quiere decir esto que las Esencias (de todo lo creado), ya pueden, por tal motivo, poseer cuerpo.

Que mucho más tarde ese Universo Mental cristaliza en forma Astral, ¡también es cierto y de toda verdad!, ¿no? Pero eso no quiere decir que las Esencias tengan Cuerpo... [...X...] ...Astral.

Que ese Universo Astral... [...X...] ...cristaliza en la forma Etérica, ¡también es cierto!

Pero no quiere decir que las Esencias tengan Cuerpo Etérico.

Y por último, viene la manifestación del Universo en su forma física; entonces las Esencias han descendido hasta el Reino Mineral, propiamente dicho.

From there they begin [the] evolutionary processes of Elemental Life, continuing towards the Vegetable, they continue into the Animal and, finally, they arrive at the "Humanoid" State.

Life, in its processes, brings[89] us here (we could say, in its processes of involutionary and evolutionary type); finally, life leaves us there, in the "Humanoid" State…

The "humanoid" is something incomplete: It is an "Elemental" with [a] (we [could] say) three-brained body, and that is all.

If the "humanoid" wants to advance a little more, to complete itself, then it must create the Superior Existential Bodies of the Being, in order to CONVERT ITSELF INTO [A] MAN, right?

Obviously, the "humanoid" always falls, converting itself, we could say, into a very animalistic creature, right?

In itself, it is animal, but (we [could] say) it is soiled with the animal passions, [thus] it develops the Ego in its nature.

Nevertheless, it must eliminate the Ego, create the Solar Bodies, and then convert itself into an authentic Man, right?

In any case, life comes to Involution, from the Absolute to the Mineral Kingdom; [and] from the Mineral Kingdom it evolves into the "human".

Desde allí comienzan procesos evolutivos de Vida Elemental, continúan hacia el Vegetal, prosiguen en el Animal y al fin, llegan al Estado "Humanoide".

La vida, en sus procesos, nos deja hasta ahí (en sus procesos, dijéramos, de tipo involucionante y evolucionante); por último, la vida nos deja ahí, hasta el Estado de "Humanoide"…

El "humanoide" es algo incompleto: Es un "Elemental" con cuerpo, dijéramos, tri-cerebrado, y eso es todo.

Si el "humanoide" quiere avanzar un poco más, completarse, entonces tiene que crearse los Cuerpos Existenciales Superiores del Ser, para CONVERTIRSE EN HOMBRE, ¿no?

Obviamente, el "humanoide" siempre cae, se convierte, dijéramos, en una criatura demasiado animalesca, ¿no?

De por sí, es animal, pero, dijéramos, se ensucia con las pasiones animales, desarrolla el Ego en su naturaleza.

Sin embargo, debe eliminar el Ego, crear los Cuerpos Solares, y entonces se convierte en un Hombre auténtico, ¿no?

En todo caso, la vida viene en Involución, desde el Absoluto hasta el Reino Mineral; desde el Reino Mineral evoluciona hasta el "humano".

---

[89] Literally 'deja' means "leave, quit; forsake, abandon; lend; forget; drop; put down; yield, produce; give up; stop"

In the "human", or (better said) the "humanoid", if it wants to GET OFF[90] OF THE WHEEL of Involutions and Evolutions (because obviously, it must do something different): [Then] it must work upon itself, it must finish CREATING ITSELF BY ITSELF, creating the Superior Existential Bodies of the Being within itself; converting itself into a true Man and into a God (within itself, working upon itself).

That is the crude reality of facts!

D. [Could] we say that the Rayasic Man (of [the] Rayas [Guna]), is he the one that is in the "Wheel of the Samsara"?

M. He is the passionate man, the man who is given[91] to animal passions…

D. Exactly!…

M. because Rayas is Passion, Sattva is Harmony, Happiness, the Beauty of the Spirit…

D. The Sattvic [Man] is the one who has arrived at the Tetragrammaton, the Man [number] Five, right?

M. Yes, when one obtains the perfect balance of the Three Gunas, within oneself, one converts oneself into what could be called a "SATTVIC MAN" ([a] Perfect Man).

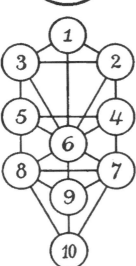

En el "humano", o el "humanoide", mejor dicho, si quiere SALIRSE DE LA RUEDA de las Involuciones y Evoluciones, pues obviamente, tiene que hacer algo distinto: Tiene que trabajar sobre sí mismo, tiene que acabar de CREARSE POR SÍ MISMO, crear los Cuerpos Existenciales Superiores del Ser dentro de sí mismo; convertirse en un Hombre verdadero y en un Dios (dentro de sí mismo, trabajando sobre sí mismo).

¡Ésa es la cruda realidad de los hechos!

D. Por decirlo así, el Hombre Rayásico (de Rayas), ¿es el que está en la "Rueda del Samsara"?

M. Es el hombre pasionario, el hombre que está entregado a las pasiones animales…

D. ¡Exacto!…

M. porque Rayas es la Pasión, Sattva es la Armonía, la Felicidad, la Belleza del Espíritu…

D. El Sáttvico, ¿es aquél que llegó al Tetragrammaton, el Hombre Cinco, no?

M. Sí, cuando uno consigue el equilibrio perfecto de las Tres Gunas, dentro de sí mismo, se convierte en lo que se llamaría un "HOMBRE SÁTTVICO" (Hombre Perfecto).

---

[90] Literally 'SALIRSE' means "bleed; leak; pull out, poke out; leave, tear, get out, get off"
[91] Literally 'entregado' means "deliver, convey; give over, give oneself up; give in, hand in; consign; submit; surrender; address; serve"

D. Master, and the process of the Essence, is this intimately related with the RAY OF CREATION?

M. Well yes, the Essence (naturally, as I said to you) first comes [into manifestation by] descending from region in region, right?

So as soon as the Milky Way exists, the Essence begins its processes of descent, right?, until [arriving at] the Mineral; from the Mineral it initiates its processes of ascent, into the "Humanoid" State.

D. Could we say [that] one must arrive (we [could] say) at the [lowest] level [of the] descent?

M. Clearly!

D. Since this is [all happeneing] in order to return again to the Absolute, it must begin the inverse process, right?

M. Inverse, yes!

TO RETURN AGAIN: To leave the World of the 48 Laws and to pass [on] to the one of 24, and soon to the one of 12, soon to the one of 6, and there to the one of 3, until [finally] approaching the Absolute.[92]

D. For that reason it is said that "to be able to ascend, first one must descend", or [one could say] that [it is necessary] to descend first to the Mineral Worlds, in order to be able to return [and] to ascend?

M. Clearly!

D. Clearly!...

D. Maestro, y el proceso de la Esencia, ¿está íntimamente relacionado con el RAYO DE LA CREACIÓN?

M. Pues sí, la Esencia (naturalmente, como te dije) primero viene descendiendo de región en región, ¿no?

Tan pronto existe la Vía Láctea, la Esencia comienza sus procesos de descenso, ¿no?, hasta el Mineral; desde el Mineral inicia sus procesos de ascenso, hasta el Estado "Humanoide".

D. ¿Tiene que llegar, digamos, hasta el nivel más descendente, digamos?

M. ¡Claro!

D. Porque es que para volver otra vez al Absoluto, ¿tiene que iniciar el proceso inverso, no?

M. ¡Inverso, sí!

REGRESAR OTRA VEZ: Salirse del Mundo de las 48 Leyes y pasar al de las 24, y luego al de las 12, luego al de las 6, y de ahí al de las 3, hasta abordar el Absoluto.[93]

D. ¿Por eso se dice que "para poder ascender, primero se tiene que descender", o sea que, ¿se desciende primero hasta los Mundos Minerales, para poder volver a ascender?

M. ¡Claro!

D. ¡Claro!...

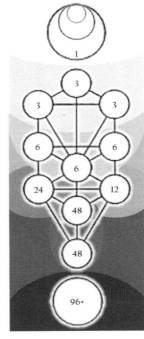

---

[92] Editor's note: For more information about this subject, see the book *Gnostic Christification* by the same publishers.

[93] Nota del editor: Para obtener más información acerca de este tema, consulte el libro *Cristificación Gnóstico* por el mismo editor.

D. "In order to be able to ascend, first it is necessary to descend" and to work in the Ninth Sphere?

M. Well, THIS IS VERY DEEP, very profound, right?

I am speaking of a First Descent, when the Universe is created, in which the Great Life comes from the Absolute into the Physical World.

At that time the Essence has had to come, then, from above [down] to the Physical World, in order to raise itself step by step[94] to the Vegetable and the Animal [and finally] to the "Humanoid" [State].

But, before [arriving] there; that is the First Descent of Life, into the Physical World.

Later, already [being] in the Physical World, the Essence is submitted[95] to the Wheel of Samsara, which is another thing!

In this Wheel that turns incessantly: 3,000 Cycles of 108 Existences each [time].

It is already different[96]: [It is] actually Elemental in the Mineral Kingdom, which is happening [to it] for the first time through the Elemental Mineral Kingdom; and it is [an] Elemental of the Elemental Mineral Kingdom which has already passed through the Mineral [state] long ago; and then it returns to pass [through the same states again] and [this] will continue happening...

D. ¿"Para poder subir, primero hay que bajar" y trabajar en la Novena Esfera?

M. Bueno, ya ESO ES MAS HONDO, más profundo, ¿no?

Yo estoy hablando de una Primera Bajada, cuando se crea el Universo, en el que la Gran Vida vino desde el Absoluto hasta el Mundo Físico.

Entonces la Esencia ha tenido que venir, pues, desde arriba hasta el Mundo Físico, para escalonarse subiendo por el Vegetal y el Animal hasta el "Humanoide".

Pero, hasta ahí; ésa es la Primera Bajada de la Vida, hasta el Mundo Físico.

Que después, ya en el Mundo Físico, queda la Esencia sometida a la Rueda del Samsara, ¡eso es otra cosa!

En esa Rueda que gira incesantemente: 3.000 Ciclos de 108 Existencias cada uno.

Ya es distinto: Hay Elementales, actualmente, en el Reino Mineral, que están pasando por primera vez por el Reino Elemental Mineral; y hay Elementales del Reino Elemental Mineral que ya pasaron por el Mineral hace mucho tiempo; y volvieron a pasar y seguirán pasando...

---

[94] Literally 'escalonarse' means "staggered, be spread, be phased, be stepped"
[95] Literally 'sometida' means "meddlesome, interfering; subject, under, submitted, undergone"
[96] Literally 'distinto' means "distinct, different; diverse, varied; several; separate"

D. Right now, I have caught sight [of] a detail!: That only with the decompensation[97] of those Three Gunas (at the time when the Dawn of this Creation begins) is when the Three Forces appear so that there is this Creation (that Holy Affirming, Holy Denying and Holy Reconciling), right?

Being the Positive, Negative and Neutral Forces, precisely so that this Creation exists.

D2. Clearly, they (those Three Forces) are what create as one.

D. And for these Three Forces to exist at the beginning, at that Dawning, [then this] is when that Ray of Creation begins (so well-known, right?) Which is, precisely, started [by] that Third Logos.

M. It is the Third Logos,

D. Clearly! It is the creative [one]; everything in harmony…

D. First is the Absolute, right?

M. Exactly!

D. It fits, we could say, all the Worlds [within itself]… Next everything comes [into existence]…

M. Well, that Third Logos is all the Suns.

D. But, after the Absolute comes all the Worlds, right?

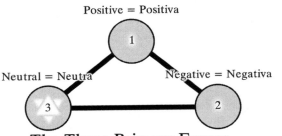

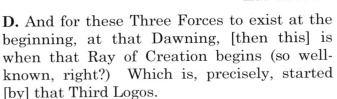

The Three Primary Forces
Las Tres Fuerzas Primarias

D. ¡Ahorita, vislumbro un detalle!: Que solamente con la descompensación de esas Tres Gunas, a la hora de que comienza la Aurora de esta Creación, es cuando tienen que aparecer las Tres Fuerzas para que haya esta Creación, ese Santo Afirmar, Santo Negar y Santo Conciliar, ¿no?

Es la Fuerza Positiva, Negativa y Neutra, precisamente para que exista esta Creación.

D2. ¡Claro, son las que crean a uno (esas Tres Fuerzas).

D. Y al existir esas Tres Fuerzas al inicio, en esta Aurora, es cuando comienza ese Rayo de la Creación (tan conocido, ¿no?) Que está, precisamente, iniciando ese Tercer Logos.

M. Es el Tercer Logos,

D. ¡Claro! Es el creativo; todo en armonía…

D. Primero es el Absoluto, ¿no?

M. ¡Exactamente!

D. Caben, digamos, todos los Mundos… Enseguida vienen todo…

M. Bueno, ese Tercer Logos es todos los Soles.

D. Pero, ¿después del Absoluto vienen todos los Mundos, ahora?

---

[97] Literally 'descompensación' means "decompensation (a loss of the ability to maintain normal or appropriate function)"

Editor's Appendix

M. [First] the Absolute, then comes all the Infinity (what is known as Infinity); then what is known, then, as all the Galaxies; then [what is known] as all the Suns; then [what is known] as the World; and so on…

Well, here I'll leave you, my estimable brethren, because I am going to enter into Meditation…

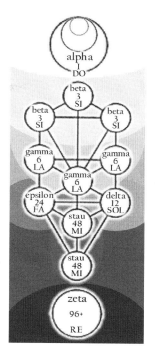

Apéndice del Editor

M. El Absoluto, luego viene todo el Infinito (lo que se conoce como Infinito); luego lo que se conoce, pues, como todas las Galaxias; luego como todos los Soles; luego como el Mundo; y así…

Bueno, hasta aquí los voy a dejar, mis estimables hermanos, porque voy a entrar en Meditación…

Extracted from the Lecture / Extraído de la Conferencia

	SATTVA	RAYAS	TAMAS
Explanation	Harmony, Beauty, [and] authentic Happiness	animal Passion, Action	Inertia
Explicación	la Armonía, la Belleza, la Felicidad auténtica	la Pasión animal, la Acción	Inercia
The Religions and Forms of Worship	adore the Devas, they render cult to the Devas (Celestial Beings, because the Devas are the same [as the] Angels or Divine Beings)	render cult to the Yakshas or Rakshasas (Beings with Supernatural Powers)	render cult to the Spirits and the Elements
Los Cultos y Adoraciones	adoran a los Devas, es decir, le rinden culto a los Devas (Seres Celestiales, porque los Devas son los mismos Ángeles o Seres Divinos).	rinden culto a los Yakshas o Rakshasas (Seres con Poderes Sobrenaturales)	rinden culto a los Espíritus y los Elementos
The Foods	foods that increase [their] vitality, energy, strength, health, happiness and appetite, and that are flavorful, [foods] that are oily, substantial, pleasant (vegetables, fruits of all types, etc.)	the bitter, acidic, salty, very hot, spicy, dry and burning foods, and [they] are those that produce weight [gain], suffering and disease...	the tasteless foods, almost decomposed, bad smelling, leftovers from the previous day, cold food and impure foods...
Los Alimentos	los alimentos que aumentan la vitalidad, energía, fuerza, salud, felicidad y apetito, y que son sabrosos, que son oleaginosos, substanciosos, agradables (las verduras, las frutas de toda especie, etc.)	los amargos, ácidos, salados, muy calientes, picantes, secos y ardientes, y son los alimentos que producen pesar, sufrimientos y enfermedad...	son los alimentos desabridos, casi descompuestos, mal olientes, restos del día anterior, comida fría y alimentos impuros

	SATTVA	RAYAS	TAMAS
Jnana	develops according to the Commandments: Concentrating themselves on Worship, only [living] for Worship, for men who do not want results (they are people that love Worship, who adore it, but who do not want egoistical results)	develops through temptation and [through] desiring the fruits, [through desiring] merit (people that practice Rites, but with some interest, not disinterestedly)	develop against the Commandments: Without Faith, without mantrams, without distributing food to the poor, and without offering their tithe to the Priests (their Rites are practically BLACK)
Jñana	se hace según los Mandamientos: Concentrándose en el Culto, sólo por el Culto, por hombres que no desean el resultados (son gentes que aman el Culto, que lo adoran, pero que no quieren resultados egoístas)	se hace por tentación y deseando los frutos, el mérito (gentes que practican Ritos, pero con algún interés, no desinteresadamente)	se hace contra los Mandamientos: Sin Fe, sin los mantrams, sin repartir alimentos a los pobres y sin ofrecer su óbolo a los Sacerdotes (son Ritos prácticamente NEGROS)
Austerity	Physical, Mental and Verbal Austerities*	fleeting, less durable, since it is passionate; it is the one that people practice by ostentation, in order to gain respect, honors and reverence; so that others say: "What a devoted person, how magnificent!"	made foolishly, causing suffering, or with the desire to damage the neighbor
Austeridad	La Austeridade Física, Mental y Verbal*	Es pasajera, poco durable, puesto que es pasionaria; es la que la gente practica por ostentación, para ganar respeto, honores y reverencias; para que otros digan: "¡Qué persona tan devota, qué magnífica!"	se hace neciamente, causándose sufrimiento, o con el deseo de dañar al prójimo

	SATTVA	**RAYAS**	**TAMAS**
Charity	done like a duty, without the idea of repayment, in due place and time, to the person who deserves it	done waiting for reward, merit, or with reluctantly	done in [an] inopportune moment, in [an] improper place, with a person who does not deserve it and [is done] with disdain
Caridad	se hace como un deber, sin la idea de retribución, en debido lugar y momento, a la persona que lo merece	se hace esperando recompensa, mérito, o de mala gana	se hace en momento inoportuno, en lugar indebido, a una persona que no lo merece y con desdén

	CORPOREAL AUSTERITY / **AUSTERIDAD CORPÓREA**	**VERBAL AUSTERITY** / **AUSTERIDAD VERBAL**	**MENTAL AUSTERITY** / **AUSTERIDAD MENTAL**
***Sattvic Austerity**	consists of the adoration of the Devas, of the Brahamins, [and] of the spiritual precepts of the Wise; in purity, uprightness, continence and not damaging, not harming anyone	consists in the form of speaking clearly, which does not produce any preoccupation; in reliability, in [an] agreeable and beneficial way of speaking, and in the daily reading of sacred texts...	consists of serenity, piety, silence, self-control and purity of heart... Being serene: indifferent before praise and condemnation, before triumph and defeat
***La Austeridad Sáttvica**	consiste en la adoración a los Devas, a los Brahamines, a los preceptos espirituales de los Sabios; en la pureza, rectitud, continencia y no dañar, no perjudicar a nadie	consiste en la forma de hablar claramente, que no produce ninguna preocupación; en la veracidad, en el modo agradable y benéfico de hablar, y en la diaria lectura de los textos sagrados...	consiste en la serenidad, piedad, silencio, autocontrol y pureza de corazón... Siendo sereno: indiferente ante la alabanza y el vituperio, ante el triunfo y la derrota

Love, Death and Resurrection

El Amor, la Muerte y la Resurrección

Extracted from the Chapter 20 of
THE PERFECT MATRIMONY
by Samael Aun Weor

...To many readers it may seem strange that we relate Love with Death and Resurrection.

In hindu[98] mythology, Love and Death are the two faces of the one same deity.

Shiva, the God of the universal creative sexual force, is at the same time the God of violent death and destruction.

The wife of Shiva also has two faces. She is Parvati and Kali at the same time.

As Parvati, she is supreme beauty, love and happiness.

As Kali or Durga, she can convert herself into death, disgrace and bitterness.

Shiva and Kali together symbolize the Tree of Knowledge, the Tree of the Science of Good and Evil.

Love and Death are twin brothers who never separate.

The path of life is formed by the hoof-prints of the horse of death.

The error of many cults and schools consists in being unilateral.

They study death but do not want to study Love, when in reality these are the two faces of deity.

Extracto del Capítulo XX de
EL MATRIMONIO PERFECTO
por Samael Aun Weor

...A muchos lectores se les hace extraño que relacionemos el Amor con la Muerte y la Resurrección.

En la mitología indostánica el Amor y la Muerte son dos caras de una misma deidad.

Shiva, el Dios de la fuerza creadora sexual universal, es al mismo tiempo el Dios de la muerte violenta y de la destrucción.

La esposa de Shiva tiene también dos caras. Ella es Parvati y Kali a la vez.

Como Parvati, es suprema belleza, amor y felicidad.

Como Kali o Durga, puede convertirse en muerte, desgracia y amargura.

Shiva y Kali juntos simbolizan el Árbol del Conocimiento, el Árbol de la Ciencia del Bien y del Mal.

El Amor y la Muerte son dos hermanos gemelos que no se separan nunca.

La senda de la vida está formada con las huellas del caballo de la muerte.

El error de muchos cultos y escuelas consiste en ser unilaterales.

Estudian la muerte pero no quieren estudiar el Amor, cuando en realidad estas son las dos caras de la deidad.

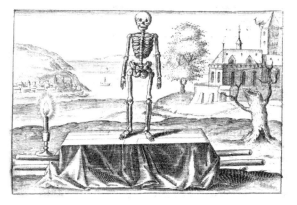

---

[98] Literally 'indostánica' means "Hindustani, of Hindustan, of the Hindu areas of India; of the people or language of Hindustan"

The diverse doctrines of the Orient and the Occident really believe that they know Love, when in fact they do not.

Love is a cosmic phenomenon in which the history of the Earth and its races are simple accidents.

Love is the mysterious magnetic and occult force which the alchemist needs in order to create the Philosopher's Stone and the Elixir of Long Life, without which Resurrection is impossible.

Love is a force that the "I" can never subordinate because Satan can never subjugate God.

The illustrious[99] ignoramuses are mistaken about the origin of Love.

The foolish[100] are mistaken about its effect[101].

It is stupid to suppose that the only objective of Love is the reproduction of the species.

Really Love unfolds[102] and develops on a very very distinct[103] plane, which the swine of materialism radically ignore.

Only an infinitesimal[104] force of Love is used for the perpetuation of the species.

What happens to the rest of the force?

Where does [it] go? Where does it unfold?

This is what the illustrious ignoramuses ignore.

Las diversas doctrinas de Oriente y Occidente creen realmente conocer el Amor, cuando en realidad no lo conocen.

El Amor es un fenómeno cósmico en el que toda la historia de la Tierra y sus razas son simples accidentes.

El Amor es la fuerza magnética misteriosa y oculta que el alkimista necesita para fabricar la Piedra Filosofal y el Elixir de Larga Vida, sin el cual la Resurrección es imposible.

El Amor es una fuerza que el yo jamás puede subordinar porque Satán jamás puede subyugar a Dios.

Los ignorantes ilustrados están equivocados sobre el origen del Amor.

Los necios se equivocan sobre su resultado.

Es estúpido suponer que el único objeto del Amor sea la reproducción de la especie.

Realmente el Amor se desenvuelve y desarrolla en un plano muy distinto que los cerdos del materialismo ignoran radicalmente.

Sólo una fuerza infinitesimal del Amor sirve para la perpetuación de la especie.

¿Qué se hace la demás fuerza?

¿Adónde va? ¿Dónde se desenvuelve?

Esto es lo que ignoran los ignorantes ilustrados.

---

[99] Literally 'ilustrados' means "improved; illustrated; enlightened; pictorial"
[100] Literally 'necios' means "silly, foolish, ignorant, stupid, bothersome, tomfool, unwise;"
[101] Literally 'resultado' means "result, effect, outcome, progeny; answer, solution;"
[102] Literally 'desenvuelve' means "unfold, unwrap, unroll; unwind; unravel, clear up, untangle, disentangle, extricate; develop; expound, explain;"
[103] Literally 'distinto' means "distinct, different; diverse, varied; several; separate"
[104] Literally 'infinitesimal' means "infinitesimal, minute, very tiny; pertaining to infinitesimals (Mathematics)"

Love is energy and this [energy] cannot be lost.

The excess energy has other uses and purposes[105] which people ignore.

The excess energy of Love is intimately related with thought, feeling and willpower.

Without sexual energy these faculties could not unfold.

The creative energy is transformed into beauty, thought, feelings, harmony, poetry, art, wisdom, etc.

The supreme transformation of creative energy produces as [a] result the awakening of the Consciousness and the Death and Resurrection of the Initiate.

Really, all the creative activity of humanity comes from the marvelous force of Love.

Love is the marvelous force that awakens the mystical powers of man.

Without Love the Resurrection of the dead is impossible.

It is urgent to once again open the temples of Love in order to once again celebrate the mystic festivals of Love.

The Serpent of Fire only awakens with the enchantments of Love.

El Amor es energía y ésta no puede perderse.

El excedente de energía tiene otros usos y finalidades que las gentes ignoran.

La energía excedente del Amor está íntimamente relacionada con el pensamiento, el sentimiento y la voluntad.

Sin la energía sexual no podrían desenvolverse esas facultades.

La energía creadora se transforma en belleza, pensamiento, sentimientos, armonía, poesía, arte, sabiduría, etc.

La suprema transformación de la energía creadora da como resultado el despertar de la Conciencia y la Muerte y Resurrección del Iniciado.

Realmente, toda la actividad creadora de la humanidad resulta de la fuerza maravillosa del Amor.

El Amor es la fuerza maravillosa que despierta los poderes místicos del hombre.

Sin el Amor la Resurrección de los muertos resulta imposible.

Es urgente abrir nuevamente los templos del Amor para celebrar nuevamente las fiestas místicas del Amor.

Sólo con los encantos del Amor despierta la Serpiente de Fuego.

---

[105] Literally 'finalidades' means "purpose, goal, objective, aim, end;"

If we want the Resurrection of the dead we first need to be devoured by the Serpent.

The person who has not been devoured[106] by the Serpent is worth nothing.

If we want the Verb to become flesh in us, we need to practice Sexual Magic intensely.

The Verb is in Sex[107].

The Lingam Yoni is the foundation of every power.

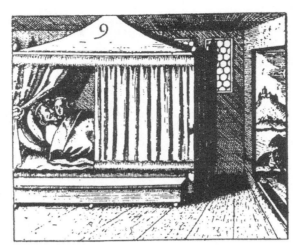

First, we need to raise the Serpent upon the staff and then be devoured by the Serpent.

Thus, we convert ourselves into Serpents.

In India, the Adepts are called Nagas, Serpents.

In Teotihuacan, Mexico, there is a marvelous temple of serpents.

Only the serpents of fire can resurrect from among the dead.

An inhabitant of a two-dimensional world, with their two-dimensional psychology believe that all the phenomena occurring in that plane would have their cause and effect there, their birth and death [in that dimension].

Such phenomena would be identical for these beings.

Si queremos la Resurrección de los muertos necesitamos ser primero devorados por la Serpiente.

Nada vale quien no ha sido tragado por la Serpiente.

Si queremos que el Verbo se haga carne en nosotros, necesitamos practicar Magia Sexual intensamente.

El Verbo está en el Sexo.

El Lingam Yoni es la base de todo poder.

Necesitamos primero levantar la Serpiente sobre la vara y después ser tragados por la Serpiente.

Así nos convertimos en Serpientes.

En la India, los Adeptos son llamados Nagas, Serpientes.

En Teotihuacan, México, existe el templo maravilloso de las serpientes.

Sólo las serpientes de fuego pueden resucitar de entre los muertos.

Un habitante del mundo bidimensional con su psicología bidimensional creería que todos los fenómenos ocurridos en su plano tendrían allí su causa y su efecto, su nacimiento y su muerte.

Los fenómenos semejantes serían para esos seres, idénticos.

---

[106] Literally 'tragado' means "swallow, gulp, swallow up, engulf, get down, gobble, gorge; devour, guzzle"

[107] Literally 'Sexo' means "sex, sexual organs". So this sentence could also be translated as "The Verb is in the Sexual Organs."

All the phenomena which came from the third dimension would be taken by these two-dimensional beings as unique facts of their two-dimensional world; they would not accept being told of a third dimension because, for them, only their flat, two-dimensional world would exist.

Nevertheless, if these flat beings would resolve to abandon their two-dimensional psychology in order to deeply comprehend the causes of all the phenomena of their world, they could then depart from it and discover with astonishment a great unknown world. The three-dimensional world.

The same thing happens with the question of Love.

People believe that Love is only for perpetuating the species.

People believe that Love is only vulgarity, carnal pleasure, violent desire, satisfaction, etc.

Only those who can see beyond these animal passions, only those who renounce this type of animal psychology can discover in other worlds and dimensions the grandeur and majesty of that which is called Love.

People sleep profoundly.

People live sleeping and dream about Love, but they have not awakened Love[108].

They sing about Love and believe that Love is what they dream.

When man awakens to Love, he makes himself conscious of Love, [and] recognizes that he was dreaming.

Then and only then does he discover the true meaning[109] of Love.

Todos los fenómenos que vinieran de la tercera dimensión serían tomados por esos seres bidimensionales como hechos únicos de su mundo bidimensional; no aceptarían que se les hablase de una tercera dimensión porque para ellos sólo existiría su mundo plano bidimensional.

Empero, si estos seres planos resolvieran abandonar su sicología bidimensional para comprender a fondo las causas de todos los fenómenos de su mundo, podrían entonces salir de él y descubrir con asombro un gran mundo desconocido. El mundo tridimensional.

Lo mismo sucede con la cuestión del Amor.

La gente sólo cree que el Amor es para perpetuar la especie.

La gente solo cree que el Amor es vulgaridad, placer carnal, deseo violento, satisfacción, etc.

Sólo quien pueda ver más allá de estas pasiones animales, solo quien renuncie a este tipo de sicología animal puede descubrir en otros mundos y dimensiones la grandeza y majestad de eso que se llama Amor.

La gente sueña profundamente.

La gente vive dormida y sueña con el Amor, pero no ha despertado al Amor.

Le canta al Amor y cree que el Amor es eso que sueña.

Cuando el hombre despierta al Amor, se hace consciente del Amor, reconoce que estaba soñando.

Entonces y sólo entonces descubre el verdadero significado del Amor.

---

[108] Literally 'despertado al Amor' means "awakened to Love"

[109] Literally 'significado' means "significance, meaning, purport, sense, purposefulness, significancy, signification;"

Only then does he discover that which before he [merely] dreamed of.

Only then does he come to know that which is called Love.

This awakening is similar to that of the man who, being far from the physical body in the Astral Body, realizes[110] that he has awakened Consciousness.

People are[111] asleep in the Astral.

When someone realizes that they are dreaming and then says, "This is a dream, I am dreaming, I am in the Astral Body, I am outside my physical body", the dream disappears as if by magic[112] and then the individual is awake in the Astral World.

A new and marvelous world appears before whosoever was dreaming their Consciousness was awakened.

Now they can know all the marvels of Nature.

So too is the awakening of Love.

Before that awakening we dream about Love.

We take those dreams as reality; we believe that we love; we live in a world of passions, romances, occasionally delicious, disillusionments, vain oaths, carnal desires, jealousies etc., etc., and we believe that this is Love.

We are dreaming and we ignore it.

Solo entonces descubre que es eso en lo cual soñaba.

Sólo entonces viene a saber qué es eso que se llama Amor.

Este despertar es semejante a aquel del hombre que, estando en Cuerpo Astral fuera de su cuerpo físico, viene a tener cuanto despierta la Conciencia.

La gente en el Astral anda soñando.

Cuando alguien se da cuenta de que está soñando dice: "Esto es un sueño, yo estoy soñando, yo estoy en Cuerpo Astral, yo estoy fuera de mi cuerpo físico", el sueño desaparece como por encanto y entonces el individuo queda despierto en el Mundo Astral.

Un mundo nuevo y maravilloso aparece ante aquél que antes soñaba, su Conciencia ha despertado.

Ahora puede conocer todas las maravillas de la Naturaleza.

Así también es el despertar del Amor.

Antes de ese despertar soñamos en el Amor.

Tomamos esos sueños por la realidad; creemos que estamos amando; vivimos en un mundo de pasiones, romances a veces deliciosos, desilusiones, vanos juramentos, deseos carnales, celos, etc., etc., y creemos que es eso el Amor.

Estamos soñando y lo ignoramos.

---

[110] Literally 'viene a tener' means "comes to have"
[111] Literally 'anda' means "go, travel; walk; function; go by"
[112] Literally 'encanto' means "charm, spell, incantation; delight, joy; sweetheart"

The Resurrection of the dead is impossible without Love, because Love and Death are two faces of the same deity.	La Resurrección de los muertos es imposible sin el Amor, porque el Amor y la Muerte son dos caras de una misma deidad.
It is necessary to awaken Love in order to attain Resurrection.	Es necesario despertar al Amor para lograr la Resurrección.
It is urgent to renounce our three-dimensional psychology and crude facts in order to discover the meaning of Love in the fourth, fifth and sixth dimensions.	Es urgente renunciar a nuestra psicología tridimensional y a los hechos groseros para descubrir el significado del Amor en las dimensiones cuarta, quinta y sexta.
Love comes from the superior dimensions.	El Amor viene de las dimensiones superiores.
Whosoever does not renounce their three-dimensional psychology will never discover the true meaning of Love, because Love does not have its origin in the three-dimensional world.	Quien no renuncia a su psicología tridimensional jamás descubrirá el verdadero significado del Amor, porque el Amor no tiene origen en el mundo tridimensional.
The flat being who does not renounce his two-dimensional psychology would believe that the only reality in the universe is lines, the color changes of the lines, [as if all of life were] on a [two-dimensional] plane, etc.	El ser plano si no renuncia a su psicología bidimensional creería que la única realidad del Universo son las líneas, los cambios de color de las líneas, en un plano, etc.
A flat being would ignore that the lines and the color changes in certain lines, could be the result of the turning of a wheel with multicolored spokes, perhaps that of a carriage.	Un ser plano ignoraría que las líneas y el cambio de color en ciertas líneas podría ser el resultado del girar de una rueda de rayos multicolores, tal vez un carruaje.
The two-dimensional being would ignore the existence of such a carriage, and with his two-dimensional psychology would not believe in such a carriage; he would only believe in the lines and the color changes seen in his world, without knowing that these are only effects of superior causes.	El ser bidimensional ignoraría la existencia de tal carruaje, y con su psicología bidimensional no creería en tal carruaje; sólo creería en las líneas y en los cambios de colores vistos en su mundo, sin saber que éstos son únicamente efectos de causas superiores.
So too are those who believe that Love is only of this three-dimensional world and who accept crude facts as the only true meaning of Love.	Así son también aquellos que creen que el Amor solo es de este mundo tridimensional y que sólo aceptan los hechos groseros como único significado verdadero del Amor.
People like this cannot discover the true meaning of Love.	Gente así no pueden descubrir el significado verdadero del Amor.

People like this cannot be devoured by the Serpent of Fire.

People like this cannot resurrect from among the dead.

All those poets, all those lovers have sung of Love, but none [of them] really knows that which is called Love.

People only dream about that which is called Love.

People have not awakened to Love.

Gentes así no pueden ser devoradas por la Serpiente de Fuego.

Gentes así no pueden resucitar de entre los muertos.

Todos los poetas, todos los enamorados le han cantado al Amor, pero ninguno sabe realmente qué es eso que se llama Amor.

La gente solo sueña en eso que se llama Amor.

La gente no ha despertado al Amor.

*Gnostic Secrets of
Esoteric and Occult Masonry*

*Secretos Gnósticos de la
Masonería Esoterica y Oculta*

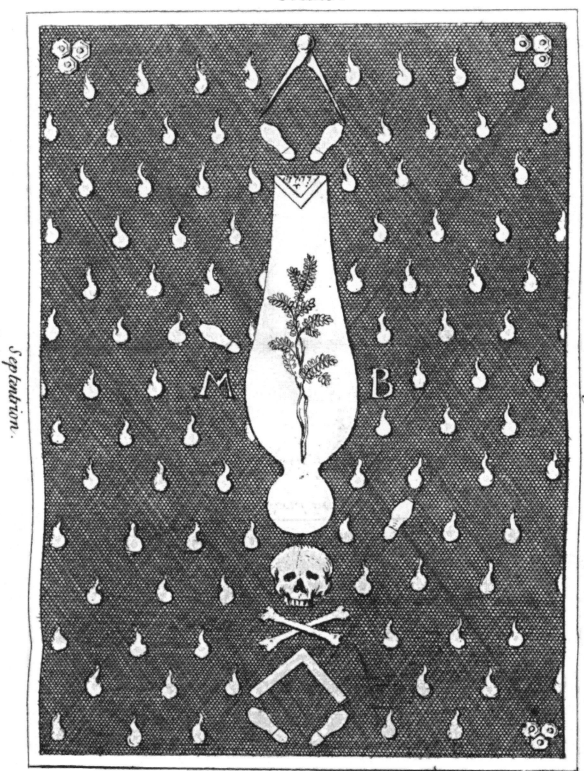

Plan de la Loge du Maitre.

Editor's Appendix

Extracted from pages 2375-2376 of
THE FIFTH GOSPEL:

"INTERVIEW ON UNIVERSITY RADIO"

...

Question. In search of the transcendental Truth, there have always appeared in the History of Humanity (which has happened many times) groups or associations that have worked with secrecy.

We could refer to the Essenes, the Cathars, the Phoenicians, the Masons, what is the relationship [that exists] between these groups and the Gnostic Association you represent, Doctor?

Answer. Well, the Gnostic Association of Cultural and Anthropological Studies, [a] Civic Association, respects all schools, organizations, sects, orders, etc., etc., etc.

But we know that if one does not work with the THREE FACTORS OF THE REVOLUTION OF THE CONSCIOUSNESS, [then] one does not reach any logical conclusion.

I emphatically refer to these three aspects which are: BIRTH, DEATH AND SACRIFICE FOR HUMANITY.

BIRTH: It is necessary to create the Man within ourselves, because the present man is a Man not yet achieved.[113]

---

[113] Editor's note: The 'Man' refers to the 'Son of Man' from the Bible, "I want you to understand the allegory: this PHOENIX BIRD is the THIRD LOGOS, our particular, individually Logoi; [the] very sacred Holy Spirit, in whose name, we always do the Gnostic Baptism. It is the Lord, it is the King of Alchemy, the Hiram Abiff of occult Masonry, who is now dead, but [who] should be born in each one of us, [and who] should resurrect in each one of us. As for the small PHOENIX [BIRD], [this] is the SON OF MAN, the Tiphereth of the hebrew Kabalah, which needs to come into the world in order to work in the Great Work of the Father." from Lecture #122 'Resurrection through Baptism' in *THE FIFTH GOSPEL*.

Apéndice del Editor

Extracto de páginas 2375-2376 de
EL QUINTO EVANGELIO:

"ENTREVISTA EN RADIO UNIVERSIDAD"

...

Pregunta. En busca de la Verdad trascendental, siempre han aparecido en la Historia de la Humanidad (lo cual ha sucedido muchas veces) grupos o asociaciones que han trabajado con carácter secreto.

Podríamos referirnos a los Esenios, a los Cátaros, a los Fenicios, a los Masones, ¿qué relación tendrían todos esos grupos con la Asociación Gnóstica que usted representa, Doctor?

Respuesta. Bueno, la Asociación Gnóstica de Estudios Antropológicos y Culturales, Asociación Civil, respeta a todas las escuelas, organizaciones, sectas, órdenes, etc., etc., etc.

Mas sabemos muy bien que si no se trabaja con los TRES FACTORES DE LA REVOLUCIÓN DE LA CONCIENCIA, no se llega a ninguna conclusión lógica.

Quiero referirme, en forma enfática, a esos tres aspectos que son: NACER, MORIR Y SACRIFICARSE POR LA HUMANIDAD.

NACER: Es necesario crear al Hombre dentro de nosotros mismos, porque el hombre actual es un Hombre no logrado todavía.[114]

---

[114] Nota del editor: El 'Hombre' se refiere al 'Hijo del Hombre' de la Biblia, "Quiero que entendáis la alegoría: ese AVE FÉNIX es el TERCER LOGOS, nuestro Logoi particular, individual; sacratísimo Espíritu Santo, en cuyo nombre, siempre, hacemos los Bautismos Gnósticos. Es el Señor, es el Rey de la Alquimia, el Hiram Abiff de la Masonería oculta, que ahora está muerto, pero debe nacer en cada uno de nosotros, debe resucitar en cada uno de nosotros. En cuanto al pequeño FENIXITO, es el HIJO DEL HOMBRE, el Tiphereth de la Kábala hebraica, que necesita venir al mundo para trabajar en la Gran Obra del Padre." del Conferencia #122 'La Resurrección a través del Bautismo' en *EL QUINTO EVANGELIO*.

I agree with what some college professor in Mexico said: "We –affirming–, are only rational mammals"... I believe that this is an correct definition.

What would be interesting, would be to create the MAN within ourselves and this is only possible by learning to TRANSMUTE OUR SEXUAL SECRETIONS, because it is through sex that we reproduce ourselves (we are children[115] of sex, we are children of a man and a woman), if we learn to transmute our Sexual Libido, as Sigmund Freud teaches us in his "Psychoanalysis", [then it] is possible to create the Man within ourselves.

Frederic Nietzsche talks to us about a SUPERMAN, but he made a very great error: He forgot about the Man.

We need to first create the Man, before we can even think about the Super-Man.

Obviously, if we transmute the SACRED SPERM, the EXIOHEHAI, we can obtain[116] CREATIVE ENERGY.

Indubitably, the Energy will condense in various forms of life.

The Creative Energy (for example, in a superior Octave) will condense as the famous ASTRAL BODY that the Ancient Sages have mentioned, which Parascelsus (Philip Theophrastus Bombastus von Hohenheim) spoke to us about.

The Astral Body is not perceived through the physical eyes, but those who have it, know they have it.

---

[115] Literally 'hijos' means "son, male child, male offspring; child; boy"
[116] Literally 'obtener' means "obtain, acquire, come by; procure, secure; earn, achieve"

One knows that [one] has an Astral Body when one can use it to transport oneself out of their physical body; when one has [it], with this vehicle, one [can] transport oneself to any place in the infinite space (this is a reality; and photographs have been taken of the Astral Body, very good pictures taken with special lenses).

And, in a much higher octave, we [could] say, in a very elevated Second Octave, the Creative Energy can condense into the form of the MENTAL BODY.

The Mental Body gives us an "Intellectual Individuality"; because [it is] one thing to fill our heads with theories and another to have [the] "spark" of the true Understanding[117] (in the most complete sense of the word).

In a much higher Third Octave, the Creative Energy will crystallize or condense into the form of the CAUSAL BODY.

Those who possess a Causal Body, or Body of Conscious Willpower, can determine circumstances at will, and are no longer victims of circumstances.

Instead, they can originate new circumstances.

Anyone who possesses the Physical, Astral, Mental and Causal Bodies is able to receive the ANIMIC, BUDDHIC or CHRISTIC PRINCIPLES (or however we want to call them) and converts themselves into [a] real Man, into [a] true Man, in the most complete meaning of the word.

---

[117] Literally 'Inteligencia' means "intelligence, knowledge; wit; brains; abilities; comprehension"

Uno sabe que tiene un Cuerpo Astral cuando puede usarlo, cuando puede viajar con él, fuera del cuerpo físico; cuando puede, con ese vehículo, transportarse a cualquier lugar del espacio infinito (es una realidad eso; y hasta se han sacado fotografías del Cuerpo Astral, muy buenas fotografías, con lentes muy finos).

Y bien, en una octava más alta, diríamos, en una Segunda Octava más elevada, la Energía Creadora puede condensar en la forma del CUERPO MENTAL.

El Cuerpo Mental nos da "Individualidad Intelectual"; porque una cosa es rellenarnos la cabeza con muchas teorías y otra cosa es tener "chispa" (en el sentido más completo de la palabra), verdadera Inteligencia.

En una Tercera Octava más alta, la Energía Creadora puede cristalizar o condensarse en la forma del CUERPO CAUSAL.

Quien posee un Cuerpo Causal, o Cuerpo de la Voluntad Consciente, puede determinar circunstancias a voluntad, ya no es víctima de las circunstancias.

Antes bien, puede originar nuevas circunstancias.

Alguien que posea los Cuerpos Físico, Astral, Mental y Causal, puede recibir los PRINCIPIOS ÉTNICOS, BÚDDHICOS o CRÍSTICOS (o como se le quiera llamar) y se convierte en Hombre real, en Hombre verdadero, en el sentido más completo de la palabra.

Those who develop their SENSE OF PSYCHOLOGICAL SELF-OBSERVATION, are able to perceive the Astral, to perceive the Mental and to perceive the Causal [worlds].

But we need to possess these Bodies in their totality[118], completely, in order to become real Men; before that instant one is nothing more than a "rational mammal", as that professor from the University of Mexico [once] said…

So, it is important to work with this Energy in order to convert ourselves into Men…

The second factor necessary is TO DISSOLVE THE EGO (the psychological "I"), to reduce it to dust, so that only the BEING remains within us.

And finally, [we need] TO RAISE THE TORCH HIGH in order to illuminate the path for others.

Any school that does not work with these Three Factors of the Revolution of the Consciousness, is obviously bottled up within theories and will not reach any conclusion.

No matter how respectable an organization may be, if they forget about these Three Factors of the Revolution of the Consciousness, [then they] serve no purpose.

I do respect all organizations, from the East to the West.

I am only referring, in [an] emphatic[119] way, to the Three Factors, and I say that if there are any Schools that do not know those Three Factors, they should learn them, and that is all…

---

[118] Literally 'en forma íntegra' means "in [an] integral form"
[119] Literally 'enfática' means "emphatic (using emphasis in speech or action)"

Extracted from the Chapter 9 of TAROT & KABALAH by Samael Aun Weor

...One must descend and one must ascend by the Luciferic ladder, we need to become Masters of both the Superior and Inferior Forces.

The Father who is in secret commands that which must be done, [and] only upon receiving the order does one descend.

Only he who FALLS loses his Initiatic degrees, not he who has DESCENDED.

Orders are received upon [the] conclusion of the work and one now no longer makes use of Sex capriciously[120]. It is the Father who is lord[121] of this act, and it is the Father from whom the order must come.

Sex does not belong to oneself, but rather to the Father.

The Law of Leviathan is that of the Mason who has already passed [through] all the Works or Esoteric Degrees and since he has already been decapitated he can not be re-capitated, he can neither be harmed from above nor from below; he lives in keeping with the Law, with the Great Law.

This is the superior knowledge of Esoteric Masonry...

Extracto del Capítulo IX de TAROT Y KÁBALA por Samael Aun Weor

...Por la escalera Luciférica hay que bajar y hay que subir, necesitamos hacernos Maestros tanto de las Fuerzas Superiores como Inferiores.

El Padre que está en secreto ordena lo que se debe hacer, sólo recibiendo una orden se baja.

Sólo pierde sus grados Iniciáticos el que CAE, no el que ha BAJADO.

Concluido el trabajo se reciben las órdenes y ya no se hace uso del Sexo en forma caprichosa. Es el Padre dueño de este acto, y del Padre tiene que venir la orden.

El Sexo no pertenece a uno sino al Padre.

La Ley de Leviatán es la de aquel Masón que ya pasó todos los Trabajos o Grados Esotéricos y como ya fue decapitado no puede ser re-decapitado, no puede recibir daño ni de arriba ni de abajo, vive en tono a la Ley, a la Gran Ley.

Este es el conocimiento superior de la Masonería Esotérica...

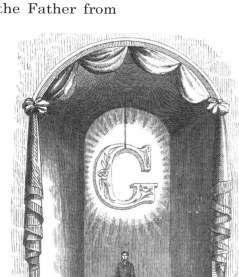

---

[120] Literally 'caprichosa' means "capricious, whimsical, fanciful; faddish"
[121] Literally 'dueño' means "owner, proprietor, landlord"

Extracted from the Chapter 3 of
AZTEC CHRISTIC MAGIC
by Samael Aun Weor

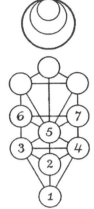

...The human being has seven bodies that interpenetrate[122] without confusion. Each one of these bodies has its own spinal medulla. There is a serpent that corresponds to each one of them.

[There are] two groups of three serpents and, in [the] middle, [is] the sublime crown of the seventh serpent, the tongue of fire that unites us with the Law, with our Intimus, with our Father.

With the first initiation of major mysteries, man lights, within himself, the Universal Fire, awakening and raising his first serpent; with the second initiation [he lights, awakens and raises] the second serpent; with the third initiation, [he lights, awakens and raises] the third serpent, and likewise until raising the seventh serpent.

The ascent of the seventh precious feathered serpent of Quetzalli through each one of the 33 vertebrae of the dorsal spine (the 33 degrees of masonry) is very slow, difficult and is only possible by means of sexual magic.

We must not allow ejaculation and [instead] we must transmute the semen that comes[123] from the testicles in the man and from the ovaries in the woman into electromagnetic energy that rises through the different conduits[124] of both in order to be united in their spinal medulla in their coccygeal gland, and from there [it] ascends to the brain converted into solar and lunar atoms.

---

[122] Literally 'compenetran' means "interpenetrate, compenetrate, permeate, penetrate"
[123] Literally 'parte' means "divide, split up; share; cut, chop; break; tear; district; abandon, depart; dole out; fly off; chapter"
[124] Literally 'conductos' means "pipe, conduit; canal, channel; duct"

Extracto del Capítulo 3 de
MAGIA CRÍSTICA AZTECA[125]
por Samael Aun Weor

...El hombre tiene siete cuerpos que se compenetran sin confundirse. Cada uno de ellos tiene su propia médula espinal. A cada una de éstas le corresponde una serpiente.

Dos grupos de tres serpientes y, en medio, la corona sublime de la séptima serpiente, la lengua de fuego que nos une con la Ley, con el Intimo, con el Padre.

Con la primera iniciación de misterios mayores el hombre enciende, en él mismo, el Fuego Universal, despierta y levanta a su primera serpiente, con la segunda iniciación a la segunda serpiente; con la tercera iniciación, a la tercera serpiente y así, hasta levantar a la séptima serpiente.

El asenso de la séptima preciosa serpiente de plumas de Quetzalli a lo largo de cada una de las 33 vértebras de la espina dorsal (los 33 grados de la masonería) es muy lento, difícil y sólo es posible por medio de la magia sexual.

No permitir la eyaculación y transmutar el semen, que parte de los testículos en el hombre y de los ovarios en la mujer, en energía electromagnética que sube por los diferentes conductos de ambos para unirse con la médula espinal en la glándula coxígea, y de allí asciende al cerebro convertida en átomos solares y lunares.

---

[125] MONOGRAFÍA Nº3 "EL DECAPITADO"

When, through the alchemy of amorous[126] sexual contact, the semen is transmuted into electromagnetic energy and makes contact in the coccygeal gland, [then] the precious feathered serpent Quetzalli awakens, exhausted[127] and raises itself, transformed in to Quetzalcoatl...

Cuando por la alquimia del contacto sexual amoroso se transmuta el semen en energía electromagnética y ésta hace contacto con la glándula coxígea, despierta, se agota y se levanta la serpiente preciosa de plumas de Quetzalli que, transformada en Quetzalcoatl...

---

[126] Literally 'amoroso' means "loving, affectionate; amorous, passionate; yearning; yielding"

[127] Literally 'agota' means "exhaust, use up; wear down; distress; frazzle; impoverish"

Extracted from pages 559-560 of
THE FIFTH GOSPEL:

"THE POWER OF CONSCIOUS FAITH"[128]

Disciple. [...X...] ...In order to create[129] Faith it is necessary to study... [...X...] ...we must work with our Divine Mother and we should practice the Sahaja Maithuna.

Well, the confusion consists of this: In your book, you talk in a passage, you mention Brutus... [...X...] ...any relation... [...X...] ...say that he practiced the Sahaja Maithuna and despite this he [still] failed... [...X...] ...thus I think that it cannot be achieved.

So, I ask [you]: If we... [...X...] ...how does one know if our Mother Kundalini does not forgive mistakes such as: Betrayal[130], adultery, lust, right?, and all that, [so] how can we develop this Consciousness, without knowing [if] what we did in previous lives, in order to create Faith, since we are weighed down[131] [by] several previous offenses for which we will not be forgiven and which will impede us from creating that Faith?

Especially seeing the last [thing] you mentioned[132] now... [...X...] ...in order to do a retrospective analysis of... [...X...]

Master. Well, with the greatest pleasure I will answer your question...

First of all, in order that there may be (we [could] say) forgiveness, in order for there to exist FORGIVENESS, there needs to be someone who asks for that forgiveness, someone who is REPENTANT[133].

---

[128] This extract is from part of a question and answer session.
[129] Literally 'fabricar' means "manufacture; create, make, produce; mass-produce; fabricate, invent"
[130] Literally 'traición' means "treason, betrayal, treachery"
[131] Literally 'arrastramos' means "drag, haul; be pulled; creep; grovel; trail; blow away; wash down"
[132] Literally 'señala' means " signalize, make prominent; mark, indicate, signal; particularize, specify"
[133] Literally 'ARREPENTIDO' means "repentant, penitent; regretful, sorry; contrite, rueful"

Extracto de páginas 559-560 de
EL QUINTO EVANGELIO:

"EL PODER DE LA FE CONSCIENTE"[134]

Discípulo. [...X...] ...Para fabricar Fe es necesario estudiar... [...X...] ...debemos de trabajar con nuestra Divina Madre y debemos practicar el Sahaja Maithuna.

Bueno, la confusión consiste en esto: En su libro, habla usted en un pasaje, menciona usted a Bruto... [...X...] ...alguna relación... [...X...] ...dice que practicó el Sahaja Maithuna y a pesar de eso fracasará... [...X...] ...con lo cual pienso yo que no podrá lograrlo.

Entonces, yo pregunto: ¿Si nosotros... [...X...] ...cómo puedo saber?, si nuestra Madre Kundalini no perdona faltas como son: La traición, el adulterio, la lujuria, ¿verdad?, y todo eso, ¿cómo podemos nosotros desarrollar esa Conciencia, sin saber qué es lo que hicimos en vidas anteriores, para poder fabricar la Fe, si ya arrastramos varias faltas anteriores que no nos van a ser perdonadas y que nos van a impedir que logremos fabricar esa Fe?

Sobre todo y viendo lo último que usted señala ahora... [...X...] ...para ser un análisis retrospectivo de... [...X...]

Maestro. Bueno, con el mayor gusto daré respuesta a tu pregunta...

Ante todo, para que haya, dijéramos, un perdón, para que exista un PERDÓN, es necesario que haya alguien que pida ese perdón, alguien que esté ARREPENTIDO.

---

[134] Este extracto de parte de a preguntas y respuestas sesiones.

How could a [person] pardon someone who has not repented?

Is it fair to forgive someone who does not repent of a crime?

But if he repents [of] the crime he committed and apologizes sincerely, [then] he can be forgiven, right?

But if he does not repent nor ask for forgiveness, if he is happy with the offense, could he or should he, really, be given a pardon that he did not ask for, and that he does not desire and that he does not want?

ANYONE CAN GIVE YOU WHAT YOU DO NOT WANT.

Further: We can not raise anyone to Heaven "whether [they] like it or not", by force, if they don't want to.

We could not teach Gnosis to another [person] if that other [person] does not accept it; we could not give a drink to a person if the person does not want it.

We can provide it, but if they do we want it, how are we to force them to drink?

This is the case of BRUTUS, right?

Brutus betrayed the Guru, and not only betrayed, but never repented of the betrayal, [he] never apologized, [he] never wanted forgiveness.

Why should [someone] be given forgiveness who has not asked [for] forgiveness?

Why should [someone] forgive someone [else] who has not repented of a crime?

If Brutus enters into [the] work in the Ninth Sphere continuing with the crime of treason, should the Divine Mother Kundalini perhaps reward betrayal?

¿Cómo podría darse un perdón a alguien que no se ha arrepentido?

¿Sería justo perdonar a quien no se arrepiente de un delito?

Pero si el que cometió el delito se arrepiente y pide perdón sinceramente, puede ser perdonado, ¿verdad?

Pero si no se arrepiente ni pide perdón, si está contento con el delito, ¿acaso se le podría o se le debería, realmente, dar un perdón que él no ha pedido, y que no lo desea y no lo quiere?

A NADIE SE LE PUEDE DAR LO QUE NO QUIERE.

Aun más: No podríamos llevar a nadie al Cielo "a la brava", a la fuerza, si ése no quiere.

No podríamos enseñarle la Gnosis a otro si ese otro no la acepta; no podríamos brindarle un refresco a una persona si la persona no lo quiere.

Podemos brindárselo, pero si no lo quiere, ¿cómo se lo podemos hacer beber a la fuerza?

Ése es el caso de BRUTO, ¿no?

Bruto traicionó al Gurú, y no solamente lo traicionó, sino que jamás se arrepintió de la traición, nunca pidió perdón, jamás deseó perdón.

¿Por qué habría de dársele perdón a alguien no pidió perdón?

¿Por qué se habría de perdonar a alguien que no se ha arrepentido de un delito?

Si Bruto entrara a trabajar en la Novena Esfera continuando con el delito de traición, ¿la Madre Divina Kundalini podría acaso recompensarle la traición?

I am sure that THE DIVINE MOTHER KUNDALINI DOES NOT REWARD CRIMES; SHE CAN FORGIVE US IF THERE IS REPENTANCE, but she will not become [an] accomplice to the crime.

If the Divine Mother can forgive crimes without the subject being repent thereof, without them having begged [for] forgiveness, then she obviously would become [an] accomplice to the crime, [and] would be criminal as well, and I do not think that God-Mother can become [an] accomplice to crime, [she could not become a] culprit[135].

Just because the subject went to work in the Ninth Sphere, and because of this the Divine Mother, inevitably, were to give a pardon for a crime which [the subject] had never repented, well no!

Because the ascent of the Sacred Fire, the ascent of the Serpent through the dorsal spine, is controlled by MERITS OF HEART.

The FIRES OF THE CARDIA CONTROL THE SPINAL FIRES, this is known [by] anyone who has studied Occult Anatomy; on the contrary, [if this were not the case, then] our Divine Mother [would] become [an] accomplice to the crime.

I know a case, whose name I will not mention.

It is the case of a lady (that does not now have a compound name) who has two husbands and practiced Sexual Magic with both, and she thinks that [everything] is going well.

I had to remove her, expel[136] her, from the Gnostic Movement, but she believes [everything] is going very well.

Yo estoy seguro que LA MADRE DIVINA KUNDALINI NO RECOMPENSA DELITOS; PUEDE PERDONARLOS SI HAY ARREPENTIMIENTO, pero ella no se convertiría en cómplice del delito.

Si la Madre Divina perdonara delitos sin que el sujeto se arrepintiese de los mismos, sin que él suplicara el perdón, entonces ella, obviamente, se convertiría en cómplice del delito, sería delincuente también, y no me parece que Dios-Madre pueda convertirse en cómplice del delito, en delincuente.

Si porque el sujeto entró a trabajar en la Novena Esfera, ya por eso la Madre Divina, forzosamente, habría de darle un perdón, por un delito del cual él jamás se arrepintió, ¡pues no!

Porque el ascenso del Fuego Sagrado, el ascenso de la Serpiente por la espina dorsal, está controlado por los MÉRITOS DEL CORAZÓN.

Los FUEGOS DEL CARDIAS CONTROLAN A LOS FUEGOS ESPINALES, eso lo sabe cualquiera que haya estudiado Anatomía Oculta; de lo contrario, nuestra Madre Divina se convertiría en cómplice del delito.

Yo conozco un caso, cuyo nombre no menciono.

Es el de una dama (que no viene ahora a colación nombrarla) que tiene dos maridos y con ambos practica Magia Sexual, y ella piensa que va muy bien.

Tuve que retirarla del Movimiento Gnóstico, expulsarla, pero ella cree que va muy bien.

---

[135] Literally 'delincuente' means "felonious, delinquent; offender, culprit, delinquent"
[136] Literally 'expulsarla' means "expel, eject; scavenge"

The first, a poor old man, [she] says she keeps "for peity[137]"; the second "because she loves [him] and wants to help so he can also Self-realize..."

Do you believe that perhaps that Sexual Magic thus, with three people, a "ball" of three people practicing Sexual Magic, will Self-realize?

Do you believe that the Divine Mother Kundalini would reward this lady for ADULTERY?

What would occur, then, [if] the Divine Mother Kundalini rewarded adultery? Impossible!, right?

In this way, then, what I have said with respect to Brutus is true.

First of all, in order for the Sacred Serpent to rise, one needs the MERITS OF THE HEART.

Each of the 33 vertebrae of the dorsal spine correspond to a Virtue or Virtues.

The Serpent could not reach[138], for example to the 10th vertebra, if the candidate was not tested beforehand.

The Serpent could not reach the 20th vertebra, if the candidate does not meet the requirements of this vertebra.

In the dorsal spine there are all 33 Degrees of Occult Masonry and it is not possible for the Serpent to rise, to pass from degree to degree, if the corresponding merits do not exist...

Al primero, un pobre vejete, dice que lo tiene "y que por piedad"; al segundo que "porque lo ama y desea ayudarlo para que él también se Autorrealice"...

¿Creen ustedes acaso que una Magia Sexual así, con tres personas, una "bola" de tres personas practicando Magia Sexual, van a Autorrealizarse?

¿Acaso creen ustedes que la Madre Divina Kundalini iría a recompensarle a esa dama el ADULTERIO?

¿En qué quedaría entonces la Madre Divina Kundalini, recompensando adulterios? ¡Imposible!, ¿verdad?

De manera pues que, entonces, lo que he dicho con respecto a Bruto es verdad.

Ante todo, para que la Serpiente Sagrada suba, se necesitan los MERITOS DEL CORAZÓN.

Cada una de las 33 vértebras de la espina dorsal corresponde a una Virtud o Virtudes.

No podría la Serpiente llegar, por ejemplo a la vértebra 10, si antes no ha sido probado el candidato.

No podría llegar la Serpiente a la vértebra 20, si el candidato no llena los requisitos de tal vértebra.

En la espina dorsal están todos los 33 Grados de la Masonería Oculta y no es posible que la Serpiente suba, pase de grado en grado, si no existen los méritos correspondientes...

---

[137] Literally 'piedad' means "piety, piousness (having or showing a dutiful spirit of reverence for God or an earnest wish to fulfill religious obligations)"
[138] Literally 'llegar' means "arrive, come; reach; roll along; land; immigrate; invade; get; travel; vaporize"

What if all murderers, drunkards, fornicators, thieves, etc.., [simply] by the fact of having worked [with] Sexual Magic can become perfect, the Serpent rising up through the spine and [thereby] they become Gods?

What kind of "Gods" would they be?

Thieving Gods?, murdering Gods, traitor Gods?

Where would the Cosmic Order of the Worlds be [then]?...

Editor's Appendix

Extracted from the Chapter 32 of THE PERFECT MATRIMONY by Samael Aun Weor

The sacred scriptures of India affirm that the navel, the heart and the throat are igneous centers of the human organism, and also add that [by] meditating on these centers we encounter the Masters Sarasvati, Lakshmi, [and] Parvati or Gauri in successive hierarchical order.

These three Masters work with the three profundities of our resplendent dragon of wisdom.

These three Masters control the forces that come from the three aspects of the Solar Logos.

Sarasvati works with the forces of the Father.

Lakshmi exerts control over the Astral Body, and Parvati exerts control over the physical body.

The Apprentice has to perfect his physical body by accustoming it to the practice of Sexual Magic with his priestess wife.

This work is very arduous and difficult.

The Companion needs to perfect his Astral Body until it becomes a useful instrument.

The Master needs to perfect his Mental Body with the power of the fire that blazes in the universal orchestration.

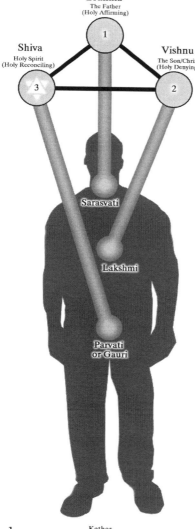

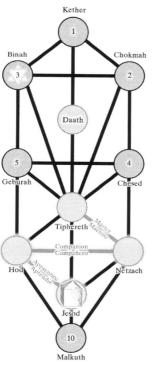

Apéndice del Editor

Extracto del Capítulo XXXII de EL MATRIMONIO PERFECTO por Samael Aun Weor

Las sagradas escrituras de la India afirman que el ombligo, el corazón y la garganta son centros ígneos del organismo humano, y añaden que meditando en dichos centros encontramos a los Maestros Saraswati, Lakshmi, Parvati o Girija en orden jerárquico sucesivo.

Estos tres Maestros trabajan con las tres profundidades de nuestro resplandeciente dragón de sabiduría.

Estos tres Maestros manejan las fuerzas que vienen de los tres aspectos del Logos Solar.

Saraswati trabaja con las fuerzas del Padre.

Lakshmi ejerce poder sobre el Cuerpo Astral y Parvati ejerce poder sobre el cuerpo físico.

El Aprendiz ha de perfeccionar su cuerpo físico acostumbrándolo a practicar Magia Sexual con la esposa sacerdotisa.

Esta labor es muy ardua y difícil.

El Compañero necesita perfeccionar su Cuerpo Astral hasta convertirlo en un instrumento útil.

El Maestro necesita perfeccionar su Cuerpo Mental con el poder del fuego que flamea entre la orquestación universal.

The Apprentice must invoke the Master Parvati to help him control the sexual organs during the practice of Sexual Magic.

The Companion must invoke Lakshmi in order to teach him how to get out in [the] Astral Body.

It is urgent to learn how to travel consciously and positively in the Astral Body.

The Master must invoke Sarasvati so that he may help him to Christify the mind.

These invocations are made during Sexual Magic.

It is necessary to invoke the forces of the Holy Spirit during Sexual Magic.

It is urgent to call the forces of the Christ so that they give rise to the birth of the Christ Astral in the depths of our interior universe.

It is indispensable to ask the forces of the Father for assistance with our mind.

We need to engender the Christ Mind.

The physical, astral and mental vehicles must become fine instruments of the Spirit.

It is indispensable to learn how to get out consciously in [the] Astral Body.

Let us remember that the mind is found within the astral.

It is urgent to visit the temples of the White Lodge consciously.

In the astral we can study at the feet of the Master.

In the following paragraphs we will teach the mantram for getting out [in] astral as taught by a sage in one of his books.

These mantrams are in the sanskrit language and the Yogis of India use them in order to get out in astral.

MANTRAM FOR ASTRAL PROJECTION

"Hare Ram.
Hare Ram, Ram Hare Hare.

Hare Cristo.
Hare Cristo, Cristo, Cristo, Hare, Hare.

Hare Murare Modup Coiptus Hare Copal Govind Mukum Sonre.

Mage Prage Yodi Kolpi Basi Parvot Tullo Hiro No Dane En Bai de Nem.

Sri Govind, Sri Govind.
Sri Govind. Sri Govind.
Ganesha Namap."

The devotee should fall asleep with the head towards the North or towards the East.

It is necessary that the devotee should first learn these Mantrams of India by heart.

The devotee should lie down dorsal decubitus (face up). Supplicate, call and invoke with all his soul the Master Lakshmi to take him out consciously and positively in the Astral Body.

It is necessary to call Lakshmi in the name of the Christ.

INVOCATION

*"In the name of the Christ,
by the glory of the Christ,
by the power of the Christ,
I call you,
Lakshmi, Lakshmi, Lakshmi.
Amen."*

This invocation is repeated thousands of times supplicating the Master Lakshmi to take you out of the physical body consciously and to teach you how to travel consciously in the Astral Body.

After making this invocation, recite the sanskrit Mantram thousands of times with the mind concentrated on the Christ.

Fall asleep calmly while making the invocation.

When you wake up, practice a retrospective exercise to remember where you were, where you walked, with whom you were speaking etc.

It is necessary to ask Lakshmi to teach you how to go consciously into the astral.

It is necessary to have patience as great as that of Saint Job to learn how to go out consciously in the Astral Body.

Let us remember that the degree of Apprentice is of seven years and that only after seven years do the first flashes of illumination begin.

We give this caution so that the student knows what to expect.

For the curious, the profane and the profaners of the Temple; it is best that they leave.

This science is not for the curious.

In accordance with how the devotee practices Sexual Magic with his priestess wife; in accordance with how his conduct becomes more and more upright; in accordance with his continuing sanctification; the splendors and powers of the Intimus (the Spirit) begin to reflect in his astral and in his mind. Then illumination comes.

This is the path; but this illumination is only after the degree of Apprentice. (We are speaking in the terminology of occult masonry).

Every true candidate prepared for illumination will be able to be recognized and verified with the square and the compass.

Después de hecha la invocación recitad los Mantram sánscritos millares de veces con la mente concentrada en el Cristo.

Adormeceos tranquilo haciendo la invocación.

Cuando despertéis del sueño practicad luego un ejercicio retrospectivo para recordar dónde estuvisteis, por dónde anduviste, con quién tuviste pláticas, etc.

Es necesario pedir a Lakshmi que os enseñe a salir conscientemente en astral.

Es necesario tener una paciencia tan grande como la del Santo Job para aprender a salir conscientemente en Cuerpo Astral.

Recordemos que el grado de Aprendiz es de siete años y que sólo después de siete años comienzan los primero relámpagos de la iluminación.

Nosotros advertimos para que los estudiantes sepan a qué atenerse.

Los curiosos, los profanos y profanadores del templo es mejor que se retiren.

Esta ciencia no es para los curiosos.

Conforme el devoto practica Magia Sexual con su esposa sacerdotisa, conforme su conducta se hace cada vez más recta, conforme se va santificando, comienzan a reflejarse en su astral y en su mente los esplendores y poderes del Intimo (el Espíritu). Entonces viene la iluminación.

Ese es el camino; empero, dicha iluminación sólo es después del grado de Aprendiz. (Estamos hablando en términos de masonería oculta).

A todo verdadero candidato preparado para la iluminación se le podrá reconocer y comprobar con la escuadra y el compás.

Editor's Appendix	Apéndice del Editor
When the Spirit and the human personality act in an orderly manner and in full harmony, the devotee is prepared for illumination.	Cuando el Espíritu y la humana personalidad actúan ordenadamente y con plena armonía, el devoto está preparado para la iluminación.
Whoever complains of lack of illumination, cannot withstand the trial of the square and the compass.	Quienes se quejan de no estar iluminados, no pueden resistir la prueba con la escuadra y el compás.
When the inferior quaternary loyally obeys the Spirit, the result is illumination.	Cuando el cuaternario inferior obedece fielmente al Espíritu, el resultado es la iluminación.

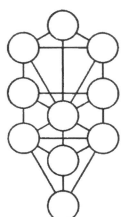

As long as the inferior quaternary does not obey the Spirit, that is to say, while the human personality does not know how to obey the Spirit, illumination is impossible.

Mientras el cuaternario inferior no obedezca al Espíritu, es decir mientras la humana persona no sepa obedecer al Espíritu es imposible la iluminación.

The devotee should purify his bedroom daily with special aromatic substances. Incense purifies the Astral Body.

El devoto debe purificar diariamente su recámara con sahumerios especiales. El incienso purifica el Cuerpo Astral.

A good incense attracts the great Masters that we need for our work.

Un buen incienso atrae a los grandes Maestros que necesitamos para nuestro trabajo.

We can mix incense with benzoin. Benzoin purifies the astral and dispels gross and sensual thoughts.

Podemos mezclar incienso con benjuí. El benjuí purifica el astral y desvanece los pensamientos groseros y sensuales.

Benzoin can be mixed with incense in a perfume censer, or all burnt within a brazier. This is the most practical.

Puede mezclarse el benjuí con el incienso dentro de un pebetero, o quemando todo entre un braserillo. Esto es lo más práctico.

The essence of roses can also be mixed with these perfumes to purify the environment.

La esencia de rosas también puede mezclarse con estos perfumes para purificar el ambiente.

It is good to remember that roses have great power. The rose is the queen of flowers.

Es bueno recordar que las rosas tienen un gran poder. La rosa es la reina de las flores.

It is necessary that the rose of the Spirit open its fragrant and delicious bud upon the cross of our body.

Es necesario que la rosa del Espíritu abra su fragante y delicioso capullo sobre la cruz de nuestro cuerpo.

We also recommend olibanum[139] to create a devotional atmosphere in the nuptial bedroom. Husband and wife should live in the midst of perfume and love.

Recordamos el olívano, también para formar ambiente devocional en la recámara nupcial. El esposo y la esposa deben vivir entre los perfumes y el amor.

---

[139] Literally 'olívano' means "olibanum, frankincense"

Incense and perfume burn delightfully in all temples [of the] hindu, pharsee, jain, shinto etc., etc.

Incense and perfumes were never absent from the temples of Greece, Rome, Persia etc.

The devotee needs much purification and sanctification in order to reach illumination.

SPECIAL INDICATION

Jesus, the Great Hierophant said, *"Help yourself and I will help you."*

So then, the gnostic student should take account of these words of the Master.

The mantrams to go out in the Astral Body as we have taught in this chapter are marvelous.

The invocation to the Master Lakshmi is magnificent, marvelous, but the Gnostic student must help himself, he must concentrate on the navel; he must fall asleep singing the mantram mentally, and when he finds himself dozing, when he feels that lassitude[140] of sleep itself he should imagine himself to be a breeze, a gas, something subtle, to feel himself to be completely aerial and gaseous, and in that state, feeling thus, aerial and subtle, to forget the heaviness of the physical body, to think that he can fly anywhere because he no longer has weight of any kind; forgetting his physical body, feeling like a cloud, [an] aroma, [a] breeze, [or a] divine breath, he should leap up from his bed.

Do not try to leap mentally; it is urgent that all this is translated into action, into concrete facts.

Once outside the physical body, leave your house and direct yourself to the Gnostic Church in the Astral Body, or to whatver place you want.

---

[140] Literally 'lasitud' means "lassitude, weariness, exhaustion"

With the Astral Body one can travel to other planets, with the Astral Body one can visit the most distant places of the Cosmos, the Mystery Temples, etc., etc...	Con Cuerpo Astral se puede viajar a otros planetas, con Cuerpo Astral se pueden visitar los sitios más lejanos del Cosmos, los Templos de Misterios, etc., etc...

Extracted from the Chapter 22 of
ESOTERIC COURSE OF KABALAH
by Samael Aun Weor

...You are IMITATUS, or rather, one who others have put on the PATH OF THE RAZOR'S EDGE.

Exert yourself to become ADEPTUS, one who is the product of their own deeds, one who conquers the Science by themselves, the Child of their own Work.[141]

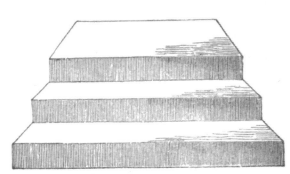

GNOSIS teaches three steps through which anyone who works in the Flaming Forge of Vulcan has to pass through, these are: PURIFICATION, ILLUMINATION, AND PERFECTION.

It so happens that curious people who enter into our Gnostic studies want illumination, [astral] projections, faculties of Clairvoyance, practical Magic, etc., and when they do not achieve this immediately, they withdraw.

No one can achieve illumination without having themselves been previously purified, only those that have achieved Purification [and] Sanctity can enter into the hall of Illumination.

There are also many curious students (they enter into our studies purely out of curiosity) who want to immediately be wise.

Paul of Tarsus stated: "WE SPEAK WISDOM AMONG THOSE THAT ARE PERFECT" [1st Corinthians 2:6].

---

[141] Editor's note: Compare "YOU MUST ACHIEVE THE DEGREE OF ADEPTUS, LEAVING BEHIND THE ANIMAL STATE, ACQUIRING CONSCIOUSNESS." from Ch. 22 of *Tarot & Kabalah*

Only those who achieve the third step are Perfect, only among them can Divine Wisdom be spoken of.

In the old Egypt of the Pharaohs, among the Occult Masons, the three steps of the Path were: APPRENTICES, COMPANIONS, MASTERS.

Candidates remained in the degree of Apprentice for seven years and sometimes longer; only when the HEIROPHANTS were completely sure of the Purification and Sanctity of the Candidates were they then able to pass them to the second stage; the first faculty that the Candidate develops is the one related with the degree of listener[143], [related with] Clairaudience and occult hearing.

Really, illumination begins only after seven years of Apprenticeship; nonetheless, Students believe that spiritual faculties are going to be immediately developed and when they realize that this subject matter is serious, then they flee; this is the sad reality, it is very rare to find someone who is prepared for Adepthood.

...

THE INTERIOR LODGE

The first duty of any Gnostic is to be sure that the LODGE is protected.

During the degree of Apprentice, the attention is focused especially on the Astral Plane.

The INTERNAL LODGE must be protected, the Astral body must be cleansed of animal passions and of all types of desires.

In the second Degree the mental Lodge must be protected, worldly thoughts must be cast out of the Temple.

---

[143] Literally 'oyentes' means "listener, hearer; auditor"

It is necessary to protect the INTERIOR LODGE very well, so that Doctrines, persons, Demons, and things do not penetrate inside the Internal Sanctuary to sabotage the GREAT WORK.

In practical life, we may see that students (apparently very serious) when they became careless, when they could not protect their own Interior Lodge, were invaded by strange people and Doctrines; often times they continue working in the FLAMING FORGE OF VULCAN, but they mixed many different methods and systems; the result of all of this was a true [Tower of] Babel, a barbaric confusion whose only purpose was to bring disorder into the INTERIOR LODGE OF THE CONSCIOUSNESS.

Therefore, it is necessary to have the interior Lodge (the authentic School of Intimate Self-Education) in perfect order.

We are absolutely sure that only one door and only one way exists: Sex, everything that is not through this way is just a miserable waste of time.[144]

Es necesario cubrir bien la LOGIA INTERIOR, para impedir que Doctrinas, personas, Demonios y cosas penetren dentro del Santuario Interno para sabotear la GRAN OBRA.

En la práctica pudimos ver que estudiantes aparentemente muy serios cuando se descuidaron, cuando no supieron cubrir su Logia Interna, fueron invadidos por gentes y Doctrinas extrañas, muchas veces continuaron trabajando en la FRAGUA ENCENDIDA DE VULCANO, pero mezclaron métodos y sistemas tan distintos, que el resultado de todo esto, fue entonces una verdadera Babel, una confusión bárbara que solo sirvió para traer desorden a la LOGIA INTERIOR DE LA CONCIENCIA.

Es necesario tener la Logia interior, en perfecto orden, la auténtica Escuela de Auto Educación Intima.

Estamos absolutamente seguros de que sólo existe una sola puerta y un solo camino, el Sexo, todo lo que no sea por allí es perder miserablemente el tiempo.[145]

---

[144] Editor's note: Compare Krumm-Heller in Section Two of *Logos Mantram Magic*: "I, who have nearly half a century of study in these matters behind me, who possess the highest degrees of masonry … declare for myself [that] in vocalization, in the use of mantrams and [of] *prayer*, [and] through the awakening of sexual secretions, exists the only path to arrive at the goal and all else, that is not here, is a miserable waste of time."

[145] Nota del editor: Comparar Krumm-Heller en la Sección Dos de *Logos Mantram Magia*: "Yo, que tengo casi medio siglo de estudio en estos asuntos, que tengo los grados más altos de la masonería … declaro que para mí en la vocalización, en el uso de los mantrams y la *oración*, mediante el despertar de las secreciones sexuales, resido el único camino de llegar a la meta y todo lo demás, que no sea por aquí, es perder lastimosamente el tiempo."

We are not against any Religion, School, Sect, Order, etc., nonetheless, we firmly know that inside our Individual Interior Lodge we must have order, so that we avoid confusion and error.

Nosotros no estamos contra ninguna Religión, Escuela, Secta, Orden, etc., empero sabemos firmemente que dentro de la Logia Interna Individual debemos tener un orden a fin de evitarnos las confusiones y el error.

Extracted from the Chapter 9 of AZTEC CHRISTIC MAGIC by Samael Aun Weor

In the ancient aztec mystery schools, after passing through the ordeals to which the candidates were submitted, they could directly work with the feathered serpent.

However, we are not stating that you have already victoriously passed these ordeals, we will see [about this] later.

Meanwhile, let us continue working with meditation. Meditation is the bread of the wise.

When the sage meditates [he is] searching for God, he searches for information or he searches for power.

There are five clues for meditation:

1. Comfortable Position[146]
2. Blank Mind
3. Concentration
4. Introversion
5. Ecstasy

Seat yourself in the most comfortable position then concentrate on your physical body and, after you have attentively examined it and realize[147] that you are not such a marvelous vehicle, discard it from your mind saying: "I am not my physical body."

Concentrate on your etheric body, identify [with] it and, once you have attentively observed its marvelous luminosity (which protrudes from the physical body forming a multicolored aura) and realize that this second body of yours is not what you are and discard it from your mind saying: "I am not my etheric body."

---

[146] Literally 'Postura' means "posture, viewpoint, standpoint; pose, position; stance; condition, state; mood, attitude"
[147] Literally 'comprobar' means "check; test; test out; substantiate, prove"

Extracto del Capítulo 9[148] de MAGIA CRÍSTICA AZTECA por Samael Aun Weor

En las antiguas escuelas de misterios aztecas, después de las pruebas a las que eran sometidos los candidatos, estos podían pasar a trabajar directamente con la serpiente emplumada.

No queremos decir con esto que usted haya pasado victoriosamente sus pruebas, eso lo veremos más adelante.

Mientras tanto, vamos a seguir trabajando con la meditación. La meditación es el pan del sabio.

Cuando el sabio medita busca a Dios, busca información o busca poder.

Cinco son las claves de la meditación.

1. Postura Cómoda
2. Mente en blanco
3. Concentración.
4. Introversión.
5. Éxtasis.

Sentado en la postura más cómoda para usted, concéntrese en su cuerpo físico y, después de examinarlo atentamente y comprobar que usted no es ese maravilloso vehículo suyo, deséchelo de su mente diciendo: Yo no soy mi cuerpo físico.

Concéntrese en su cuerpo etérico, identifíquelo y, después de observar atentamente su bellísima luminosidad que sobresale del cuerpo físico formando un aura multicolor y comprobar que usted no es ese su segundo cuerpo, deséchelo de su mente diciendo: Yo no soy mi cuerpo etérico.

---

[148] MONOGRAFÍA N°7 "LA MEDITACIÓN"

Introvert[149] yourself more and concentrate, first on your astral body and then on your mental body.

The astral and mental bodies are the two columns of the masonic temples: Jakin and Boaz, which have their foundation in the cubic stone of Yesod, the etheric body.

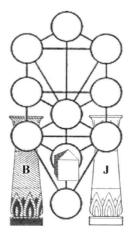

Concentrate yourself well upon these two bodies and, after you realize that you are neither one of them and that they are only two more of your instruments of expression, discard them from your mind saying: "I am not my astral body. I am not my mental body."

Discard your four bodies of sin to arrive at this stage of your meditation and pass through the two columns —white and black— of the temple which is your living body and upon which is written the "password": 'INRI' with characters of fire.

Divide[150] this word into two syllables and vocalize one immediately after the other, as follows:

IIIIIIIIINNNNNNN-RRRRRRRIIIIIIIII

Then, go and wander around the world of the mist[151] of fire without your four material vehicles.

Adéntrese más en usted mismo y concéntrese primero en su cuerpo astral y después en su cuerpo mental.

Estos cuerpos son las dos columnas de los templos masónicos: Jakín y Boaz, cuya base fundamental es la piedra cúbica de Jesod, el cuerpo etérico.

Concéntrese bien en estos dos cuerpos y, después de comprobar que usted no es ninguno de ellos y que sólo son dos más de sus instrumentos de expresión, deséchelos de su mente diciendo: Yo no soy mi cuerpo astral. Yo no soy mi cuerpo mental.

Despójese de sus cuatro cuerpos de pecado al llegar a esta etapa de su meditación y pase por en medio de las dos columnas -blanca y negra- del templo que es su cuerpo viviente y en las cuales está escrita con caracteres de fuego la "palabra de pase": INRI.

Descomponga esta palabra en dos sílabas y vocalícelas una inmediatamente después de la otra así:

IIIIIIIIINNNNNNN-RRRRRRRIIIIIIIII

A continuación sálgase a vagar por el mundo de la niebla de fuego sin sus cuatro vehículos materiales.

---

[149] Literally 'Adéntrese' means "Delve, Immerse yourself, Step inside, Get inside"
[150] Literally 'Descomponga' means "discompose, confuse; disorganize, disarrange; decompose, separate into simpler compounds, rot"
[151] Literally 'niebla' means "mist, fog"

Return to your body in order to keep working on your meditation and concentrate again on the black column of your living temple, your astral body; try to hear the sharp[152] sound of the cricket that we talked about in chapter 4[153] – this sharp sound is the essence of the lost word INRI – and without missing a moment of listening to this sharp sound, (that is now emerging from within the cells of your brain) concentrate on the white column, your mental body.

Do not stop, keep meditating.

Now, concentrate on your body of willpower until you attain consciousness of it and, when you have realized that you are neither this nor the other bodies, discard it from your mind saying: "I am not my body of willpower."

Now take a further step forward in your meditation.

Concentrate on your body of consciousness; identify [with] it and realize that you are not it, that it is only another [one] of your marvelous vehicles of expression, and discard it, saying: "I am not my body of consciousness either."

Then you will ask yourself: "Who am I?"

A sweet and affable voice will answer you: "You are me[154], the Intimus, the reflection of the internal Christ[155], you and I are one."

---

[152] Literally 'agudo' means "sharp, acute, keen; quick-witted, perceptive; pitched half a step higher (Music); eager, willing"

[153] From Ch. 4 of the same book "The chirping must come from within the cells of your brain. If this practice is done correctly, you will soon be in transition between vigil and sleep. Increase the drowsiness and the sound of the crickets' chirping by using your willpower. Then get up from your bed…"

[154] Literally 'Tú eres yo' means "You are I"

[155] Literally 'yo Cristo' means "Christ I" or "Christ self", but the Editors have choosen to translate this as "internal Christ" in an effort to not confuse the reader, since the Spanish term 'yo' is often used in Gnostic Psychology as "I" when referring to the Ego, Myself, or Psychological Aggregate which must be eliminated.

Regrese a su cuerpo para seguir trabajando, concéntrese nuevamente en la columna negra de su templo viviente, su cuerpo astral, trate de escuchar el agudo canto del grillo del que hablamos en el capítulo IV[156] -agudo canto que es la esencia de la palabra perdida INRI- y sin dejar de escuchar ese agudo canto, que ahora sale de entre las celdillas de su cerebro, concéntrese en la columna blanca, su cuerpo mental.

No se detenga, siga meditando.

Concéntrese en su cuerpo de voluntad hasta que tenga conciencia del mismo y, cuando haya comprobado que usted no es ese otro de sus cuerpos, deséchelo de su mente diciendo: Yo no soy mi cuerpo de voluntad.

Dé un paso más en su meditación.

Concéntrese en su cuerpo de conciencia, identifíquelo y comprueba que usted no es él, que se trata de otro de sus maravillosos vehículos de expresión, y deséchelo diciendo: Yo no soy mi cuerpo de conciencia.

Entonces preguntará usted: ¿Quién soy yo?

Una voz muy queda y dulce le contestará: Tú eres yo, el Intimo, el reflejo del yo Cristo[157], tú y yo somos uno.

---

[156] Del Cap. IV del mismo libro "El canto debe salir por entre sus celdillas cerebrales. Si la práctica es correcta, pronto estará usted en la transición que existe entre la vigilia y el sueño. Adormézcase más y aumente la resonancia del canto del grillo por medio de su voluntad. Entonces, levántese de su lecho..."

[157] Nota del Editor: El 'yo Christo' es el "Christo Intimo"

In those moments try to identify yourself with your Internal Christ, feel that you are him and say: "I am He... I am He... I am He..."

When reaching this state of consciousness mentally pronounce the Mantram **PANDER**; Decompose this Mantram into two syllables and pronounce one immediately after the other, prolonging the sound of each syllable.

This Mantram will help you to recognize yourself within your internal Christ.

With this daily introversion you will awaken your consciousness to such a degree that during the sleep [of your physical body], you will act in the astral body with spontaneity and lucidity as [you would] in [your] physical body.

And when in your ecstasy, through your sincerity and devotion, you are allowed to visit the nuclei upon which the universe is based – speaking allegorically, these nuclei look like holes – you will then be able to contemplate the Divine Majesty of the Absolute.

Internal meditation accelerates the awakening of the feathered serpent, whose ascension liberates the initiate from the wheel of births; but, it is necessary to help its ascension by meditating first on Ida and then on Pingala, [which are the] currents of fire – [the one on the] left is negative, and [the one on the] right is positive – so that they ascend upward (on each side of the spinal medulla) to the pituitary chakra and which preceeds, in their ascension, the sacred fire of Quetzalcoatl.

During sleep all of us move within the astral body, but unconsciously; this happens so that the etheric body can have the opportunity to repair the weakened physical body; however, you must learn how to travel within the astral body at will, consciously and as frequently as you wish.

En ese momento trate de identificarse con su Cristo Interno; siéntase ser Él; dígase: Yo soy Él... Yo soy Él... Yo soy Él...

Al alcanzar ese estado de conciencia pronuncie mentalmente el Mantram **PANDER;** Descomponga este Mantram en dos sílabas y pronúncielas una inmediatamente después de la otra alargando el sonido.

Este Mantram le ayudará a identificarse con su Cristo interno.

Con la introversión diaria logrará despertar su conciencia a tal grado que durante el sueño actuará en cuerpo astral con la misma naturalidad y lucidez que en cuerpo físico.

Y cuando, por su sinceridad y devoción, en su éxtasis se le permita visitar los núcleos sobre los cuales se fundamenta el universo -que alegóricamente hablando parecen agujeros- podrá contemplar la Divina Majestad del Absoluto.

La meditación interna acelera el despertar de la serpiente emplumada, cuya ascensión libera al iniciado de la rueda de nacimientos, pero hay que ayudar a su ascensión meditando primero en Idá y después en Pingalá, corrientes de fuego -negativa a la izquierda y positiva a la derecha- que suben a los lados de la médula espinal hasta el chakra pituitario y que preceden, en su ascensión, a la del fuego sagrado de Quetzalcoatl.

Para dar oportunidad al etérico, que durante el sueño se dedica a reparar el desgaste del cuerpo físico, todos salimos en cuerpo astral; pero usted debe salir en cuerpo astral a voluntad, conscientemente y cuantas veces lo desee.

In the astral plane we will submit you to the ordeals so that we can get to know your qualities and defects; nonetheless, if in spite of all the exercises that we have given you, you cannot travel within your astral body at will, then we recommend that you practice internal meditation tenaciously.

This is how you will recuperate the natural power of controlling[158] your astral body, a power that you have lost for now.

Practice

Before falling asleep, lay down on your bed and perform the following for no less than thirty minutes each day for at least seven days: feel that the sacred fire of the Holy Spirit is penetrating your body through the pineal chakra; thus during its descent, your pituitary, laryngeal, cardiac and solar chakras will be put into motion accordingly; keep descending towards your prostatic [or uterine] chakra making it spin from left to right, thus making it shine with the beautiful resplendence of a lotus of fire in movement.

Every morning, after you wash, stand facing the east (as we recommended in the former chapter[159]) and vocalize the mantrams **INRI** and **PANDER** until you become familiarized with them; likewise, early in all mornings chant one of the syllables which we have taught in the previous chapters.[160]

As an exercise of this chapter vocalize the syllable **AN** as follows:

AAAAAAAAAAANNNNNNNNNN

---

[158] Literally 'manejar' means "handle, manage; run, operate, work; use; tend; drive; steer"

[159] From the Ch. 8 of *Aztec Christic Magic*: "After bathing in the morning, before and during sunrise, stand facing the east or imagine that in the heavens the Sun is a fiery rose in the middle of an enormous golden cross and that thousands of rays of light come from it and penetrate into your body through your solar plexus; at the same time chant the syllable UN … Soon, with these practices, the sense of telepathy will be awakened within you."

[160] Editor's note: The syllables used were IN, EN, ON, and UN

Extracted from 'ANALYTICAL SUMMARY OF THIS COURSE' in ZODIACAL COURSE by Samael Aun Weor

...The Dragons of Wisdom are formed with the Science of the Serpent, and the "Tree-Dragon" is the same Wisdom of the Serpent.

The Akash was able to circulate through the canal of Sushumna and its two aspects flow through Ida and Pingala, this is the Brahmanic Cord.

The Cords Ida and Pingala, are the two columns, J and B of Masonry, called Jachin and Boaz.

The Solar and Lunar Forces rise through both nervous canals, which when making contact at the coccyx, awakening "**Hiram**", the Divine Fire which constitutes the Temple of Solomon (the Intimus).

"**Hiram**" is also a mantram of the Kundalini.

The **H** is pronounced like a sigh.

The **I** is vocalized like this: **iiiiiii**; and the rest [is pronounced] like this: **rrrrrrraaaaaaaaaammmmmmmm**.

The Fire has Seven Degrees of Power, which are the Seven degrees of Power of the Fire, the Seven Steps of Knowledge.

Sexual magic converts us into Omnipotent Dragons of Fire...

Extracto del 'RESUMEN ANALÍTICO DEL PRESENTE CURSO' de CURSO ZODICAL por Samael Aun Weor

...Los Dragones de la Sabiduría se forman con la Ciencia de la Serpiente, y el "Árbol-Dragón" es la misma Sabiduría de la Culebra.

El Akasha puro circula por el canal de Susumná y sus dos aspectos fluyen por Idá y Pingalá, éste es el Cordón Brahmánico.

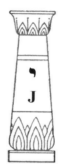

Los Cordones de Idá y Pingalá son las dos columnas J y B de la Masonería, llamadas Jachín y Boaz.

Por entre ambos canales nerviosos suben las Fuerzas Solares y Lunares, que cuando hacen contacto en el coxis, despierta "**Hiram**", el Fuego Divino que construye el Templo para Salomón (el Intimo).

"**Hiram**" es también un mantram del Kundalini.

La **H** se pronuncia como un suspiro.

La **I** se vocaliza así: **iiiiiii**; y el resto así: **rrrrrrraaaaaaaaaammmmmmmm**.

El Fuego tiene Siete Grados de Poder, que son los Siete Grados de Poder del Fuego, las Siete Escalas del Conocimiento.

La Magia-Sexual nos convierte en Dragones Omnipotentes del Fuego...

Extracted from 'SCORPIO' in ZODIACAL COURSE by Samael Aun Weor

...The Spinal Medulla with its two nervous cords is the Brahmatic cord.

The Spinal Medulla is the rod of Brahma, Aaron's Rod, the Staff of the Patriarchs, the Rod of Moses, the Sceptre of the Divine Kings, and the Bamboo Cane of 7 knots of the Yogis from India.

The secret to awakening the Kundalini is in the miracle that Christ did at the Wedding of Cana.

"The transmutation of water into wine" is accomplished in nuptials during the trance of Sexual Magic, with refrained effort, Water (Semen) will be transmuted into [the] Wine of Alchemical Light.

When the Solar and Lunar Atoms of our Seminal Energy make contact in the Center of the Coccyx, then the Snake begins to move, producing a great pain in the coccyx; it breaks the membranous pocket and enters the spinal medulla through an orifice which remains closed in common[163] people.

The vapors that rise from the Semen open[164] that orifice, which is the door of the Sushumna Canal.

This canal advances along the Spinal Medulla to the end of the cervical vertebrae; thereby the Igneous Serpent or Liquid Fire of the Kundalini rises.

This Sacred Fire rises along a fine string that serves as a conductor within the canal of the medulla.

Extracto del 'ESCORPIO' de CURSO ZODICAL por Samael Aun Weor

...La Médula Espinal con sus dos cordones nerviosos, es el Cordón Brahmánico.

La Médula Espinal es el bastón de Brahma, la Vara de Aarón, el Bastón de los Patriarcas, la Vara de Moisés, el Cetro de los Reyes Divinos, y la Caña de Bambú de 7 nudos de los Yoguis de la India.

En el milagro que Cristo hizo en la Boda de Canaán, está el secreto para despertar el Kundalini.

"La trasmutación del agua en vino", se realiza en bodas durante el trance de la Magia Sexual, con el esfuerzo refrenado, el Agua (Semen) se trasmutará en Vino de luz del Alquimista.

Cuando los Átomos Solares y Lunares de nuestra Energía Seminal hacen contacto en el Centro del Coxis, entonces la Culebra comienza a moverse, produciendo un gran dolor en el coxis; rompe la bolsa membranosa y entra en la médula por un orificio que en personas comunes y corrientes permanece cerrado.

Los vapores que se levantan del Semen destapan ese orificio, que es la puerta del Canal de Susumná.

Este canal avanza a lo largo de la Médula Espinal hasta el final de las vértebras cervicales; por allí sube la Culebra Ígnea o Fuego Líquido del Kundalini.

Ese Fuego Sagrado sube por un fino hilo que le sirve de conductor dentro del canal de la médula.

---

[163] Literally 'comunes' means "common, shared, belonging to more than one; ordinary; usual, frequent; public; mediocre, of the masses"
[164] Literally 'destapan' means "open; uncover"

| Editor's Appendix | Apéndice del Editor |

The ascension of the Kundalini is regulated by the Fires of the Heart.

In occultism, the spinal vertebrae are called: "Canyons or Pyramids".

Each Canyon has its occult name and its powers.

The Spinal Column has 33 Canyons and 33 Divine Atoms.

The ascent of the Kundalini is carried out "Canyon by Canyon", "Degree by Degree".

Each Canyon costs[165] terrible tests[166] in the Physical plane and in the Astral plane.

This is the path of unutterable[167] bitterness and martyrdom.

The nervous branches, which communicate the Chakras with the medulla, part from the fine cord of the medulla.

The Kundalini sets fire to all the Lotus Flowers or Chakras of our organism as it rises "Canyon by Canyon".

Through the 33 Canyons, we pass through the Chambers of the Great Masonic Lodge of the Astral Plane.

The External Chambers are the Minor Mysteries, and the Internal Chambers are the Major Mysteries.

The disciple should learn the Masonic salutes from his own Intimus: the "Internal Master" should teach them to him.

El ascenso del Kundalini está regulado por los Fuegos del Corazón.

Las vértebras espinales son llamadas en ocultismo: "Cañones o Pirámides".

Cada Cañón tiene su nombre oculto y sus poderes.

La Columna Espinal tiene 33 Cañones y 33 Átomos Divinos.

El ascenso del Kundalini se realiza "Cañón por Cañón", "Grado por Grado".

Cada Cañón cuesta terribles pruebas en el plano Físico y en el plano Astral.

Este es el camino de la amargura y del martirio indecible.

Del fino hilo de la médula parten los ramos nerviosos que comunican a los Chakras con la médula.

El Kundalini enciende todas las Flores de Loto o Chakras de nuestro organismo, conforme va subiendo "Cañón por Cañón".

A través de los 33 Cañones, pasamos por todas las Cámaras de la Gran Logia Masónica del Mundo Astral.

Las Cámaras Externas son los Misterios Menores, y las Cámaras Internas son los Misterios Mayores.

El discípulo debe aprender los saludos masones, de su propio Intimo: el "Maestro Interno" deberá enseñárselos.

---

[165] Literally 'cuesta' means "cost; charge; knock back; slope, incline; rise, ascent; upgrade, acclivity; hill"
[166] Literally 'Pruebas' means "evidence, proof; test, exam; experiment, trial; audition; demonstration; correction"
[167] Literally 'indecible' means "unspeakable, unutterable; nameless"

The thickness of the Kundalini will depend on the amount of stored Sexual Energy.

The color of the Kundalini depends on the psychological idiosyncrasy of the disciple.

The Kundalini rises in accordance with the practice of Sexual Magic and in accordance with our process of Sanctification, for as we have said, the ascension depends upon the Merits of the Heart.

We have to sum up our Defects and dedicate 2 months to each Defect in successive order, until we put an end to all the defects.

This simple rule is the key to making the Kundalini rise, because then the disciple comes out triumphant in all the astral and physical Tests, and wins the Canyons quickly one after the other.

A single Ejaculation or Sexual Discharge is enough for a fuse to be burnt, that is to say, for the nervous cord through which the Kundalini ascends, to fail; then the fire falls one or two Canyons according to the magnitude of the fault, and, consequently, one loses the acquired powers.

Our Lord the Christ told me: "The disciple should not let himself fall, he has to struggle very much in order to recover what has been lost".

Throughout the Initiations of Minor Mysteries, the disciple has to pass through the entire tragedy of Golgotha; finally [the disciple] will climb the Golgotha[168] of High Initiation, where he will be fused with his Intimus and convert himself into a Master of the White Lodge...

El grosor del Kundalini depende de la cantidad de Energía Sexual almacenada.

El color del Kundalini depende de la idiosincrasia psicológica del discípulo.

El Kundalini sube conforme vamos practicando Magia Sexual y conforme nos vamos Santificando, porque como dijimos, el ascenso depende de los Méritos del Corazón.

Hay que sumar los Defectos propios y dedicarle 2 meses a cada Defecto en orden sucesivo, hasta acabar con todos los defectos.

Esta sencilla regla es la clave para hacer subir el Kundalini, porque entonces el discípulo sale triunfante en todas las Pruebas astrales y físicas, y se gana los Cañones rápidamente uno tras otro.

Una sola Eyaculación o Derrame Seminal basta para que se queme un fusible, es decir para que se funda el hilo nervioso por donde sube el Kundalini; entonces el fuego cae a uno o dos o más Cañones según la magnitud de la falta, y por consiguiente pierde los poderes adquiridos.

Nuestro Señor el Cristo me dijo: "El discípulo no se debe dejar caer, porque el discípulo que se deja caer, tiene que luchar muchísimo para recuperar lo perdido".

A través de las Iniciaciones de Misterios Menores, el discípulo tiene que pasar por toda la tragedia del Gólgota; al fin subirá al Gólgota de la Alta Iniciación, donde se fusionará con su Intimo y se convertirá en Maestro de la Logia Blanca...

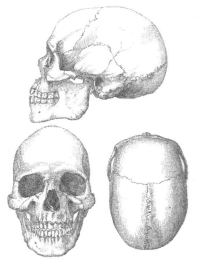

---

[168] The Greek word Golgotha is Γολγοθᾶ *gol-goth-ah'* and is of Chaldee origin; it means: the skull; Golgotha, a knoll near Jerusalem. The Hebrew word is גלגלת *gulgoleth* or *gul-go'-leth* and means a skull (as round); by implication a head (in enumeration of persons): - head, every man, poll, skull.

Extract from pages 2651-2652 of
THE FIFTH GOSPEL:

"ETHICAL AND ESOTERIC RECOMMENDATIONS"

...

Disciple. My dad got into the Masonic Lodge.

Master. Well this is very different, the Masonic Lodge is very different.

The Masonic Lodge, then, is not a religion, it is not one (we [could] say) it does not have a fixed canon of thought, right.

There are people [who belong to the Masons] from different Schools, and Orders and Sects and everything.

It seems, rather, [like] a club.

D. A club, exactly, Master! You are absolutely right.

M. Masonic Initiation is, then, very good, I am not saying that no, [actually it] is tremendous[169], right?

When he who enters [decides to] enter [therein], then, they receive the Masonic Initiation.

After such [a] tremendous Initiation, then, [one] awaits something grandiose, right?

Because [after] an initiation of that stature, then [a] man is thinking as if what he is going to receive will be golden grains of pure Wisdom.

...

---

[169] Literally 'formidable' means "formidable, redoubtable, dreadful; tremendous; bully; mean"

Extracto de páginas 2651-2652 de
EL QUINTO EVANGELIO:

"RECOMENDACIONES ÉTICAS Y ESOTÉRICAS"

...

Discípulo. Mi papá se metía en la Logia Masónica.

Maestro. Bueno esto es muy distinto, la Logia Masónica es muy distinta.

La Logia Masónica, pues, no es una religión, no es un, dijéramos, no tiene un canon de pensamiento fijo, no.

Allí van gentes de distintas Escuelas, y Ordenes, y Sectas y todo eso.

Parece, más bien, un club.

D. ¡Un club, exactamente, Maestro! Tiene usted toda la razón.

M. La Iniciación Masónica es, pues, muy buena, yo no digo que no, es formidable, ¿no?

Cuando entra el que entra, pues, recibe la Iniciación Masónica.

Después de tan tremenda Iniciación, pues, aguarda algo grandioso, ¿no?

Pues una Iniciación de esa talla, pues hombre, es como para pensar que lo que se va a recibir van a ser puros granos de oro de pura Sabiduría.

...

M. The crude reality of facts is that they [the Masons] know nothing.

I say this with all honesty.

I am also [a] Master Mason, officially (we [could] say) recognized, right?

But in the name of truth, I told them that I will never return to those Masonic Workshops.

Because when I came to work they were divided..., they were divided, [and] ended up dividing into two camps, and finally, they closed[170] the Lodges, they ended[171] [them], they had to shut them down.

Great tempests[172] were formed: Some came with me and others against me, and [the Lodges] ended up divided into two camps.

That is, until it became [a] dangerous thing.

Conclusion: Best not to return.

[Or else] end up dying there.

But yes ... [...X...] ... marvelous[173].

It is unfortunate[174], then, that the brother Masons know nothing.

Until the "G" is put there by Gnosis.

In the triangle there is the "G" of Gnosis signifying Gnosis, but they do not know it.

[Masonic] Initiation is magnificent.

---

[170] Literally 'acababan' means "finish, terminate, end; be terminated; conclude, bring to an end; destroy; defeat; complete, perfect; add the finishing touches"
[171] Literally 'terminaban' means "terminate, end, conclude, stop, discontinue, abort"
[172] Literally 'borrascas' means "storm, tempest; exhausted mine"
[173] Literally 'maravilla' means "marvel, wonder, wondrous thing; marigold, plant with orange or yellow flowers"
[174] Literally 'lamentable' means "lamentable, regrettable, unfortunate, deplorable; mournful"

M. La cruda realidad de los hechos es que ellos no saben nada.

Y lo digo con toda la franqueza.

Yo también soy Maestro Masón, oficialmente, dijéramos, reconocido, ¿no?

Pero en nombre de la verdad, les digo que no volví jamás en esos Talleres Masónicos.

Porque cuando yo llegaba a trabajar se dividían..., se dividían, terminaban divididos en dos bandos, y por último, se acababan las Logias, terminaban, tenían que clausurarlas.

Se formaban las grandes borrascas: Unos se venían conmigo y otros contra mí, y terminaba eso dividido en dos bandos.

Es decir, se ponía hasta peligrosa la cosa.

Conclusión: Mejor no volver.

Punto final y que ahí muera.

Pero eso sí... [...X...] ...a la maravilla.

Es lamentable, pues, que los hermanos masones ya nada sepan.

Hasta la "G" está puesta ahí de la Gnosis.

En el triángulo ahí está la "G" de la Gnosis, significa Gnosis; pero no saben.

La Iniciación es magnífica.

The Initiation for the degree of Master [is] tremendous[175]: They put you inside [a] symbolic coffin, meaning that in order to be [a] Master one must die in oneself.

There you have it from a wooden coffin, the whole Lodge dressed in black and the whole thing, and then they take [you] out of there and the ceremony...

D. And they end up[176] more "alive" than before[177]. [Laughs].

M. Yes, but it turns out [to be] very good, symbolically, [it] says it all!

But let's see what they know.

Nothing! What is spoken [of] in [the] Lodge?

From tiresome politics, boring things that have no relation according to value; they know nothing.

They don't have (we [could] say) knowledge of Initiations.

Signs: There are signs that belong to Esoteric Traditions, and there are others that [even] they do not understand.

From Masonry I know all that, and I can say on behalf of the Truth that they have already lost the Esoteric Tradition.

True Masonry was the one that existed in Egypt, which existed in Jerusalem; there, if there was [an authentic] Masonry, [it was the] Masonry of the Great Mysteries...

La Iniciación del grado de Maestro formidable: Lo meten a uno entre el ataúd simbólico, significando que para llegar a ser Maestro tiene que morir en sí mismo.

Ahí lo tienen entre un ataúd de madera, toda la Logia vestida de negro y toda la cosa, y luego lo sacan de ahí y la ceremonia...

D. Y lo sacan más "vivo" todavía. [Risas].

M. Sí, pero resulta que, ¡muy bueno, simbólico, dice todo!

Pero vamos a ver qué es lo que sabe.

¡Nada! ¿Qué se habla en Logia?

De la política cansona, aburridora, cosas que no tienen ningún valor; no saben nada.

No tienen, dijéramos, el conocimiento de las Iniciaciones.

Saludos: Hay saludos que pertenecen a Tradiciones Esotéricas, y hay otros que ni ellos mismos los entienden.

Yo de Masonería me conozco todo eso, y puedo decirles en nombre de la Verdad que ya perdieron la Tradición Esotérica.

La verdadera Masonería fue la que existió en Egipto, la que existió en Jerusalén; ahí si hubo Masonería, Masonería de los Grandes Misterios...

---

[175] Literally 'formidable' means "formidable, redoubtable, dreadful; tremendous; bully; mean"
[176] Literally 'sacan' means "take out, remove; bring out; draw out, extract; get; take; bring up; let; produce; educe, deduce; protract"
[177] Literally 'todavía' means "still, yet; as yet"

Extracted from Chapter 11 of
YES THERE IS HELL, YES THERE IS [A] DEVIL, YES THERE IS KARMA
by Samael Aun Weor

...

Question: Venerable Master, in the Masonic Order to which I belong, it is said that Religion helps man to die and that Masonry helps man to live; therefore I believe that the majority of Masons that I know, do not know what religion is and confuse it with something totally negative. Since we are dealing with violence against God, would you like to give us the correct concept of what "religion" means[178]?

Answer: Good friend who has asked the question, dear sir, people who are listening to me: "religion" comes from the latin word "religare" that means to re-link the soul with God

Masonry is not properly [called] a Religion; it is more a Universal type of Fraternity.

However it would be recommended that such a deserving institution study the "Science of Religion".

We are not suggesting, in any way, that someone be affiliated to any particular school; everyone is free to think as you want.

We only limit ourselves to advise the study of the Science of Religion.

The latter is precisely Gnosticism in its purest form, Wisdom of [a] Divine type, Profound Analytical Esotericism, Transcendental Occultism.

---

[178] Literally 'significa' means "mean, signify; imply; spell; amount"

Question: Permit me to insist, beloved Master; since I have heard in another talk within the Gnostic Teachings that the Universe was created by seven Masonic Lodges and this undoubtedly links Primitive Masonry with the Father; this being the reason why I have the concept that in synthesis, Masonry is the common denominator of all religions and therefore it comes from Gnosis. Could you clarify this for me?

Answer: Dear sir, those who have profoundly studied the Masonry of a Ragon or of Leadbeater, know very well that Occult [or] Esoteric Masonry existed not only under the porticoes of the Temple of Jerusalem, but also in ancient Egypt and in submerged Atlantis.

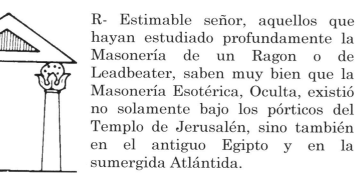

Unfortunately, that honorable Institution, entered into the involutive circle, descending, with the Age of Kali Yuga or the Iron Age in which we actually find ourselves.

However, it is ostensible that in the future Sixth Great Race, [Masonry] will have a brilliant mission to fulfill precisely when the powerful esoteric civilizations of the past resurrect

We do not deny the Divine origin of such [an] Institution.

We already know that the Seven Cosmocrators officiate with [their] Holy Liturgy in the dawn of the Great Day, when they fecundated the Chaotic Matter so that life would surge[179] [forth].

---

[179] Literally 'surgiera' means "appear, arise, emerge; intervene; crop up"

From century to century, through the different "Cosmic Rounds", the "Workshops" became denser and denser each time, until they finally arrived at the state in which they are presently[180] found.

We recommend to the Masonic Brothers to study in depth the Esotericism of Solomon and the Divine Wisdom of the Land of the Pharaohs.

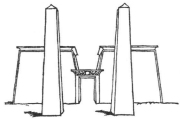

It is necessary, it is urgent that the Masonic Brothers do not fall into the Marxist-Leninist [type of] skepticism, [the] dialectic of fools, [that they] do not pronounce themselves against the Divinity, because this (besides being contrary to an Esoteric Order of Divine origin) will inevitably lead them to the Seventh Dantestic Circle, the tenebrous region of the Violent against God.

...

De siglo en siglo, a través de las distintas "Rondas Cósmicas", los "Talleres" se fueron volviendo cada vez más y más densos, hasta llegar por último al estado en que actualmente se encuentran.

Nosotros recomendamos a los Hermanos Masones, estudien a fondo el Esoterismo de Salomón y la Sabiduría Divina de la Tierra de los Faraones.

Es necesario, es urgente que los Hermanos Masones no caigan en el escepticismo Marxista-Leninista, dialéctica de tontos, no se pronuncien contra la Divinidad, porque esto, además de ser contrario a una Orden Esotérica de origen Divinal, les conduciría inevitablemente al Séptimo Círculo Dantesco, tenebrosa región de los Violentos contra Dios.

...

---

[180] Literally 'actualmente' means "at present, now; nowadays, at the present time; actually"

Speculation of the Editors regarding some Masonic Signs

Especulación de los Editores sobre algunos Signos Masónica

First Degree

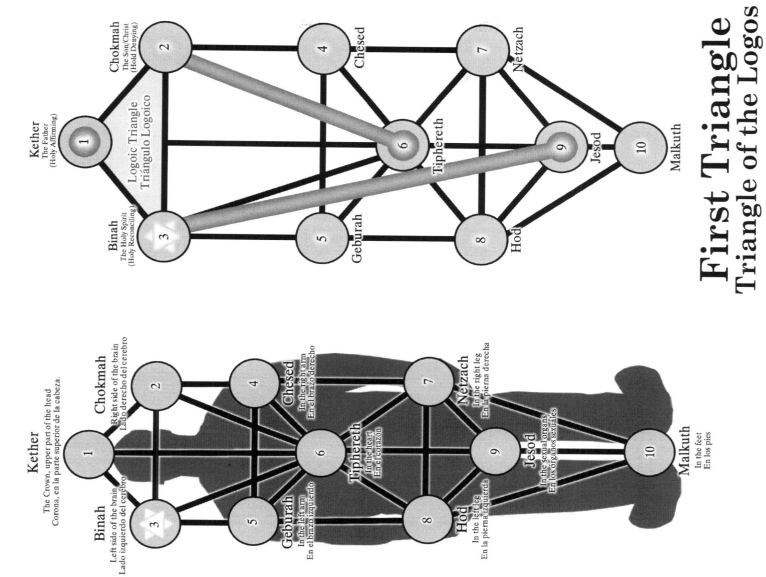

SIGN OF AN ENTERED APPRENTICE

Second Degree

Second Triangle
Ethical Triangle

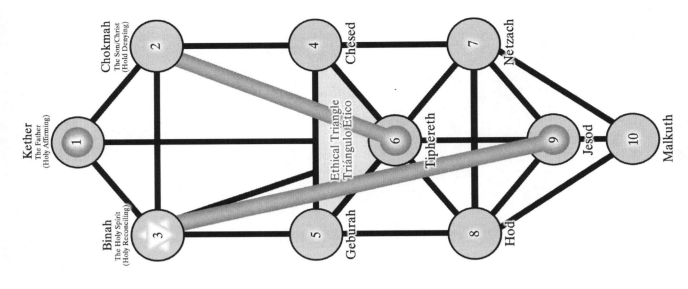
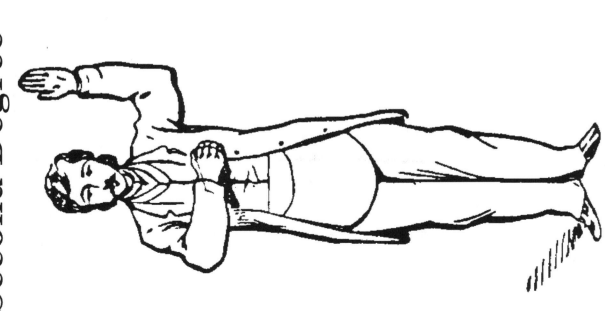

Third Degree

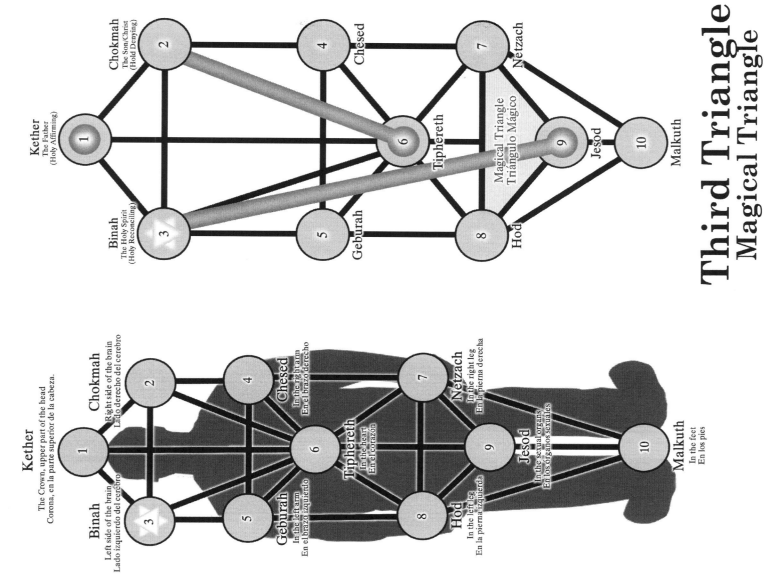

SIGN OF A MASTER MASON

אֵלַי בְּנֵי אַלְמָנָה elai bene al'manah, *huc venite filii viduæ*

"Let us remember the sign of help[181] for the third degree or that of [the] MASTER.

The interlaced hands are placed over the head, at the level of the forehead[182] with the palms facing outwards[183], [while] pronouncing at the same time, "Unto me, children of the widow!"

In Hebrew, "ELAI B'NE AL'MANAH".

All masons must come to the rescue when hearing this cry, in order to help the brother [who is] in misfortune and grant him their protection in all cases and circumstances of life."

-from Ch. 40 from *The Magic Runes*

"Recordemos el signo de socorro del grado tercero o sea de MAESTRO.

Se ponen las manos entrelazadas sobre la cabeza, a la altura de la frente con las palmas hacia afuera, pronunciando al mismo tiempo: ¡A mí los hijos de la viuda!

En Hebreo, "ELAI B' NE AL' MANAH".

A este grito deben acudir a socorrer al hermano en desgracia, todos los masones y prestarle su protección en todos los casos y circunstancias de la vida."

-de Cap. 40 del *Magia Runica*

---

[181] Literally 'socorro' means "succor, relief, aid, help; rescue"
[182] Literally 'frente' means "forehead, brow; front, fore; line"
[183] Literally 'afuera' means "out-of-door; out, outside; without"

***Some Names of God
in Masonry***

***Algunos Nombres de Dios
en la Masonría***

In the 14° of *Thuileur des trente-trois degrés de l'écossisme de rit ancien dit accepté* (1813) by François-Henri-Stanislas de L'Aulnaye (on page 94) we have the following information given, "The twelve great names of God placed upon the twelve stones of the Rational [Breastplate of the High Priest[1]], are:

Name	Hebrew	Meaning Given	Translation of Meaning	French note	Translation of note
Melek		*Rex*	King	sur la Sardoine	on the Sardius
Gomel		*Retribuens*	Retribution or Reward	sur la Topase.	on the Topaz
Adar		*Magnificus*	Magnificent	sur l'Émeraude.	on the Emerald
Éloah		*Deus fortis*	strong God	sur l'Escarboucle.	on the Carbuncle
Hain		*Fons, oculus*	Spring, eye	sur le Saphir.	on the Sapphire
Elchai		*Deus vivens*	living God	sur le Diamant.	on the Diamond
Élohim		*Dii*	Gods	sur le Lyncure.	on the Ligure
El		*Fortis*	Strength	sur l'Agathe.	on the Agate
Iaho		*IAΩ*	IAO	sur l'Amethyste.	on the Amethyst
Ischgob		*Pater excelsus*	most high Father	sur la Chrysolithe.	on the Chrysolite
Adonai		*Domini*	Lord	sur l'Onyx.	on the Onyx
Iehovah		*Sum qui sum*	I am who I am	sur le Berylle.	on the Beryl

---

[1] See Exodus 28:17-20 "And thou shalt set in it settings of stones, even four rows of stones: the first row shall be a **sardius**, a **topaz**, and a **carbuncle**: this shall be the first row. And the second row shall be an **emerald**, a **sapphire**, and a **diamond**. And the third row a **ligure**, an **agate**, and an **amethyst**. And the fourth row a **beryl**, and an **onyx**, and a **jasper**: they shall be set in gold in their inclosings. And the stones shall be with the names of the children of Israel, twelve, according to their names, like the engravings of a signet; every one with his name shall they be according to the twelve tribes."
And compare with Revelations 21:19-20 "And the foundations of the wall of the city were garnished with all manner of precious stones. The first foundation was **jasper**; the second, **sapphire**; the third, a **chalcedony**; the fourth, an **emerald**; The fifth, **sardonyx**; the sixth, **sardius**; the seventh, **chrysolite**; the eighth, **beryl**; the ninth, a **topaz**; the tenth, a **chrysoprasus**; the eleventh, a **jacinth**; the twelfth, an **amethyst**."

In the 14° of the same book (p.94-95), we also have the follow list given, "The twenty names of God, in alphabetical order." which corresponds very closely to a list given by Claude André Vuillaume (on page 40) at the end of the 'Instruction Préliminaire' ['Preliminary Instruction'] in his *Manuel maçonnique ou Tuileur de tous les rites de maçonnerie pratiques en France* (1820) which Vuillaume calls "TABLE OF THE NAMES OF GOD, corresponding to each of the letters of the Hebrew Alphabet."

Associated Hebrew Letter	Name given by L'Aulnaye	Hebrew given by L'Aulnaye	Meaning given by L'Aulnaye	Pronunciation given by Vuillaume	Names given by Vuillaume	Signification given by Vuillaume
א	Ehieh	אֶהְיֶה	*Sum, Ero*	Eh'ieh	אֶהְיֶה	*Ero.*
ב	Bachour	בָּחוּר	*Electus, Juvenis*	Bahhour	בָּחוּר	*Electus, Juvenis, Delectus.*
ג	Gadol	גָּדֹל	*Magnus*	Ghadol	גָּדֹל	*Magnus.*
ד	Dagoul	דָּגוּל	*Insignis*	Daghoul	דָּגוּל	*Insignis.*
ה	Hadour	הָדוּר	*Formosus, Majestuosus*	Hadour	הָדוּר	*Formosus, Majestuosus.*
ו	Vezio	וְזִיו	*Cum Splendors*	[not given]	[not given]	[not given][2]
ז	Zakai	זַכַּי	*Purus, Mundus*	Zacchaï	זַכַּי	*Purus, Mundus.*
ח	Chasid	חָסִיד	*Misericors*	Hhasid	חָסִיד	*Misericors, Pius.*
ט	Tehor	טָהוֹר	*Mundus, Purus*	Tahor	טָהוֹר	*Mundus.*
י	Jah	יָהּ	*Deus*	Jah	יָהּ	*Deus.*
כ	Kabbir	כַּבִּיר	*Potens*	Cabbir	כַּבִּיר	*Potens.*

---

[2] Instead of giving a name, Vuillaume says: 'Le vav n'étant qu'un signe copulatif [et] ne commence aucun mot radical.' meaning "The vau is but a copulative sign [and] does not begin any radical" meaning that he does not assign a name of God to the letter vau.

Associated Hebrew Letter	Name given by de L'Aulnaye	Hebrew given by L'Aulnaye	Meaning given by L'Aulnaye	Pronunciation given by Vuillaume	Names given by Vuillaume	Signification given by Vuillaume
ל	Limmud	לִמֻּד	*Doctus*	Limmud	לִמֻּד	*Doctus.*
מ	Meborak	מְבֹרָךְ	*Benedictus*	Meborach	מְבֹרָךְ	*Benedictus.*
ן	Nora	נוֹרָא	*Formidabilis*	Nora	נוֹרָא	*Formidabilis.*
ס	Somek	סוֹמֵךְ	*Fulciens, firmans*	Somech	סוֹמֵךְ	*Fulciens, Firmans.*
ע	Hazaz	עִזּוּז	*Fortis*	Ngazouz	עִזּוּז	*Potentia.*
פ	Phodeh	פּוֹדֶה	*Redemptor*	Phodeh	פּוֹדֶה	*Redemptor.*
צ	Tsedek	צֶדֶק	*Justus*	Tsedek	צֶדֶק	*Justicia.*
ק	Kodesch	קֹדֶשׁ	*Sanctus*	Kodesch	קֹדֶשׁ	*Sanctitas.*
ר	Rodeh	רֹדֶה	*Imperans*	Rahhoum	רַחוּם	*Clemens.*
ש	Schaddai	שַׁדַּי	*Omnipotens*	Schaddai	שַׁדַּי	*Omnipotens.*
ת	Thechinnah	תְּחִנָּה	*Gratiosus*	Thamim	תָּמִים	*Perfectus.*

Some Masonic Words of Interest

Algunas Palabras Masónicas de Interés

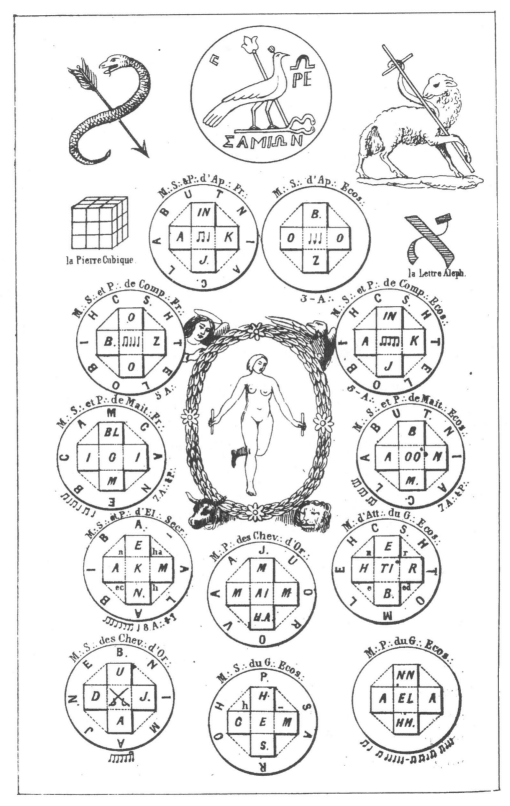

Le Sceau de Cagliostro, le Sceau de la Junon Samienne, le Sceau Apocalyptique et les douze Sceaux de la pierre cubique, autour de la Clé du Tarot.

Editor's Note about these Words

The purpose of including this section is:

1. to give evidence of the extensive use of Hebrew (which also implies the Kabalah) in Masonry,
2. to provide an easy way to look up esoteric Hebrew words that one may encounter and understand their meaning, and
3. to provide a way for those who would like to investigate what Arnoldo Krumm-Heller implies in his book *Logos, Mantram, Magic*.

In the section entitled 'EVERYTHING RADIATES', Krumm-Heller says the following:

"The Mahatma Subramanya Aiyar, guru of the Suddha Dharma Mandala Vidyalaya Society, gives to its members **certain mantram**, [that] is to say, certain syllables which they are to repeat in the evening and [which] were taken from Indian literature.

Had he been with me in Mexico, he would have fallen back in surprise at seeing what the Mayas already knew, and what was given [to certain Society members] in Madras [India] is second-hand.

An Initiate of the Middle Ages has also done an illustration on this theme, and if these were not done prior to the Columbian epoch one would have believed that it was plagiarized.

Masons will find words which are passwords in the order."

This excerpt seems to imply that at least some Masonic "passwords" are also mantrams.

Nota del Editor sobre estas Palabras

El propósito de incluir esta sección es:

1. para dar pruebas de uso extensivo de hebreo (lo que también implica la Kabalah) en la Masonería,
2. para proporcionar una manera fácil de buscar palabras hebreas esotéricas que uno puede encontrar y comprender su significado, y
3. para proporcionar una manera para aquellos que quieran investigar lo que implica Arnoldo Krumm-Heller en su libro *Logos, Mantram, Magia*.

En la sección titulada 'TODO IRRADIA', Krumm-Heller dice lo siguiente:

« El Mahatma Subramanya Aiyar, guía de la Sociedad Suddha Dharma Mandala Vidyalaya, da a sus miembros **ciertos mantram**, es decir, ciertas sílabas que deben repetir de noche y los sacó de la literatura inda.

Si hubiese estado conmigo en México se habría caído de espalda al ver que los conocían ya los Mayas y lo que ellos dan en Madras, es de su segunda mano.

Un Iniciado de la edad media ha hecho dibujos sobre esta materia y si no hubiese sido que son anteriores a la época colombiana, se podría creer que hubiesen sido plagiados.

Los masones encontrarán palabras que son de pase en la orden. »

Este fragmento parece dar a entender que al menos algunos "palabras de pase" Masónicas son también mantrams.

Editor's Appendix	Apéndice del Editor
Not all of the words given here are "passwords", but all of them are found in the French books *Thuileur des trente-trois degrés de l'écossisme de rit ancien dit accepté [Tyler of the thirty-three degrees of the ancient and accepted scottish rite]* (1813) by François-Henri-Stanislas de L'Aulnaye and *Manuel maçonnique or Tuileur de tous les rites de maçonnerie pratiques en France [Masonic Manual or Tyler of all the rites of masonry practiced in France]* (1820) by Claude André Vuillaume. Between these books, the following rites are covered: French Rite, Scottish Rite, Egyptian (Misraim) Rite, and the Adoptive Rite.	No todas las palabras que se dan aquí son "palabras de pase", pero todas se encuentran en los libros franceses *Thuileur des trente-trois degrés de l'écossisme de rit ancien dit accepté [El Tejador de los treinta y tres grados del rito escocés antiguo y aceptado]* (1813) por François-Henri-Stanislas de L'Aulnaye y *Manuel maçonnique or Tuileur de tous les rites de maçonnerie pratiques en France [Manual masónico o Tejador de todos los ritos de masonería practicada en Francia]* (1820) por Claude André Vuillaume. Entre estos libros están cubiertos los ritos siguientes: Rito Francés, Rito Escocés, Rito Egipcio (de Mizraím) y el Rito Adoptivo.
There are about 496 words or phrases listed, of which 403 (81%) are definitively Hebrew, 35 (8%) are of unknown origin, 26 (5%) are French, 14 (2%) are Latin, 10 (2%) are Greek, and 4 (1%) are English.	Hay 496 palabras o frases, de los cuales 403 (81%) son definitivamente Hebreo, 35 (8%) son de origen desconocido, 26 (5%) son Franceses, 14 (2%) son Latina, 10 (2%) son Griego y 4 (1%) son en Inglés.

Corrupted Name	Rectified Name	Name in Original Language(s)	Latin Meaning of Name	Masonic Significance of Name	Translated Significance
Aaron	AHARON	אַהֲרֹן	mons, sive montanus		[mountain, or mountains]
Abadon	ABADDON	אֲבַדּוֹן en grec ἈΒΑΔΔΩΝ Ἀπολλύων Απολυον	Exterminans, vel perditio, aut destruens	qui Extermine ; nom de l'ange de l'abime (Voy. Apocal., c. 9, v. 11)	(He) who Exterminates; name of the Angel of the Abyss (See Rev. 9:11)
	ABAD	אֲבַד	Periit, desperiit	Nom de l'ange de l'abime (Apoc. 9:11)	Name of the angel of the Abyss (Rev. 9:11)
Abaïm	ABARIM, OU GABARIM	עֲבָרִים	transitus		[transition]
	ABDA, OU GABDA	עַבְדָּא	Servus, aut servitus		[slave, or slavery]
Abdamon	HABDAMON.	עַבְדָּמוֹן	Servus turboe	Serviteur	Servant
Abdenago	GABDENAGOU	עַבְדְּנְגוֹ	fervus anxius		[anxious fever]
Abibalc, or Abibalag	ABI BALAH.	אֲבִי בָלַה	destruens patrem	qui détruit le Père ;	(He) who destroys the Father
Abif	ABI.	אֲבִי	Pater	Père ;	Father
Abbraak				Roi sans tâche	King without blemish
Abbrak	ABRA, OU ABRAG	אַבְרָע	malus pater		[evil father]
Abyram, or Abiram	ABI RAMAH	אֲבִי רָמָה	dejiciens patrem	qui renverse le Père ;	(He) who overturns the Father
	ACACIA	[not given][3]			[name of a thorny bush]

---

[3] François-Henri-Stanislas de L'Aulnaye says to see his other book *Récapitulation de toute la maçonnerie, ou Description et explication de l'hiéroglyphe universel du maître des maîtres* [*Recapitulation of all masonry, or Description and explanation of the universal hieroglyph of the master of masters*] (1812) for a description of this word.

Corrupted Name	Rectified Name	Name in Original Language(s)	Latin Meaning of Name	Masonic Significance of Name	Translated Significance
Acan	HAKAN.	עָקָן	conterens	qui Brise	(He) who Breaks
Acaron Sitone	ACHARON SCHILTON, OU AHHARON SCHIL'TON	אַחֲרוֹן שִׁלְטוֹן	novissimum imperium	Empire tout nouveau	Totally new empire
	ACHAR, OU HAKAR	עָכָר	conturbans		[disturbing]
Achal, or Acal	UKAL.	אֻכָל	Comedens ; Comedit	qui Mange	(He) who Eats
Achias	ACHIIAH.	[Hebrew, but not given]		Frère du Seigneur ;	Brother of the Lord ;
Achirab or Achirob	ACHITOUB	אֲחִיטוּב	frater bonitatis	Frère de bonté	Brother of kindness
Acob	HAKOUB	[Hebrew, but not given]		Frauduleux ;	Fraudulent ;
	ADAM	אָדָם	humus, terra		[soil/ground, earth]
Ader Aderim	ADIR ADIRIM.	אַדִּיר אַדִּירִים	Gloriosus inter floriosos, vei magnificus inter magnificos		[Glorious, Magnificent]
	ADON	אֲדוֹן		Seigneur[4]	Lord ; [Singular form of Adonai]
	ADONAÏ	אֲדֹנָי	Dii	les Seigneurs	the Lords (or Gods)

[4] "Ce mot Adon, racine, ou plutot singuliere de l'Adonai ou grand Dieu adrogyne des Hebreux, l'est également de l'Adonis des Pheniciens, et le lecteur a sans doute plus d'une fois remarque que ces fetes fameuses ou les habitants de la Phenicie, apres avoir rempli l'air de leur gemissement, faisoient eclater une joie immoderee, se celebroient a la meme epoque ou les nouveaux Chretiens, leur imitateurs, placerent leur brillante fête de Paques, precedee de la trists liturgie des Tenebres; tant il est vrai que toutes les religions sont une, et se reduisent au culte do la nature et des diverses parties qui la composent." from p.24-25

Corrupted Name	Rectified Name	Name in Original Language(s)	Latin Meaning of Name	Masonic Significance of Name	Translated Significance or Name
	ADONAÏ – ABRA	[Hebrew, but not given]			[see individual words]
	ADONIRAM	אֲדֹנִירָם	Dominus excelsus	Seigneur élevé	Elevated Lord
Adouph	HADOUR	הָדוּר	Formosus, Majestuosus	Majestueux	Majestic
	AGGÉE	חַגַּי	Festivus, solemnis		[Festive, solemn]
	AH ! SEIGNEUR, MON DIEU.	[French]			Ah ! Lord, my God.
Aign	HAIN	עַיִן	Fons, oculus	Œil, fontaine	Eye, Fountain
Albra	[see Abra]	[corruption of Hebrew]			[See ABRA]
	ALSIMPHOS	[not given]			
Alleluia	HALLELOUIAH	הַלְלוּיָהּ	dominum laudate	Louez de Seigneur	Praise of the Lord
	ALLIANCE, PROMESSE, SAINTETÉ	[French]			Alliance, Promise, Holiness
	ALLEZ-VOUS LOIN ?	[French]			Are you going far ?
	ALPHA, OMEGA	Α Ω			[Beginning and the End]
Emerek	AMARIAH	אֲמַרְיָה	eloquens	Homme vrai	True man, eloquent
	AMAL SAGGHI	עָמָל שַׂגִּיא	Labor magus		Great work
Amana	EMENETH	אֱמֶנֶת	veritas	Vérité	Truth
	AMEN	אָמֵן	firmum sit	Dieu le veuille	God likes it

Corrupted Name	Rectified Name	Name in Original Language(s)	Latin Meaning of Name	Masonic Significance of Name	Translated Significance or Name
	A MOI, LES ENFANTS DE LA VERITE	אֱלַי בְּנֵי אֱמֶת ou לִי *elaï beniémeth*		*Cri*	*Cry* ["To me, the children of the truth"]
	A MOI, LES ENFANTS DE LA VEUVE	אֱלַי בְּנֵי אַלְמָנָה *elaï bene al'manah*	*huc venite filii viduae*	*Cri de Secours des Maçons*	*Masonic Cry for Help* ["To me, children of the widow"]
Anonias, *or* Ananias	ANIGAM, *OU* GANIGAM	עֲנִיִּים	*Afflictio populi*		[suffering of the people]
	HANANIAH.	חֲנַנְיָה		*Divination du Seigneur*	*Divination of the Lord*
Aniam	ANIHAM.	אֲנִיעָם	*Fortitudo populi*	*Force du People*	*Strength of the People*
	ANTIVICH—ARDAS	[not given]			
	APOLLYON.	ἈΠΟΛΛΥΩΝ			[See ABADDON]
A		[French or English]		*Architecte*	*Architect*
	ARCHITRUM	[Latin]			[the feast]
Ardarel		[Hebrew, but not given]		*Ange du Feu*	*Angle of Fire*
Assard	HAZAZ	חָזָז	*Fortis*	*Fort*	*Hard, strong*
Athersata	THIRSCHATHA, *OU* HATHIR'SCHATHA	הַתִּרְשָׁתָא אֲתִרְשָׁתָא	*contemplans annum, vel tempus.*	*Échanson ou Venez et Buvez*	*Echanson or Come and Drink*
	ATHA CONANTHA	אַתָּה כּוֹנַנְתָּ עוֹלָם מִקֶּדֶם		*Tu as construi le monde dès commencement*	*You have constructed the world from the beginning*
	AVERRONS	[not given]			

Corrupted Name	Rectified Name	Name in Original Language(s)	Latin Meaning of Name	Masonic Significance of Name	Translated Significance of Name
Avreca Adonaï Recolgetho Tamilh Thabritath Rephi.	ABORKAH ETH ADONAÏ BEKOL HETH:THAMIDTHE HILLATHO BEPHI.	אברכה את אדני בכל עת תמיד תהלתו בפי	*Benedicam dominum omni in tempore semper lause jus in ore meo*	*Je bénirai le Ser en tout temps ; sa louange sera toujours dans ma bouche.*	*I will bless the Lord at all times; his praise will always be in my mouth.* [see Psalm 34:1]
Azarias	HAZARIAH, *OU* GAZARIAH	עזריה	*Auxilium Dei*	*Secours du Seigneur*	Rescue of the Lord
Baana	BAHANAH	[Hebrew, but not given]		*Pauvre*	Poor
Baclim	BEHALIM	בעלים	*Domini, proediti*	*Préfets*	*Magistrate*
Banahamel jon hamey	BAHABAH AHHALLEK IM HEANI	באהבה אחלק עם עני	*In dilectione dividam cum paupero*		[? with love, divide when poor ?]
Baharaba	BAHIR-ABBA	בהיר-אבא	*pater candidus*		white father
Bagulcal	BEGOAL KOL, *OU* BEGOHAL KOL, *OU* BEGOGAL CHOL, *OU* BEGOAL-CHOL	בגעל כל	*in abominatine omnium*	*Tout est expliqué*	*Everything is explained*
Bagulcal Pharascal	BEGOAL KOL PHARAS KOL.	בגעל כל פרש כל	*in abjectione omne, explicatum est omne*	*Tout est expliqué, tout est dans l'abjection*	Everything is explained, everything is in abjection [or humiliation]
Bakol	BACHOUR	בחור	*Electus, Juvenis*	*Juste*	Just

Corrupted Name	Rectified Name	Name in Original Language(s)	Latin Meaning of Name	Masonic Significance of Name	Translated Significance of Name
Balthazar	BELSCHATSAR, OU BELTESCHATRAR, OU BEL'TSCHATZAR	בֵּלְשַׁאצַּר		qui ne Thesaurise point	(He) who never collects [see Daniel 1:7]
B.D.S.P.H.G.F.		[French]		Beauté, Divinité, Sagesse, Puissance, Honneur, Gloire, Force.	Beauty, Divinity, Wisdom, Power, Honor, Glory, Strength
Bea Macmaha Rababack, or Beamacheh Bacarah	BEA MACMEH BAMEARAH	בְּעָא מַכֵּה בַּמְּעָרָה	quoerit interfectorum vel percussorum spelunca.	Dieu soit loué ! nous avons trouvé !	God is praised ! we have found !
Benaca, or Bekankan	BEN HAKAR, OU BEN-AKAR	בֶּן־הָקָר	sterilitatis filius	fils de la Stérilité	son of sterility
Benrerins	BEN CHORIM	[Hebrew, but not given]	nobilis		[noble]
	BANAÏN	בָּנָאִין		Architectes	Architects
Belba	BABEL	בָּבֶל	in confusione	Tour de confusion	Tour of confusion
Balthazar	BELSCHATZAR	בֵּלְשַׁאצַּר			[king of Babylon]
Benaya	BENAIAH	בְּנָיָהוּ	filius domini	fils de la Maître	son of Master
Benchanael jon Hamey	BAAHABAH ACHALLEK HIM HEHANI.	בְּאַהֲבָה עִם הֶעָנִי אֲחַלֵּק	pro dilectione dividam cum paupero	je Partagerai par amour avec le pauvre.	I will share through love with the poor
Bencorim	BENCHORIM	בֶּנְחוֹרִים	Nobilum filius	le fils des Nobles	son of the Nobles
Bencorim achard Jakinai	BENCHORIM HAKAR IAKINAÏ	[Hebrew, but not given]		le fils des Nobles est ferme devant celui qui trouble tout.	the son of the Nobles is enclosed infront he who trouble all.

Corrupted Name	Rectified Name	Name in Original Language(s)	Latin Meaning of Name	Masonic Significance of Name	Translated Significance of Name
B.A.I.	BENCHORIM HAKAR/AKAR IAKINAÏ	[see above]			[see above]
Bendecar, ou Ben-Dacha	BENDAKA	בן דכא	contritionis filius	fils de la Contrition	son of Contrition
	BEN-IAH	בן יה	filius Dei	fils du Fort	[son of God]
Bengaber, or Ben-gabel	BEN-GHEBER	בן גבר	filius fortis ; filius hominis		son of the strong or strong son
Benjamin	BINJAMIN	בנימין	Dextroe filius, sive oetatum		[right son, or age]
Berich	BERITH	ברית	pactum	alliance	alliance
Berit Neder Aliam	BERITH NEDER ELIHAM	[Hebrew, but not given]		Vœu d'alliance avec le Peuple de Dieu, ou avec le Dieu du peuple.	Vow of alliance with the People of God, or with the God of the people.
	BERITH NEDER ABRAHAM	[Hebrew, but not given]			[see individual words]
Berit Neder Selemouth	BERITH NEDER SCHELEMOTH.	ברית נדר שלמות	Foedus votum integroe	Alliance, Promesse, Perfection ; ou Vœu d'alliance complète.	Alliance, Promise, Perfection
B.N.S.	BERITH NEDER SCHELEMOTH.	[see above]			[see above]
Betha-Bara	BETH-ABARA OU BETH-GABARA	בית עברה	Domus transitus	Masion de passage	House of passage
Bezéléel, or Beseleel	BETSALEL.	בצלאל	In umbra dei	Dans l'Ombre de Dieu	In the Shadow of God

Corrupted Name	Rectified Name	Name in Original Language(s)	Latin Meaning of Name	Masonic Significance of Name	Translated Significance of Name
Bigva	BIGOAI	[Hebrew, but not given]		Intrinsèque	Intrinsic [or Inherent]
Bilsan	BILSCHAN	[Hebrew, but not given]		qui Scrute	(He) who scrutinizes
	BALBEK	[not given]		Nom du plus fameux des temples consacrés en l'honneur de l'Eternel.	Name of the most famous of the temples consecrated in honor of the Eternal.
Booz	BOHAZ	בעז	in fortitudine	en Force	in Strength
	BROACHING-TURHAL	[not given]		Marteau à pointe	Hammer to tip
Cain	KAÏN	קין		Possession	Possession
	CAIN, ACHAN, UNNI	[Hebrew, but not given]			[see individual words]
Camael	CHAMALIEL, OU HHAMALIEL	חמליאל	Indulgentia Dei	Indulgence de Dieu	Indulgence of God
	CANA	קנא	zelus, æmulatio	zele	zeal
Casmaran		[Hebrew, but not given]		ange de l'Air	angel of the Air
Ceplane	TSEPHON	צפון	reconditus	Caché	Hidden
Chabire	KABBIR	כביר	Potens	Puissant	Powerful
Charlabah	SCHOR LABAN	שור לבן	Albus Bos	Bœuf blanc (candeur)	White Cow
	CHARITÉ	[French]			Charity
	CHATITA	[Hebrew, but not given]		Pécheur	Sinner / Fisherman
Chaumex	SOMEK	סמך	Fulciens, firmans	Brillant	Brilliant
	CHEBOD	כבד	majestas, honor		[majesty, honor]

394

Corrupted Name	Rectified Name	Name in Original Language(s)	Latin Meaning of Name	Masonic Significance of Name	Translated Significance of Name
	CHEROUB	כְּרוּב	aratrum, caulis		[plow, stem/stalk]
	CHEROUBIN, OU CHEROUBIM	כְּרוּבִין כְּרוּבִים	aratrum, caulis	des image qui ont la figure humaine, avec des ailes, et representent des anges	images which have the human figure, with wings, and represent angels
Chemal Binem Rabira	GHEMOUL BINAH THEBOUNAH	גְּמוּל בִּינָה תְּבוּנָה	Prudentia, Intelligentia, Prudentia	Prudence, Intelligence, Justice	Prudence, Intelligence, Justice
Chi chal-hagedah culam kedoschim voub'thocham Adonai		כִּי כָל־הָעֵדָה כֻּלָּם קְדֹשִׁים וּבְתוֹכָם יְהוָה	quia omnis multitude sanctorum est		[For all the saints] [see Num 16:3]
Choemul seal	HAMAL SAGHIA	עָמָל שַׂגִּיא	labor magnus	grand Travail	Great Work/Labor
Choumer	HORMAH	חָרְמָה	Destruction, sive anathema, sive dedicatum, aut consecreatum		[Destruction, or devoted, or dedicated, or consecrated]
	CHORIM, OU HHORIM	חֹרִים	Nobiles	Nobles	Noble
	CHOTSEBIM	חֹצְבִים	coesores	Tailleurs de pierres	Stone Cutters
Codesq	KODESCH	קֹדֶשׁ	Sanctus	Saint	Holy
	CONSUMMATUM EST.	[Latin]	Consummatum est	[not given]	it is finished
C.D.T.I.C.		[French]		Corinthien, Dorique, Toscan, Ionique, Composite.	Corinthian, ... [these are types of columns]

Corrupted Name	Rectified Name	Name in Original Language(s)	Latin Meaning of Name	Masonic Significance of Name	Translated Significance of Name
Cosa	CHOSAH	[Hebrew, but not given]		Fort	Strong
Cyrus	CHORESCH		Quasi miser, quasi hoeres, aut venter	Dimanche, Ézéchiel	Sunday, Ezekiel
D.	DANIEL		Judicium Dei		[Judgement of God]
Demscoy – Hiram Abi	DE MOLAY – HIRAM-ABI	[not given]			[names of persons]
Deus sacratus machem	DEUS SACRATUS NOKEM		Deus sanctus / Sacratus ultor	Dieu sacré, vengeur	Sacred God, avenger
	DIEU LE VEUT.	[French]			God wills it
	DIEU VOUS ASSISTE.	[French]			God assists you
Dougla	DAGOUL.		Insignis	Insigne	Insignia
	EDOM		sanguineus	Sanglant	Bloody or Bleeding
	EDUL-PEN-CAGU			Fais ce que tu voudrais qui te fût fait.	Do what you want which should be done.
Eich	ISCHI, OU JSCH'GI		Salus ; Salus mea	Salut	Salvation
Eiec	EHIEH, OU EHEIAH		Sum, ero	Je suis, je serai.	I am, I will be
	EL			Dieu	God
	EL-ADON		dominus fortis		[Lord of strength]
	EL-ASSER		Deus victor		[God of victory]
Elehi	EL-CHAI		Deus vivens	Dieu vivant	living God

Corrupted Name	Rectified Name	Name in Original Language(s)	Latin Meaning of Name	Masonic Significance of Name	Translated Significance of Name
Elehanam, or Eleanam, or Elehanam	EL HHANAN, OU EL-CHANAN	אֵל חָן, אֵל־חָנָן, אֱלְחָנָן	gratia dei, misericors Deus		grace of god, merciful God
Eliab		[Hebrew, but not given]		Dieu fort	strong God
Eliacim	ELIAKIM	אֶלְיָקִים	Dei resurectio		[God's resurrection]
Eliael	ELIEL	אֱלִיאֵל	Dei fortitudo	Force du Seigneur	Strength of the Savior
	ELIAH	אֵלִיָּה אֵלִיָּ	Fortis	voyez Oliab.	see Oliab
Elie	HELIIAH	אֵלִיָּה	Deus fortis	Dieu fort	strong God
Elion	HELION	ΗΛΙΩΝ		Soleil	(the) Sun
Elios	HELIOS	ΗΛΙΟΣ		Soleil	(the) Sun
Eloa	ELOAH	אֱלוֹהַּ	Deus fortis	Dieu	God [strong God]
	ELLAH- ALLAH, ADONAÏ- ELLAH, JEHOVAH	[Hebrew, but not given]			[see individual words]
Eloena	ELOHAI	אֱלֹהַי	Deus meus		[my God]
Eloim	ELOHIM	אֱלֹהִים	Dii	les Dieux	the Gods
El-meler	EL-MELECH	אֵל־מֶלֶךְ	rex fortus		[strong king]

Corrupted Name	Rectified Name	Name in Original Language(s)	Latin Meaning of Name	Masonic Significance of Name	Translated Significance of Name
Emereck	AMARIAH.	אֲמַרְיָה	eloquens ; verbum domini	Éloquent, homme vrai	Eloquent, true man
	EMETZ	אֶמֶץ	fortitudo		[strength]
	EMETH VEEMOUNA	אֶמֶת וֶאֱמוּנָא	veritas et firmitas		[truth and firmness]
Emmanuel	HIMMANOUEL	עִמָּנוּאֵל	Deus nobiscum	Dieu est avec nous	God is with us
Emmunack, or Emmunac	EMOUNAH	אֱמוּנָה	veritas; Fides, firmitas	Vérité	Truth
Endiague-Lestercy, or Lestercy		[not hebrew]			
Enoch	CHANOK	חָנֹךְ	dedicatus	Consacré	Consecrated
Enos	ENOS	אֱנוֹשׁ		fils de Seth, fils d'Adam	son of Seth, son of Adam
Esdras	HEZRA	אֶזְרָא	Adjutorum	Adjuteur	Helper
Esie	VESIO	וֵסִיוֹ	Cum Splendors	Splendidement	Splendidly
	ESPÉRER, VEILLER, ET NE POINT PARLER.	[French]			Hope, will and speak not at all.
Eubulus	EUBULOS	[Greek]	prudens	prudens	prudence
Eva	HHAVAH	חַוָּה	vita		[Life]
	EZÉCHIEL	יְחֶזְקֵאל	Fortitudo Dei		[Strength of God]
	FÉIX-FÉAX	[not given]		Academie or École de vertus	Academy or School of virtues
	FIDES-SALUS	[Latin]			[Faith-Health]

Corrupted Name	Rectified Name	Name in Original Language(s)	Latin Meaning of Name	Masonic Significance of Name	Translated Significance of Name
	FRÉDÉRIC – DE PRUSSE	[French]			Fredrick of Prussia
Frédéric trois-Noé		[French]			Fredrick the 3rd - Noah
Fréd. trois-roi de Prusse		[French]			Fredrick the 3rd - King of Prussia
Furlac		[Hebrew, but not given]		ange de la Terre	*angel of the Earth*
	FOI, ESPÉRANCE, CHARITÉ.	[French]			Faith, Hope, Charity
G		[not hebrew]		God (Dieu), Géométrie, Garimont, Guimont, etc.	God, Geometry, Garimont, Guimont, etc.
Gabaon	GHIBHON	גִּבְעוֹן	*collis* or *habitaculum excelsum*	*Lieu éléve*[5]	*Raised (or Elevated) place [or hill]*[6]
Gabaon-notade.	GHIBHON NOTEL	גִּבְעוֹן נוֹטֵל		*Ami-Parfait, Élu.*	Perfect-Friend, Elect.
	GABRIEL	גַּבְרִיאֵל	*Fortitudo Dei; Vir Dei*	*Force de Dieu*	*Strength of God*
Gadon		[not given]			[might be a person's last name]
Galaad	GHILHAD, OU GAL-GED	גַּל-עֵד	*Tumulus testis*	*réunion de Témoignages*	*reunion of the Testimonies*
Garimont		[not given]			[the last name of a person, who was the "patriarch of Jerusalem" around 1150]

[5] "En recevant le nom de *Gabaon*, le *Maître*, veut-on dire, contracte l'obligation de *garder* dans son cœur *les secrets* de l'ordre, avec autant de fidélité que les Gabaonites, réconciliés depuis avec les enfants d'Israël, en mirent à garder le dépôt qui leur était confié." –du page 21 de *Thuileur des trente-trois degrés*...

[6] "In receiving the name of *Gabaon*, the *Master*, one could say, contracts the obligation of *keeping* in their heart *the secrets* of the order, with as much fidelity as the Gabaonites, reconciled since with the children of Israel, by starting out guarding the depot which was entrusted to them." –from p.21 of *Thuileur des trente-trois degrés*...

Corrupted Name	Rectified Name	Name in Original Language(s)	Latin Meaning of Name	Masonic Significance of Name	Translated Significance of Name
Géometros Xincheu Yzirie, Ivah, Hiram, Stolkin.	JZRACHIAH, JEHOVAH, HIRAM, STOLKIN, GÉOMÈTRES-ARCHITECTES	[not given]			[see individual words]
Gezac	GHEZER	גֶּזֶר	Proescissio, sive divisio aut sententia		[Procession, division or sentence]
Giblim	GHEBOLIM	גְּבֻלִים	Termini	les Termes	the Terms, Limit or End[7] [also see Gabaon]
	GHETH	גַּת	torcular		[press]
	GHETH – JEHOVAH	[Hebrew, but not given]			[see individual words]
	GHOMEL	גֹּמֵל	beneficus		[beneficent]
	GHOMEL BINAH THEBOUNAR	גֹּמֵל בִּינָה תְבוּנָה	Retributio, intelligentia, prudentia		[Retribution, intelligence, prudence]
	GHOMEL – JEHOVAH	[Hebrew, but not given]			[see individual words]
	GHEDOL HAGHEDOLIM	גָּדוֹל הַגְּדוֹלִים	Magnus inter magnos		[Great among the great]
Giblim-Gabaon		[Hebrew, but not given]			[see individual words]
Gnhelion Bagulionim	GELION BAGELONIM	עֶלְיוֹן בָּעֶלְיוֹנִים	sublime inter sublimos		[sublime among the most sublime]
	GHIBOR GHEBORIM.	גִּבּוֹר גִּבּוֹרִים	potens inter potentes		[power among the powerful]

---

[7] See page 24 more more information about "Ghiblim"

Corrupted Name	Rectified Name	Name in Original Language(s)	Latin Meaning of Name	Masonic Significance of Name	Translated Significance of Name
	GLOIRE A DIEU ET AU SOUVERAIN	[French]			Glory to God and to the Sovereign
Godel	GADOL	גָּדוֹל	Magnus	Grand	Great
Gomez	GOMEL	גֹּמֵל	retribuens	Qui donne à chacun suivant ses œuvres.	One who gives to each according to his works
Guimont		[not given]		le même que Garimont	the same as Garimont
	HABACUC	חֲבַקּוּק	Amplector		[embrace]
	HABBAMAH	הַבָּמָה	fanum excelsum		[shrine of high place]
Habin/Iabin	HABIN	הָבִין	Intelligus		[Understanding, also see IABIN]
Hada	ADAR	אָדָר	Magnificus	Magnifique	Magnificent
Hadar	ADAR	[see above]		Mois des Hébreux	Month of the Hebrews
	HARAM, OU HARAMA	הָרָם	consecratus		[consecrated]
Haramanath	HAROUMAPH	הָרוּמַף	Destruction, sive anathema oris		Destruction, or cursed mouth
	HARODIM	הֹרְדִים	Proesidentes	Présidents	Presidents
Haudek	PHODEH	פֹּדֶה	Redemptor	Rédempteur	Redeemer
	HAVER	חָבֵר		Collegue, ami	Collegue, friend
Havoth-Jair	CHAVOTH-JAÏR	חַוֹּת יָאִיר	oppida illuminationis	L'éclatante lumière de la vérité a dessillé mes yeux	The bright light of truth has openned my eyes
Heleham	ELIHAM, OU ELIGAM, OU ELIAM	אֱלִיעָם	Deus populi or dei populus	Dieu du people, ou Peuple de Dieu	God of the people or People of God

Corrupted Name	Rectified Name	Name in Original Language(s)	Latin Meaning of Name	Masonic Significance of Name	Translated Significance of Name
Heleanam	El Chanan	אלחנן	Miscericors deus	Grâce de Dieu, Dieu miséricordieux	Grace of God, merciful God
Helial	Eliiah, ou Heliiah	אֵלִיָּה	deus fortis	Dieu Fort	Strong God
	Helion	ΉΛΙΩΝ		Soleil	Sun
	Helios, Méné, Tetragrammaton	[Greek]			
Heni	Hunni	עֲנִי	miserabilis	Misérable	Miserable
H.	Henoch	חֲנוֹךְ			[Enoch]
Heredon	Herodom, ou Heredum	[not given]		des héritiers	from/of the heirs [or inheritors]
Hezed	Chasid	חָסִיד	Miscericors[8]	Miséricordieux	Merciful
Hasids	Hasidim	חֲסִידִים	virtuosi		[virtuous]
Hezer	Hezer, ou Ezer, ou Gezer	עֵזֶר		de secours	for help
	Hichah, ou Hikah	הִכָּה	Percussit		[Defeated/Struck]
Hiram	Chiram, ou Chouram	חִירָם חוּרָם	celsitudo vitum, candidus	Vie élevée, Candide	Elevated life, White/Candid [Note : Hiram is called "Chouram" in 1st & 2nd Chronicles]
Hiram	Hiram Abi	[Hebrew, but not given]	Hiram pater	Hiram père	Father Hiram [Note : see 2nd Chronicles 2:13]

---

[8] The latin meaning is given as "virtuosus" (p.364) in *Manuel Maçonnique*

Corrupted Name	Rectified Name	Name in Original Language(s)	Latin Meaning of Name	Masonic Significance of Name	Translated Significance of Name
Hobbheu	HEZER	עֵזֶר	de secours	Secours	Rescue/Help
Hochmah	HOKMAH	חָכְמָה	Sapientia		[Wisdom]
	HUR	חוּר	libertas	liberté	liberty
Houzzé	HUZZA	[not given]	Vivat	Vive le Roi	(Long) Live the King
	HUMANITÉ	[French]			Humanity
Ia vaurum hamen, or Ya vaurum hamen	JAABOROU-HAMMAIM	יַעֲבֹרוּ הַמַּיִם	aquoe transibunt		[passage of water]
Jabaniac or Jabamiah	HABAMAH, OU HABBAMAH	הַבָּמָה	Fanum, excelsum	Lieu saint, élevé	Holy place, elevated (or raised)
Ieceschah	IABESCHEH	יַבֶּשֶׁה	arida terra		[dry land]
Jahaben	JABIN	יָבִין	Filius Dei	[fils de Dieu]	[son of God, see Judges 4:2]
Jabulum [or Johabulum, Jibulum, Jibellum]	IOBEL, OU ZEBULOUN				[see JOBEL and ZÉBULOUN]
	JACOB, OU JAGAKOB	יַעֲקֹב	supplantator		[trip/supplantor]
Jachin, or Jakin	IAKIN	יָכִין	Firmus, Stabilis, Rectus	Ferme[9]	Firm[10]
Jakin, Jakinik, Jakinaï	JACHIN, JACHINIK, JACHINAÏ	[Hebrew, but not given]			[see individual words]

[9] "Le mot *Iakin* signifie encore, en hébreu, *Préparation*. Cette acception convient parfaitement au degré de l'Apprenti, qui n'est qu'une *préparation* à la *Maîtrise*." —du page 11 de *Thuileur des trente-trois degrés*...
[10] "The word *Iakin* signifies also, in hebrew, *Preparation*. This meaning perfectly agrees with the degree of *Apprentice*, which is but a preparation for *Mastership*." —from p.11 of *Thuileur des trente-trois degrés*...

Corrupted Name	Rectified Name	Name in Original Language(s)	Latin Meaning of Name	Masonic Significance of Name	Translated Significance of Name
Jakinik	JACHINIK	[Hebrew, but not given]			
Jakinaï	JACHINAÏ	יְכִינִי		*Voyez Jachin*	*See Jachin*
J. B. M.		[Hebrew and/or Latin]		*Iakin-Boaz-Makbena. Jacobus-Burdundus-Molai*	[see individual words]
Jea	IAH	יָהּ	*deus*	*Dieu*	*God*
Jahobe	IAHEB, *OU* JAHEB	יָהֵב יָהֵב	*Concedens*	*qui accorde*	*(He) who bestows*
Jakinaï	IAKINAI	יְכִינַי		*le pluriel de Iakin*	*the plural of Iakin*
Jaïm-Adonai	JAMIN-ADONAÏ	יָמִין	*Dexter*		[Right]
Jamaich	JAMMIM, *OU* IAMMIM	יָמִים	*Maria*		[Mary/the Seas]
Iao	IAHO, *OU* JHAO	יהו	*Existens*		[Existence (IAΩ or IAO)]
Japhet, or Japheth	IAPHETH	יָפֶת	*pulcher*	*Beau, persudant*	*Beautiful [or Handsom], persudant*
Joppé	JAPHO, *OU* JAFFA	יָפוֹ	*pulchritudo*		[Beauty, see Joshua 19:46]
Iea	IAH	יָהּ	*deus*	*Dieu*	*God*
	JE COMPASSE JUSQU'AU SOLEIL	[French]			*I encompass the sun*
Jehobe	ISCHGOB	אִשְׁגֹב	*Pater excelsus*	*Père élevé*	*most high Father*
Jehovah	IEHOVAH	יְהֹוָה	*sum qui sum*	*Je suis celui qui suis*	*I am that he that is*
J.H.V.	IEHOVAH	[see above]			[see above]

404

Corrupted Name	Rectified Name	Name in Original Language(s)	Latin Meaning of Name	Masonic Significance of Name	Translated Significance of Name
Jehovah-Jakin		[Hebrew, but not given]			[see individual words]
Jecksone	JACKS-SON	[English]		fils de Jacques	Jack's son [also see Stolkin]
	JEKSAN	יקשן	duricies sive scandalum	nom d'un des fils d'Abraham et de Céthura	name of one of the sons of Abraham and Cethura [also see "JACKS-SON"]
	JELCON, JELOUN, ZEPHOFRAS	[not given]			[see individual words]
Jerusalem	JEROUSCHALAIM	יְרוּשָׁלַיִם	hereditas pacis		[inheritance of peace]
	JE SUIS – NOUS SOMMES	[French]			I am – We are
Jibulum		[Hebrew, but not given]		Voyez Jabulum	See Jabulum
I.L.		[Latin]	Invenit Leonem		[Lion has found]
	JOBEL	יוֹבֵל	Jubilans		[Jubilation]
J.N.R.J.	I.N.R.I.	׳, נ, ר, ׳ Iammim..... מים (Maria) Nour........ נור (Ignis) Rouach..... רוח (Ventus) Iebeschah.. יבשה (Arida, Terra)		Iesus Nazarenus Rex Iudoeorum; Judee-Nazareth-Raphael-Juda; Ignem Natura Regenerando Integrat; Igne Natura Renovatur Integra; Igne Nitrum Roris Invenitur; Iammin, Nour, Rouach, Iabescheh, etc.	Jesus the Nazarene King of the Jews; Judeah-Nazarus-Raphael- Judah; (the) Fire Renews Nature Integrally; ... (etc.)

Corrupted Name	Rectified Name	Name in Original Language(s)	Latin Meaning of Name	Masonic Significance of Name	Translated Significance of Name
	JOHANNES RALP, *OU* JOANNES RALP	[not given]		*nom du fondateur de l'ordre*	*name of the founder of the order*
	JOÏADA	יְהוֹיָדָע	*Domini scientia*		[knowledge of the Lord]
	ISIS-OSIRIS	[not given]		*pour exprimer la nature, selon les anciens Egyptiens*	*(used) to express nature according to the ancient Egyptians*
	ISRAEL	יִשְׂרָאֵל	*proevalens com Deo*		[Prevail with God]
J.V.I.L.G.		[Latin]		*J. Ustrinam Invenit Leonem G.*	*J. Fire Found Lion G.*
I.V.I.O.L.		[Latin]		*Inveni Veritatem In Ore Leonis ou Inveni Verbum In Ore Leonis*	*I have found the truth in the mouth of the Lion or I have found the Verb in the mouth of the Lion*
Joaben, or Johaben	IABIN HABIN	יָבִין הָבִין		*Intelligent*	*Intelligent*
Jocabert		[not given]			[see Johaber]
Jod	IOD	י	*Principium*	*Principe [ou unité]*	*Principle [or unity]*
Johaber		[not given]		*Nom du Frère Curieux*	*Name of the Curious Brother*
Joïada	IOIADAH	[Hebrew, but not given]		*Connoissance de Dieu*	*Knowledge of God*
J.	JONAS	יוֹנָה	*columba*		[dove]
	JORAM	יוֹרָם	*Excelsus*		[High]

Corrupted Name	Rectified Name	Name in Original Language(s)	Latin Meaning of Name	Masonic Significance of Name	Translated Significance of Name
Josué	IESUAH	יֵשׁוּעַ	Salvator	Sauveur	Savior
Jovah	JEHOVAH	[Hebrew, but not given]			[see IEHOVAH]
Ischi	ISCHGI	יִשְׁעִי	salus mea		[my salvation]
	ISRACHIAH, IEHOVAH, HIRAM, STOLKIN, GÉOMÈTRE, ARCHITECTE	[Hebrew and French]			[see individual words]
Jubelum		[Hebrew, but not given]		Voy. Jabulum	See Jabulum
Jubil	IOBEL	יֹבֵל	jubiloeum	qui donne la Joie	(He) who gives Joy
	JUDA, ADONAÏ, JEHOVAH	[Hebrew, but not given]			[see individual words]
Juda-Benjamin	IEHOUDAH-BINIAMIN	יְהוּדָה בִּנְיָמִין	dextroe filius laudatio		Righthand son [of] Praise
Judea-ia	IEHOUDAH-IAH	[Hebrew, but not given]		Louange à Dieu	Praise be to God
Judith	JEHOUDITH	יְהוּדִית	laudans		[praise]
	JUSTICE-ÉQUITÉ ; AINSI SOIT-IL.	[French]			Justice-Equality, so be it
Ivah, or Jvah	IEHOVAH	[Hebrew, but not given]			[see IEHOVAH]
Ivoran	IORAM	יוֹרָם	Excelsus	élevé	Elevated (or raised)

Corrupted Name	Rectified Name	Name in Original Language(s)	Latin Meaning of Name	Masonic Significance of Name	Translated Significance of Name
Izirie	IZRACHIAH, OU JZRACH-IAH, OU IZ'RAHH-IAH	יִזְרַחְיָה	Oriens dominus; orientur Dominus	Dieu Levant	Raising (or elevating) God
Kados	KADOSCH, OU KODESCH	קדש	Sanctus, Consecratus, Purificatus	Saint	Saint
	KADOSCH, JEHOVAH	[Hebrew, but not given]			[see individual words]
	KADESCHNOU	קָדְשֵׁנוּ	sanctitas nostras		[our sanctity]
Kadosch L'Adonai	KADESCH L'ADONAI	קֶדֶשׁ לַיהוָה	Sanctum domino	consacré au Seigneur (Exod. chap. 28, v. 36)	consecrated to the Lord (see Exodus 28:36)
Ki	CHAÏ, OU HHAÏ	חי	vivans	Vivant	Living
	KIBBOUTZ IJSCHIM	קִבּוּץ אִישִׁים	collection virorum		[collection of men]
Kiriès	KYRIE	Κγριε , de Κύριος	Dominus	Seigneur!	Lord!
Ky, or Civi, or Caki	KIVI	כְּרַע ou כִּי	Inclinare	fléchissez le genou	Blend the knee
	KAI	כֵּא	stat, vel surgit ad standum	Levez-vous	Raise yourself or get up
L.	Leo	[Latin]			[Lion]
Lamma Sabactani	LAMMAH SCHEBAKTHANI	לָמָה שְׁבַקְתָּנִי	Ut quid dereliquisti me?	Seigneur, je n'ai péché que parce que vous m'avez abondonné.	Lord, I have only sinned because you abandoned me.
	LAMECH	למך	Pauper		[poor]

Corrupted Name	Rectified Name	Name in Original Language(s)	Latin Meaning of Name	Masonic Significance of Name	Translated Significance of Name
	LA VERTU UNIT CE QUE LA MORT NE PEUT SEPARER	[French]			Virtue unites what death can not separate
	LEGOLAM	לְעוֹלָם	Semper		[always]
	LEGOLAM IHEEH ADAM	לְעוֹלָם יִהְיֶה אָדָם	Semper erit homo		[always be a man]
Lemoud	LIMMUD	לִמּוּד	Doctus	Savant	Knower
Liban	LEBANON	לְבָנוֹן		Blanc, Encens	white, inscence
	LIBERTAS	[Latin]			[Liberty]
L.S.A.A.C.D.X.Z.A. S.N.S.C.I.M.B.O.		[not given]		Liban, Salomon, Abda, Adoniram, Cyrus, Darius, Xercès, Zorobabel, Ananias, Sidonius, Noé, Sem, Cham, Japheth, Moïse, Beseleel, Ooliab.	[see individual words]
L.D.P.		[French or Latin]		Liberté De Passer, Lilia Desture Pedibus	Liberty to Pass[11]

---

[11] Editor's note: Eliphas Levi gives alternate meanings for these three letters (L.D.P.) in his writings: "The name of God [יהוה] is complete in three letters, because the fourth repeats the second. Three letters also represent the plentitude of the Masonic science L∴D∴P∴. Three letters summarize the science of Solomon א מ ת. L∴D∴P∴ signifies for the profane: 'Liberty to pass' and this inscription is placed upon a symbolic bridge, which communicates the earth of exile with the homeland. For the simple initiates, it is 'Liberty of thought'. For the initiates of the highest degrees it is: 'Liberty, Duty, Power'. Aleph [א], Mem [מ], Tav [ת], compose a word which is read: 'Ameth' and which signifies: Truth and Peace." —from letter #47 (dated March 19th, 1862) from Levi to his student Baron Spédalieri.

"The triagram L∴P∴D∴ ... means *liberty, power, duty*; it also signifies *light, proportion, density*; [and] *law, principle and right*. The free-masons have changed the order of these letters, and write them L∴D∴P∴; they make of these initials in the words *liberty of thought*, which they inscribe upon a symbolic bridge, [and] read them for the profane as: *liberty to pass*." —from Ch.2 entitled 'MARVELOUS PERONALITIES OF THE 18th CENTURY' in Book 6 of *History of Magic* (1860).

Corrupted Name	Rectified Name	Name in Original Language(s)	Latin Meaning of Name	Masonic Significance of Name	Translated Significance of Name
Maaca	LOUEZ LE SEIGNEUR	[French]			Praise the Lord
	MAHAKAH	מַעֲכָה	compressus	Comprimé	Compressed
Macbenac	MAK BENAH	מָךְ בֶּנָה	ædificantis putredo, ou filius putrificationis ou ædificantis interfectio	La chair quitte les os[12]	The flesh leaves (or comes away from) the bones.[13]
Mahabin, or Makobin	MACHOBIM	מַכֹאבִים	dolores	C'est lui, il est mort!	Its him, he is dead!

[12] "D'abord, on ne doit point écrire *Macbenac*; il faut dire, en deux mots, Mak Benah, ou Mak Bena. Les deux premiers, *Mak Benah* sont formés de מָךְ בָּנָה qui signifient : *ædificantis putredo*, ou *filius putrificationis* ; racines בָּנָה et בֵּן.

Les mots Mak Bena se forment de מַכְבְּנָא qui signifie : *Percussio, interfectio ædificantis*; racine בְּנָה ou מַכְּא, Chald.

La première interprétation (*ædificantis putredo*) se rapproche beaucoup de celle que l'on donne communément; elle a même avec la légende maçonnique, une conformité frappante. La seconde (*filius putrificationis*) ne paraîtra pas moins naturelle à ceux qui connoissent les vérités cachées sous les emblêmes maçonniques. Car, sous tous les rapports connus des *Enfans de la veuve*, le *Maître* peut être dit le *Fils de la mort*, dont la *putréfaction* est l'image et le résultat, comme elle est en même temps le principe de la vie, la condition nécessaire au développement des êtres. Enfin, la troisième interprétation (*ædificantis interfectio*), à laquelle nous pensons que l'on doit donner la préférence, s'accorde parfaitement avec la fin tragique d'Hiram, et c'est celle qu'ont adoptée les Rose-Croix de Kilwining." —des pages 18-19 de *Thuileur des trente-trois degrés*...

[13] "First of all, it should only be written *Macbenac*; one must say, in two words, Mak Benah, or Mak Bena. The first two, *Mak Benah* are formed from מָךְ בָּנָה which signifies: *ædificantis putredo*, or *filius putrificationis*; [from the] roots בָּנָה and בֵּן.

The words Mak Bena are formed from מַכְבְּנָא which signifies: *Percussio, interfectio ædificantis*; [from the] *Chaldean* root בְּנָה of מַכְּא.

The first interpretation (*ædificantis putredo*) brings us close to that which is commonly given; it even [makes sense] with the masonic legend, a striking conformity. The second (*filius putrificationis*) will not appear [any] less natural to those who know the truths hidden under the masonic emblems. Since, under all the known relationships of the *Children of the widow*, the *Master* can be called the *Son of death*, of which the *putrfaction* is the image and the result, as it is at the same time the principle of life, the condition necessary for the development of beings. Finally, the third interpretation (*ædificantis interfectio*), to which we think that one should give their preference, is in perfect accordance with the tragic end of Hiram, and it is that which the Rose-Cross of Kilwining have adopted." —from p.18-19 of *Thuileur des trente-trois degrés*...

Corrupted Name	Rectified Name	Name in Original Language(s)	Latin Meaning of Name	Masonic Significance of Name	Translated Significance of Name
Makakmaï	MACHBANAÏ-ISRAEL	מַכְבַּנַּי יִשְׂרָאֵל	Humiliation filii, vel oedificationis	(premier mot) nom d'un des princes Hébreux qui se réunirent à David	(first word) name of one of the Hebrew princes who reunites with David
M.B.	M	[not given]		Moabon	Moabon [or MakBenah]
M.B.	MAK BENA	מַכְבֵּנָא	percussion, interfectio ædificantis		[see "MAK BENAH" and also 1st Chronicles 2:49]
Macmaharababack	MAKEH MEHARAH BEHA	מַכֵּה מְעָרָה בָּהּ	quaesivit Spelunca Interfector	Il a cherché le meurtier dans la caverne	He sought the murderer in the cave
Magacacia	MAGACHAH, OU MAACHAH	מַעֲכָה	compressus		[compress, embrace]
Mahabin	MAKOBIM	מַכְאוֹבִים	dolores	les Douleurs	Pain / Suffering
	MAH SCHEMECHA	מַה שְּׁמֶךָ	qui vocare ?		[who to call ?]
	MAH SCHIM'CHA	מַה שִּׁמְךָ	Quid tibi nomen ?		[What is your name ?]
Maharsul	MAHER SCHALAL CHASCH BAZ	מַהֵר שָׁלָל חָשׁ בַּז	Praedam accelerans spolium festinans	qui hate les dépouilles, qui accélère la proie	(He) who rushes the slough, who hastens the prey
Mahuzen	MACHSIM, OU MAH'SCHIM	מַחְסִים	tacentes	Les Silentieux	The Silencer
Malachias	MALAKI, OU MALACHIE	מַלְאָכִי	Angelus	Ange	Angel
Manchem	MENACHEM, OU MENAHHEM	מְנַחֵם	Consolator	Consolateur	Comforter
Mardochée	MORDOKAI	[Hebrew, but not given]		Contrition amère	bitter Contrition

Corrupted Name	Rectified Name	Name in Original Language(s)	Latin Meaning of Name	Masonic Significance of Name	Translated Significance of Name
	Mathoc	מָתוֹק	Dulcis		[sweet]
Mebaurel	Meborak	מְבֹרָךְ	Benedictus	Béni	Blessed
Melech	Melek	מֶלֶךְ		Roi	King
	Melek-Schlomoh	[Hebrew, but not given]	Rex pacificus		[king of peace]
	Mekaton	מְקָטֹן			
	Menatschim	מְנַצְּחִים	proefecti	Préfets	Prefect (or magistrate)
Menès	Mené	מֵהֹנָה		Lune	(the) Moon
Menias	Menni, ou Mennith	מְנִי	proeparatio		[prepared]
Michel	Mikael, ou Michael	מִיכָאֵל	Pauper Dei	qui est comme Dieu	(He) who is like God
Mi-chamicha Bealim Adonai	Mika-Mikah Bealim Adonaï	מִי־כָמֹכָה בָּאֵלִים יְהוָה	Quis similes tui in fortibus, Domine?		[Who among the gods is like unto thee, O Lord? [see Exodus 15:1]
	Mihino	[not given]			
Missac	Missach	מִשָׂח	Sapiens		[Wise]
	Mischkan, ou Misch'chan	מִשְׁכָּן	habitaculum	Tabernacle	Tabernacle
	Mischtar	מִשְׁטָר	dominium. ministerium	Pouvoir	Power
	Miscphereth	[Hebrew, but not given]		Fontaine	Fountain

Corrupted Name	Rectified Name	Name in Original Language(s)	Latin Meaning of Name	Masonic Significance of Name	Translated Significance of Name
	MITHREDATH	[Hebrew, but not given]		qui explique la Loi	(He) who explains the Law
	MOAB	מוֹאָב	A Pater	du Père	from the Father [also see Genesis 19:36-37]
	MOABITE	[Hebrew, but not given]			
Mahabone	MOABON	מוֹאָבוֹן	A Pater	[Fils] du Père[14]	[Son] of the Father[15] [also see "MOAB"]
Mahhabone	MAHABON	מַהְאָבוֹן			"This signifies rotten, or decayed almost to the Bone."[16]
Moabon-Hiram-Jehovah		[Hebrew, but not given]			[see individual words]
Mont-Liban		[French]			Mount Lebanon
Moria	MORIIAH, OU MORIAH	מוֹרִיָּה מוֹרִיָּה	Myrrha Domini	Myrrhe du Seigneur	Myrrh of the Lord
Modim	MADIM	מָדִים	mensuae		[measure]
Motech	MATHOK	מָתוֹק	Dulcedo	Douceur	Sweetness
Moyse, or Moïse	MOSCHEH	מֹשֶׁה	assumptus	Enlevé	Raised [or Elevated]

[14] "Par ce mot *Moabon*, on a voulu exprimer qu'un Franc-Maçon devient, par le fait de sa reception, le *Fils* et le successeur d'Hiram qu'il doit desormais regarder comme son *Père* adoptif et régénérateur." —du page 16 de *Thuileur des trente-trois degrés*...

[15] "It is wished to express, by this word *Moabon*, that a Free-Mason becomes, by the fact of his reception, the *Son* and the successor of Hiram whom he must henceforth see as his adoptive and regenerative *Father*." —from p.16 of *Thuileur des trente-trois degrés*...

[16] This entry for 'Mahhabone' is from p. 67 of *The Three Distinct Knocks* (1760) by W____ O____ V____ n : Member of a Lodge in England at this Time

Corrupted Name	Rectified Name	Name in Original Language(s)	Latin Meaning of Name	Masonic Significance of Name	Translated Significance of Name
Nabucodonosor	NEBUKADNETSAR, *OU* NEBUCHODONOSOR	נְבוּכַדְנֶאצַּר		*Gémissement du jugement de Misère*	*Wailing for the judgment of Misery*
Nabuzardan, or Nabouzardan	NEBOUZARADAN	נְבוּזַרְאֲדָן	*princeps exercitus*	*Prophétie du jugement étranger.*	*Prophecy of strange judgment.*
	NACHAMANI	[Hebrew, but not given]		*Consolateur*	*Consolation*
	NAC-MAROOZ	נַכְמָרוֹז	*rebellum percussit*		[defeated/struck rebel]
	NACHUM	[Hebrew, but not given]		*Consolateur*	*Consolation*
	LES NATHINÉENS	נְתִינִים	*donati*		[given]
	NATURE-VÉRITÉ	[French]			Nature-Truth
Naural	NORA	נוֹרָא	*Formidabilis*	*Formidable*	*Incredible*
	NECHUSTHAN, *OU* NECHUSCHTHAN, *OU* NEHHUS'TAN,	נְחֻשְׁתָּן	*Aeneus, Serpens, Augurans*	*Serpent, oracle*	*Serpent, oracle*
	NEC PRODITOR NEC PRODITUR INNOCENS FOVET.	[Latin: Nec Proditor, nec Proditur, Innocens Feret]		[*Ni Traître, ni Trahi, mais Innocent il Supportera*]	[*Neither Traitor, nor Betrayed, but Innocent he will support*]
	NEHEMIAS	[not given]			
Necar	NIKAR	נִקָּר	*perforavit*		*Perforated [or pierced through]*
Nechah	NEKAH	[Hebrew, but not given]			
Necum	NEKAM	נָקָם		*Vengeance*	*Vengence*
Necum Adonaï	NEKAM ADONAÏ	נְקֹם אֲדֹנָי		*Vengeance, Seigneur*	*Vengeance, Lord*

414

Corrupted Name	Rectified Name	Name in Original Language(s)	Latin Meaning of Name	Masonic Significance of Name	Translated Significance of Name
N.A.	Nekam Adonaï	[see above]			[see above]
	Nekamah	נְקָמָה	ultio	Vengeance	Vengeance
Necum Balim	Nekamah Baelim, ou Nikam Makah Behalim	נְקָמָה בָּאֵלִים	ultio inter fortes; explicatum est omne	Vengeance parmi les forts ; Vengeance, Meurtre, Elus	Vengeance through efforts ; Vengeance, Death, Illumination
	Nekam – Menahhem	[Hebrew, but not given]			[see individual words]
Necum Necar	Nekam Nikar, ou Nikar Nekam	נְקָם נִכָּר	Vengeance perforavit	Vengeance! Il a frappé ou Il a frappé ! vengeance	Vengeance! He has struck or He has struck ! Vengeance
N.N.	Neikar Nekam	[see above]			
	Neder	נֶדֶר	Votum	promesse, vœu	promise, swear
Nehemias	Nehemiah	נְחֶמְיָה	Solatio Dei	Consolation de Dieu	Consolation of God
Nemehaniack	Nechemiah	נְחֶמְיָה	Solatio Dei	Consolation de Dieu	Consolation of God
Nica Maca	Nekam Mahah, Nekam-Macchah	נְקָם מַכָּה	Percussio ultio	Vengeance, meurtre	Vengence, murder
N.M. [or N.K.M.K. or Nika Maka, etc.]	Nekam Mahah	[see above]			[see above]
	Nimakimiah	[Hebrew, but not given]			
Noé or Noë	Noach	נֹחַ		Repos	Rest

Corrupted Name	Rectified Name	Name in Original Language(s)	Latin Meaning of Name	Masonic Significance of Name	Translated Significance of Name
	Noemi, ou Nogemi	נֹעֲמִי	Pulchra, sive decora		[Beautiful, or handsome]
Neeman	Noeman, ou Nogeman	נֹעֲמָן	Pulcher, sive decorus, aut motum proeparans		[Beautiful, or handsome, or the motion of preparing]
Machem	Nokem	נֹקֵם	ultor		[avenger]
Nojkes		[English (anagram)]		anagr. de Jeksone pour Jaks-son	Anagram for Jackson
Noni		[not given]			
Notade	Notel	נֹטֵל	Proeponens	qui préfère	(He) who prefers
Nouvaik	Nopheth	נֹפֶת	Favus		[Honeycomb]
	Nour	נוּר	ignis		[fire]
Obed	Hobed, ou Gobed	הֹבֵד עֹבֵד	Servus; Serviens	Serviteur	Servant
Obededdon	Hobed Edom	[Hebrew, but not given]		Serviteur de l'Homme	Servant of Man
	Oheb Eloah	אֹהֵב אֱלוֹהַּ	Deum amans		[loving God]
	Oheb Kerobo	אֹהֵב קְרֹבוֹ	Propinquum ei amans		[close to one's lover]
Och	Ohel	אֹהֶל	tabernaculum, sive tentorium, aut splendor		[the tabernacle, or tent, or brightness]

Corrupted Name	Rectified Name	Name in Original Language(s)	Latin Meaning of Name	Masonic Significance of Name	Translated Significance of Name
Olis, *or* Otis	OHOLLI	אהלי	*Incipiens, sive frater mihi*		[Starting, or a brother to me]
Oliab, *or* Ooliab	AHOLIAB	אהליאב	*Tabernaculum, seu potius pater Tabernaculi*	*Tabernacle du père, ou Père du tabernacle*	Tabernacle of the Father or Father of the Tabernacle
Oniam	ANIHAN	אני הם	*Fortitudo populi*	*Force du Peuple*	Strength of the People
Oseb Eloa	OHEB ELOAH	אהב אלוה	*Deum amans*	*qui aime Dieu*	(He) who loves God
Oseb Scharabel, *or* Oseb Scherabal	OHEB KEROBO	אהב קרבו	*propinquum ei amans*	*qui aime son Prochein ou Amour du Prochain*	(He) who loves his neighbor or Love of the Neighbor
Osée	HOSCHEAH	הושע	*salvator*	*Sauveur*	Savior
Oziah	GOSIAH	עזיה	*fortitudo domini*		[strength of the Lord]
Paulcal Pharascal	PHAAL KOL PHARAS KOL.	פעל כל פרש כל	*operatum est omne, explicatum est omne*	*tout est Opéré, tout est Expliqué*	Everything is Done (or Operated), everything is Explained
	PHAAL-CHOL, PHARASCH-CHOL, NEKAM-MACCHAH	[not given]		*séparés, réunis, pour la vengeance*	Separates, reunited, for vengence
Paulcal Pharat Kados	PHOHAL PHERED KADOSCH	פעל פרד קדוש	*sanctum separavit opus*	*la Sainteté de ses œuvres l'a Séparé*	The Sanctity of his works has Separated him
Perignan		[not given]		[*nom de l'inconnu*]	[name of the unknown]
Perpend-aster	PERPEN-ASTER	[not given]		*Pierre Angulaire*	Corner Stone
	PHALAMOS – ARBAS	[not given]			

417

Corrupted Name	Rectified Name	Name in Original Language(s)	Latin Meaning of Name	Masonic Significance of Name	Translated Significance of Name
	PHALEG	פָּלֶג	divisio seu confusio	Confusion	Confusion [through division]
Phaudeck	PHODEH	פֹדֶה	Redemptor	Rédempteur	Redeemer
	PRUDENCE, VALEUR, FERMETÉ	[French]			Prudence, Valor, Firmness
Rabacim	RAB BANAÏN	רַב בָּנַאִין	Oedificantium magister	Maître des Architects	Master of the Architects
R.M.	RAB BANAIN (R.N.)	[see above]			[see above]
	RAM	רָם		élevé	raised (or elevated)
Ramach	RAMAH	רָמָה	projecit		[projected/thrown/cast]
	RAPHAEL	רְפָאֵל	Medecina Dei	Médecine de Dieu	Doctor of God
Raphodon	REPHIDIM	רְפִידִים	reclinatoria	Nom du lieu où les Israélites firent leur dixième campement après leur sortie d'Égypte.	Name of the place where the Israelites had their tenth encampment after their departure from Egypt
Razabassi	RAZAH BETSIIAH, OU RAZAH BETSJIAH	רָזָה בְצִיָּה	in solitudine exterminavit ; macis in solitudine	Il Extermina dans la Solitude	He Exterminates in Solitude
R	RAZAH BETSIIAH	[see above]			[see above]
Reblata	RIBLATAH	[Hebrew, but not given]		Rixe (la ville d'Antioche)	Rixe (the town of Antioche)
Rechamias	RAHAMIAH	[Hebrew, but not given]		Tonnant	Thunderous
	RETSEH, OU RETSAH	רְצַח	occidio		[slaughter/extermination]

418

Corrupted Name	Rectified Name	Name in Original Language(s)	Latin Meaning of Name	Masonic Significance of Name	Translated Significance of Name
Rodeck	RODEH	רֹדֶה	Imperans	qui Commande	(He) who Commands
	ROUACH, OU ROUAHH	רוּחַ	ventus		[wind]
	ROZNIM, OU ROZ'NIM	רֹזְנִים	Principes	les Princes	the Princes
S.A.L.I.X.N.O.N.I.		[Hebrew, but not given]		Malachias, Zorobabel, Nehemias, Hobben, Phaleg, Joïada, Ooliab, Josué, Esdras	[see individual words]
Sabael	SABBAL	סַבָּל	onus	Poids pris pour Patience Portefaix	Weight taken for Patience Carried
	SAGESSE, FORCE, BEAUTÉ, ALARME	[French]			Wisdom, Strength, Beauty, Alarm.
Sachaï	ZAKAÏ	זַכַּי	Purus, Mundus	Pur	Pure
Sadaï	SCHADDAI	שַׁדַּי	Omnipotens	Tout-puissant	All powerful
Salatiel	SCHEALTHIEL	שְׁאַלְתִּיאֵל	Dei postulatus	Postulé de Dieu	Postulate of God
	SALIX-NONI-TENGU	[not given]			[see individual words]
Schilo Schalom abi	SCHALAL SCHALOM ABI	שְׁלַל שָׁלוֹם אֲבִי	Diripuit pacem patri		[Plundered the father of peace]
Salome, Salom, or Salem	SCHALLUM, OU SCHALLOUM, OU SCHALOM	שַׁלּוּם שָׁלוֹם	Pax, prosperitas	Pacifique	Peaceful [Peace, prosperity]
Salomon	SCHELOMOH	שְׁלֹמֹה	pacificus	Pacifique	Peaceful

Corrupted Name	Rectified Name	Name in Original Language(s)	Latin Meaning of Name	Masonic Significance of Name	Translated Significance of Name
Salathiel	SCHALTHIEL	שְׁאַלְתִּיאֵל	Deo postulatus		[required God]
Saphi	SCHUPHI	[Hebrew, but not given]		qui Indique	(He) who Indicates
Saraias	SERAIAH	[Hebrew, but not given]		Cantique du Seigneur	Canticle (or Song) of the Lord
Suchel	SCHECHEL	שֶׂכֶל	intelligentia		[intelligence]
Schibolet, or Schiboleth, or Shibboleth, etc.	SCHIBBOLETH	שִׁבֹּלֶת	spica	Épi; Nobreaux comme des épis de bled.[17]	Ear (of wheat or corn); Numerous like the ears of wheat[18]
Schoeumul Seol, or Choemul Seal	HAMAL SAGHIA	חָמָל שַׂגִיא		grand Travail	Great work
Sedech	TSEDEK	צֶדֶק	Justus	Juste	Just [or Right/Righteous]
Sedidias, or Sedecias	TSEDIKIOU	צִדְקִיָּהוּ	Justus Domini, vel justitia Domini	Juste	Just [The Lord is just, or justice of the Lord]

[17] "Ce mot signifie également un *Épi* et un *Fleuve*. On sait qu'il servit de mot du guet aux habitants de Galaad, dans la guerre qu'ils eurent à soutenir, sous Jephté, contre les Ephraïmites, lesquels ne pouvoient pas prononcer le *Schin* hébreu. Les Francs-Maçons ont choisi l'acception d'*Épi*, et traduisent *Schibboleth* par *nombreux comme des Epis de blé*, ce qu'ils appliquent aux Membres de leur ordre." —du page 11 de *Thuileur des trente-trois degrés*...
[18] "This word equally signifies *Ear [of wheat or corn]* and a *River*. It is known that it served as a watch-word to the inhabitants of Galaad, in the war that they sustained, under Jephte, against the Ephraimites, who could not pronounce the Hebrew [letter] *Shin*. The Free-Masons have chosen to accept the *Ear [of wheat or corn]*, and translate *Schibboleth* as *numerous like the Ears of wheat*, which applies to the Members of their order." —from p. 11 of *Thuileur des trente-trois degrés*... "The entire power is found enveloped within the seed, who's symbol is the ear of wheat." —from Ch.8 of *Esoteric Course of Kabalah* by Samael Aun Weor. The Hebrew term "shibboleth" literally means the part of a plant containing grains, but metaphorically "shibboleth" refers 'to a word, sound, or custom unfamiliar with its significance may not pronounce or perform correctly relative to those who are familiar with it' and therefore is used to identify foreigners or those who do not belong to a particular class or group of people.

Corrupted Name	Rectified Name	Name in Original Language(s)	Latin Meaning of Name	Masonic Significance of Name	Translated Significance of Name
Sekinac	SCHEKINAH	שְׁכִינָה	Majestas, seu praesentia Dei	Présence de Dieu, l'Esprit-Saint	Presence of God, the Holy Spirit
Selemias	SCHELEMIAH	[Hebrew, but not given]		Paix du Seigneur	Peace of the Lord
	SCHELEMOTH	שְׁלֵמוֹת	Integroe	integer, pur, inaltéré	integral, pure, unaltered
Sephora	TSEPHORAH	צִפֹּרָה	Avis, vel, bel passer		[Bird, or war bird]
Semamphorach	SCHEM HAMMEPHORAS	שֵׁם הַמְפֹרָשׁ	Nomen explicatum, expansum, pronuntiatum.	Nom bien Expliqué, le nom entendu	Well explained name, the name heard
	SCHEMED	שֶׁמֶד	destruction		[destruction]
	SEM, CHAM, JAPHETH	שֵׁם חָם יֶפֶת		Renommée, Noir, Beau	Renamed, Black, Hanson
Sidrach	SCHIDRACH	שִׁדְרַךְ	Mamella tenera		[tender Breast]
Sidonius	TSIDONI	צִידֹנִי	venator	Chasseur, Sidonien	Hunter, Sidonien
Sillex	SCHILO	שִׁילֹה	Pax	Paix	Peace
Sipim		סִפִּים	Vestibula, seu loca introitus templi		[Vestibules/Porches, or the entrance of the temple]
Soin	TSIION	צִיּוֹן	Monumentum; acervus, aut tumulus	Monument, Tombeau	Monument, Tomb
Sobai	SCHOBAI	[Hebrew, but not given]		Conversion	Conversion

421

Corrupted Name	Rectified Name	Name in Original Language(s)	Latin Meaning of Name	Masonic Significance of Name	Translated Significance of Name
Sophonie, *or* Sophonias	TSEPHANIAH	צְפַנְיָה	*Scrotum Domini*	*Secret du Seigneur*	*Secret of the Lord*
	SOPHIA	[Greek]		*sagesse*	*wisdom*
	SCHOR-LABAN	שׁוֹר לָבָן	*Bos albus*		[white ox]
	SPES	[not given]			
S.M.A.	Sidrach, Missac, Abdenago	[Hebrew, but not given]			[see individual words]
S.S.S.	Stella, Sedet, Soli	[Latin and French]		*Science, Saggesse, Sainteté*	*Stella Sedet Soli* or Science, Wisdom, Holiness
Starbuzanai	SCHETHAR BOZENAÏ	שְׁתַר בּוֹזְנַי	*Contemnentes me putrefaciens*	*Conspuant ceux qui me méprisent*	Booing those who dispise me
Sterkin,	STIBILUM	antimone [des philosophes]		*La première Matière de toutes les choses*	The first Material of all things
	STOLKIN	[Hebrew, but not given]			[see Jeksonne]
Stolkin-Emerek	STOLKIN	[see above]			[see above and also see "AMARIAH"]
	LE TABERNACLE DES VERITES REVELEES	[French]			The Tabernacle of Truths Revealed
Tabaor	TEBACH	טֶבַח	*occisio*	*Meurtre*	*Murder*
Takental	TECHINNAH, *OU* THECHINNAH	תְּחִנָּה	*Gratiosus*	*Gracieux*	*Gracious*
Talliud		[Hebrew, but not given]		*ange de l'Eau*	angel of the Water
	TELMON	[Hebrew, but not given]		*present de Rosée*	present of the Dew

Corrupted Name	Rectified Name	Name in Original Language(s)	Latin Meaning of Name	Masonic Significance of Name	Translated Significance of Name
Tangu	T.E.N.G.U.	[acronym]		T = Beseleel, E = Ooliab, N = Mahuzem, G = Garimont U = Amariah	[see individual words]
	TAROFARI	[not given]			
Tebel	TEBETH, OR TEVETH	טֶבֶת		dixième mois des Hébreux	10th Hebrew month
Teor	TEHOR	טָהוֹר	Mundus, Purus	Pur	Pure
Telsa cades	TSEDAKAH	צְדָקָה	Justitia, eleemosina	Justice	Justice
	TETRAGRAMMATON	[Greek]		nom de Dieu en quatre lettres	name of God in four letters
	THAMEDI	תְּמִידִי	perpetuo		[perpetuate]
Thalmudim	THALMOUD	תַּלְמוּד	eruditio, donctrina		[literature, doctrine]
	THEMID	תָּמִיד	semper; jugiter		[always, continuously]
	TITO	Grec. Τιτος lat. TITUS	honorabilis; cognomento justi	le chef ou le prince des 3600 chefs que Salomon aviat établis sur les ouvries du Temple	the chief or prince of the chief which Solomon established over the workmen of the Temple
Toffet	THOPHEL	תֹּפֶל	ruina	Ruine	Ruin
Toub Banai Amalabec	TOUB BAHANI HAMAL ABEL.	טוּב בָּנַי עֲמַל אָבֵל	Bonum in afflictione labor lugentis	le Travail soulage le malheureux dans l'affliction	the Work relieves the unfortunate in (their) affliction
Tsohin	TSOHIM, OU TSOGIM	צֹעִים	Peregrinantes	les Voyageurs	The Travelers

Corrupted Name	Rectified Name	Name in Original Language(s)	Latin Meaning of Name	Masonic Significance of Name	Translated Significance of Name
	TUBALCAIN	תובלקין			"The Signification of this is, that he was the Inventor of Brass, Iron and other Metals..."[19]
Tubalcain	THOUBAL-KAÏN, OU THUBALKAIN	חובל קין	Possesio Orbis	Possession du Monde[20]	Possessor of the World[21]
U.I.L.		[Latin]	Uti Inveni Leonem		[Use the Lion I have found]
	UR	אר	ignis	[feu]	[fire]
Uriel	OURIEL	אוריאל	ignis domini; ignis Dei	Feu de Dieu	Fire of God
Hurim, Thumin	URIM-THUMIM	אורים תמים	illuminations – perfections		[illumination – perfection]
U - Thu	URIM-THUMIM	[see above]			[see above]
	VAYECHOULOU, OU VAJECHULOU	ויכלו	perfecti sunt.		[were finished] [see Genesis 2:1]
	VAINCRE OU MOURIR	[French]			Vanquish or die
	VEZIO	יזיו	Cum Splendors		With the Splendors

---

[19] This entry for 'Tubalcain' is from p. 67 of *The Three Distinct Knocks* (1760) by W_____O_____V_____n : Member of a Lodge in England at this Time, and it continues: "...His father was the Father of Music: He rose from Cain, of the Fifth Generation; and his son Tubalcain, becain excellent in all Metals, which Hiram improved. See the Fourth Chapter of Genesis."
[20] "...Tubalcaïn fut, suivant l'Ecriture, le premier qui forgea les métaux. Mais, si l'on réfléchit à la signification des deux mots hébreux, on reçonnoîtra facilement, dans leur assemblage, le vœu secret de l'Hiérophante, du Templier, du FrancMaçon, de tout sectaire mystérieux, celui de *gouverner le monde* par ses principes et même par ses loix..." –du page 17 de *Thuileur des trente-trois degrés*...
[21] "...Tubalcain was, according to Scripture, the first who forged metals. But, if we reflect on the significance of the two Hebrew words, we will easily recognize in their assembly, the secret vow of the Hierophant, of the Templar, of the Free-Mason, [and] of all mysterious sectarian [societies], that of the *governer [of] the world* through his principles and even by his laws..." –from p.17 of *Thuileur des trente-trois degrés*...

Corrupted Name	Rectified Name	Name in Original Language(s)	Latin Meaning of Name	Masonic Significance of Name	Translated Significance of Name
	VIRTUTE ET SILENTIO	[Latin]			[Virtue and Silence]
	VIVAT	[Latin]		Applaudissement des Maçons	Masonic Applaud [Note: literally this Latin word means 'Live' or 'Alive']
	VINGT–VIGNT-TROIS	[French]			Twenty-twenty-three
	WHAT SHALL WE MAKE WITH THE STONE ? HEAVE IT OVER.	[English]		Que ferons-nous de cette pierre ? Portons-la plus loin	What shall we (do) with this stone? Carry it furthur
Xincheu		[not given]		Siége de l'Ame	Seat of the Soul
Ya Vaurum Ammen	IAHABOROU HAMMAIM	יעברו המים	aquas transibunt	Ils passeront les Eaux	They will pass the Waters
Yva	IVAH	[Hebrew, but not given]		par syncope, pour Iehovah	A syncope for Iehovah
Yzirie	IZRACHIAH	יזרחיה	oriens dominus	Dieu Levant	Raising (or Elevating) God
	ZAKAI	זכי	Purus, Mundus		[Pure, World]
Zabulon	ZÉBULOUN	זבלון		Habitacle par excellence: le ciel, la demeure de Dieu	Cockpit/Cabin par excellence; heaven, the abode of God
Zacharie	ZEKARIAH	זכריה	Memoria Domini	Mémoire du Seigneur	Memory of the Savior
Zekenins, or Zadikin	TZADIKIM	צדיקים	justi		[just/righteous]
Zanabosan		[not given]			

Corrupted Name	Rectified Name	Name in Original Language(s)	Latin Meaning of Name	Masonic Significance of Name	Translated Significance of Name
	ZAO	[not given]		Nom de la nature, que tous les peuples anciens ont vénérée comme symbole de la divinité.	[The] name of nature, which all the ancient people have venerated as [a] symbol of divinity.
Zaphiel	TSAPHIEL	צפאל	Absconditus Deus; Mirans Deus	Dieu caché	hidden God
Zaraias	ZERACHIAH	זרחיה	Oriens Dominus	Dieu Levant	Raising (or Elevating) God
Zarakiel	ZERACHIEL, OU Z'RAHHIEL	זרחיאל	Oriens Deus	Dieu Levant	Raising (or Elevating) God
Zedidiac	ZEBADIAH	זבדיה	victima dei	Victime de Dieu	Victim of God
Zerbal, or Zerbel	SEREB-IAH, OU SCHEREB-IAH	שרביה	praevalens cum domino	Nom du capitaine des Gardes d'Hiram / de Salomon	Name of Hiram's / Solomon's captain of the Guards
Zizon	ZIZA	זיזא	Splendor ; resplendens	Splendeur	Splendor
Z.	ZIZA	[see above]			[see above]
Zorobabel	ZERUBABEL, OU ZERUBBABEL	זרבבל	dispersion confusionis	Dispersion de la Confusion	Dispersion of Confusion

426

Some Masonic Plates, Codes and Alphabets

Algunas Laminas, Código, y Alfabetos Masónicos

The Cubic Stone

from *Le Rameau D'Or D'Éleusis* [*The Golden Branch of Eleusis*] (1863) by Jacques-Etienne Marconis

Note: the following 2 images were not together in the text.

La Piedra Cúbica

de *Le Rameau D'Or D'Éleusis* [*La Rama Dorada de Eleusis*] (1863) por Jacques-Etienne Marconis

Nota: las siguientes 2 imágenes no estaban juntos en el texto.

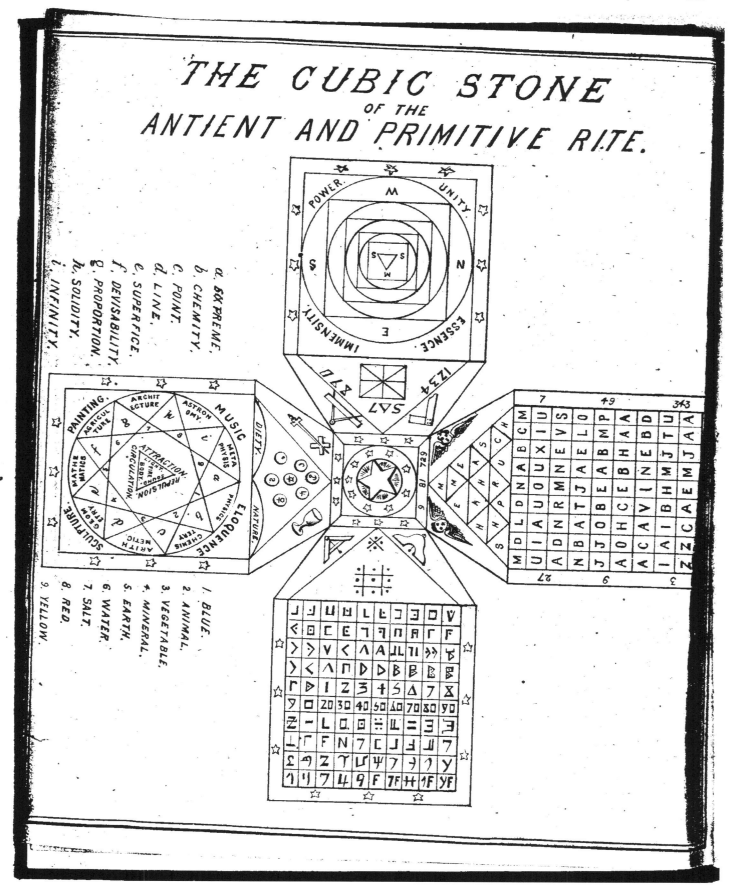

Pierre Cubique [The Cubic Stone]

from *Le Rameau D'Or D'Éleusis* [*The Golden Branch of Eleusis*] (1863) by Jacques-Etienne Marconis

Note: these 2 images were not together in the text.

Pierre Cubique [La Piedra Cúbica]

de *Le Rameau D'Or D'Éleusis* [*The Golden Branch of Eleusis*] (1863) de Jacques-Etienne Marconis

Nota: las siguientes 2 imágenes no estaban juntos en el texto.

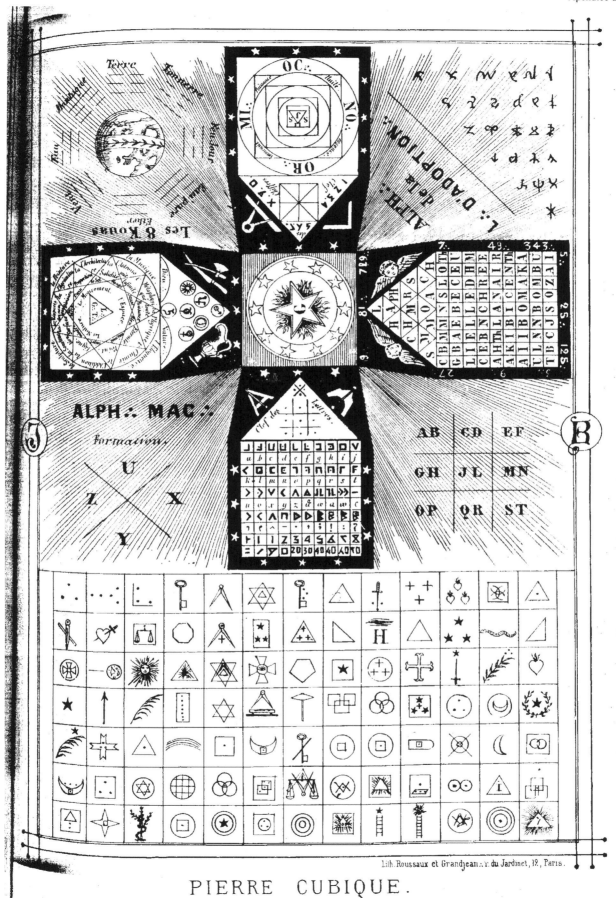

PIERRE CUBIQUE.

Les Quatre Faces de la Pierre Cubique du Grade Ecossais du Régime du G∴ Or∴ de France
[The Four Faces of the Cubic Stone of the Scottish Degree from the Plan of the G∴ Or∴ of France]

from *Manuel général de la Maçonnerie comprenant les sept grades du Rit Français* [*General Manual of Masonry including the seven degrees of the French Rite*] (1856) by Antoine Guillaume Chéreau (edited by André Teissier)

Note: this image goes along with an explanation (on pages 47-65 of the same book) which is given between the 5th and 6th degrees of the French Rite.

Les Quatre Faces de la Pierre Cubique du Grade Ecossais du Régime du G∴ Or∴ de France
[Las Cuatro Caras de la piedra cúbica de la Licenciatura escocesa del Plan del G∴ Or∴ de Francia]

de *Manuel général de la Maçonnerie comprenant les sept grades du Rit Français* [*Manual General de la Masonería incluyendo los siete grados del Rito Francés*] (1856) de Antoine Guillaume Chéreau (editado por André Teissier)

Nota: esta imagen va acompañada de una explicación (en las páginas 47-65 del mismo libro) que se da entre los grados quinto y sexto del Rito francés.

Pierre Cubique [The Cubic Stone]

from *Manuel Maçonnique ou Tuileur des Divers Rites de Maçonnerie Pratiqués en France* [*Masonic Manual or Tyler of the Diverse Rites of Masonry Practiced in France*] (1830[184]) by Claude André Vuillaume

Note: the first 4 images where together in the text.

1) Top and back side

Pierre Cubique [La Piedra Cúbica]

del *Manuel Maçonnique ou Tuileur des Divers Rites de Maçonnerie Pratiqués en France* [*Manual masónico o Tyler de los diversos ritos de la masonería se practica en Francia*] (1830[185]) de Claude André Vuillaume

Nota: Las primeras 4 imágenes donde juntos en el texto.

1) Parte superior y posterior

---

[184] The First Edition was published in 1820

[185] La primera edición fue publicada en 1820

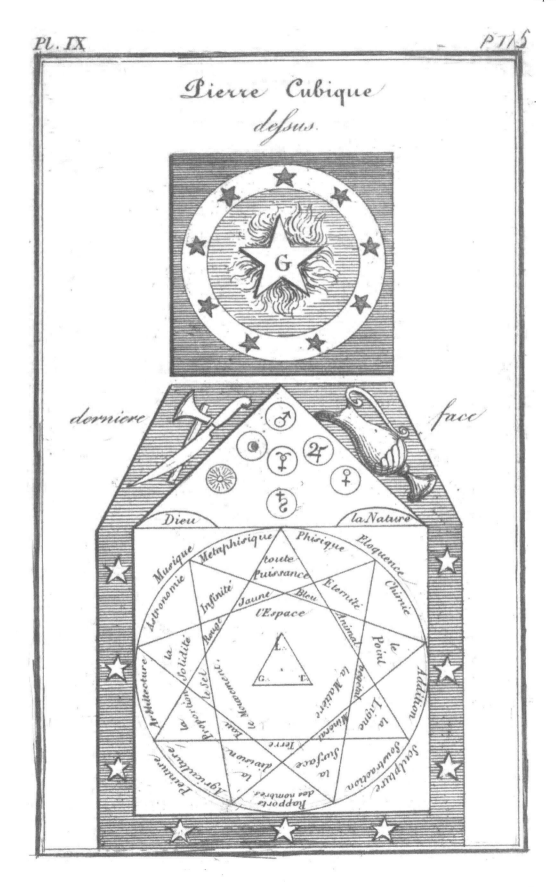

Pierre Cubique [The Cubic Stone]

from *Manuel Maçonnique ou Tuileur des Divers Rites de Maçonnerie Pratiqués en France* [*Masonic Manual or Tyler of the Diverse Rites of Masonry Practiced in France*] (1830[186]) by Claude André Vuillaume

Note: the first 4 images where together in the text.

   2) Left side

Pierre Cubique [La Piedra Cúbica]

del *Manuel Maçonnique ou Tuileur des Divers Rites de Maçonnerie Pratiqués en France* [*Manual masónico o Tyler de los diversos ritos de la masonería se practica en Francia*] (1830[187]) de Claude André Vuillaume

Nota: Las primeras 4 imágenes donde juntos en el texto.

   2) El lado izquierdo

---

[186] The First Edition was published in 1820

[187] La primera edición fue publicada en 1820

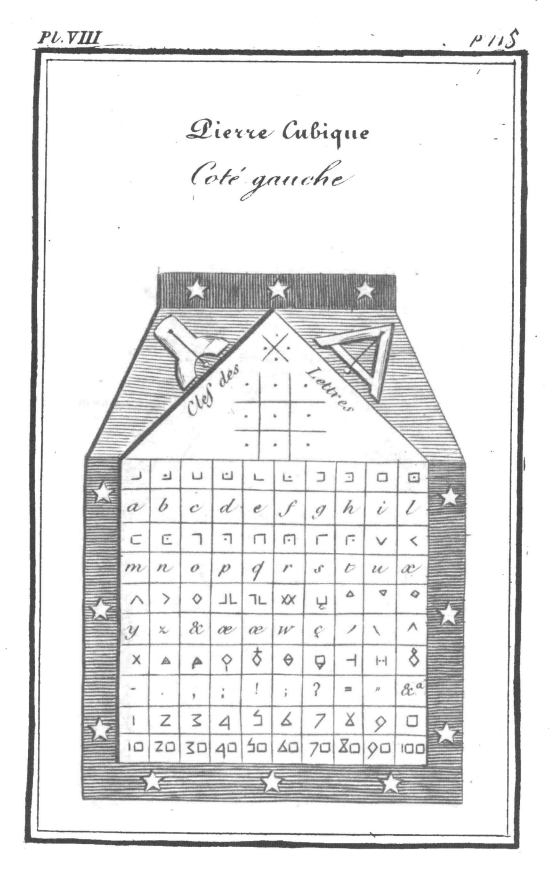

Pierre Cubique [The Cubic Stone]
 	
from *Manuel Maçonnique ou Tuileur des Divers Rites de Maçonnerie Pratiqués en France* [*Masonic Manual or Tyler of the Diverse Rites of Masonry Practiced in France*] (1830[188]) by Claude André Vuillaume
 	
Note: the first 4 images where together in the text.
 	
   3) Right side
	Pierre Cubique [La Piedra Cúbica]
	
	del *Manuel Maçonnique ou Tuileur des Divers Rites de Maçonnerie Pratiqués en France* [*Manual masónico o Tyler de los diversos ritos de la masonería se practica en Francia*] (1830[189]) de Claude André Vuillaume
	
	Nota: Las primeras 4 imágenes donde juntos en el texto.
	
	   3) El lado derecho

---

[188] The First Edition was published in 1820

[189] La primera edición fue publicada en 1820

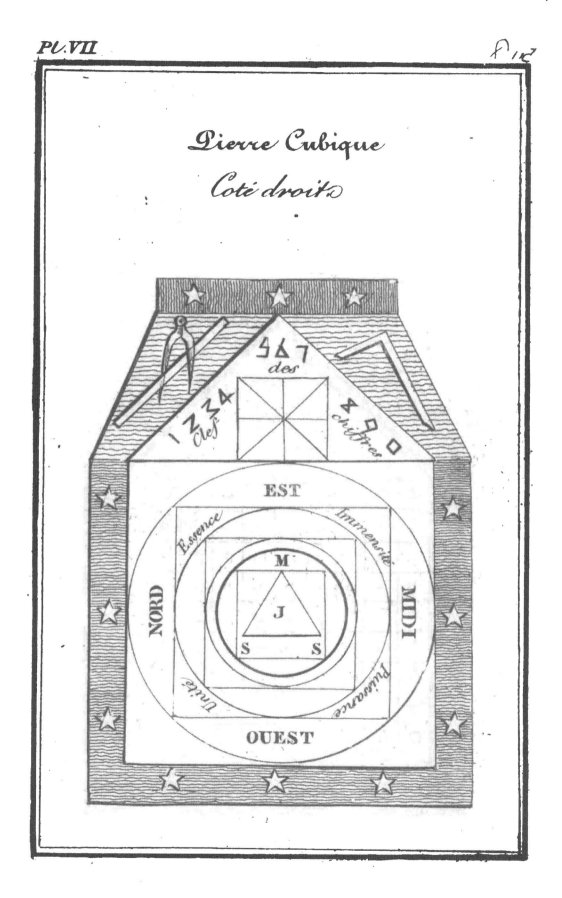

Pierre Cubique [The Cubic Stone]

from *Manuel Maçonnique ou Tuileur des Divers Rites de Maçonnerie Pratiqués en France* [*Masonic Manual or Tyler of the Diverse Rites of Masonry Practiced in France*] (1830[190]) by Claude André Vuillaume

Note: the first 4 images where together in the text.

4) 1st side [Front side]

Pierre Cubique [La Piedra Cúbica]

del *Manuel Maçonnique ou Tuileur des Divers Rites de Maçonnerie Pratiqués en France* [*Manual masónico o Tyler de los diversos ritos de la masonería se practica en Francia*] (1830[191]) de Claude André Vuillaume

Nota: Las primeras 4 imágenes donde juntos en el texto.

4) Primera parte [Anverso]

---

[190] The First Edition was published in 1820

[191] La primera edición fue publicada en 1820

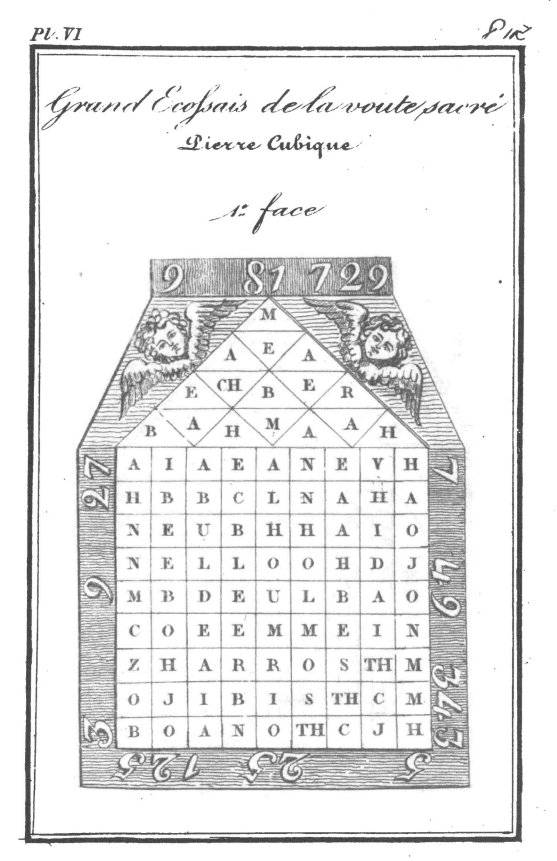

Pierre Cubique [The Cubic Stone]

from *Manuel Maçonnique ou Tuileur des Divers Rites de Maçonnerie Pratiqués en France* [*Masonic Manual or Tyler of the Diverse Rites of Masonry Practiced in France*] (1830[192]) by Claude André Vuillaume

Note: these last 2 images were both independent (it is not clear what they correspond to exactly).

5) Scottish Square of the French Rite

Pierre Cubique [La Piedra Cúbica]

del *Manuel Maçonnique ou Tuileur des Divers Rites de Maçonnerie Pratiqués en France* [*Manual masónico o Tyler de los diversos ritos de la masonería se practica en Francia*] (1830[193]) de Claude André Vuillaume

Nota: estas 2 últimas imágenes fueron independiente (no está claro lo que se corresponden con exactamente).

5) Cuadrado Escoceso del Rito Francés

---

[192] The First Edition was published in 1820

[193] La primera edición fue publicada en 1820

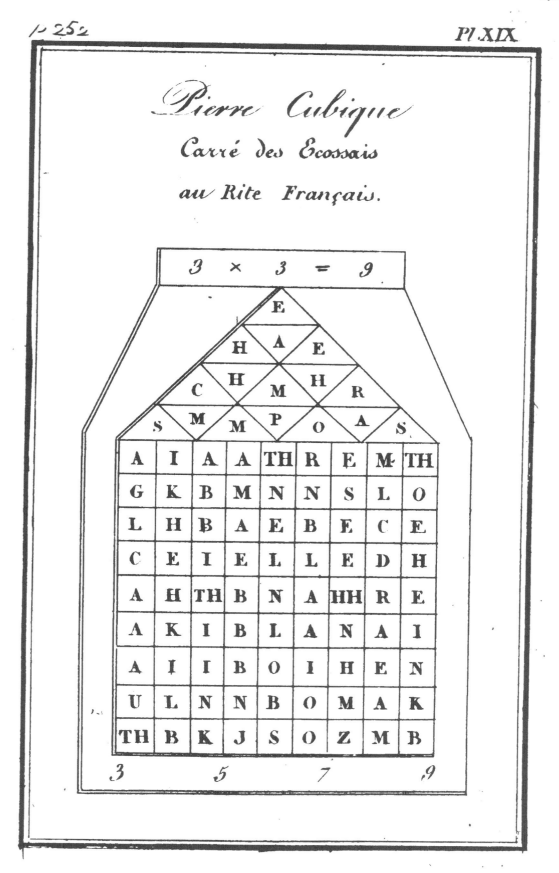

Pierre Cubique [The Cubic Stone]

from *Manuel Maçonnique ou Tuileur des Divers Rites de Maçonnerie Pratiqués en France* [*Masonic Manual or Tyler of the Diverse Rites of Masonry Practiced in France*] (1830[194]) by Claude André Vuillaume

Note: these last 2 images were both independent (it is not clear what they correspond to exactly).

6) Hieroglyphic Square of the Knights Kadosch

Pierre Cubique [La Piedra Cúbica]

del *Manuel Maçonnique ou Tuileur des Divers Rites de Maçonnerie Pratiqués en France* [*Manual masónico o Tyler de los diversos ritos de la masonería se practica en Francia*] (1830[195]) de Claude André Vuillaume

Nota: estas 2 últimas imágenes fueron independiente (no está claro lo que se corresponden con exactamente).

6) Jeroglífica Cuadrado del Caballeros Kadosch

---

[194] The First Edition was published in 1820

[195] La primera edición fue publicada en 1820

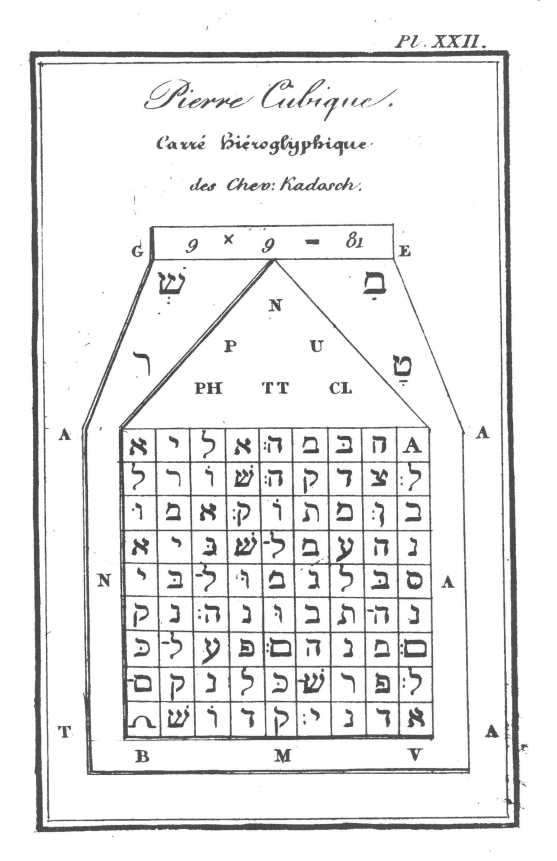

Carré Rectifié [The Rectified Square]

from *Thuileur des trente-trois degrés de l'écossisme de rit ancien dit accepté* [Tyler of the thirty three degrees of the ancient and accepted scottish rite] (1813) by François-Henri-Stanislas de L'Aulnaye

Note: these first 2 images where together in the text.

1) [The Rectified Square] of the Sacred Scottish Vault

Carré Rectifié [El Cuadrado Rectificado]

del *Thuileur des trente-trois degrés de l'écossisme de rit ancien dit accepté* [Tyler de los treinta y tres grados del Rito Escocés Antiguo y Aceptado] (1813) por François-Henri-Stanislas de L'Aulnaye

Nota: estas 2 primeras imágenes en las juntas en el texto.

1) [El Cuadrado Rectificado] del Sagrada Bóveda Escocesa

CARRÉ RECTIFIÉ
de l'Ecossois de la Voute Sacrée.

D	M	U	E	M	A	A	B	A
E	E	L	L	I	N	K	H	V
N	L	U	O	B	A	A	A	O
H	E	B	B	O	N	M	R	H
T	H	A	I	K	A	I	A	E
I	C	J	H	A	H	A	H	J
R	S	H	C	M	C	N	E	A
E	R	T	S	H	L	O	M	H
B	E	O	M	T	E	D	H	E

Pl. IV.

Carré Rectifié [The Rectified Square]

from *Thuileur des trente-trois degrés de l'écossisme de rit ancien dit accepté* [Tyler of the thirty three degrees of the ancient and accepted scottish rite] (1813) by François-Henri-Stanislas de L'Aulnaye

Note: these first 2 images where together in the text.

2) Face of the Cubic Stone Rectified

Carré Rectifié [El Cuadrado Rectificado]

del *Thuileur des trente-trois degrés de l'écossisme de rit ancien dit accepté* [Tyler de los treinta y tres grados del Rito Escocés Antiguo y Aceptado] (1813) por François-Henri-Stanislas de L'Aulnaye

Nota: estas 2 primeras imágenes en las juntas en el texto.

2) Cara de la Piedra Cúbica Rectificado

Pl. I.

FACE DE LA PIERRE CUBIQUE, *Rectifiée*.

			E				
		H	A	E			
	C	H	M	H	R		
S	M	M	P	O	A	S	

A	B	A	A	TH	R	E	M	TH
G	K	A	M	N	N	S	L	O
E	H	B	L	E	B	E	C	E
C	TH	I	E	A	L	E	D	H
A	H	B	B	N	H	CH	R	E
A	K	I	O	L	A	N	A	I
A	I	I	B	H	I	A	E	N
OU	L	N	N	O	A	M	B	K
TH	B	K	I	S	L	Z	M	I

Carré Rectifié [The Rectified Square]

from *Thuileur des trente-trois degrés de l'écossisme de rit ancien dit accepté* [*Tyler of the thirty three degrees of the ancient and accepted scottish rite*] (1813) by François-Henri-Stanislas de L'Aulnaye

Note: these last 3 images were all together.

3) Hierogliphic Square of the Knights Kadosch

Carré Rectifié [El Cuadrado Rectificado]

del *Thuileur des trente-trois degrés de l'écossisme de rit ancien dit accepté* [*Tyler de los treinta y tres grados del Rito Escocés Antiguo y Aceptado*] (1813) por François-Henri-Stanislas de L'Aulnaye

Nota: estas 3 últimas imágenes fueron todos juntos.

3) Jeroglífica Cuadrada del Caballeros Kadosch

Pl. IX.

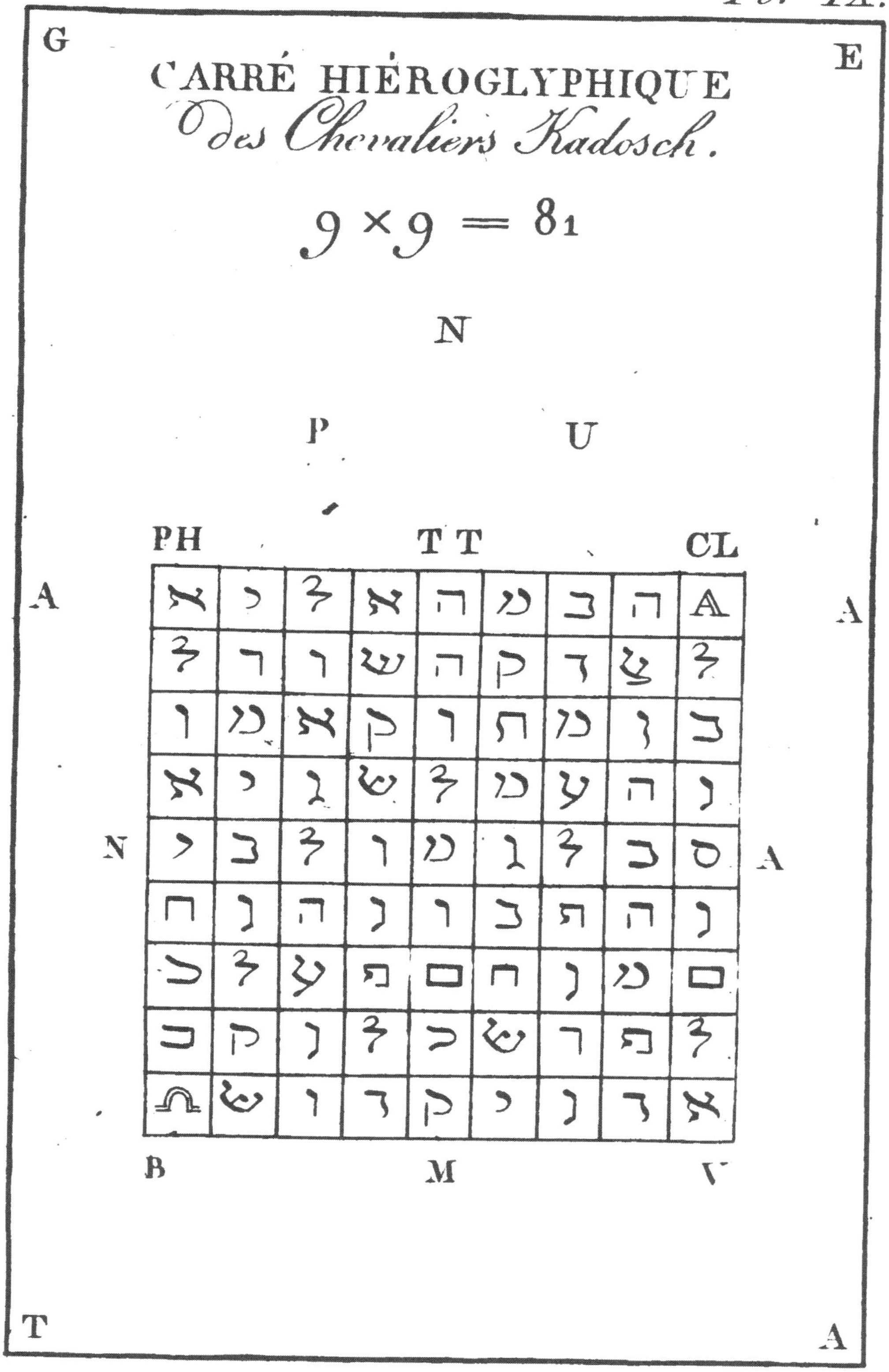
G
E
CARRÉ HIÉROGLYPHIQUE
des Chevaliers Kadosch.
9 × 9 = 81
N
P
U
PH
T T
CL
A
A
N
A
B
M
V
T
A

Carré Rectifié [The Rectified Square]

from *Thuileur des trente-trois degrés de l'écossisme de rit ancien dit accepté* [*Tyler of the thirty three degrees of the ancient and accepted scottish rite*] (1813) by François-Henri-Stanislas de L'Aulnaye

Note: these last 3 images were all together.

4) Great Universal Square containing in its 144 boxes, all the sacred words of the eight degrees of france (including the perfect master), and of the Knight Kadosch.

Carré Rectifié [El Cuadrado Rectificado]

del *Thuileur des trente-trois degrés de l'écossisme de rit ancien dit accepté* [*Tyler de los treinta y tres grados del Rito Escocés Antiguo y Aceptado*] (1813) por François-Henri-Stanislas de L'Aulnaye

Nota: estas 3 últimas imágenes fueron todos juntos.

4) Gran Cuadrado Universal que contenía en sus 144 cajas, todas las palabras sagradas de los ocho grados de Francia (incluyendo el maestro perfecto), y del Caballero Kadosch.

Pl. X.

GRAND CARRÉ UNIVERSEL,

contenant, dans ses 144 cases,
tous les mots sacrés des huit grades de france
(y compris le maitre parfait),
et du Chevalier Kadosch.

ז	י	ק	ל	ב	ו	ת	ז	י	כ	י	A
א	נ	ב	כ	מ	ח	ל	ב	ש	ז	ע	ב
נ	ב	ל	ה	ו	ה	י	ס	י	ל	ב	ג
ש	ע	ל	ב	י	ב	א	ס	ק	נ	ז	ו
ז	נ	ח	ל	א	ש	ר	ו	פ	מ	ה	ם
ת	ו	מ	ל	ש	ר	ד	נ	ת	כ	ר	ב
י	ז	כ	מ	י	נ	ב	ה	ד	ו	ה	י
י	ר	נ	י	ם	י	מ	ה	ו	ר	ב	ע
ב	ה	ע	ש	ו	ה	ל	א	ו	נ	מ	ע
נ	מ	ם	ח	נ	ל	א	י	ל	א	ה	מ
ל	כ	ש	ר	פ	ל	כ	ל	ע	פ	ס	ח
[illegible]	ש	ו	ד	ק	י	נ	ד	א	ם	ק	נ

Carré Rectifié [The Rectified Square]

from *Thuileur des trente-trois degrés de l'écossisme de rit ancien dit accepté* [Tyler of the thirty three degrees of the ancient and accepted scottish rite] (1813) by François-Henri-Stanislas de L'Aulnaye

Note: these last 3 images were all together.

5) The Same Universal Square in Vulgar Characters

Carré Rectifié [El Cuadrado Rectificado]

del *Thuileur des trente-trois degrés de l'écossisme de rit ancien dit accepté* [Tyler de los treinta y tres grados del Rito Escocés Antiguo y Aceptado] (1813) por François-Henri-Stanislas de L'Aulnaye

Nota: estas 3 últimas imágenes fueron todos juntos.

5) El Mismo Cuadrado Universal de Caracteres Vulgar

Pl. XI.

LE MÊME CARRÉ UNIVERSEL,

en Caracteres Vulgaires.

H	A	M	E	SCH	E	N	A	M	M	O	A	L	K	M
N	O	H	I	L	E	L	E	I	E	PH	L	S	N	E
S	E	U	A	N	P	A	I	K	N	N	A	PH	K	O
SCH	E	D	D	B	R	A	H	E	A	O	A	A	A	O
K	E	L	E	A	O	I	X	H	L	M	C	O	L	R
V	A	M	CH	R	H	R	H	V	A	K	A	H	H	K
I	A	M	H	A	SCH	B	O	I	O	B	Y	D	A	E
A	B	H	A	A	N	E	I	U	M	B	A	R	O	M
I	K	L	L	B	M	A	L	N	H	M	I	M	I	N
B	B	B	I	I	I	M	N	E	I	A	A	S	A	E
L	O	O	E	M	B	B	E	B	M	A	M	N	H	H
O	K	H	L	N	I	A	A	PH	E	O	M	M	O	O
I	U	A	A	E	A	E	N	L	O	R	TH	I	A	U
A	N	B	I	Z	TH	G	H	N	A	R	I	I	N	I
I	K	TH	A	N	SCH	M	H	O	E	H	A	TH	E	I

Alphabets et Hiéroglyphes Maçonnique [Masonic Alphabets and Hieroglyphics]

from *Le Sanctuaire de Memphis ou Hermès* [*The Sanctuary of Memphis or Hermes*] (1849) by Jacques-Etienne Marconis

Note: these 4 images were all together in the text.

1) Masonic Alphabets, Numbers, Months, and the Eight Kuas of Fo-Hi [Fo-Xi]

Alphabets et Hiéroglyphes Maçonnique [Alfabetos Masónicos y Jeroglíficos]

de *Le Sanctuaire de Memphis ou Hermès* [*El Santuario de Memphis o Hermes*] (1849) de Jacques-Etienne Marconis

Nota: estas 4 imágenes estaban todos juntos en el texto.

1) Alfabetos Masónicos, Números, Meses y los Ocho Kuas de Fo-Hi [Fo-Xi]

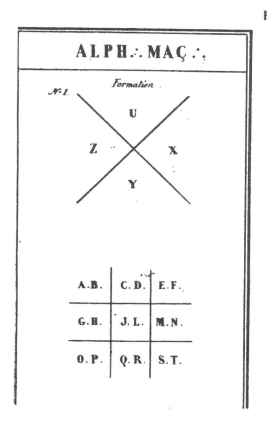
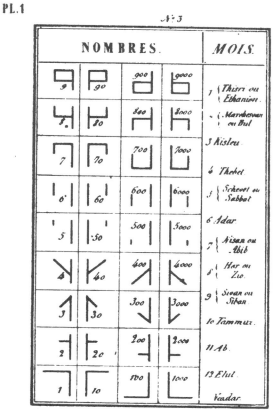

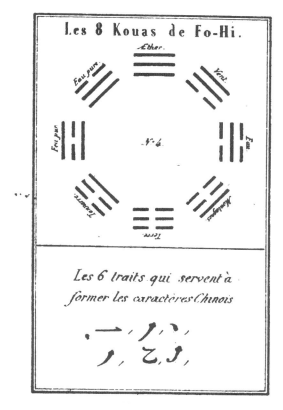

Alphabets et Hiéroglyphes Maçonnique [Masonic Alphabets and Hieroglyphics]

from *Le Sanctuaire de Memphis ou Hermès* [*The Sanctuary of Memphis or Hermes*] (1849) by Jacques-Etienne Marconis

Note: these 4 images were all together in the text.

> 2) Alphabet of the Grand Inspector Inquisitor Commander, Hieroglyphics of the Sublime Royal Prince of the Secret, Hieroglyphics of the Grand Inspector Inquisitor Commander, Alphabet of the Masonic Adoptive Rite.

Alphabets et Hiéroglyphes Maçonnique [Alfabetos masónicos y jeroglíficos]

de *Le Sanctuaire de Memphis ou Hermès* [*El Santuario de Memphis o Hermes*] (1849) de Jacques-Etienne Marconis

Nota: estas 4 imágenes estaban todos juntos en el texto.

> 2) Alfabeto de la Gran Inspector Inquisidor Comendador, Jeroglíficas de la Príncipe Sublime del Regio Secreto, Jeroglíficas del Gran Inspector Inquisidor Comandante, Alfabeto del Rito Masónico Adoptivo.

Pl. 2.

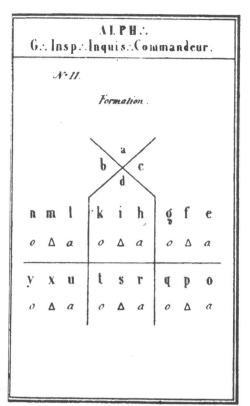

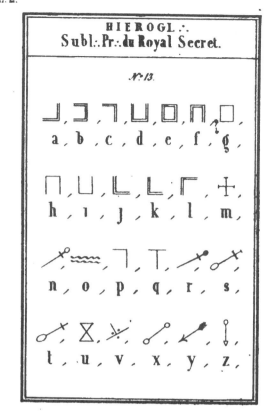

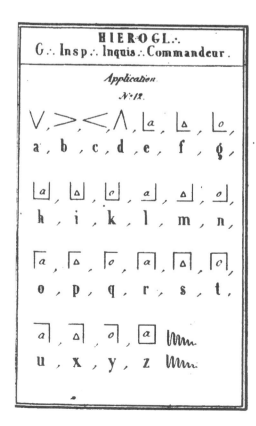

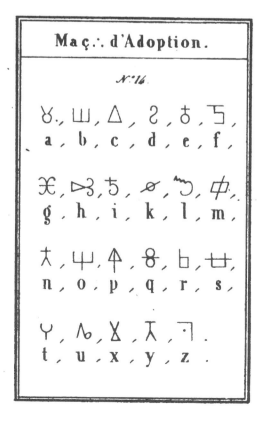

Alphabets et Hiéroglyphes Maçonnique [Masonic Alphabets and Hieroglyphics]

from *Le Sanctuaire de Memphis ou Hermès* [*The Sanctuary of Memphis or Hermes*] (1849) by Jacques-Etienne Marconis

Note: these 4 images were all together in the text.

3) Hierogliphics of the Sublime Prince of the Rose Cross, Numbers of the Knights of the Rose Cross of Hierdom, Rectified Square of the Sacred Scottish Vault.

   Numbers of the Chief of the Tabernacle, Numbers of the Knights of Kadosch, Hierogliphics of the Knights Kasocsh.

Alphabets et Hiéroglyphes Maçonnique [Alfabetos masónicos y jeroglíficos]

de *Le Sanctuaire de Memphis ou Hermès* [*El Santuario de Memphis o Hermes*] (1849) de Jacques-Etienne Marconis

Nota: estas 4 imágenes estaban todos juntos en el texto.

3) Jeroglíficas de la Sublime Príncipe de la Rosa Cruz, Números de las Caballeros de la Rosa Cruz de Hierdom, Cuadrado Rectificado de la Sagrada Bóveda Escocesa.

   Números del Jefe del Tabernáculo, los Números de los Caballeros de Kadosch, Jeroglíficas del Kasocsh Caballeros.

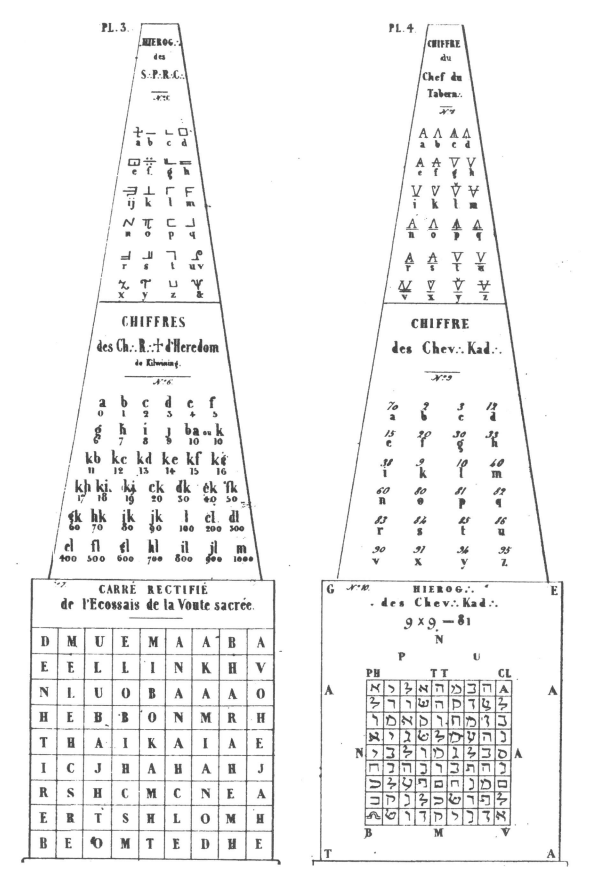

Alphabets et Hiéroglyphes Maçonnique [Masonic Alphabets and Hieroglyphics]

from *Le Sanctuaire de Memphis ou Hermès* [*The Sanctuary of Memphis or Hermes*] (1849) by Jacques-Etienne Marconis

Note: these 4 images were all together in the text.

4) Alphabet [using Hebrew letters to represent Latin characters].

Masonic Order of the Oriental Rite of Memphis: 3 Hieroglyphic Alphabets (Sub. Phil. Herm., Sage of the Pyramids, and Prince of Truth)

Numbers [using Hebrew letters to represent numbers] and New Numbers [which appear to be Chinese characters].

4 Hieroglyphic Alphabets (Sacred Doctrine of the Vedas, S.P.L.D. Mason, S.M.G.D. Work, S. Knight of the Kneph)

Ancient Numbers

Alphabets et Hiéroglyphes Maçonnique [Alfabetos masónicos y jeroglíficos]

de *Le Sanctuaire de Memphis ou Hermès* [*El Santuario de Memphis o Hermes*] (1849) de Jacques-Etienne Marconis

Nota: estas 4 imágenes estaban todos juntos en el texto.

4) Alfabeto [con letras Hebreas para representar caracteres Latinos].

Orden Masónica del Rito Oriental de Memphis: 3 Alfabetos Jeroglíficos (Sub. Phil Herm, Sabio de las Pirámides, y el Príncipe de la Verdad).

Números [con letras hebreas para representar números] y Nuevos Números [que parecen ser los caracteres Chinos].

4 Alfabetos Jeroglíficos (Doctrina Sagrada de los Vedas, Mason S.P.L.D., Trabajo S.M.G.D., S. Caballero de la Kneph)

Números Antiguos

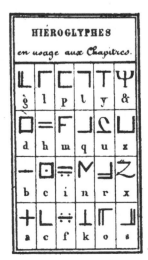

C. — ALPHABET MAÇONNIQUE.

1. SYSTÈME FRANÇAIS.

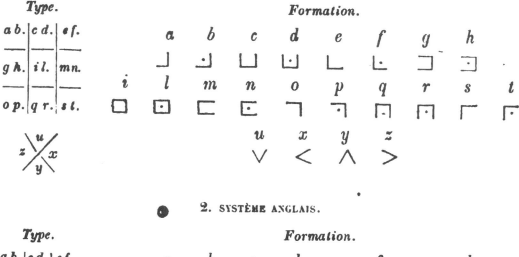

2. SYSTÈME ANGLAIS.

Ces deux alphabets sont des modifications de l'alphabet primitif, qui, lui-même avait ses variantes. On voit, en effet, par de vieux documents français, que la première figure du type n° **1**, c'est-à-dire celle qui est formée de deux lignes perpendiculaires et de deux horizontales, servait seule de base dans l'origine à tout l'alphabet, et que les signes qui en étaient tirés ne répondaient pas aux mêmes lettres de l'alphabet vulgaire que les signes actuels. Un document publié il y a quelques années en Hollande en caractères maçonniques, diffère également, quant à la valeur des signes, de l'alphabet moderne.

Voici les types de ces deux alphabets anciens. On en formera facilement la décomposition. On remarquera que, dans les cases où il se trouve deux lettres, la première se forme seulement des lignes de la portion de la figure qui lui est propre; et la seconde, de la même portion de figure avec un point au centre. Lorsque la case contient trois lettres, la dernière se forme en mettant deux points au centre.

ANCIEN TYPE FRANÇAIS.

f g.	*a i.*	*o u.*
g p.	*r s.* *t. .*	*d h.* *z. .*
e n.	*e l* *x. .*	*b m.* *y. .*

ANCIEN TYPE HOLLANDAIS.

a l. *u. .*	*b m.* *v. .*	*c n.* *x. .*
d o.	*e p.*	*f q.*
g r.	*h s.*	*i t.*

Editor's Appendix

French Masonic Alphabets and Codes

Serial Order	Letter(s)	Actual French System	Ancient French System	Rose Cross Princes	Sublime Prince of the Royal Secret	Grand Inspector Inquisitor Commander	Order of Felicity or Adoptive Rite	Chiefs or Princes of the Tabernacle	Rose Cross of Kilwining	Knights Kadosch
1	A								0	70 70
2	B								1	2 2
3	C								2	3 3
4	D								3	12 12
5	E								4	15 15
6	F								5	20 20
7	G								6	30 30
8	H								7	33 33
9	I								8	38 38
10	J								9	
11	K								10	9 9
12	L								11	10 10
13	M								12	40 40
14	N								13	60 60
15	O								14	80 80
16	P								15	81 81
17	Q								16	82 82
18	R								17	83 83
19	S								18	84 84
20	T								19	85 85
21	U								20	86 86
22	V								21	90
23	X								22	90 91
24	Y								23	91 94
25	Z								24	94 95
26										
27	&									95

Source: "Manuel Maçonnique" (1820, 1830) by Claude André Vuillaume,
"Le Sanctuaire de Memphis ou Hermès" (1849) by Jacques-Etienne Marconis, and
"Thuileur des trente trois degrés" (1813) by François-Henri-Stanislas de L'Aulnaye

Memphis Rite Masonic Alphabets and Codes

Serial Order	Letter(s)	Hebrew Letters	Sub. Phil. Herm.	Sages of the Pyramids	Prince of the Truth	Sacred Doctrine of the Vedas	S.P.L.D. Masonic Hierogliphics	S.M.G.D. Work	S. Knight of the Kneph
1	A	א							
2	B	ב							
3	C								
4	D	ד							
5	E	ה							
6	F								
7	G	גה							
8	H	ח							
9	I								
10	J	י							
11	K	קכ							
12	L	ל							
13	M	מם							
14	N	נן							
15	O	וֹ							
16	P	פ							
17	Q								
18	R	ר							
19	S	ס							
20	T	ת							
21	U								
22	V	ו							
23	X								
24	Y								
25	Z	ז							
	sch	ש							
	ts	ע							

Source: "Le Sanctuaire de Memphis ou Hermès" (1849) by Jacques-Etienne Marconis

Editor's Appendix | Apéndice del Editor

Additional Masonic and Esoteric Alphabets

Numeric Value	Kabalistic Value	Square Hebrew	Hebrew Letter Name	Cipher Hebrew	Postel's Samaritan	Mackey/Pike Masonic Samaritan	Pike's Masonic Pheonecian	"Celestial" or "Angelic" Hebrew	"Passing the River" Hebrew	Alphabet of the Magi
1	1	א	Aleph							
2	2	ב	Beth							
3	3	ג	Gimel							
4	4	ד	Dalet							
5	5	ה	Heh							
6	6	ו	Vau							
7	7	ז	Zayin							
8	8	ח	Cheth							
9	9	ט	Teth							
10	10	י	Yod/Jod							
11	20	כ	Kaf/Kaph							
12	30	ל	Lamed							
13	40	מ	Mem/Men							
14	50	נ	Nun							
15	60	ס	Samech							
16	70	ע	Ayin							
17	80	פ	Pei							
18	90	צ	Tzadik							
19	100	ק	Kuf/Qoph							
20	200	ר	Resh/Reish							
21	300	ש	Shin							
22	400	ת	Tav							
23	(500)	ך	final Kaph							
24	(600)	ם	final Mem							
25	(700)	ן	final Nun							
26	(800)	ף	final Pei							
27	(900)	ץ	final Tzadik							

"Nearly all of the significant words in the Masonic rituals are of Hebrew origin, and in writing them in the rituals the Hebrew letters are frequently used."
- Albert Mackey

*Sources: "Linguarum Duodecim Characteribus Differentium Alphabetum Introductio" (1547) by Guillaume Postel, "An Encyclopædia of Freemasonry and its Kindred Sciences" (1874) by Albert Mackey, "Book of the Words" (1878) by Albert Pike, "Peculium Abrae" (1523) by Abraham de Balmis, "Champ Fleury" (1529) by Geoffroy Tory, and "Traicté des chiffres" (1587) by Blaise de Vigenère

Editor's Appendix — Apéndice del Editor

High Masonic Alphabet of the Egyptian Magi

Numeric Value	Kabalistic Value	Square Hebrew	Hebrew Letter Name	Alphabet of the Magi	Egyptian Magi Letter Name	Corresponding Modern Letter	High Masonic Letter Meaning
1	1	א	Aleph		Athoïm	A	the Magus
2	2	ב	Beth		Beïnthin	B	the Door to the occult Sanctuary
3	3	ג	Gimel		Gomor	G	Isis
4	4	ד	Dalet		Dinaïn	D	the cubic Stone
5	5	ה	Heh		Eni	E	the Master of the Arcana
6	6	ו	Vau		Ur	U,V	the Two Paths
7	7	ז	Zayin		Zaïn	Z	the Chariot of Osiris
8	8	ח	Cheth		Hélétha	H	Themis [law & order]
9	9	ט	Teth		Théla	Th	the veiled Lamp
10	10	י	Yod/Jod		Ioïthi	I,J,Y	the Sphinx
11	20	כ	Kaf/Kaph		Caïtha	C,K	the tamed Lion
12	30	ל	Lamed		Luzaïn	L	the Sacrifice
13	40	מ	Mem/Men		Mataloth	M	the Sickle
14	50	נ	Nun		Naïn	N	the Solar Genie
15	60	ס	Samech		Xirôn	X	Typhon
16	70	ע	Ayin		Olélath	O	the fulminated Tower
17	80	פ	Pei		Pilôn	P	the Star of the Magi
18	90	צ	Tzadik		Tsadi	Ts	Twilight
19	100	ק	Kuf/Qoph		Quitolath	Q	the resplendant Light
20	200	ר	Resh/Reish		Rasith	R	the Waking of the Dead
21	300	ש	Shin		Sichen	S	the Crocodile
22	400	ת	Tav		Thoth	T	the Crown of the Magi
23	(500)	ך	final Kaph				
24	(600)	ם	final Mem				
25	(700)	ן	final Nun				
26	(800)	ף	final Pei				
27	(900)	ץ	final Tzadik				

"...American high-masons ...used the letters of a secret magical alphabet to mark the divisions of a document... Each letter has a corresponding hierogliphic, a secret, a symbolic name and a motto..."
- Docteur Bataille [Gabriel Jogand-Pagès]

*Sources: "Traicté des chiffres ou Secrètes manières d'escrire" (1587) by Blaise de Vigenère, and 'L'Alphabet du Magism Palladique dit Alphabet des Mages d'Égypte' by Docteur Bataille [Gabriel Jogand-Pagès] in "REVUE MENSUELLE Religieuse, Politique, Scientifique" from Issue No. 3 (March 1894)

Esoteric & Kabalistic Hebrew Letter Associations

Numeric Value	Kabalistic Value	Square Hebrew:	Hebrew Letter Name:	Meaning of Letter:	Divine Attribute:	Intellectual, Sidereal, and Elementary Worlds:
1	1	א	Aleph	Doctrine	God of the Infinite	Seraphim
2	2	ב	Beth	House	God of Wisdom	Cherubim
3	3	ג	Gimel	Retribution	God of Retribution	Thones
4	4	ד	Dalet	Door	God of the Doors of Light	Dominions
5	5	ה	Heh	Indication	God of Eternity	Potencies
6	6	ו	Vau/Vav	Hook	Creator God	Virtues
7	7	ז	Zayin	Weapons	God of Splendors	Principalities
8	8	ח	Cheth	Life	Living God	Archangels
9	9	ט	Teth	Good, Disgrace, Avoidance	God of Goodness	Angels
10	10	י	Yod/Jod	Principle, Very Happy	Principle God	First Mobile
11	20	כ	Kaf/Kaph	Palm of the Hand	Immutable God	Heaven of the Fixed Stars
12	30	ל	Lamed	Discipline	God of Alliance or God of the 30 Paths of Wisdom	Saturn
13	40	מ	Mem/Men	Spot, Blotch	Mysterious God	Jupiter
14	50	נ	Nun	Fish	God of the 50 Gates of Intelligence	Mars
15	60	ס	Samech	Help, Support	God of Light	Sun
16	70	ע	Ayin	Heaven, Fountain, Color	Beneficial God	Venus
17	80	פ	Pei	Mouth, Decree	God of Eloquence	Mercury
18	90	צ	Tzadik	Hunting	God of Justice	Moon
19	100	ק	Kuf/Qoph	Revolution, Singe	God of Uprightness	Fire
20	200	ר	Resh/Reish	Head, Chief, Poverty	Chief God, Soul of the World	Air
21	300	ש	Shin	Teeth, Ivory, Reef	God, Founder of the world; Savior God	Water
22	400	ת	Tau/Tav	Cross, Sign, End	God, End of Everything	Earth
23	(500)	ך	final Kaph			Mineral
24	(600)	ם	final Mem			Vegetable
25	(700)	ן	final Nun			Terrestrial Animals
26	(800)	ף	final Pei			Aquatic Animals
27	(900)	ץ	final Tzadik			Microcosmos

"Histoire generale et particuliere des religions et du culte de tous les peuples du monde tant anciens que modernes" (1791) by Francois-Henri-Stanislas De L'Aulnaye

Daath Gnosis: Bilingual Translations

"The Book of the Virgin of Carmel" by Samael Aun Weor

"Universal Charity" by Samael Aun Weor

"Gnostic Christification" by Samael Aun Weor

"Logos Mantram Magic" by Krumm-Heller (Huiracocha)

"The Reconciliation of Science and Religion" by Eliphas Levi

"The Bible of Liberty" by Eliphas Levi

"The Initiatic Path in the Arcanum of the Tarot & Kabalah" by Samael Aun Weor

"Esoteric Course of Kabalah" by Samael Aun Weor

"Magic, Alchemy and the Great Work" by Samael Aun Weor

"Dogma of High Magic" by Eliphas Levi

"The Awakening of Man" by Samael Aun Weor

"Gnostic Rosicrucian Astrology" by Krumm-Heller (Huiracocha)

"The Kabalistic and Occult Philosophy of Eliphas Levi" Vol.1 by Eliphas Levi *

"Gnostic Rosicrucian Kabalah" by Krumm-Heller (Huiracocha) *

"Ritual of High Magic" by Eliphas Levi *

* Current projects for future publication from Daath Gnostic Publishing

Daath Gnosis: Reprints[1]

"The Psychology of Man's Possible Evolution" by P.D. Ouspensky *(English-Español)*

"In Search of the Miraculous" Vol. 1 & 2 by P.D. Ouspensky *(English-Español)*

"Mystical Kabalah" by Dion Fortune *(English - Español)*

"Rito Memphis y Misraim Guias del Aprendiz, Compañero, y Maestro" by Memphis y Misraim Argentina *(Español)*

"The Theosophical ZOHAR" by Nurho de Manahar *(English)*

"The Oragean Version" by C. Daly King *(English)*

"La Science Cabalistique" by Lazare Lenain *(Français)* *

"The Fourth Way" by P.D. Ouspensky *(English - Español)* *

Daath Gnosis: Study Guides

"Gnostic Egyptian Tarot Coloring Book" *(English - Español)*

"The Gnostic Kabalistic Verb" *(English - Español)*

"The Gnostic and Esoteric Mysteries of Freemasonry, Lucifer and the Great Work" *(English - Español)*

"The Kabalistic and Occult Tarot of Eliphas Levi" *(English)*

"Esoteric Studies in Masonry" Vol. 1 *(English - Français)*

* Current projects for future publication from Daath Gnostic Publishing

---

[1] These are books which were 1) either originally in English and have been republished by Daath Gnosis in order to either make them bilingual or 2) provide access to difficult to find documents in their original language.

A word about "**Daath Gnostic Publishing – Art, Science, Philosophy and Mysticism (A.S.P.M)**" and our motivation:

> In an attempt to integrate the large amount of enlightening material on the subject of GNOSIS into the English language and to provide a way:
> - for non-English speakers to give lectures & assignments to English speaking students (and vice versa) and be able to reference specific topics or quotes, and
> - for English speakers to access materials previously unavailable in English (or not critically translated into English)
>
> we have decided to translate and publish these materials for the serious Gnostic Students.

Almost all our publications are bilingual, giving access to the original source material and the translation so that the reader can decide for themselves what the meaning of each sentence is.

We are also working on Study Guides that are a combination of Gnostic Materials from multiple sources which provide further insight when taken together.

Because of the need for a practical GNOSIS in these revolutionary times, we have focused on, and continue to benefit from, the writing and teachings of Samael Aun Weor. We encourage you to study his materials, they are wonderful.

In *Endocrinology and Criminology* (1959), at the end of Ch. 15, he says:

"Before delivering ourselves to the development of occult powers, we need to study ourselves and make a persona-logical and psycho-pathological diagnosis of our own personality.	"Antes de entregarnos al desarrollo de los poderes ocultos necesitamos estudiarnos a sí mismos, y hacer un diagnóstico persona-lógico y psico-patológico de nuestra propia personalidad.
After discovering our own particular Psycho-bio-typo-logical "I", it is necessary for us to reform ourselves with intellectual culture.	Después de haber descubierto nuestro propio yo Psico-Biotipológico, necesitamos reformarnos con la cultura intelectual.
A Pedagogic[2] Psychotherapy is necessary in order to reform ourselves.	Necesitamos una Psicoterapia Pedagógica para reformarnos.

---

[2] Pedagogy: 1) the function or work of a teacher; teaching. 2) the art or science of teaching; education; instructional methods.

The four gospels of Jesus Christ are the best Pedagogic Psychotherapy.

It is necessary to totally study and practice all the teachings contained in the four gospels of Jesus Christ.

Only after reforming ourselves morally can we deliver ourselves to the development of the chakras, discs or magnetic wheels, of the astral body.

It is also urgent to study the best authors of Theosophy, Rosicrucianism, Psychology, Yoga, etc., etc."

In *The Seven Words* (1953), about a third of the way through, he says:

"I dare to affirm that all the books which have been written in the world on Theosophism, Rosicrucianism, Spiritualism, etc., are completely antiquated for the new AQUARIAN Era, and therefore they should be revised in order to extract from them only what is essential.

Here I, AUN WEOR, deliver to humanity, the authentic message that the WHITE LODGE sends to humanity for the new AQUARIAN Era.

God has delivered to men the wisdom of the Serpent. What more do they want?

This science is not mine; this science is from God; my person is not worth anything; the work is everything, I am nothing but an emissary."

So let us practice the Science of the Serpent, *la magia amorosa*, while we study and extract only what is essential from the Esoteric texts of the past, in order to synthesize the truth within ourselves.

If you are interested:
- in receiving a list of our currently available materials,
- or would like to suggest a better translation for anything we publish,
- or if you would like to take the responsibility and time to translate or proofread a chapter or a book (in English, French or Spanish),
- or would like to suggest or submit materials for publication,
- or would like to inquire about purchasing Gnostic Tarot Deck(s)

please send us an email at:

GnosticStudies@gmail.com

Or join our group for the latest updates:
http://groups.yahoo.com/group/DaathGnosis/